MW00806147

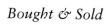

Bought & Sold

Bought & Sold

Living and Losing the Good Life
in Socialist Yugoslavia

PATRICK HYDER PATTERSON

Cornell University Press
ITHACA AND LONDON

First published 2011 by Cornell University Press

Printed in the United States of America

Library of Congress Cataloging-in-Publication Data

Patterson, Patrick Hyder, 1963–
    Bought and sold : living and losing the good life in socialist Yugoslavia /
Patrick Hyder Patterson.
      p. cm.
    Includes bibliographical references and index.
    ISBN 978-0-8014-5004-4 (cloth : alk. paper)
    1. Consumer behavior—Social aspects—Yugoslavia.   2. Consumption (Economics)—
Social aspects—Yugoslavia.   3. Socialism and culture—Yugoslavia.   I. Title.
    HF5415.33.Y8P38   2012
    306.309497'09045—dc23   2011022273

Cornell University Press strives to use environmentally responsible suppliers and materials to the fullest extent possible in the publishing of its books. Such materials include vegetable-based, low-VOC inks and acid-free papers that are recycled, totally chlorine-free, or partly composed of nonwood fibers. For further information, visit our website at www.cornellpress.cornell.edu.

Cloth printing   10 9 8 7 6 5 4 3 2 1

for John Fine,

    who has always been, as much as anyone,

for all of what once was Yugoslavia,

    and

for all of its people

Contents

Acknowledgments

Yugoslavia is hard to understand. To the extent that I have been able to make some sense of it, that success is built on the extraordinary work done by other scholars. The list could go on and on, but I do want to offer special thanks to those Yugoslav specialists from whom I have learned so much over the years, through so many lively conversations about Yugoslavia and about this project, including John Lampe, Wendy Bracewell, Sabrina Ramet, Paul Shoup, Gale Stokes, Carole Rogel, Brigitte Le Normand, Vladimir Kulić, Hannes Grandits, Nicole Lindstrom, Igor Duda, Maja Mikula, Karin Taylor, Elissa Helms, Paula Pickering, Emily Greble, Zoran Milutinović, Arnold Suppan, Katherine Sredl, Peter Vodopivec, Dejan Djokić, Božo Repe, Nick Miller, Ellen Comisso, and the late Dennison Rusinow. I am also grateful for the insights, inspiration, and support I have gained from conversations with what has turned out to be a truly remarkable collection of colleagues—and friends—in the broader circles of East European and Balkan history. Here, too, I cannot hope to acknowledge everyone who deserves it, but I do want to mention the help I have received from Holly Case, Mary Neuburger, John Connelly, Padraic Kenney, Norman Naimark, Martha Lampland, Jonathan Zatlin, Paulina Bren, Brad Abrams, Andrea Orzoff, György (Gyuri) Péteri, Bruce Berglund, Paul Hanebrink, Karl Hall, Kimberly Elman Zarecor, Eagle Glassheim, Irina Gigova, and Pieter Judson. Mark Pittaway, who died all too soon just before I finished this book, was a source of constant inspiration and enthusiasm for all of us who seek to understand the history of everyday life in socialist society. Like so many others, I will always miss his generosity, vitality, insight, and friendship.

I owe a tremendous debt to the advisers and friends at the University of Michigan who helped me launch this project. John V. A. Fine Jr., a wonderful mentor in every sense of the word, was always there to offer me his superb guidance, his inexhaustible warmth, camaraderie, and *Menschlichkeit,* his masterful command of Balkan historiography, and his profound feeling for the intricacies of the Yugoslav experience, along with remarkable latitude and freedom to frame the project and the argument as I judged best. Raymond Grew, as ever, encouraged me in the toughest, friendliest, liveliest, and most helpful way, pushing me to try to write a history that would be big and ambitious and durable, challenging me to conceptualize Yugoslavia's consumer culture on my own terms, and at the same time making sure that I was alert to the temptations of interpretative overreach. I have always prospered by relying on Brian Porter-Szűcs for his sharp critical eye and his attention to the interpretative problems that matter most in our field; his sense for the historiographical questions and controversies that have made for good work on Eastern Europe and the Balkans is unmatched. Zvi Gitelman, with his inimitable sparkle, gave me a great model to try to live up to in my own work and proved especially artful at nudging me to make my arguments more economical, more clear, and more tightly connected to the larger arcs of East European history and politics. Others at Michigan were incredibly valuable, too. Stephanie Platz and Fran Blouin were always there with a real concern for both my present and my future. Rashi Jackman, Meghan Hays, and Donna Parmalee were great companions who continually enriched my understanding of the Yugoslavs and the Balkans. And Janet Crayne was not just an indispensable guide to Balkan sources but a great friend as well. All of these people, and many others, helped me no end.

I have been fortunate to have colleagues at the University of California, San Diego, who have been unfailingly supportive, but I should single out Frank Biess, David Luft, Bob Edelman, and Tom Gallant for their guidance, their wisdom, their encouragement, their keen critical sense, and their very useful suggestions for improving my work. In ways too numerous to mention, Ann Craig, Steve Cassedy, and Mollie Martinek kept me moving along and saw to it that I would be able to make a lasting and happy home here. Cathy Gere, Ev Meade, Armin Owzar, Matthew Herbst, Heidi Keller-Lapp, and Nancy Kwak have done double duty as intellectual comrades and good friends. Susan Sullivan Nakigane has proved a delight as a student, sounding board, and interlocutor. The tenacious and talented research assistance I have received from Nataša Garić-Humphrey has been invaluable.

My research went forward smoothly thanks to the very helpful staffs of academic institutions across the former Yugoslavia: in Belgrade, the Arhiv Jugoslavije, the Narodna Biblioteka Srbije, and the Muzej Grada Beograda; in Zagreb, the Hrvatski Državni Arhiv and the Nacionalna i Sveučilišna Knjižnica; and in Ljubljana, the Muzej Novejše Zgodovine, the Inštitut za Novejšo Zgodovino, the Inštitut za Narodnostna Vprašanja, the Arhiv Republike Slovenije, and the Narodna in Univerzitetna Knjižnica. Ivanka Ponikvar and the staff of the American Center in Ljubljana ensured that my time there as a Fulbright scholar was both profitable and pleasurable. My work abroad was made much more successful through the assistance and advice given by Rudi Rizman, Jože Vogrinc, Miha Javornik, Mitja Žagar, and Jerneja Petrič, and I am grateful to Maca Jogan, Janez Damjan, Zlatko Jančič, Alenka Puhar, and Jana Novak for sharing their perspectives on Yugoslav commercial promotion and consumer culture. Special thanks are owed to Borislav Buca Mitrović, who got in touch with me after seeing his own work cited in one of my earlier articles and, over the course of a number of delightful conversations in Belgrade, shared with me his deep personal understanding of the day-to-day practice of Yugoslav advertising and marketing, a real insider's perspective that I could not have hoped to get otherwise.

Portions of the material in chapter 3 can be found in modified form in a previous publication: "Truth Half Told: Finding the Perfect Pitch for Advertising and Marketing in Socialist Yugoslavia, 1950–1991," *Enterprise & Society: The International Journal of Business History* 4, no. 2 (June 2003): 179–225. I thank Oxford Journals and *Enterprise & Society* for allowing me to reprint this material here.

Unless otherwise noted, all translations from foreign languages in this book are mine. I thank Paul Shoup for directing me toward Matija Bećković's revealing meditations on the contemporary Yugoslav condition. For an alternative translation of Bećković's "On Yugoslavs," see Matija Bećković and Dušan Radović, *Che: A Permanent Tragedy/Random Targets*, trans. Drenka Willen (New York: Harcourt Brace Jovanovich, 1970), 75–77, at 75–76; the sensitive translation and reading in Sharon Zukin, *Beyond Marx and Tito: Theory and Practice in Yugoslav Socialism* (New York: Cambridge University Press, 1975), 112–114; and the references in Dusko Doder, *The Yugoslavs* (New York: Random House, 1978), 60. My understanding of Bećković's essay is indebted to these interpreters.

Research and publication expenses were funded with the generous support of postdoctoral grants and fellowships from the National Research Competition of the National Council for Eurasian and East European Research (NCEEER), the Southeast European Studies Program of the American Council of Learned Societies (ACLS), and the Individual Advanced Research Opportunities Program of the International Research and Exchanges Board (IREX). The color illustrations in this volume were made possible by the anonymous founder of the UC San Diego Dean of Arts and Humanities Fund for Innovation and by Chris and Warren Hellman, sponsors of UC San Diego's Hellman Fellowships. Additional support for earlier stages of my research came from the J. William Fulbright Foreign Scholarship program, the UC San Diego Faculty Career Development Program, the Bernadotte E. Schmitt Grants of the American Historical Association, the Ministry for Education, Science, and Sport of the Republic of Slovenia, and the University of Michigan's Rackham Predoctoral Fellowships, Mellon Candidacy Fellowships, and Regents' Fellowships. Grants from the Business History Conference and the Center for Russian and East European Studies at Stanford University offered me valuable opportunities to present the work in its formative phases. And there will always be a special place in my heart for the University of Virginia, which funded my early work in Serbo-Croatian with a Foreign Language and Area Studies (FLAS) fellowship back in 1987, during my final year of law school, and thereby nurtured the fascination with Yugoslavia and its people that would, in the end, pull me away from a decade-long career in legal work and put me on the path that I have found so rewarding. I extend my warmest thanks to each of these sponsors.

The book came together seamlessly and quickly thanks to the outstanding work of the staff at Cornell University Press. I have been fortunate beyond my greatest hopes to have John Ackerman as my editor, and his sure judgment and invariably useful critical comments, along with those so carefully and generously provided by the anonymous readers of my manuscript, have made my account much, much better. Karen Laun and Rita Bernhard saw to it that the preparation of the final text was as smooth as possible, and I have been fortunate to rely on Bruce Tindall here in San Diego for expert indexing.

My friends and family have been a wonderful source of encouragement and happiness throughout the process of writing this book. Hyder Patterson, Wilma Patterson, Carole Knight, Jane Hobbs, and the late Ersa Patterson were with me from the beginning. Clark Hantzmon, Bob Geraci, and Daniel Deudney were more than just friends, helping me from the start to think more creatively about the project. I am also thankful for the support I have received from many other friends as well, and among them I must single out Susan Larsen, Jane Rhodes, Lynn Hudson, Gary Phillips, Cynthia Chris, Miles Kahler, Steven Schwarz, Igor Koršič, Jani Bačnik, Dejan Rebernik, Iztok Božič, Matjaž Marinč, and Sašo Štravs. And, as always, I owe the most to Michael Gorman.

To all these people, I am grateful. Much of the credit for this enterprise is rightly theirs; all the errors are my own.

A Note on Archival Sources

This book makes reference to sources from the Arhiv Jugoslavije (Archive of Yugoslavia) in Belgrade and the Hrvatski Državni Arhiv (Croatian State Archive) in Zagreb. Archival materials are cited in the notes with the initials of the archive (either AJ or HDA) followed by the number of the archival *fond* and then by the number of the folder/box/register/archival unit within that *fond*. For example, for documents from box 53 of *fond* 229, Savez trgovinskih komora, held in the Arhiv Jugoslavije: AJ-229–53. In most if not all cases individual pages within an archival unit have not been numbered in the course of archival processing to date, so references to individual archival documents have been cited when possible with details as to titles, authors, and dates sufficient to facilitate identification.

Prologue
The Good Life and the Yugoslav Dream

Yugoslavs take in more than they produce, and they spend more than they take in. How?!

Rather nicely, actually! For whatever it is that the modest opportunities of the present phase are not able to offer them, they use a magic wand to pull it out of their top hats—or their everyday hats, or their caps, or the folding caps they wear as soldiers....

Yugoslavs have liberated themselves. They have gotten rid of some of their traditional complexes. And they are now breathing in deeply and grabbing, just grabbing. So, on this volcanic territory of constant uprisings and illegality, a new illegal movement has broken out—a movement for happiness, for a little house surrounded by flowers, for a bathroom lined with tiles, for sedans and deodorants.

—Matija Bećković, "O Jugoslovenima" [On the Yugoslavs], 1969

Reflecting on socialism in Yugoslavia at the close of its first decade, Milovan Djilas complained that his country's Communist Party and state officials had betrayed the promise of their own revolution by creating a New Class: an exclusive coterie of apparatchiks seduced by the material trappings of the power they enjoyed, entrenched in their control of the nation's income and resources, and, as a result, utterly at odds with the time-honored communist ideal of a classless society. Djilas, once one of Tito's closest associates and later the Yugoslav dissident par excellence, used his book *The New Class* to deliver a blistering indictment of the bureaucracy that had emerged in the years after the Communists' rise to power. The implications were nothing short of damning: the governing élites had gone far beyond ousting the hated bourgeoisie (not that there had been all that much of a bourgeoisie to hate in Yugoslavia) and had, in effect, taken the place of their traditional enemies, reserving to themselves a privileged lifestyle previously available only to the wealthy few, who, in a place as poor as Yugoslavia, had always been very few indeed.[1]

Source for the epigraph: Matija Bećković, "O Jugoslovenima," in Bećković, *Dr Janez Paćuka o meduvremenu* (Novi Sad: Matica srpska, 1969), 81, 82–83.

1. Milovan Djilas, *The New Class: An Analysis of the Communist System* (New York, 1957).

Following its appearance in 1957, *The New Class* did its share to reinforce one of the stock Cold War stereotypes of communist injustice, the aloof fat cat of the party-state *nomenklatura* arriving in a rare private automobile to buy luxury goods in a restricted-access, foreign-currency store. But, by the late 1960s, the Yugoslav Communists had gone on to create yet another New Class, this one also defined in large part by its access to and control over material goods. Members of this segment of society busied themselves shopping for, buying, and enjoying all the tangible things and intangible experiences that their newfound positions of economic privilege afforded them. They outfitted their homes and apartments with sleek, modern furniture modeled on the hottest and freshest ideas from Scandinavia. They planned renovated kitchens furnished with up-to-date appliances and laid out in popular styles that aspired to the latest European design standards. This new New Class watched television in pleasant living rooms and listened to popular music on modern hi-fi systems. As if their comfortable apartments and homes were not enough, they busily set about building weekend houses in the mountains and along the spectacular Adriatic seacoast. They thumbed through magazines on automobiles and home improvement and entertainment and fashion, and they followed the trends emanating from the style centers of Western Europe and the United States. They laundered their new clothes in new washing machines installed in their new and modern bathrooms. They snapped up perfumes and skin creams and makeup and detergents and all manner of other cosmetics and household items. They ate well and drank freely and smoked a lot, with appetites stirred by their keen awareness of all the finer things European markets had to offer.

They traveled, too. They saved a portion of their paychecks to buy automobiles, modest but serviceable, and in those little cars Yugoslav families journeyed about energetically on holiday around their own country and across Europe—and not just to the "fraternal" states of communist Eastern Europe but to the West as well, typically making those visits to "the lands of developed capitalism" without any restriction more serious than a budget.

This second New Class of Yugoslavs was caught up in the pursuit of what may fairly be called the Yugoslav Dream, an embrace of the pleasures and virtues of material abundance that sought at once to mirror and rival the American Dream of postwar prosperity. Yet for the new New Class, the Good Life was more than just a dream. It held its share of illusions, to be sure, but it was no mere deception or escapist fantasy. It was real, tangible, and immediate—something that could be seen across Yugoslavia in advertisements and the popular press, purchased in the stores and supermarkets, and brought home to enjoy and display.

In stark contrast to the comparatively narrow circle of bureaucrats that Djilas had described, the New Class of the economically privileged that emerged in the 1960s was by no means a small, restricted group of the powerful, well-connected, and influential. Quite to the contrary, all this fervid and altogether conspicuous consumption had rapidly become the domain of more or less ordinary Yugoslav citizens. To be sure, serious differences in earnings and disposable income persisted, and the Yugoslav Dream would always remain unattainable for many people. But the new life of plentiful pleasures and comparative comfort was within reach for *enough* of the population to sustain it as a realistic hope even for those who could not at the moment share fully in the dream. In other words, the emergent vision of consumer abundance was sufficiently grounded in social and economic realities to give it substantial legitimacy as a dominant cultural model for the country as a whole and to make it genuinely, and peculiarly, Yugoslav. This capacity to create a widely shared, truly *popular* culture made the new engagement with consumption a novel and profoundly significant force in Yugoslav history—and, indeed, in the history of socialism. And that it could take root across the staggeringly varied Yugoslav federation made the new consumer culture all the more important. Such unifying forces were a rarity in this society, where ethnic, linguistic, religious, cultural, and economic differences long hampered the development of pan-Yugoslav values, attitudes, customs, and identities.

Sustained both through the decisions of political and business leaders and through the everyday acts of ordinary shoppers and consumers, Yugoslavia's remarkable culture of consumption formed a great part—arguably the greatest part—of what made the society's experiment in socialism so distinctive. In addition, the shared celebration and pursuit of abundance was what made the venture, at least for a time, so successful.

But this was also what made the Yugoslav experiment so precarious: in ways we are only now beginning to appreciate, the failure of the Yugoslav Dream—the thwarted expectation of a Good Life that would be ever more available, ever more pleasing—was an essential part of what ultimately brought socialism to an end and tore the country apart. To understand what happened to Yugoslavia, and to the communist project in Yugoslavia, we need to appreciate the nature and power of the Yugoslav Dream and, beyond that, to ask just how the new vision of the Good Life was created, how it was lived, and what it meant for Yugoslav society—to ask, in other words, how it was bought and sold. To come to that understanding is the purpose of this book.

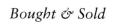

Bought & Sold

Introduction
Getting It
Making Sense of Socialist Consumer Culture

In the past year, our average Yugoslav woman has had a lot of temptations. Every month a new detergent. It's not easy to take a political stand and choose between Yeti and Mixal.
　　—New Year's greetings "To the Average Woman in the SFRY [Socialist Federal Republic of Yugoslavia]," *Svijet* [World], 1 January 1968

　　This book explains something that was simply not supposed to happen: for all their emphasis on material prosperity and social welfare, socialist states were not supposed to generate "consumer societies" where shoppers' desires supplanted genuine human needs and where the symbolic, expressive, cultural value of the goods and services purchased became a primary factor of individual and group identity. And yet, as shown here, these things did happen in socialist Yugoslavia, with extraordinary consequences for both the life and the death of the Yugoslav experiment in reformist socialism and multiethnic federalism.

　　Though it is easy enough to forget this fact given the sad fate of Yugoslavia in the 1990s, our subject is a country with a system of government that many once considered to be the best of all possible socialisms: a bold and noble, if flawed, experiment in tolerance and flexibility. Ultimately that experiment failed, it is true, but if we care to understand what Yugoslavia once was, we forget that tolerance and flexibility at our peril. Those virtues are, at any rate, central to the story told here. With regard to consumption, Yugoslav socialism did indeed prove to be open, experimental, and extraordinarily amenable to practices and values that the political leaders and economic managers of other communist states were much more likely to squelch in short order as undesirable ideological deviations.

　　The results were striking and the implications profound. From the mid-1950s on the political climate in Yugoslavia permitted, and later even encouraged, the growth of a deep and complicated relationship with shopping, spending, acquiring, and enjoying, a relationship that engaged the public on a day-to-day basis through the enthusiastic and surprisingly

---

Source for the epigraph: Zoran Zec, "Novogodišnja pisma Zorana Zeca," *Svijet* no. 1, 1 January 1968, 8–9, at 9.

unrestrained use of "rational," "scientific," and "modern" styles of commerce and communication. Socialist Yugoslavia thus moved toward the creation of a consumer society: for a growing number of its people, the experience of consumption began to take on a set of meanings that no longer bore a strong relationship to the mere fulfillment of basic material needs. The acquisition of various consumer goods and services, and the consumption of experiences like holiday getaways, moviegoing, dancing and drinking in discotheques, and foreign travel, all gradually became a more central concern of social life in Yugoslavia. At the same time the status, satisfaction, and self-understanding of individuals in the society were increasingly linked to the ways in which they consumed such goods, services, and experiences.

By the late 1960s a marked shift toward these characteristic modes of thought and action—that is, toward the way of life that scholars and critics have typically identified as "consumerism"—was well under way. Commercial advertising, for example, had come to play a strikingly more prominent role in the daily lives of Yugoslavs than it did in other European socialist countries, although it did not yet rival the full-scale promotion seen in Britain, for example. (Applying the designation "Yugoslavs" may now trigger objections in parts of what used to be the socialist federation. But the use of the term here and indeed throughout the book is, in fact, justified by the very frames of reference that were assumed and deployed across the country by party and state officials, businesses, advertisers, and indeed most contributors to public discourse, including ordinary citizens: at issue then, as now, were *Yugoslav* consumers, a *Yugoslav* market, *Yugoslav* shopping opportunities, a *Yugoslav* popular culture.) A fundamental qualitative shift in the modes and messages of advertising compounded the dramatic expansion in the sheer volume of the ads themselves, as they became more difficult to distinguish from the styles and techniques employed in Western Europe and in the United States, which had long been the most important incubator of advertising theory and practice. Alongside the growth of advertising in its strict sense came a parallel expansion of the broader concept of marketing, and with it crept in a new ideology—radically new in the socialist context—of the role of business and the essential nature of the relationship between producers, distributors, and consumers. The principal modes of retailing began to change as well, and though the country never saw anything quite so free-wheeling and aggressive as the American style of merchandising, Yugoslav enterprises did begin to discard their very traditional business practices in favor of techniques that played to the notion that shopping and purchasing should be a pleasing expression of the consumer's individuality. As a result, self-service shops, supermarkets, and department stores that aspired to Western ideals of luxury, choice, satisfaction, and modernity started to spring up across Yugoslavia beginning as early as the late 1950s.

As a consequence of all this rapid change, shopping and buying captured a steadily larger share of the public imagination. Given the prevailing stereotypes about the grim and gray everyday of communism, it bears mentioning that this heavy emphasis on shopping in Yugoslavia was not the product of ordeals like those that year after year faced buyers looking for the most basic items in the stores of the Soviet Union and other less prosperous communist countries. Extreme scarcity, too, can lend an unusually powerful valence to consumption activity, but it yields a very different calculus of consumption and a very different consumer culture.[1] Yugoslavia never shook off all its worries about shortages, but scarcity is not what made the Yugoslav experience so novel and so surprising.

Instead, the heightened concern with consumption and its power that gripped Yugoslav society speaks to a transformed terrain for the day-to-day operation of socialist economics: new conditions of abundance, and with them a fundamental shift in the meaning of the experience of finding, choosing, purchasing, and using consumer commodities. In the stores themselves, the selection and quality available to purchasers improved substantially. With consumers being offered, at least in many instances, a real choice between competing manufacturers both domestic and foreign, producers began to feel some genuine pressures to respond to market forces, just as government policy had intended, and the most aggressive enterprises explored ways to use the new arts of advertising, marketing, and retailing to secure their competitive position and establish brand loyalty among the customers they targeted. What had not too long before been shopping for sustenance was now becoming, in a more prosperous, more open, and more competitive Yugoslavia, shopping for satisfaction, self-expression, and status, prompting critics to fret that instead of the anticipated "classless society" the country was now veering toward a culture of status marking and group differentiation of the sort that Pierre Bourdieu would later describe in his analysis of consumption and taste.[2]

None of this would sound all that surprising if what was being described here was the evolution of a consumerist orientation in an economy geared to the principles and values of market-driven capitalist production. But in a socialist society whose leaders had fought relentlessly to divorce culture from the norms of Western capitalism, and whose citizens had been taught to ground their identities not on their participation in markets as consumers but rather on their rights and responsibilities as producers, the rise of a genuine consumer culture resembling that seen in the West was, to put it mildly, rather unexpected.

Changes of this magnitude demand explanations. Accordingly, this project has necessarily involved a search for evidence that may deepen our understanding of how, by whom, and with precisely what intentions the consumerist

---

1. For a very different sort of consumer culture in conditions of great scarcity, see Liviu Chelcea, "The Culture of Shortage during State Socialism: Consumption Practices in a Romanian Village in the 1980s," *Cultural Studies* 16, no. 1 (2002): 16–43.

2. Pierre Bourdieu, *Distinction: A Social Critique of the Judgment of Taste* (Cambridge, Mass., 1984).

course was bought and sold—how it was chosen, advocated, approved, and put into practice. As explained in the chapters that follow, Yugoslav consumerism and the mass culture that embodied it were the products of a complicated back-and-forth between party-state representatives, businesspeople and enterprise leaders, and ordinary members of the consuming public, all of them deeply involved in the continual cycle of buying and selling.

Open for Business? The Effects of Western Exposure

The analysis presented in these pages stresses Yugoslavia's openness to Western cultural, ideological, and commercial influences. It is impossible to understand properly the growth and spread of consumerist values in the country without taking full account of its distinctive cross-border cultural fluidity. If we are concerned with the development of advertising, marketing, and retailing, for example, it is critical to acknowledge the extent to which many of the ideas and techniques of these industries—and the ideology of business that underlay those ideas and techniques—were transnational in the truest and most rigorous sense of the term: directly imported from the capitalist West through a variety of channels such as scholarly and trade literature, professional exchanges, international conferences, and trade fairs. The most ardent advocates and "sellers" of an expansion of the consumerist orientation in Yugoslavia, the country's advertising and marketing specialists, had largely unrestricted access to foreign business literature and, like other Yugoslavs, were free to travel abroad. They read voraciously and traveled widely, and they eagerly sought out their peers from Western Europe and the United States, engaging in what would be called "networking" in today's business argot. In the process, they brought home ideas essential to the making of a new way of doing business in Yugoslavia, a new culture of the market, and, indeed, a new way of living.[3] But no matter how dedicated these ad men were (and these circles remained, like the rest of the Yugoslav political and economic establishment, preponderantly male), there was a limit to what they and the market culture they promoted could achieve in the absence of a strong response from below, that is, from the ranks of ordinary buyers and browsers who interacted with the business-driven culture of the market and, in the process, produced a broader popular *consumer* culture.

An even greater practical consequence of the regime's permissiveness with regard to foreign travel was the extensive cross-border shopping traffic that developed at points of easy contact with Western commerce. Yugoslavs

---

3. The transfer of ideas about business will be a major concern of subsequent chapters. Increasingly it is also an important focus of business history and cultural history more generally. On the links between popular culture and the ideologies that may inhere in commercial publicity, see, for example, William J. Bird Jr., *"Better Living": Advertising, Media, and the New Vocabulary of Business Leadership, 1935–1955* (Evanston, Ill., 1999).

became frequent day-trippers to towns just over their borders with Italy and Austria (and, to a lesser extent, Greece). Croats around Zagreb and Slovenes near Maribor, for example, could easily travel to Graz in Austria for household items, groceries, and appliances that were unavailable or more expensive in Yugoslavia; Slovenes living in or around Ljubljana could be over the Alps and in the shopping centers of Klagenfurt in an hour or so. People in Macedonia and southern Serbia had fairly easy access to the markets and shops of Thessaloniki. And Yugoslavs of every variety poured into Trieste to buy all sorts of Western items. In particular, shoppers in Trieste were keen to bring back more fashionable clothes than they believed could be had back at home. The stream of customers into Italy was so reliable that many Triestine shopkeepers learned enough Serbo-Croatian to lubricate their business transactions with the busloads of shoppers from the East.[4]

Obviously the very fact that there remained a perceived need to go shopping abroad suggests that not all was perfect at home. But given that the country in question here was communist, it should perhaps be noted that throughout all this border-hopping, defection was never a major worry. Things were not perfect at home, but they were good enough. So Yugoslav shoppers left, and they came right back. And because of what they saw and experienced while abroad, when they did return they brought back considerably more than just the day's haul of consumer goods.

Though it was almost certainly of less direct practical consequence than the bustling cross-border shopping trade, we should not discount the more subtle effects of another phenomenon, holiday tourism to the West. As Yugoslavs became wealthier in the 1960s and 1970s, they enthusiastically took advantage of their unusual freedom to travel. Needing no visas to visit practically any country in Europe by the mid-1960s—a happy outcome of their state's peculiar geopolitical positioning between the two Cold War blocs—they began streaming out of Yugoslavia on longer vacations, bringing back new "European" goods, new experiences of life as participants in the Western whirl of advertising and shopping, and new ideas about what their own national economy might be expected to offer consumers. The concrete contributions of these sorts of leisure excursions to the West, of course, are difficult to measure with any great certainty. Still, abundant evidence suggests that these experiences also played a significant role in shaping the country's emerging consumer culture. So, too, did the availability of Western media in Yugoslavia. On the pages of imported newspapers and magazines, and soon even in the domestic press, ordinary Yugoslavs could see for themselves what the competing system promised its consumers. Some

4. On the significance of this cross-border shopping, see Wendy Bracewell, "Adventures in the Marketplace: Yugoslav Travel Writing and Tourism in the 1950s–1960s," in *Turizm: The Russian and East European Tourist under Capitalism and Socialism*, ed. Anne E. Gorsuch and Diane P. Koenker (Ithaca, 2006), 248–265; Alenka Švab, "Consuming Western Image of Well-Being—Shopping Tourism in Socialist Slovenia," *Cultural Studies* 16, no. 1 (2002): 63–79.

Slovenes, moreover, could receive Italian and Austrian television and radio broadcasts, and, with time, popular American television shows were shown, to avid audiences, on Yugoslav channels. Consequently, in the last decades of the socialist period the Yugoslav public was even more closely connected to the experience of daily life in the shoppers' paradise of the West.

Another potent contribution to the reorientation of public values toward consumerism was the cultural and ideological importation that accompanied Yugoslavia's massive export of *Gastarbeiter* labor to Western Europe. Hundreds of thousands of Yugoslavs left the country for work in the West. Usually men unaccompanied by their families, and often from the poorer parts of Yugoslavia, these workers typically returned home from time to time. When they returned, they came back schooled in Western consumer culture. Having lived under a different social and economic paradigm, they were more acutely aware of its costs, but they had also seen what it had to offer. They had watched hundreds if not thousands of television commercials, seen newspapers and magazines full of well-crafted and seductive advertisements, been drawn in by dazzling shop-window displays, and checked out the extensive selection of consumer items in the stores themselves. Everyday life in the West gave these guest workers a host of opportunities to judge for themselves which features of the capitalist way of life were better or worse than what they had been able to expect back home. Their comparatively well-paid work abroad meant that when they returned home they had greater disposable income—often dramatically more—and new ideas about how to spend that money. Moreover, they often left behind a substantial portion of these funds in Yugoslavia for their families to spend.

These exchanges of labor, hard currency, and ideas had profound and enduring implications for the domestic development of consumer culture. In both geographic and socioeconomic terms, there was an important cascading effect to all these *Gastarbeiter* contacts: through them, the benefits of German, Swiss, Austrian, and Scandinavian wealth spilled downward to the poorer strata of Yugoslav society, while the evolving demographics of the labor flows ultimately carried the values and styles of Western consumerism deep into the historically underdeveloped Yugoslav South, helping to overcome, at least to some extent, the obstacles that a lower standard of living and sheer physical distance had imposed.

All That YU Can Be: The Possibilities of the Good Life for Yugoslav History

Because it was so remarkably open to the mixing of cultural elements associated with both socialist and capitalist ways of life, Yugoslavia presents a fascinating case study of the historical development of consumerist mentalities and the emergence of consumer society. Here this book ventures onto new ground: with the exception of a small cluster of recent studies of the German Democratic Republic[5] and a scattering of works on other countries, typically limited in scope and accessible only to those with a command of the languages of the region, the otherwise massive scholarship on consumption and culture has largely overlooked the societies of Eastern Europe.[6] There has been a flurry of cultural-critical studies on the post-Soviet landscape, but explicitly historical work on the consumer experience in the Soviet Union is still in its infancy, despite some promising new analyses, particularly in the area of retail trade, and a welcome emphasis on the lives of ordinary citizens sparked in no small part by Sheila Fitzpatrick's landmark *Everyday Stalinism*.[7] As for Yugoslavia itself, the country's political and economic history have been well covered in traditional terms,[8] but when it comes to the relationship between that history and the widespread culture of consumption that made Yugoslavia so different and so promising, very few of the central questions have been asked, and very little of the story has been told, though a few exceptional contributions have started to bring at least some of these issues to light, as seen notably in the recent work of such scholars as Croatian historian Igor Duda, Slovenian media studies and communication specialist Breda Luthar, and Serbian historian Predrag J. Marković.[9]

Yugoslavia's engagement with consumption—so important to Yugoslavs themselves and so noticeable to foreigners who visited the country—thus

---

5. The only case for which an appropriate foundational scholarship has developed is that of East Germany, although it is still far from comprehensive. Key monographic contributions include Philipp Heldmann, *Herrschaft, Wirtschaft, Anoraks: Konsumpolitik in der DDR der Sechzigerjahre* (Göttingen, 2004); Ina Merkel, *Utopie und Bedürfnis: die Geschichte der Konsumkultur in der DDR* (Cologne, 1999); Mark Landsman, *Dictatorship and Demand: The Politics of Consumerism in East Germany* (Cambridge, Mass., 2005); Philip J. Bryson, *The Consumer under Socialist Planning: The East German Case* (New York, 1984). See also Jonathan R. Zatlin, *The Currency of Socialism: Money and Political Culture in East Germany* (New York, 2007).

6. The most important contributions to the extant literature are cited throughout this book in connection with the various specific subjects at issue.

7. See Sheila Fitzpatrick, *Everyday Stalinism: Ordinary Life in Extraordinary Times: Soviet Russia in the 1930s* (New York, 1999), esp. chap. 2, "Hard Times," 40–66. Dynamics similar to those Fitzpatrick describes persisted through the state-socialist period. See also Catriona Kelly, "Ordinary Life in Extraordinary Times: Chronicles of the Quotidian in Russia and the Soviet Union," *Kritika: Explorations in Russian and Eurasian History* 3, no. 4 (fall 2002): 631–651.

8. See, for example, Carol S. Lilly, *Power and Persuasion: Ideology and Rhetoric in Communist Yugoslavia, 1944–1953* (Boulder, Colo., 2001); John R. Lampe, *Yugoslavia as History: Twice There Was a Country*, 2d ed. (Cambridge, 2000). A provocative and forcefully argued new interpretation, grounded in theories of regime stability and attuned to the central problem of the legitimacy of the various Yugoslav governments, is Sabrina P. Ramet, *The Three Yugoslavias: State-Building and Legitimation, 1918–2005* (Washington, D.C., 2006).

9. E.g., Igor Duda, *Pronađeno blagostanje: svakodnevni život i potrošačka kultura u Hrvatskoj 1970-ih i 1980-ih* (Zagreb, 2010); Duda, *U potrazi za odmorom i blagostanjem: O povijesti dokolice i potrošačkog društva u Hrvatskoj 1950-ih i 1960-ih* (Zagreb: 2005); Duda, "Tehnika narodu! Trajna dobra, potrošnja i slobodno vrijeme u socijalističkoj Hrvatskoj," *Časopis za suvremenu povijest* 37, no. 2 (2005): 371–392; Breda Luthar, "Remembering Socialism: On Desire, Consumption and Surveillance," *Journal of Consumer Culture* 6, no. 2 (2006): 229–259.

remains largely obscured from the historical record.[10] A prime mission here must therefore be to characterize and interpret the texture of the consumer experience as it unfolded. Another chief aim is to look carefully at questions of agency, origin, and causation. The study therefore seeks, for example, to determine how it was that those who governed Yugoslavia began to tolerate and even welcome some aspects of consumerism. In simplest terms, of course, the Yugoslav consumer culture grew out of the party's experimentation with market mechanisms through its much ballyhooed system of "socialist self-management" [*samoupravljanje*]. In part, the search for an answer can and must build upon the body of scholarship concerning that innovation, which, happily, is rich indeed.[11]

But we have to go beyond those simple and convenient terms to understand what really happened in, and to, Yugoslavia. Self-management meant the injection of, at most, limited and imperfect market forces into the Yugoslav economy. What has to be explicated here, however, is the proliferation of a rich (some said extravagant) consumer culture and the movement toward the values and behaviors associated with consumer society. Can the option for self-management explain that? It cannot. There is little reason to conclude that the drift toward full-fledged consumerism was a foreordained consequence of the move to self-management socialism, as some Yugoslav critics worried at the time. The Yugoslav economic and political system was remarkably more open than its counterparts in the rest of socialist Europe, and the effect of market forces was indeed real, if significantly constrained by a lack of the political will to let unprofitable enterprises fail. Yet despite all this maneuvering room for producers, distributors, advertisers, and consumers, the fundamental political realities of communist governance in Yugoslavia meant that the society and its institutions were still very amenable to state direction and would remain so even during the final years of sometimes chaotic decentralization.

Given the persistence of at least the potential for real and meaningful political control, another key problem arises. The emergence of a radically new cultural orientation toward shopping, buying, and consuming forces us to inquire whether, so to speak, anyone was minding the store. In other words,

---

10. Studies focused on everyday life as such in the socialist world are still comparatively rare, but there are signs of a new and rapid expansion. See, for example, David Crowley and Susan E. Reid, eds., *Socialist Spaces: Sites of Everyday Life in the Eastern Bloc* (Oxford, 2002).

11. See, for example, Susan L. Woodward, *Socialist Unemployment: The Political Economy of Yugoslavia, 1945–1990* (Princeton, N.J., 1995); Laura D'Andrea Tyson, *The Yugoslav Economic System and Its Performance in the 1970s* (Berkeley, 1980); Aleksander Bajt, *Alternativna ekonomska politika* (Zagreb, 1986); Bajt, *Osnovi ekonomske politike i analize* (Zagreb, 1979); Branko Horvat, *The Yugoslav Economic System* (Armonk, N.Y., 1976); Horvat, *Jugoslavenska privreda, 1965–1983* (Ljubljana, 1984); Deborah Duff Milenkovitch, *Plan and Market in Yugoslav Economic Thought* (New Haven, Conn., 1971). An essential background work is John R. Lampe and Marvin R. Jackson, *Balkan Economic History, 1550–1950: From Imperial Borderlands to Developing Nations* (Bloomington, 1982).

we must ask to what extent the creation of a consumer culture in this sort of society reflected a *deliberate* strategy on the part of government decision makers, and to what extent this new culture developed more or less on its own, "from below," perhaps attesting to the power of modern capitalist practices to shape social relations according to their own internal logic.

Underscoring the ascendant concern for consumers as historical agents, Frank Trentmann, who sees in modern history nothing less than "the evolution of the consumer into a master category of collective and individual identity," has sought to redirect our attention to the processes whereby *consumers as such* emerged as vital subjects of modernity, concluding that "before there could be a popular notion of consumer sovereignty, the consumer had to be cultivated."[12] There is much truth to that observation, yet the comparatively late eruption of these larger world-historical processes in Yugoslavia and elsewhere in the communist world meant that the two developments had to take place simultaneously. Yugoslav consumers were being "made"—by retailers, advertising and marketing specialists, business planners and other experts, government and party officials, and not least by themselves and their compatriots—at the same time that the concept of their "sovereign" place in the nation's economic system was starting to take root.

Occasionally, and especially early on, ordinary Yugoslavs showed some disinclination to be transformed into the new consuming types that businesses, state agencies, and the media imagined would be so useful to the development of the economy and of the society as a whole. For example, as Igor Duda documents in his examination of the culture of tourism in Croatia in the 1950s and 1960s, selling the idea of "modern" leisure consumption was by no means a sure thing. And so, in 1958, the ninety beds of a resort that one major textile enterprise maintained on Rab (a little charmer of an island with, today, a thriving tourist industry) proved to be, as Duda reveals, "still too many for the five thousand Varteks workers who would rather have stayed at home" or opted for short bus excursions that let them sleep in their own beds. "When it was time to head off for annual vacation at the seaside, even if it was free, they were able to say, 'No, thank you, comrades. In my thirty years of work I have still never spent my vacation at the sea. That's not for me.'"[13] Not all new consumption habits came easily.

Yet despite such occasional bumps in the road, what is most remarkable is the way in which most ordinary Yugoslavs indeed were, sooner or later, sold on the virtues and pleasures of consumption and thus effectively made into

---

12. Frank Trentmann, "Knowing Consumers—Histories, Identities, Practices: An Introduction," in *The Making of the Consumer: Knowledge, Power, and Identity in the Modern World,* ed. Frank Trentmann (Oxford, 2006), 2, 9.

13. References are to Duda, *U potrazi za blagostanjem,* 86–87, citing "Društvena tribina: Nije uzrok samo u novcu, *Vjesnik,* 19 June 1958. Mary Neuburger finds that the Bulgarian state had similar difficulties in enticing Muslim women into new roles as "modern" consuming women. Neuburger, "Veils, *Shalvari,* and Matters of Dress: Unravelling the Fabric of Women's

consumers: engaged, curious, resourceful, enthusiastic, and demanding. The advent of this sort of consumer, and this sort of consumerism, carried with it great implications for the legitimacy of the Yugoslav regime—and, ultimately, for the success and failure of the Yugoslav experiment. During the country's years of remarkable prosperity, the Communists benefited from a more secure position in the minds of the public. This book shows how the new consumerist orientation served to reinforce an understanding of Yugoslav socialism as the ultimate benefactor of the new bounty for shoppers, leading some critics to allege that it was deployed for just such ends. A heady consumer culture proved to be a major part of what gave the Yugoslav socialist experiment its life and its legitimacy, but by raising public expectations and placing a heightened value on ever expanding access to consumer goods, it made the economic disintegration that came in the late 1970s and 1980s even more unbearable, thereby contributing to the ouster of the Communists.[14]

The linkages between consumer culture and yet another central problem in Yugoslav history, the national question, are no less tantalizing. The account presented here illustrates how people across the federation could typically experience the new abundance as Yugoslav citizens, that is, as beneficiaries of federal-level policy and of a flexible, innovative, specifically Yugoslav kind of state socialism—rather than as, say, ethnic Slovenes, Croats, Magyars, and so forth, or as citizens of a given republic or residents of a given region. At the same time, however, not all areas of the country shared in the newfound prosperity to the same extent, and the rise of a consumerist culture may, in fact, have created popular expectations that could not be satisfied in the poorer parts of the country, thereby exacerbating the north/south split and compounding centrifugal tensions.

Now that the former Yugoslav republics have gone their own way, each has embraced at least to some degree a version of Western consumerism—if

---

Lives in Communist Bulgaria," in *Style and Socialism: Modernity and Material Culture in Post-War Eastern Europe,* ed. Susan E. Reid and David Crowley (Oxford, 2000), 169–187.

14. In this connection, my interpretations will draw upon, and I hope make some contribution to, the substantial body of critical literature that has addressed the relationship between material wealth and individual satisfaction. Some scholars, especially economists, have deemed a positive correlation between the two to be certain, even self-evident. See Colin Campbell, "Consumption: The New Wave of Research in the Humanities and Social Sciences," in *To Have Possessions: A Handbook on Ownership and Property* (special issue), *Journal of Social Behavior and Personality* 6, no. 6 (1991): 57–74. But other studies, elaborating the early critics' misgivings about the potential social costs of consumerism, have recast the issue as quite problematic indeed. See, for example, Richard Easterlin, "Will Raising the Incomes of All Increase the Happiness of All?" *Journal of Economic Behavior and Organization* 27 (1995): 35–48; Easterlin, "Does Economic Growth Improve the Human Lot?" in *Nations and Households in Economic Growth: Essays in Honor of Moses Abramovitz,* ed. Paul David and Melvin Reder (New York, 1974), 89–125; William Leiss, *The Limits of Satisfaction: An Essay on the Problem of Needs and Commodities* (Toronto, 1976); Daniel Miller, *Material Culture and Mass Consumption* (Oxford, 1987).

not always the political and economic norms of Western liberal democracy that are often assumed (erroneously) to go hand in hand with consumerist capitalism. As a result, the years since the dissolution of the Yugoslav federation in 1991 have seen an upwelling of new critical attention focused on the troubling consequences of what in some places has been a headlong rush toward consumer society.[15] The approach taken in these works often suggests that the presence of consumer society in what used to be Yugoslavia has been a matter of a post-socialist—and thus capitalist—*creatio ex nihilo*.[16] One of the chief implications of my analysis is that this was anything but the case. The immediate concern here, however, is not with "what came after" but instead to explore the complex developments that laid a solid groundwork for the later entrenchment of consumerist values across former Yugoslavia. Still, the very fact that domestic critics are now so attuned to the power of consumerism in the remnants of Yugoslavia suggests the importance of efforts to probe the nature of consumer culture in the predecessor state and to comprehend, insofar as is possible, what came before.

Getting There Is Half the Fun: The Conceptual Value of Socialist Consumer Culture

As the foregoing suggests, a careful study of consumer culture ought to yield insights that will allow us to re-chart the broader currents of Yugoslavia's own history—reason enough to take the phenomenon seriously. Yet the focus on Yugoslavia should ultimately contribute to a greater understanding of the significance of consumer culture in the modern world as well. It probably stretches the facts too far to conclude, as did Milovan Djilas at the close of the 1980s, long after his fall from grace, that "Yugoslavia is the laboratory of all Communism," but it surely was an extraordinary testing ground for socialist politics and economics and for left-revisionist efforts to create new social forms that might avoid some of the worst ills and excesses of both

---

15. See, for example, the special issue of one of Slovenia's most prominent cultural reviews devoted to consumption issues: *Potrošnja: zasebne prakse, javni užitki* (special issue), *Časopis za kritiko znanosti* 26, no. 189 (1998).

16. A welcome exception is Katherine Sredl, "Consumption and Class during and after State Socialism," in *Research in Consumer Behavior*, Vol. 11, *Consumer Culture Theory*, ed. Russell Belk and John Sherry (Oxford, 2007), 187–205. On the importance of past and present consumption practice to the post-Soviet experience, see, for example, Caroline Humphrey, *The Unmaking of Soviet Life: Everyday Economies after Socialism* (Ithaca, 2002); Adele Marie Barker, ed., *Consuming Russia: Popular Culture, Sex, and Society since Gorbachev* (Durham, N.C., 1999); Nancy Condee and Vladimir Padunov, "The ABC of Russian Consumer Culture: Readings, Ratings, and Real Estate," in *Soviet Hieroglyphics: Visual Culture in Late Twentieth-Century Russia*, ed. Nancy Condee (Bloomington, 1995), 130–172. See also Ruth Mandel and Caroline Humphrey, eds., *Markets and Moralities: Ethnographies of Postsocialism* (Oxford, 2002).

Cold War paradigms.[17] As such, it was a site of experimentation that had, then as now, world-historical significance.

Most immediately, this case holds important implications for the history of socialism and its capitalist competitor.[18] As critics within Yugoslavia frequently complained, the country's culture of consumption was marked by many outward similarities to the classic consumer societies of the capitalist West. All this change was remarkable for just how "un-communist" it felt. As such, the choice of Yugoslavia helps us begin testing the traditional identification of consumer society with capitalism. Because the growth of consumer culture has been so florid in capitalist economies, and especially in the consummate dreamland of consumerist abandon, the United States, there has been insufficient attention to the question of whether other, *non*-capitalist economic systems might themselves produce something resembling Western-style consumer culture. This book seeks to help redress that imbalance and to take our conceptualization of consumption in the new directions needed.

Real and meaningful differences are at work here. For all the points of contact and comparison, Yugoslavia never became anything like the "Consumers' Republic" that Lizabeth Cohen has described in her study of the postwar United States. Always remaining far more problematic in the prevailing public discourse, consumption was never clearly articulated as a *duty* of citizenship, as had been the case in America. Instead consumption continued, more predictably and comfortably, in its familiar status as a *reward*. And though some of those who sold the consumer ideal bore strong resemblances to the economic and political actors emphasized in Cohen's account, the citizen's participation in consumption was never widely understood to have anything like the power and virtue of "delivering not only economic prosperity but also loftier social and political ambitions for a more equal, free, and democratic nation."[19]

We might ask, then, whether Yugoslavia ended up generating a genuinely, distinctively, perhaps even purely "socialist" version of consumer culture. The answer is that it did not: although the country's economic system remained socialist, the *culture* of consumption that arose there was, in truth, a hybrid form. Socialist values and socialist economic relationships certainly did shape and restrain the development of Yugoslavia's consumer culture, but the shared public experience was also marked by cultural norms and forms derived from the capitalist West and, arguably, by values and practices that resulted from the sheer variety and abundance of the Yugoslav consumer market as it evolved. Consumer culture, in other words, sprang from varied sources and often proved capable of growing and moving independently of the socialist

17. Milovan Djilas, quoted in Robert D. Kaplan, *Balkan Ghosts: A Journey through History* (New York, 1993), 76.

18. On the East-West competition in Germany, see David F. Crew, ed., *Consuming Germany in the Cold War* (Oxford, 2003).

19. Lizabeth Cohen, *A Consumers' Republic: The Politics of Mass Consumption in Postwar America* (New York, 2003), 13.

economic basis of the Yugoslav system. These findings challenge the assumed necessity of capitalism and, at the same time, call into question Marx's original assessment of culture as "superstructure," that is, as the reflection, the instrument, and above all the product of underlying production relations.

Recent scholarship on consumption frequently centers on the means by which consumer society tends to grow and spread.[20] Given the history of consumption in the modern world, it is certainly quite reasonable that this would be an overarching concern for many observers, and indeed the effort to determine just how modern consumerism cropped up in a new and unusual environment is an important focus of this book. But the extant literature on consumer society tends to treat the phenomenon as too much the unstoppable steamroller. Commentators seem so awed by its (admittedly awesome) capacity for replication and diffusion that there has been a comparative neglect of the mechanisms that may serve to hold consumerist values in check. This work seeks to help remedy that problem by pairing an examination of the processes of propagation with a fresh look at the possibilities for *resisting* consumer society.

The potential rewards are clear. As Victoria de Grazia has observed in her far-reaching review of the transfer of American business and consumer values to Europe (or, more precisely, to Western Europe), the state-socialist system, through the leadership of the Soviet Union, "came to be regarded as offering the leading global alternative to the hegemony of American consumer culture for practically the entire period from 1945 to its disintegration in the late 1980s."[21] Yet if the "consumer revolution" of capitalism's "irresistible empire" was to be resisted anywhere, it was in Eastern Europe and the Soviet Union. Here again the Yugoslav example, where consumerism met with both forceful support and forceful opposition inside and outside the channels of official power, proves especially enlightening.

For this and other critical questions in the global history of consumption and consumerism—origins, mechanisms, constraints, and consequences— many open issues remain, and considerable work awaits us, but in the search for answers that can reach beyond the limitations of the familiar ground of Western capitalism, there is no better place to start than Yugoslavia.

What Is to Be Done? The Framework of This Analysis

Addressing the entirety of the socialist period from 1945 to 1991, the analysis here highlights the period of the hottest action and most rapid change in the 1960s and 1970s. To establish the varying social, cultural, and political

---

20. On the globalizing force of the advertising industry and its products, see Armand Mattelart, *Advertising International: The Privatisation of Public Space* (London, 1991).

21. Victoria de Grazia, *Irresistible Empire: America's Advance through 20th-Century Europe* (Cambridge, Mass., 2005), 11.

meanings of consumption, I have consulted an unusually broad variety of sources from across the Yugoslav federation, including both the familiar stuff of history writing and other items that, though they figure less often in conventional accounts, turn out to have great probative value when the questions at hand center, as here, on the nature and origins of popular culture and business culture. These materials include government, party, and business-organization archives; political, academic, and journalistic commentary; a large and surprisingly lively selection of trade journals and related literature; conference papers, addresses, and presentations by industry specialists, political figures, and cultural critics; economic analyses of consumption policy; textbooks on marketing, retailing, and advertising for high school and university students; ordinary consumers' complaints and letters to magazine editors; literary, film, and television representations of consumer culture; museum collections of everyday consumer items and other works of material culture; colorful newspaper and magazine coverage of consumption and shopping opportunities at home and abroad; and, of course, a rich collection of advertisements and other promotional materials.

Archival approaches to the questions posed in this book have proved extremely revealing at times, but they remain, for a variety of reasons, limited. Precious little of the evidence that matters to the history of culture and everyday life ever made it to the archives in the first place. This problem was (and is) bad enough for most times and locales, but it was exacerbated by patterns and practices typical of communist society, where civil society was weak, individuals and private groups had little opportunity or incentive to generate an archival record, and party and government organs concentrated on documenting their work according to a very specific Marxist-materialist logic that devalued culture generally and popular culture in particular. We are left with an officially sanctioned record that sees "history" the way a state (and a very statist state at that) saw it in the late twentieth century: heavy on nuts-and-bolts economic data and high-level administrative action, light to nonexistent on the thoughts, desires, values, feelings, and experiences of ordinary citizens.

Fortunately there are other places to turn. Materials from the fields of advertising, marketing, and retailing have survived as some of the best evidence of the ways in which this particular society promoted and practiced consumption. This literature of Yugoslav commercial promotion is enormous and yet until now essentially untapped.[22] Close attention must also go to the parallel development of increasingly sophisticated retailing techniques: specialty shops, service establishments, restaurants, and cafés that tried to track the hottest European and American fashions, modern

---

22. The most significant of the very rare exceptions in the secondary scholarship on the subject include two older studies: S. W. Topham, *Advertising and Socialist Self-Management in Yugoslavia* (Bradford, U.K., 1984); and Philip Hanson, *Advertising and Socialism* (White Plains, N.Y., 1974).

department stores that emulated Western styles of advertising and display, and bright, well-stocked supermarkets that served up a Yugoslav version of household abundance that could stand up reasonably well on its own, even if it could not fully match the offerings available in the West.

The relationship between the unusual consumerism that we encounter here and the more familiar Western capitalist variety can never be far from our minds in this story and has a critical bearing on the effort to capture and make sense of the historical experience of those who built and shared in Yugoslavia's consumer-society-in-the-making. I confront these problems as neither a committed opponent of nor apologist for Western capitalist practice. That said, the book does address the Yugoslav case with a healthy skepticism about many of the implicit and explicit promises of modern consumer culture, along with an awareness that consumerism may hold out the false assurance of a Good Life that on closer inspection seems, if not evil, then at least not all that good. The consumer experience may indeed offer what the Hungarian sociologist and cultural critic Elémer Hankiss calls "the toothpaste of immortality," a fundamentally deceptive mental, moral, and emotional engagement with consumer commodities that transforms them from utilitarian, need-based banalities into dream concoctions that promise to place us "in the center of beauty, wealth, and success, in the midst of the jet set, where the real people live and the real things happen" and even let us "enter the sacred fields of eternity."[23]

At the same time, however, it seems only proper to temper this sort of skepticism with a respectful recognition that consumerism in Yugoslavia grew, in no small way, out of people's very honest desires and aspirations for a life they understood as better. To buy, to keep, perchance to dream: sometimes consumers really did find a little happiness in the opportunity to escape the woes of their workaday world through the pleasures of consumption.

Scholars therefore risk a serious error when they adopt a critical stance either reflexively hostile toward or dismissive of the consumer experience in modern society. Don Slater has it right when he observes that "what was—and still is—the most infuriating problem in consumption studies is moralism, whether the great condemnations or the great neo-liberal (or postmodern) apologias."[24] These phenomena are, to be sure, fraught with problems for the ordinary people who strive, often without success, to participate in all the promised pleasures. Illusions there are aplenty, and yet not all is illusion. For all its potential to deceive and divert, the modern consumer society nevertheless remains one that holds out to its members the prospect of certain very real rewards. Accordingly, this account looks for guidance

23. Elémer Hankiss, *The Toothpaste of Immortality: Self-Construction in the Consumer Age* (Washington, D.C., 2006), 29–30.

24. "Moments and Movements in the Study of Consumer Culture: A Discussion between Daniel Miller and Don Slater," *Journal of Consumer Culture* 7, no. 1 (2007): 5–23, at 7. See also Matthew Hilton, "The Legacy of Luxury: Moralities of Consumption since the 18th Century," *Journal of Consumer Culture* 4, no. 1 (2004): 101–123.

both to the works of those who have lamented the deceptions and sacrifices that may accompany the fetishistic pursuit of commodities,[25] beginning with the *Ursprung* of the socialist anti-consumerist critique in the work of Karl Marx, and to the interpretations of scholars who have seen in the new modes of consumer culture the promise of genuinely satisfying material abundance and the potential for individuals to create fresh, imaginative, new self-conceptions that cast aside the constraints of tired traditionalism and orthodoxy.[26]

From these points of departure, the study tackles in turn each of the most important aspects of Yugoslav consumer culture. Chapter 1, "Living It," traces the spectacular transformation of Yugoslav society that took place in the 1960s and 1970s, showing how, after a major shift of government priorities, the country became something truly unique in the state-socialist world—a place where the Good Life seemed, for the first time, to be available to ordinary people who worked and lived in a system that held out an alternative to Western capitalism's "Affluent Society." The next chapter, "Making It," focuses on the prime shapers of market culture, stressing the pivotal role played by specialists in advertising, retailing, and marketing, and by media institutions, especially television and the popular press. Chapter 3, "Selling It," demonstrates how, beginning as early as the 1950s, the representatives of these commercial trades went about legitimizing the appeal of (and to) consumerist values, working hard to "sell" the new consumer orientation to government authorities, party politicians, business leaders, and ordinary consumers.

Although this promotional campaign had its successes, Yugoslavia nonetheless became a site of heated controversy over consumerism and its consequences. The battle was fiery and furious—and, at times, wonderfully acerbic and entertaining. Chapter 4, "Fearing It," assays the mainstream Marxist critique of the ongoing consumerist shift, and the chapter that follows, "Taming It," shows how the state authorities' response often did not match the intensity of the public debate, tending instead toward a pattern of fitful accommodation and resistance, with remarkable toleration punctuated by

---

25. Classic critical analyses include, for example, Thorstein Veblen, *The Theory of the Leisure Class* (Boston, 1973 [1899]); Vance Packard, *The Hidden Persuaders* (New York, 1957); John Kenneth Galbraith, *The Affluent Society* (New York, 1958); and Leiss, *The Limits of Satisfaction.* I deal with the enormous critical literature of recent decades on an issue-specific basis throughout the remaining chapters of this book.

26. A useful collection of perspectives on these debates is Russell Keat, Nigel Whiteley, and Nicholas Abercrombie, eds., *The Authority of the Consumer* (London: Routledge, 1994). See also, for example, Stuart Ewen, *Captains of Consciousness: Advertising and the Social Roots of Consumer Culture,* 25th anniversary edition (New York: Basic Books, 2001); Simon N. Patten, *The Consumption of Wealth* (Philadelphia, 1899); Warren I. Susman, *Culture as History: The Transformation of American Society in the Twentieth Century* (New York, 1984); William Leach, "Transformations in a Culture of Consumption: Women and Department Stores, 1890–1925," *Journal of American History* 71 (September 1984): 319–342; Stanley Lebergott, *Pursuing Happiness: American Consumers in the Twentieth Century* (Princeton, N.J., 1993).

occasional ideological assaults for the purposes of discipline and restraint. A harsher and more relentless resistance to consumerist values forms the focus of Chapter 6, "Fighting It," which considers the implications of the aggressively egalitarian, anti-market Marxist humanism of the *Praxis* revisionists, who advanced the radical claim that Yugoslavia's consumerist orientation had been used as a new "opiate of the masses," adopted deliberately in order to quell popular discontent and enforce a form of barely noticeable social discipline.[27] Chapter 7, "Loving It," proves why the critics had found so much to resist. Ordinary Yugoslavs often really were "sold" on what the Yugoslav system promised to deliver: they loved their consumer culture, and they celebrated their chance to participate in it. The final chapter, "Needing It," offers further answers to the difficult question of what the movement toward consumerism meant for the making and unmaking of the Yugoslav experiment in reformist socialism and multiethnic comity. The epilogue, "Missing It," explores how and why it is precisely the country's unusual consumer culture that lies at the heart of today's wonderfully creative (and stubbornly resistant) Yugo-Nostalgia, in which consumerist pleasure and abundance represent one of the few aspects of the communist experience that can now be approached as something "safe" to remember. With so much to be forgotten, the Good Life of the past seems all the more appealing now as an unusually effective sort of social glue, a history that can be claimed happily as "ours" whether the speakers are Catholic or Orthodox, Slovene or Macedonian, Bosnian Serb or Bosnian Muslim. And so "Yugoslavia" is not yet gone: it lives on through the widely shared recollection of the once so attainable Yugoslav Dream.

Did this country's consumer culture matter? Did it play a part in the life and death of Yugoslavia? The record demonstrates that it did. Because the ideal of consumer abundance was so eagerly bought and so successfully sold, and because that ideal became the basis of a vibrant popular culture when it was given life in the everyday desires, thoughts, and values that were shared by ordinary people, Yugoslavia first flourished when times were good, then faltered when it became clear that ever increasing abundance could not prove sustainable. Because the culture of plenty and pleasure had been so much of what made the country a success and held it together, the undoing of that culture in the 1980s was felt all the more acutely when Yugoslavia at last fragmented and fell to pieces.

Given the violence that swallowed up the country in the 1990s, there is the danger that we will now forget there ever was a Yugoslav Dream. It is fair

---

27. Western opposition to consumerism, especially the Frankfurt School's denunciations of the "culture industry" of capitalist mass media and advertising, deeply influenced the Yugoslav critics. See, for example, Max Horkheimer and Theodor W. Adorno, "The Culture Industry: Enlightenment as Mass Deception," in Adorno and Horkheimer, *Dialectic of Enlightenment: Philosophical Fragments*, ed. Gunzelin Schmid Noerr, trans. Edmund Jephcott (Stanford, 2002), 94–136.

to wonder whether the arrival of the Good Life in this unlikely locale was all more or less an illusion, in the end signifying nothing. But a close look at the evidence leads to the contrary conclusion. The Yugoslav Dream was real enough, and for enough real Yugoslavs, to change the course of Yugoslav history. Doing justice to Yugoslav history, therefore, must mean making an honest and thorough effort to understand that reality. This book, then, aims to establish just what that Yugoslav vision of the Good Life was, where it came from, and what sort of difference it made for the people who built it, lived it, and saw it die.

1 Living It

Yugoslavia's Economic Miracle

The lady of the house is a short, well-built woman with a kerchief on her head, and for her forty years very young looking. She is occupied with her copper coffee mill and her *džezva* [the traditional copper Turkish coffee pot]. Finally, she sits down at the table as well and pours the coffee. [I ask:] "In your home is it a regular habit to drink coffee?" "Earlier it wasn't. At one time we only drank coffee when someone got a package from America. But in the last few years no one can be without coffee."

We took a look at newspaper headlines, selected at random, to help us remember what once made us happy, and it seemed impossible to us that all this could so quickly become just an ordinary, normal everyday way of living.
—selections from *Svijet*, December 1966

By the mid-1960s millions of ordinary Yugoslavs were eagerly participating in a burgeoning culture of consumerism that made their society quite unlike anything else in the contemporary socialist world. Not much earlier, however, a Yugoslav version of consumer society would have been all but unimaginable. In the years from 1945 to 1950 the country looked much like any other communist state. This was a period of authoritarian political control and centralized economic decision making. But beginning in 1950 the Yugoslav leadership set out on an exceptional new path. The next fifteen years would see the establishment and elaboration of an innovative new system of "workers' self-management," accompanied by decentralization, liberalization, and the first tentative moves toward the adoption of market mechanisms. These tendencies would be intensified during a third phase that began in 1965, when new legal reforms brought about a more far-reaching engagement with the market.

For most of the next decade and a half Yugoslavs would enjoy a dramatic increase in living standards and the further loosening of party control. Along

---

Sources for the epigraphs, respectively: Ivo Košutić, "Želje počinja sa fridžiderom" (interview with farm wife Maca Mankas from the village of Lekenik in the Sava river valley), *Svijet* no 24, 15 December 1966, 8–9, at 8; Pero Zlatar, "Vremeplov standarda," *Svijet* no. 23, 1 December 1966, 4–5, at 5.

with these developments came the consolidation of a vital and influential advertising and marketing industry that had emerged shortly after the reforms of the early 1950s, a process explored in detail in the next two chapters. As a result of the work of these advertising specialists and the new political and economic climate, this period also witnessed the development of something truly extraordinary in the socialist context: a rich, complex, and lively mass culture that, according to its critics, amounted to nothing less than a Yugoslav variant of consumer society very much akin to the classic phenomenon seen in the developed West. The Yugoslav economic miracle would unravel quickly at the end of the 1970s, however, and with Tito's death in 1980 the final dissolution of the Yugoslav Dream began. Economic hardship now mixed with growing regional and ethnic tensions and a resentment toward the lingering authoritarianism of communist leadership to produce a situation in which almost everyone in the country was, in one way or another, seriously dissatisfied with the status quo and impatient for change. It is easy to overlook this fact now, but not too long before, many ordinary Yugoslavs had been fairly content with their lot: certainly eager for more freedom and opportunity, and hungry for even more of the prosperity they had quickly learned to enjoy, but when all was said and done, not so aggrieved that they voiced any demand for radical, systemic change. In short order, by the late 1980s, such demands were everywhere, and they were fueled to no small degree by the developments detailed here: the distinctive Yugoslav experience of modern consumer culture.

Command Performance: Consumption and the Planned Economy, 1945–1950

For the first five years after the Communists took power, however, Yugoslavia was not the kind of country where citizens could make demands on their leaders, at least not without running great risks. Yugoslav governance, in fact, looked very much like its counterparts elsewhere in the emerging Soviet bloc: strict, centralist, and oppressive. The country's population and its infrastructure had been devastated during the war, the result both of conflicts with the occupying forces of the Axis and of internecine warfare among various competing Yugoslav factions. Much of the small industrial base that Serbia had developed before the war, for example, was destroyed or expropriated by the German occupiers. Slovenian and Croatian industrial capacity fared somewhat better under fascist management of one sort or another, and such enterprises were, as a result, among the first and easiest targets for nationalization as the new government set about establishing state control over the economy with a vengeance, in some cases quite literally.[1] The German occupation of Serbia thus exacerbated tendencies toward

---

1. Lampe and Jackson, *Balkan Economic History, 1550–1950*, 569–570.

differential economic development that would ultimately play a significant role in the destruction of the Yugoslav federation in 1991.

But despite a few bright spots, when the Communists began consolidating their power, they inherited an economy that was, for the most part, in ruins. Accordingly, among their first tasks was rebuilding the country's industrial infrastructure and productive capacity, which had not been particularly impressive even *before* the war. Tito and his allies pursued that end with a vigor and an ideological fervor that many consider unmatched by communist authorities in any of the other emerging socialist states of postwar Europe. Having achieved substantial popular legitimacy through their struggles as resistance leaders, the country's new rulers enjoyed more of a mandate to implement radical change than their counterparts elsewhere. The strategy of stealth and subterfuge seen in other East European states was not nearly so evident here because it was not nearly so necessary: in Yugoslavia during the last half of the 1940s, Communists had the freedom to act more communist. Accordingly, they embarked almost immediately on a zealous transformation of the country's economy and social structure.

"At the heart of the Yugoslav Communist ethos," as Robert Donia and John Fine observe apropos of this initial phase, "was a profound desire to follow the example of the Soviet Union."[2] Yugoslav policy during the first five years of the new state bore the deep imprint of Soviet practice and ideology. The initial template for the government's efforts in the economic sphere was therefore the Stalinist model of centralized, top-down planning. A policy of very strict political and ideological control, which extended to practically all areas of Yugoslav life during this period, reinforced the campaign to restructure the economy. Yugoslavia's communist leaders, schooled in the USSR or through their work in the Comintern, the Soviet-dominated international communist organization, had acquired the Soviet penchant for elaborate and comprehensive central planning. That orientation was evident from the start, most notably in the state's first Five-Year Plan for 1947–1952. Prepared in 1946 under the guidance of Boris Kidrič, Tito's choice to craft the new state's economic policy, the plan by most accounts amounted to an exercise in unadulterated Stalinist wishful thinking. It was, as John Lampe has observed, "as immensely detailed as it was wildly ambitious."[3] Supported and implemented, at least in theory, by a far-flung bureaucratic structure meant to harvest and mill the minutiae of economic performance across the country, the plan was also staggeringly burdensome, and in more ways than one: the annual plan documentation weighed in at three thousand pounds, emblematic of a system that was, as Fred Singleton remarked,

2. Robert J. Donia and John V. A. Fine Jr., *Bosnia and Hercegovina: A Tradition Betrayed* (New York, 1994), 158. The authors caution, however, that although Tito's respect for the Soviet model was deep and genuine, his ambition was for *Yugoslavs,* under his leadership, to rebuild their country following the examples of Lenin and Stalin. Tito certainly was of no mind to simply implement decisions made by a Soviet overlord. Ibid.

3. Lampe, *Yugoslavia as History,* 238.

"clogged by masses of paper containing information which bore little resemblance to the realities of the situation."[4]

The new economic policy reflected familiar Stalinist approaches not only in its methods but in its aims as well. Following the rapid nationalization of manufacturing assets, economic activity was oriented toward the rapid development of heavy industrial production, in the classic Soviet style. An immediate land reform was followed by much more aggressive efforts at coercive agricultural collectivization beginning in 1949 (but later forsaken). In one critical way, however, Yugoslavia became a glaring exception even during this period, marked as it was by otherwise unblemished orthopraxy. Since the end of the war, Tito's independent style had proved too independent for some. His determination to guide Yugoslav affairs occasionally caused him to run afoul of Stalin's equally adamant insistence on dictating communist policy beyond the Soviet Union. The reasons for the conflict were numerous and complex, and they are mostly peripheral to the present investigation of market culture and its broader social and political consequences. Many sore points, for example, centered on Yugoslavia's apparently unwelcome influence and prestige in Balkan affairs. Whatever their source, the disagreements multiplied, coming to a head on 28 June 1948, when Yugoslavia was expelled from the Cominform, the Soviet-controlled "information bureau" for the coordination of the international communist movement that had been created in September of the previous year and headquartered, significantly, in Belgrade.

But while the triggers for the dispute arose mainly in the realm of foreign relations, the break with the Soviets would, over time, have profound implications for the country's domestic politics as well as its economic and cultural life. Ultimately the consequences of the rift would touch even matters only tangentially connected to foreign policy. More immediately, however, the break with the Soviets had a nearly crippling effect on Yugoslav foreign trade. Whereas in 1948 approximately half the country's imports and exports went to the Soviet bloc, that figure fell in 1949 to around 15 percent, and trade with these states was nil for the next four years.[5] Very quickly Western countries saw the opportunity to exploit the breach, and aid from these unlikely supporters, particularly from the United States, began pouring in to help Yugoslavia weather the storm. Increased trade with the capitalist world would follow shortly. Thus began a fundamental reorientation of the country's geopolitical position, a development that itself ultimately contributed to the rise of its consumer culture, although it would certainly have been difficult to foresee such an outcome at this very early stage. In these years Yugoslavia's new openness to the developed capitalist countries was perhaps a necessity, but it was still cautious, grudging, and very slight.

---

4. Fred Singleton, *A Short History of the Yugoslav Peoples* (Cambridge, 1985), 218.
5. Ibid., 219.

I left hearing about how good they lived in socialism though all 3 which had hong hocks of the correct 9/1c investigator (Hdnm 2 606, 200

Living It | 23

It must be remembered that Tito's proximate interest was in securing the requisite financial assistance to help Yugoslavia survive without aid from its former benefactor; there was no early suggestion of any fundamental departure from familiar Stalinist modes. The turn toward the West was thus noteworthy for its immediate significance in international relations but not, or at least not yet, for any corollary effects on ideology, economic relations, culture, and the daily lives of ordinary citizens.

Indeed, until 1950 the policies pursued by Yugoslav communist leaders remained quite faithful to the models established by their erstwhile Soviet patrons. If a tight alliance with the Soviet bloc was quickly disappearing as an option for Yugoslav Communists in the wake of the 1948 split, the country's leaders at first seemed reluctant to acknowledge that fact, and they worked hard to reestablish their credentials and return to the fold. Both during that campaign and even later, once such efforts had proved futile, the party leaders grouped around Tito seemed determined to establish themselves as ultra-orthodox—thoroughly conformist if not Cominformist—and to hew as closely as possible to the already clearly demarcated lines of Marxist-Leninist thought and practice so as to eliminate any doubts as to the ideological propriety of their positions.

In these times of economic austerity and ideological severity, consumption policy was not among the Yugoslav Communists' chief worries. In this respect, too, they differed little from new communist leaders in other states. Productive capacity was what really mattered. Consumption, to be sure, was something of a concern, but only in a strictly limited and modest sense: the government faced a difficult task in guaranteeing even basic needs such as food and housing. Further slighted by the planners' bias toward heavy industry, consumption policy was geared toward meeting minimal existential standards. Anything more was not only a practical impossibility given the desperate state of the economy but was also clearly contrary to the established norms of Soviet socialist policy.

This initial period of communist governance is therefore most instructive as a foil for the dramatically different developments that came later. Looking at socialist Yugoslavia during these years, it is hard to imagine that only two decades later the country would be embroiled in debates over "consumer society," the undesirable implications of Yugoslav affluence, and the power of advertising to seduce consumers into suspiciously Western-looking modes of thought and behavior.

In the late 1940s, all that was so remote as to be unthinkable. Advertising during the first years of Yugoslav socialism continued to figure as a subspecies of "propaganda," a broader and obviously much more familiar socialist genre of mass communication, and one shot through with ideological implications. In the unfavorable ideological and economic climate, the consumer culture that did exist was geared toward making the best of scarcity. The significance of personal consumption and the bleak prospects for advertising and marketing work would change dramatically over the next fifteen years, however, as Yugoslav policy now started to stray in novel and unabashedly unorthodox, or at least un-Soviet, directions. As time passed after the 1948 expulsion from the Cominform, it soon became more clear that there would be no quick and easy return to the good graces of the USSR, although efforts to effect a rapprochement continued nevertheless. As a result, the country's leaders began defining a new strategy that would attempt to secure Yugoslavia's position by deliberately taking the country away from Soviet models in critical ways. The departure was "critical" in more than one sense of the word: once committed to the new course, Yugoslav leaders largely abandoned their earlier efforts to win back and appease the Soviet Union and its dependents. Instead, they sought to build public support at home by underscoring their differences with Stalinism and defiantly defending the Yugoslav tack as the truer Marxist path.

The Shape of Things to Come: Self-Management and the Consumer Shift, 1950–1965

Beginning in 1950, as part of this larger effort to strengthen the sense of an ideological break with the USSR and define a separate Yugoslav road toward the construction of socialism, the government began steering the country away from the rigidly centralized methods of state control that had been the centerpiece of economic policy during the previous five years. In June of that year came the first law establishing the foundations of "workers' self-management," a practical and ideological innovation that would become the cornerstone of the Yugoslav political system for the next four decades. This 1950 statute, the Basic Law on the Management of State Economic Enterprises by Working Collectives, did not by itself signal any substantial injection of market mechanisms into Yugoslav economic practice. It was instead more significant for launching a protracted, fitful process of decentralizing Yugoslav administration and economic management. The results of that process would ultimately prove quite dramatic, setting the Yugoslav system apart from the rest of the communist world. The beginnings were, however, rather modest.

Theoretically, at least, this first legal reform of Yugoslav self-management socialism gave elected workers' councils final authority over the operations of the enterprises in which they worked. But importantly, it also left broad powers to enterprise managers as well. Although by the terms of the statute these managers were to be chosen by and responsible to the councils, many directors controlled the operations of their enterprises without much interference from the nominally sovereign councils. Accordingly, even very early on, the legal framework of self-management appears to have left enough practical leeway to directors and their staffs to encourage the development of a pattern of deference to managerial authority. That tendency would characterize (some would say plague) the self-management system for as long as it existed, notwithstanding further refinements of the law and the occasional furor over the undue influence of enterprise directors.[6] Even well into the 1970s Communists were complaining that the accumulation of managerial power and prerogatives was, in effect, subverting self-management. Typical of this antagonism, for example, was the assertion made in internal documents of the Central Committee of the Bosnian party organization that too much of the Yugoslav system had fallen under the influence of "bureaucratic-managerial-technocratic ideas."[7] Paradoxically, perhaps, the one power the workers' councils did retain, and did use, was the right to fire enterprise employees as unnecessary or uneconomic. Such dismissals, however, should by no means be taken as clear responses to market forces, as mass firings are typically at least asserted to be in capitalist economies. Often enough, they appear to have been a means of ensuring that bonuses could be paid to those more privileged employees who were not sacked. Almost as rapidly as they could, workers' councils began using their power to award substantial bonuses to enterprise workers instead of investing surpluses in the expansion of productive capacity, as market considerations might have indicated.[8]

Other legal reforms elaborating the theoretical and practical bases of self-management soon followed, and a series of gradual moves toward an acceptance of the importance of markets ensued, as evidenced, for example, in another law of January 1951 that geared certain prices to market forces. The strict and painstaking central control that had marked the first Five-Year Plan of 1947–1951 was abandoned, giving way to less formal planning in the 1950s. As John Lampe wryly notes, the first Five-Year Plan was also the *last* Five-Year Plan, at least in the strict Soviet sense, and the two long-term plans that followed during this period, for 1957–1961 and 1961–1965,

---

6. The tension between managerial authority and the power of the governing councils remained a major issue of concern. A succinct analysis of the workings of self-management in the enterprises is found in Fred Singleton, *Twentieth Century Yugoslavia* (New York, 1976), see, esp., 126–132. As Singleton notes, the councils in the earliest scheme had little practical authority. Managers tended to call the shots, and they were, we should recall, "agents of the state and, ultimately, of the Party." Ibid., 128. As a result, "the economy was still managed from the centre, and as long as this situation remained there was no possibility of achieving either autonomy for the enterprise or workers' control within the enterprise." Ibid. Over time, however, enterprises came to enjoy more autonomy and, to some extent at least, a greater degree of worker control.

7. Internal informational materials for Central Committee use, Odjeljenje za informacije i dokumentaciju Centralnog komiteta Saveza komunista Bosne i Hercegovine, *Političke aktuelnosti*, no. 2 (29 January 1970): 9. Hrvatski Državni Arhiv, collection Centralni komitet, Savez komunista Hrvatske, HDA-1220-4142.

8. Lampe points out that these bonuses sometimes came at the cost of jobs: in 1951 workers' councils dismissed many unskilled employees, with the result that social-sector unemployment rates exceeded 5%. Lampe, *Yugoslavia as History*, 252. Susan Woodward explores the causes and consequences of Yugoslavia's persistent problems with excess labor in *Socialist Unemployment*.

proved quite different in their terms, methods, and goals.[9] The third Five-Year Plan for 1961–1965 thus attempted to introduce additional market incentives, most notably in the tax treatment of enterprise earnings.[10] Paralleling these developments in the economic sphere, the communist leadership began a long, slow, and hesitant process of relaxing its hitherto rigid political control over the administration of the state and over Yugoslav life more generally. In November 1952, for example, at its Sixth Congress, the Communist Party officially became the League of Communists of Yugoslavia. In party ideology as in economic theory, the rhetorical emphasis would now be on the voluntaristic, associational quality of Yugoslavia's institutions. This move, too, was designed to heighten the apparent distinctions between the new, flexible, specifically Yugoslav style of communism and the old, dictatorial, "administrative," and "bureaucratic" methods of Stalinist governance. The gesture was symbolic, yet it symbolized something quite real. Yugoslav communist leaders were indeed intent on loosening—slightly—their control over the society. They certainly did not intend to give up the party's traditional "leading role," so central to any Marxist-Leninist conception of the proper place of a communist vanguard come to power, but they were, at the same time, genuinely convinced that Yugoslav society would benefit from a lighter touch, from a more open and tolerant style, and from an effort to engage the citizenry more broadly in the project of governing the state, running the economy, and building socialism. The process was never radical, and high-placed conservatives who feared a fundamental loss of control always held it in check. Yugoslav Communists never abandoned the basic principles of Marxist-Leninist governance. Nevertheless, they did succeed in making "democratic centralism" a bit more democratic and a lot less centralist. The results of their efforts were yet another reason why the Yugoslav variety was quite unlike the forms of socialism found elsewhere during this time.

---

9. Lampe, *Yugoslavia as History*, 238.

10. See Dušan Bilandžić, *Historija Socijalističke Federativne Republike Jugoslavije: glavni procesi*, 2d ed. (Zagreb, 1979), 247–250. Bilandžić believes that except for these changes in taxation, the "new economic system" of 1961 did not live up to its billing. "All other areas of the economic system remained as they were: practically nothing changed in the system and policy of pricing, and the government continued to set prices for approximately 70% of all products and thus determined the material position of individual economic sectors; the system of currency exchange and foreign trade . . . stayed firmly in the hands of the central state apparatus, which continued as before to regulate foreign trade; the monetary-credit mechanism did not change . . . nor did the system of planning change, from the plans of the federation to the plans of the local community authorities [*komuna*]." Ibid., 249. Lampe, however, sees the 1961 transfer of most short-term enterprise credit to local banks as a very significant change: he notes that these reforms and a concomitant devaluation of the dinar sparked inflationary pressures that would never fully disappear, and that, as a result, the government began backing away from the market. Lampe, *Yugoslavia as History*, 278. On the importance of the 1961 banking reforms to the operation of market mechanisms, see also Singleton, *Twentieth Century Yugoslavia*, 152–155. At least theoretically, Singleton notes, the allocation of investment was now supposed to be determined on the basis of economic rather than political criteria. Ibid., 153.

For all this newfound administrative flexibility (and there would be more to come), self-management socialism was still clearly a form of socialism, though some irate left-wing critics both inside Yugoslavia and abroad would soon question that seemingly unexceptionable assertion. Neither the party nor the country's enterprises rushed toward pure, unrestrained markets. As we seek to understand the larger political and economic context for the development of the advertising and marketing industry in Yugoslavia, and for related questions of consumption and consumer culture—subjects that all implicate the practical and ideological significance of the market—it is important to recognize the very partial and uncertain nature of these initial reforms. As John Lampe observes, the makeover of Yugoslav economic management proceeded more tentatively and with less connection to market mechanisms than many Western commentators were inclined to believe at the time.[11] Susan Woodward's analysis reinforces this point: "The idea that 'economic' methods represented a choice for the 'market,'" she argues, "was true only in the sense that prices were freed in retail goods markets." There was, moreover, "no market allocation of factors of production in the 'new economic system'—the employment contracts, concept of socialist work communities, and workers' councils all aimed to *im*mobilize the workforce."[12]

The party took up the tools of the market only very gingerly at first, and always with a cautious eye to preserving the appearance of Marxist purity if at all possible. This sidelong approach was evident, for example, in the preparation of a new constitution that, in 1953, superseded the original of seven years past. After the break with Stalin, the existing document had proved to be a discomfitingly faithful, not to say slavish, copy of the Soviet model. To drive home the idea of Yugoslav exceptionalism and codify its emergence, something new and different seemed necessary. To these ends, the new constitution explicitly integrated the workers' councils into the structures of the state administration, while other provisions revamped the federal and local administrative apparatus to make it at least nominally more democratic and representative.

Yet if Yugoslav practice by this point had already departed decisively from Soviet styles, the country's leadership and the government's political orientation were, without doubt, socialist through and through. Soviet doctrine was being transformed into a distinctive new Yugoslav ideology, a decidedly *socialist* conception that claimed to be more faithful to the original vision laid out by Marx. It was in this spirit, for example, that the new constitution defined the country as, first and foremost, a union of *producers*.[13] Economic

---

11. Lampe, *Yugoslavia as History*, 250.
12. Woodward, *Socialist Unemployment*, 162 (emphasis in original).
13. Aleksa Djilas, *The Contested Country: Yugoslav Unity and Communist Revolution, 1919–1953* (Cambridge, Mass., 1991), 178.

theory and political theory thus remained inextricably linked and indisputably Marxist. Class was paramount, and class was, naturally, a function of a person's position in the system of production. At this point, the idea that ordinary Yugoslav citizens might ground their socioeconomic identities on some basis other than their roles as workers and producers—something that many domestic commentators would later identify as a chief consequence of the country's drift toward consumer society—was unimagined and, for the party leadership, probably unimaginable. (Ethno-national loyalties, in contrast, were seen to pose a threat to class solidarity, and no small part of Yugoslav statecraft was calculated to smother those sentiments or at least hold them in some sort of manageable abeyance.) Finally, although decentralization may have been the order of the day, the market was still not much in evidence. In this respect, too, Yugoslav socialism remained reliably socialist.

Moreover, even decentralization itself was still rather limited during these first years. The reforms reduced, but certainly did not abolish, centralized planning. Consumption policy, in particular, remained strongly influenced by the predisposition toward planning.[14] Although enterprises were, with time, granted significant autonomy both in theory and practice, other aspects of party ideology constrained their activities in important ways. As A. Ross Johnson notes, in this early phase of the development of self-management, the party continually emphasized that companies, and the workers' councils that governed them, were always to remain subject to "social control." Self-management was imposed and implemented "from above," and indeed it never lost this fundamentally Marxist-Leninist quality. Democratization, then, proved very limited, and the party leadership undertook the shift to workers' councils with an eye toward strengthening, not relinquishing, its own power. The Communists had, as Johnson observes, "no intention of abolishing central economic authority or the Party's own 'leading role' in the economy."[15]

Over the course of this second period, however, an emphasis on the potential benefits of market mechanisms would slowly be amalgamated into the prevailing understanding of what the self-management system implied. Opinions about what self-management should include, of course, were highly varied, and arguments over these matters continued right up to the dissolution of the federation in 1991. Ultimately, however, it seems fair to conclude that the initial emphasis on economic decentralization seen in the early 1950s proved less important than the new and increasingly daring

---

14. For evidence concerning Yugoslav approaches to consumption planning during this period, see, for example, Dušan Čobeljić, *Problemi planiranja lične potrošnje* (Belgrade, 1958).

15. A. Ross Johnson, *The Transformation of Communist Ideology: The Yugoslav Case, 1945–1953* (Cambridge, Mass., 1972), 172.

departures from the basic premises of the command economy that followed somewhat later:

> Accompanied by much organizational experimentation, a new, market-oriented economic system gradually emerged in which the enterprise enjoyed significant economic independence. The firm was free to plan its production and to sell its products on the market, within the framework of a centrally determined macroeconomic preference scale imposed by what became a regulative instead of directive state economic bureaucracy. Integrally related to this structural change was the abandonment of forced industrialization in favor of more balanced economic growth.[16]

The legal and administrative scheme of self-management, it should be noted, was extraordinarily complex and, furthermore, was subject to constant tinkering and amendment. Any effort to serve up "self-management-in-a-nutshell" requires some oversimplification and is thus bound to disappoint, but Johnson's characterization is right as to the essentials and succeeds as well as most. The key point is this: within the constraints suggested, Yugoslav firms were now at liberty to pursue the rewards of the market.

Again, however, some cautionary remarks are in order. There is (and was) a critical difference between being free to respond to some or all of the signals of modified, tempered markets and being forced to live (or die) according to the movements of some unrestrained "invisible hand." In this regard, we should be mindful of Susan Woodward's conclusion that it may be fundamentally misleading to describe the system that emerged in Yugoslavia as "market socialism," as some have done. Yugoslav practice, as Woodward points out, rejected market principles in a number of important ways:

> The leaders' concept of *socialist commodity production* was not a market economy, although final goods ("commodities") markets operated largely by a free price mechanism and consumer demand was meant to be the primary incentive to producers.... [T]he market did not apply to factors of production—labor, capital and intermediate goods, raw materials, credit in the form of working and venture capital—although monetary prices were assigned to facilitate allocation and comparative valuation and a rent was charged on fixed capital and borrowed funds.... Price regulation was used in place of a production plan in order to achieve balanced development as well as monetary equilibrium by influencing incentives to producers, so that the government kept the price of factors of production, necessities (such as grains), and strategic goods relatively low and allowed prices of manufactures and consumable goods to respond to demand.

---

16. Ibid., 165.

The issues have been clouded, Woodward concludes, by the difficulty of labeling this unusual sort of system. Quite rightly she stresses that a *non-planned* socialist economy cannot simply be assumed to be a *market* economy.[17] Yugoslav enterprises found themselves in an assuredly socialist economic environment but one that was nevertheless quite unusual, complex, and, with regard to the nature and influence of markets, uneven.[18] In this context, marked by continual political pressures and mixed, often contradictory business motivations, there began a long process of differentiation among Yugoslav companies, with results as varied as the system itself. The structure of economic management and the political consequences of enterprise failure meant that, in practice, companies would be buffered against the harsher imperatives of the market, but if the management of a given firm chose to exercise its autonomy so as to act in a more competitive, market-oriented way, it could indeed do so.

In these circumstances, Yugoslav enterprises had considerable freedom to respond to market incentives, and indeed some did just that. As early as the first decade after the introduction of self-management, and well before the reinforcement of market reforms in 1965, some firms evinced a disposition to seek marketplace advantages. The number of business-enterprise documents in federal-level archival collections is limited, but those that have been preserved show that even in these early years there was a remarkable amount of jostling for market position and higher profits, some of it quite aggressive at times.[19] Along these lines, for example, two Croatian marketers of, respectively, televisions and refrigerators lodged protests with the Croatian Chamber of Commerce in 1959, complaining that import-wholesale firms were keeping prices artificially inflated for these highly sought-after products. The seller of refrigerators, for example, insisted that wholesalers' discriminatory treatment had resulted in wild retail price variations of up to 20,000 dinars, angering customers, while the television merchant claimed that its importer source had sought to fix a price of 220,000 dinars for a Hungarian-made television set that, the retailer insisted, could be sold profitably on the Yugoslav market for only 160,000 dinars. When the TV

---

17. References are to Woodward, *Socialist Unemployment*, 169–170.

18. As Branko Horvat notes, the system was not "mixed" in the sense that it combined *private* capital with government management of the economy. Proposals to permit some sort of private investment in the process of production were occasionally floated, but the party steadfastly and continually resisted any such changes. Yugoslav socialism was thus not a blend of capitalism and socialism but rather a mixture of socialist-style economic management with elements of a market economy. The mixture, however, was inconstant: it changed over time and, importantly, could even be adjusted "on the ground" at the level of the individual enterprise. Horvat, *An Essay on Yugoslav Society* (White Plains, N.Y., 1969 [1967]), 92.

19. For materials on Yugoslav retailing in the early decades of socialism, see, generally, the files of the Savez trgovinskih komora, Yugoslavia's Federation of Chambers of Commerce, held in the Arhiv Jugoslavije, the former federal archive in Belgrade. AJ-229-53, AJ-229-87, AJ-229-162.

retailer attempted to import the sets using another source, the Belgrade-based wholesaler quashed the deal, asserting exclusivity rights. This was rough play indeed.[20]

Firms were not really *required* to act like market participants, however.[21] Government investment and, in particular, bank credits were available to cushion enterprises against budget shortfalls owing to poor, uncompetitive performance.[22] In this respect, we encounter yet another example of the ambiguous, flexible, uneven nature of Yugoslav socialism. Even self-management itself, the sacrosanct centerpiece of Yugoslavia's distinctive path and the subject of almost endless theorizing and speechifying in party circles, showed something of the same indeterminate quality. As Aleksa Djilas has observed, the idea might be deployed to all sorts of political ends: "Like many other central concepts in the ideology of Yugoslav Communism, self-management could be interpreted in almost any way, if the relationship of power so allowed it."[23] Yet, with these important caveats in mind, it is still fair to conclude that the acknowledgment of the importance of markets—theoretically, if not always practically—played a more significant role than is often recognized in standard historical treatments of the Yugoslav economy in the 1950s. Indeed, this move would have tremendous consequences for the evolution of market culture that is our prime concern here. The legitimization of the market as a new presence in the country's ideological landscape meant that proponents of other innovations that relied on the logic of the market for their persuasive force could, from then on, stake their claims more boldly, using the justification that their proposals were in full accordance with the essential premises of self-management. As analyzed in the following chapters, this was precisely what happened in the case of advertising and marketing work, where the explicit linkage of the industry's agenda with the market implications of self-management surfaced as early as the mid-1950s—in other words, almost immediately.

---

20. Letter from Rajka Žečević, Secretary of the Trgovinska komora NR Hrvatske to the Savez trgovinskih komora, 30 October 1959. Arhiv Jugoslavije, collection Savez trgovinskih komora, AJ-229-87. Such incidents led to a proposal from the Croatian Chamber of Commerce that the broader, all-Yugoslav Chamber, through the Yugoslav State Secretariat for Commercial Trade [Državni sekretarijat za poslove robnog prometa], move to place a ceiling on prices of imported goods in order to insure that they would reach the market with more accessible prices. Ibid., 2. AJ-229-87.

21. Describing the institutional terrain of Yugoslav business in the early 1950s, Lampe concludes that most firms, in fact, failed to respond to the continued decentralization of decision making introduced in 1952–1953: "Only a minority were developing the market mentality for serving customer needs that carried many West European firms forward by this time." Lampe, *Yugoslavia as History*, 276.

22. Lampe and Jackson note that Yugoslav commercial credit, though theoretically confined to the issuance of short-term loans, quickly became a device for the country's banking system to funnel large, frequent, and long-term infusions of cash to enterprises. Lampe and Jackson, *Balkan Economic History*, 598.

23. Djilas, *The Contested Country*, 177.

Often enough, what was at issue was the force of "the market" and not genuine, more or less unfettered market forces. But we should remember that the concept of the market did not have a single, undisputed, unproblematic meaning even within the relatively limited confines of Yugoslav economic and political parlance. Quite to the contrary, for all the many invocations of the market, the meaning of the concept differed depending on who was using the term and when.[24] Those who were the prime movers behind Yugoslavia's remarkable culture of commercial promotion tended, despite considerable deference to socialist values and to the idea of the country's "unique circumstances," to harbor understandings of the market that were, at bottom, thoroughly imbued with assumptions developed and refined through years of capitalist practice.

Inclinations of that sort, however, would not go unopposed. Resistance to the consumerist orientation represented, in fact, just one element of a broader political debate over the proper role of market forces in a socialist economy. From the beginning, the advance of the market was checked by traditionalist opinion that sought to minimize the intrusion of practices tainted by capitalism.

One of the central dynamics of Yugoslav politics during the early to mid-1960s was precisely this controversy over the wisdom of further market reforms. With the determined support of Aleksandar Ranković, a former Partisan leader and Central Committee member who had been a particularly heavy-handed director of the UDBA, Yugoslavia's answer to the Soviet KGB, the conservatives struggled with the pro-market exponents of "liberalism" (a characterization with such strong negative connotations in Yugoslav socialist usage that it would have been tantamount to slander had it not been essentially truthful). The controversy remained unresolved until 1965, when the "liberals" carried the day and managed to secure the enactment of more aggressive market reforms. Ranković himself would be disgraced in a scandal and excluded from any position of power in 1966, eliminating an important source of opposition to the pro-market agenda, but hostilities between the camps would nonetheless smolder for years, with the party leadership, most notably Tito and his chief theoretician Edvard Kardelj, tipping the balance first one way and then another, wavering between the two orientations as the economic and political terrain shifted.

One additional aspect of this initial phase of reforms must be mentioned, as it had the collateral effect of stimulating interest in advertising and marketing practice, and thus, in turn, of bolstering market culture and increasing the authority of those who built it. As part of the reorientation of Yugoslavia's economic policy toward the market and its foreign policy toward a nonaligned, betwixt-and-between stance, there also came a significant shift of

---

24. Woodward, *Socialist Unemployment,* 170–171.

export efforts toward the West. Entry into these new markets required a rethinking of strategies, and with this came a heightened sensitivity to the potential value of advertising and market analysis. Of course, Yugoslav success was in many cases determined by other, more basic market factors, not least among them the price advantages that came with the country's cheaper labor. This said, industry literature makes it clear that many Yugoslav enterprises recognized that advertising, marketing, and public relations could be an important part of their efforts on the international scene. In particular, they felt that something had to be done, and quickly, to remedy the comparatively backward state of the country's talent in these fields. The new venues in which Yugoslav companies now hoped to compete, they reasoned, were already occupied by established Western firms using very capable agencies that could draw on years of experience. Yugoslavia needed to catch up fast. The evidence further suggests that government authorities shared this interest in promoting advertising for exports, especially since the sales appeals, with their potentially corrupting messages, would not be aimed at the domestic population.

During this second phase of economic and political development, the Yugoslav economy turned in results that were, in the aggregate and with a few significant exceptions, remarkably strong. Approximately five years of economic stagnation followed the Soviet-bloc embargo that resulted from the 1948 cleavage, but after 1953 production began to increase substantially again, with very noticeable (and very welcome) effects on living standards.[25] Per capita GDP increased by 54 percent between 1950 and 1960. Annualized rates of growth were equally robust: from 1952 to 1960, real GDP grew at a rate of 6.7 percent, whereas from 1961 to 1965, the rate was just slightly lower (and still impressive) at 6.2 percent. For the same periods, consumption grew at rates of 4.8 percent and 4.7 percent, respectively. Real personal income, which had increased only modestly in 1952–1960 at a rate of 1 percent per annum, exploded during the following five years, growing at an annual rate of 9 percent.[26] Significantly, personal consumption was one of the areas in which Yugoslav performance during the period of the second Five-Year Plan for 1957–1961 substantially exceeded the target figures: whereas the plan contemplated a growth in personal consumption ranging

---

25. Bilandžić, *Historija Socijalističke Federativne Republike Jugoslavije*, 389. As Bilandžić notes, the early postwar years had been a time of "revolutionary egalitarianism" and the "leveling" of individual incomes and living standards (a practice often simply identified in Yugoslav parlance by the Russian term *uravnilovka*). In the 1950s, however, this quickly started to give way to increased social differentiation. Ibid. That development, as explained later, would strongly color the debate over the culture of the market.

26. Lampe, *Yugoslavia as History*, 275, citing Vinod Dubey, *Yugoslavia: Development with Decentralization* (Baltimore, 1975), 54–60, 385–386. More detailed data for the period under consideration, with comparative figures for other socialist countries and indicia of regional differentiation within Yugoslavia, are presented in Bilandžić, *Historija Socijalističke Federativne Republike Jugoslavije*, 281–293.

from 34 percent to 40 percent, actual consumption increased by 45.8 percent during this brief span.[27]

By some indexes, however, Yugoslavia remained a comparatively underdeveloped society. In the same period, from 1950 to 1960, the number of radio receivers increased at a dramatic rate, more than tripling, but still remained at a comparatively low seventy-eight sets per one thousand persons. Similarly, the proportion of automobile ownership increased sevenfold but still amounted to only 2.9 cars per one thousand persons.[28] (Over the course of the following decade, however, growth in these areas would be much more substantial in absolute terms.)

With this impressive expansion, the Yugoslav economy was undergoing a fundamental transformation. Even in this second period of fairly modest and tentative market reform, we see a clear departure from the heavily regulated "distributive" model that had been designed to remedy the relative deprivation of the immediate postwar years. Through the introduction of self-management and the experimentation with market mechanisms that it permitted, the operation of the Yugoslav economy began to gravitate toward a new concept, one in which the needs and preferences of ordinary consumers were, in theory at least, supposed to play a major role in guiding the production of the country's enterprises. Developments along these lines would be even more dramatic in the years to come, but Dušan Bilandžić, one of Yugoslavia's most prominent historians during the socialist period, is correct in interpreting this first decade of self-management as the beginning of a fundamental change in the orientation of the country's economy, a change that would have serious social implications as well. A well-connected party member in his own right, and thus someone with a stake in the long-term success of the communist venture, Bilandžić concluded that by the end of the 1950s the country had "already embarked on the path to consumer society."[29] It would arrive there, he said, by the beginning of the 1970s.

The causes and consequences of that surprising turn of events are the focus of the remaining chapters of the book. To set these social and cultural changes in proper context, however, we turn now to an examination of the

27. Singleton, *A Short History of the Yugoslav Peoples,* 233, citing *Social Plan for the Development of Yugoslavia* (Belgrade, 1961), 47.

28. Lampe, *Yugoslavia as History,* 289, citing Dubey, *Yugoslavia,* 54–60; and *Jugoslavija, 1945–1985: Statistički prikaz* (Belgrade, 1986), 52. A more detailed analysis of the growth and composition of Yugoslav consumption is presented in Josip Štahan, *Strukturne promjene i razvojne tendencije osobne potrošnje u Jugoslaviji u razdoblju od 1953. do 1967. godine* (Zagreb, 1970).

29. Bilandžić, *Historija Socijalističke Federativne Republike Jugoslavije,* 389. Appearing as they do in one of the most influential standard works of contemporary Yugoslav historiography, comments like these make the work by Bilandžić something more than just a very useful secondary source with a pronounced emphasis on economic performance. Originally published in 1978—as it happened, just at the end of the Golden Age of Yugoslav consumerism—the book turns out to be an extraordinarily revealing period piece as well, full of insights into the concerns of the times.

seemingly miraculous economic performance that made possible this transformation, and all the talk of "consumer society."

As Good as It Gets: High Times and Free Spending, 1965–1980

The economic reform that Yugoslavia implemented beginning in 1965 was, as John Lampe points out, "the most ambitious set of market-oriented changes undertaken anywhere in the Communist world prior to 1989."[30] Like much of Yugoslav policy, the reform package was a dauntingly complicated affair. Its details need not detain us here for long, but the main lines of the legislative scheme are instructive. Perhaps most significant, the new measures substantially reduced taxes on enterprise earnings; firms would now be able to keep approximately 70 percent of their net income, whereas before they had retained less than half.[31] In other words, the incentive for companies to make a profit was strengthened considerably. (As explained later, this in itself was a controversial move: depending on the eye of the beholder, the profit motive could be seen as either a beneficial and necessary spur to efficiency or as the root of most evil.) Reformers had also sought to end the administrative determination of prices, but the extraordinary inflation of the times (over 20% in 1964) hobbled that effort, and, in the end, the 1965 reform simply ratified a variety of quite substantial price increases and then imposed ongoing price controls on most commodities. Accordingly, as Fred Singleton observed, "the long-term objective of establishing market relations as the determinant of prices still elude[d] the reformers."[32] In another important move, the country's financial system was reworked to a great extent, moving control of investment funds away from local communal banks and consolidating it with regional institutions that were supposed to issue their loans with genuine commercial considerations in mind.[33]

Other efforts toward market-oriented reform followed over the next few years, although the momentum was reversed after 1972 when the once ascendant "liberals" in the party leadership of several republics, notably Slovenia, Croatia, and Serbia, were removed and replaced with more traditionalist types who held no great enthusiasm for a closer embrace of the market. One of the thorniest issues for Yugoslav policy during these years (earlier and

---

30. Lampe, *Yugoslavia as History*, 261.
31. The reforms of 1965 are described in Lampe, *Yugoslavia as History*, 282–283. For a more detailed treatment, see Bilandžić, *Historija Socijalističke Federativne Republike Jugoslavije*, 305–319.
32. Singleton, *Twentieth Century Yugoslavia*, 160. Singleton's work, written when the reform was still new and its effects the subject of great curiosity and debate, offers a particularly useful overview of the provisions of the reform package. On price policy, see 159–162.
33. On the banking and investment provisions, see ibid., 154–159.

later as well) was the question of worker incomes and their relationship to enterprise profitability. Here the hard lessons of the market proved difficult to take. Given the system of worker control, there arose a fundamental and unresolved tension between the firm's need to use a portion of its profits as investment capital and the workers' obvious interest in using those profits to boost their salaries. This problem became the subject of considerable debate, with some arguing that workers' councils would indeed be able to forgo bonuses for the prospect of higher incomes over the long run. In practice, however, things often worked out differently, with immediate self-interest coming first. "Arguments that sound convincing to academic economists," as Singleton noted when the controversy was still fresh, "may be looked at in a different light by the shop-floor worker when he comes to cast his vote in favour of either jam today or pie in the sky."[34]

Attempts to recalibrate the jam-to-pie quotient to achieve more satisfactory results continued following the 1965 reforms. Beginning in 1971 there were intensified efforts to make worker control more real and to tie that responsibility more directly to the wages paid to enterprise employees. Commenting on recent developments from his vantage point in the mid-1970s, Bogdan Denitch pointed out that these changes made the idea of workforce responsibility somewhat less abstract: in 1972, for example, more than five hundred thousand workers were receiving only 80 percent of the incomes to which they would normally have been entitled because their firms were unprofitable. "As a result," Denitch concluded, "pressure to remove inefficient managers has obviously increased and a growing demand for an almost day-to-day accountability by the managers is becoming institutionalized in the more successful collectives."[35] We should remember, however, that countervailing forces were constantly working to make the idea of workforce responsibility a good deal *more* abstract, and not every collective was emulating the practices and strategies of the most successful. Fiscal discipline in the enterprises suffered from continual pressures, basically political, to avoid layoffs and to keep enterprise budgets flush with cash via heavy borrowing if necessary, as was frequently the case. Whether their firms were actually operating economically or not, poor managers could often protect their positions by keeping workers on the payroll and wages high.

Such anti-market pressures intensified after the enactment in 1976 of another major overhaul of the self-management scheme, one designed as an extension of the thoroughgoing decentralization effected by the new constitution adopted in 1974. The 1976 Law on Associated Labor radically revised the structure of enterprise governance, breaking up the existing

---

34. Ibid., 163; on the debate over incomes policy that accompanied the 1965 reforms, see ibid., 162–164.
35. Bogdan Denis Denitch, *The Legitimation of a Revolution: The Yugoslav Case* (New Haven, Conn., 1976), 155–156.

workers' councils into considerably smaller units dubbed Basic Organizations of Associated Labor. On its surface it was primarily a labor-relations reform, but the Law on Associated Labor also had an important connection to the use of market mechanisms: one guiding purpose was to increase enterprise efficiency by changing the accounting process in order to make the smallest possible production units answerable for their own, independent performance.[36]

As executed, however, it yielded only mixed results. While Yugoslav law may have contemplated more unpleasant outcomes, actual practice tended to shield workers from the consequences of underperformance even if it may have been the result of bad enterprise decisions or an obliviousness to market considerations. Ultimately Yugoslav enterprises operated under a system of what economist János Kornai has memorably analyzed as "soft-budget" constraints,[37] with the government always on standby, as Laura D'Andrea Tyson put it in her seminal work on the system, to bail out ailing or failing companies "as effective lender and supporter of last resort."[38]

This detour into the workings of enterprise profitability under self-management might seem to take us rather far afield from issues of market culture and consumer culture, but there is a critical connection between the two domains. As a practical matter, the availability of loans and investments from the state to smooth out the bumps for underperforming enterprises meant that those firms, and thus the economy as a whole, were never subjected directly and completely to the unwelcome outcomes that market forces could bring. Yugoslav companies *could* respond to market incentives; they were not really required to do so. The market in Yugoslavia thus remained suspended somewhere between theory and practice. Some enterprises actually did attempt to gear their production decisions to market dynamics, while others sought shelter from those forces.

Here again a proper sense of balance is required. The Yugoslav economy was indeed plagued with many real incentives for underperformance and was constantly subject to politically motivated interference. Yet as John Lampe, one of the most attentive and insightful analysts of Yugoslavia and its economy, reminds us, there is a great danger that the post-mortem fascination with the defects of the system will produce an incomplete and unduly grim picture, masking the fact that many Yugoslav firms, in dramatic contrast to their analogues in other socialist countries, really did function on the

---

36. See Woodward, *Socialist Unemployment*, 277.

37. On the nature of "soft-budget" constraints and their presence in other socialist economies, see János Kornai, *The Socialist System: The Political Economy of Communism* (Princeton, N.J., 1992); for Kornai's unremittingly dim assessment of the Yugoslav case, and of self-management generally as "one of the dead ends of the reform process," see 461–473.

38. Tyson, *The Yugoslav Economic System*, 49. Lampe is particularly stern in his assessment of lax Yugoslav credit policies, which often worked to undo the salutary discipline of market reforms. "Too many enterprises," he concludes, "had come to rely on short-term credits from their local communal bank, increasingly rolled-over on demand to become *de facto* long-term credits." Lampe, *Yugoslavia as History*, 281.

basis of market principles, or at least tried to do so within the constraints they faced.[39] Any effort to account for the development and influence of consumerism and market culture in Yugoslavia requires an understanding of these critical aspects of the system and, no less important, a recognition of its many successes.

As a result of this uneven and indeterminate pattern of practice, the various arts of commercial promotion that proved so critical to the construction of market culture—advertising, marketing, retailing, and public relations—ended up in an odd and uncertain position: useful and sought-after, yet neither entirely necessary nor entirely welcome. Clearly, by the beginning of this third phase of the development of the Yugoslav economy, the theoretical embrace of the market, coupled with a growing practical demand for real and effective commercial promotion at least among some of the more ambitious and forward-looking enterprises, had already opened a fairly wide field of activity for advertising and marketing work. By the early 1960s these disciplines had earned at least an essential minimum level of legitimacy—although, as explained later, they were never uncontroversial. Following the 1965 reforms, interest in these business services increased dramatically.

Along with the market reforms of this third period came a truly remarkable rise in living standards. Remembering some Golden Age of Yugoslavia may ask us to forget too much, but if the country indeed ever did enjoy such a time, it would have been in the years from about 1965 to 1978.[40] To be sure, there were always signs of trouble, some of them consciously ignored, but even with the benefit of hindsight and a miserable acquaintance with what came later, it is worth remembering that this was, in many ways, a happy interlude. It was at this time that the Yugoslav Dream was the most real for the most people.

Many indicators of economic performance were very encouraging indeed. During the heady years from 1960 to 1970, for example, the country's gross domestic product grew by an annual average of 6.8%; the corresponding figure for 1970–1976 was almost as impressive at 6.3 percent.[41] That growth

39. Lampe, *Yugoslavia as History*, 312.

40. On the transformation of Yugoslav society more generally during the 1960s and 1970s, with reference to changing consumption regimes and issues of everyday life, see Predrag J. Markovic, *Beograd između Istoka i Zapada, 1941–1965* (Belgrade, 1996); Marković, "Ideologija standarda Jugoslovenskog režima 1948–1965," *Tokovi istorije: Časopis Instituta za noviju istoriju Srbije,* nos. 1/2 (1996): 7–20; Marković, *Trajnost i promena: društvena istorija socijalističke i postsocijalističke svakodnevice u Jugoslaviji i Srbiji* (Belgrade, 2007). For interesting insights into the everyday life of the capital during the 1960s, see Darko Ćirić et al., *Beograd šezdesetih godina XX veka* (Belgrade, 2003).

41. Tyson, *The Yugoslav Economic System*, 33, citing International Bank for Reconstruction and Development (IBRD), *World Development Report, 1978.* Industrial growth was more rapid than in the more advanced countries of the Soviet bloc (except for Poland), and it was more than double the rate of growth seen in developed industrial economies. Ibid.

translated into concrete gains for ordinary Yugoslavs, too. Real net income per worker in the social sector of the economy grew at an annual average rate of 6.8 percent from 1960 to 1970, and from 1970 to 1979 the annual rate of real growth was still a respectable 2.1 percent.[42] Perhaps most important, consumption also increased rapidly during this period: from 1971 to 1975, for example, the annual average growth rate in private consumption was 5.3 percent. Later in the decade, increases in consumption were even more vigorous: from 1976 to 1977 the rate was 5.7 percent, and in 1978 consumption increased by 7.4 percent.[43] Accordingly, Yugoslavs' ability to purchase modern consumer goods also rose rapidly. Radio ownership grew from 78 receivers per thousand persons in 1960 to 166 sets per thousand ten years later. Whereas there had been only 2.9 cars per thousand persons in 1960, that number had skyrocketed to 35 per thousand in 1970.[44] This was a modest figure in absolute terms, of course, but an indicator of impressive growth nonetheless.

Substantial regional differences in development clouded this otherwise fairly rosy picture. Despite considerable growth in real terms and government policy efforts to remedy the imbalance, the expansion of the Yugoslav economy still tended to help most those who needed help the least. Croatia, Vojvodina, and especially Slovenia began the process more secure and ended up wealthier still; Montenegro, Bosnia-Herzegovina, and Kosovo started off in serious deprivation and always remained comparatively poor (see Tables 2.1 and 2.2).[45] This differential development exacerbated not only regional and ethnic tensions but also a fundamental division between the urban and rural parts of the country, a split that Bogdan Denitch in 1976 termed "the most significant single cleavage in Yugoslav society as a whole."[46]

Taken on the whole, however, the indicators of economic performance during this period lend concrete support to the less rigorous but just as emphatic conclusions expressed by many visitors to the country and, even more important, by many Yugoslavs themselves. Without a doubt, the country was experiencing an extraordinary transformation, and a new, consumerist way of life was filtering outward even to the poorest rural areas. It was this

---

42. Lampe, *Yugoslavia as History*, 317, citing Harold Lydall, *Yugoslavia in Crisis* (Oxford, 1989), 41.

43. Tyson, *The Yugoslav Economic System*, 32, citing various official Yugoslav statistical reports.

44. Lampe, *Yugoslavia as History*, 289, citing Dubey, *Yugoslavia*, 54–60, and *Jugoslavija, 1945–1985*, 52.

45. See also Bilandžić, *Historija Socijalističke Federativne Republike Jugoslavije*, 292.

46. Denitch, *The Legitimation of a Revolution*, 19. Denitch further noted that the peasant way of life was subject to fairly intense pressure during the postwar period, especially by the mass media, "which define the only desirable existence as urban and modern." Ibid. Later events, of course, may call into question whether the urban-rural divide was, in fact, the most significant fracture line in Yugoslav society, but it is nevertheless clear that such divisions amplified the ethnic conflicts of the 1980s and 1990s.

Table 1.1 Ownership of consumer goods, 1968 (by republic or autonomous region)

Item	Yugoslavia	Bosnia-Herzegovina	Montenegro	Croatia	Macedonia	Slovenia	Serbia	Serbia without provinces	Vojvodina	Kosovo
Stove, gas or electric	37.7*	22.5	37.0	41.0	42.7	48.4	37.6	37.9	40.5	27.6
Hot-water heater	15.8	6.5	5.3	18.5	19.3	36.6	11.5	13.7	6.5	11.6
Refrigerator	25.2	7.6	18.5	30.8	27.3	41.3	23.9	26.4	22.0	13.0
Vacuum cleaner	15.1	6.7	4.7	18.4	12.0	27.5	13.9	15.1	12.2	10.6
Radio/transistor	68.5	52.6	50.3	74.5	65.4	89.3	66.6	66.9	74.0	43.6
Record player	18.2	15.1	14.0	20.2	15.4	22.2	17.7	17.7	20.6	9.7
Television	28.2	14.6	12.3	31.5	34.2	40.0	27.8	27.4	30.7	22.2
Washing machine	10.9	3.4	1.4	14.4	8.2	35.7	5.5	5.9	5.9	20.
Room furniture, set	80.2	43.1	44.6	104.1	57.5	117.8	75.8	67.1	110.5	34.2
Kitchen furniture, set	57.6	51.2	46.2	68.6	36.8	77.0	52.6	48.3	71.1	27.9
Camera	8.9	3.0	2.6	10.6	9.4	20.1	7.1	7.8	6.9	3.8
Motorcycle, moped	6.7	2.9	1.8	6.7	3.3	21.9	5.2	3.6	10.4	0.7
Automobile	7.9	2.6	4.5	9.5	8.2	18.5	6.1	7.1	5.0	3.9

*Number of items per 100 households.
Source: Adapted from Josip Štahan, Životni standard i osobna potrošnja u Jugoslaviji (Zagreb: Ekonomski institut Zagreb, 1973), 93.

Table 1.2 Ownership of consumer goods, 1968 (by socioeconomic category)

Item	Total population	Agricultural households	Mixed households	Nonagricultural households
Stove, gas or electric	37.7*	5.0	21.1	64.3
Hot-water heater	15.8	1.2	4.1	29.7
Refrigerator	25.2	2.2	10.6	45.4
Vacuum cleaner	15.1	0.1	3.0	29.5
Radio/transistor	68.5	43.7	68.5	82.2
Record player	18.2	5.6	14.7	26.9
Television	28.2	2.4	13.5	20.1
Washing machine	10.9	0.8	3.9	20.1
Room furniture, set	80.2	46.4	65.6	106.4
Kitchen furniture, set	57.6	33.2	53.8	73.1
Camera	8.9	0.7	2.8	16.5
Motorcycle, moped	6.7	4.4	9.3	6.6
Automobile	7.9	0.6	3.6	14.2

*Number of items per 100 households.
Source: Adapted from Josip Štahan, *Životni standard i osobna potrošnja u Jugoslaviji* (Zagreb: Ekonomski institut Zagreb, 1973), 70.

rapturous, almost frenzied rush to spend and acquire that the Montenegrin-Serb poet and writer Matija Bećković had in mind at the time when he marveled at his compatriots, now "liberated" and "grabbing, just grabbing."[47]

As significant as these developments were in absolute terms, the comparative dimensions of these changes were even more extraordinary. The Yugoslav economy, and with it Yugoslav society as a whole, had quickly evolved into something strikingly different from the more narrowly circumscribed order found in the Soviet-bloc states and other communist countries. The federation was transformed into what Mirko Tepavac has called "the showcase of socialism," a development that was all the more surprising given the comparatively "backward" status of the Yugoslav lands before the 1960s.[48] Now the country managed to eclipse (in popular perception if not always in the hard numbers) even those parts of the communist world that had embarked on the postwar push for economic progress with a much better base for consumption-oriented manufacturing. Coupled with the similarly exceptional personal freedoms that ordinary Yugoslavs enjoyed, these changes in living standards soon caught the attention of the rest of the world. The distinctions were unmistakable: "Yugoslavia was the only country that was

47. Bećković, "O Jugoslovenima," 82.
48. Mirko Tepavac, "Tito: 1945–1980," in *Burn This House: The Making and Unmaking of Yugoslavia*, ed. Jasmina Udovički and James Ridgeway (Durham, N.C., 1997), 71.

well off, indeed rather comfortable, under Communism, above all in regard to its living standard. Many inside and outside the country thought Yugoslavia had succeeded in finding an original road for socialism."[49] The revolution in personal consumption was a major source, if not indeed the sine qua non, of that curiosity and excitement.

With the country's new economic, social, and political openness, the experience of other countries was becoming relevant for Yugoslavia in all sorts of ways, but, just as important, many at the time sincerely believed that the Yugoslav experience was profoundly relevant for the rest of the world. It is now apparent that Yugoslavia since the 1950s was steadily becoming integrated—some would say enmeshed—in the economic and cultural structures of a world-system dominated by capital and capitalism. But back in the 1960s and 1970s, the Yugoslav case was more notable for its successes than its limitations and was, moreover, a paradigm with its own quite serious ambitions to the vast international reach that is now so often termed "globalization."

Notwithstanding the many necessary qualifications and the objections and reservations of contemporary critics, Yugoslav life on the whole did change for the better during the 1960s and 1970s. To a significant extent, these changes were the product of the more flexible, consumer-oriented economic system. More problematically, they were also built on massive loans. Enterprises borrowed frequently and heavily in order to keep salaries high and workers' wallets full, while the state itself became disturbingly dependent on foreign credit from the West, money that was often funneled downward to enterprises through credit and investment mechanisms, thus helping to artificially boost living standards and fueling consumer demand.[50] There were, moreover, no significant opportunities for private citizens to invest surplus wealth, so money that accumulated was in many cases just as well spent right away, especially once high inflation started to eat away at the purchasing power of wages already received.

Certain other peculiarities of the Yugoslav socialist system also encouraged this remarkable growth of personal consumption. In particular, housing and health care costs were set extremely low, leaving citizens with more disposable income. To illustrate the effects of low-cost housing on consumption, consider these figures: in 1966 a worker earning the average personal income would have had to work 16 hours to pay the monthly rent on an average apartment of fifty square meters. Simply to buy a pair of men's leather shoes, however, she would have had to work longer—almost 18 hours. To purchase a refrigerator would have required 449 hours of work, and buying

49. Tepavac, "Tito: 1945–1980," 71.

50. Lampe characterizes much of the growth of the Yugoslav economy through the 1970s as the result of a "borrowing binge." The country's foreign debt rose from about $2 billion in 1968 to $20 billion by 1982. Lampe, *Yugoslavia as History*, 315. See also Woodward, *Socialist Unemployment*, 302.

that most coveted of modern conveniences, a television, would have required a whopping 629 hours of work.[51]

Efforts to purchase these items clearly required substantial sacrifices and hard work, and in many cases workers held down extra jobs in order to increase their living standards. In relative terms, however, things were getting much better for the average Yugoslav worker. In case after case, from food to clothing to appliances, the work time required in 1966 represented just a fraction—and for some items such as refrigerators, radios, and televisions, a very small fraction—of the corresponding figures for 1963 and 1956.

For most Yugoslavs, this was a period of increasing satisfaction and perhaps even more steeply rising expectations. For those troubled by the appearance of a new and suspiciously unsocialist-looking consumer orientation, however, it was a deeply unsettling time. The fall of Ranković and the temporary victory of "liberalism" had by no means managed to snuff out all opposition to the 1965 reforms. Others continued to agitate against them, against the new deference to consumer satisfaction, and against the pro-market ideology that the government's new policies seemed to endorse. The party leadership itself continued to harbor misgivings about the consequences of market reforms. Edvard Kardelj, in particular, was leery of expanding the influence of market mechanisms, and Tito himself was certainly no enthusiast.

By 1972 the pro-market forces were nevertheless clearly in retreat. "The mood," Fred Singleton observed, "was one of caution and of a return to the ideological certainties of the past."[52] With the Tenth Party Congress of 1974, the rhetoric of communist leaders suggested a newfound suspicion of the market. Further decentralization of administration in both government and the enterprises now seemed the better remedy to the country's lingering difficulties. Reversing course, or at least braking hard, party doctrine now stressed the growing demand for self-managing labor to

> gain control over the laws of commodity production and for society consciously and appropriately to guide and rectify market trends, thus diminishing the possibility of adverse influences being generated by the action of blind forces in socio-economic development and relations. The League of Communists must combat conceptions and tendencies to consider that market relations should be formed spontaneously, and socio-economic problems can be solved by the market's automatic operation.[53]

Clearly, by the mid-1970s, many Yugoslavs in positions of power believed that the country had gone far enough, and perhaps too far, toward the establishment of a market economy.

---

51. Štahan, *Strukturne promjene i razvojne tendencije osobne potrošnje u Jugoslaviji u razdoblju od 1953. do 1967. godine*, 62.

52. Singleton, *Twentieth-Century Yugoslavia*, 296.

53. Ibid., 284, quoting *Socialist Thought and Practice* 6–7 (1974): 43–44.

Criticisms of this sort later subsided to some extent but never disappeared. Notwithstanding fears that the market in Yugoslavia was out of control—or perhaps, more aptly, that the market itself was now *in* control—it is important to realize that despite the real and dramatic nature of the reforms initiated in 1965, market mechanisms always remained imperfect, limited, and partial. As remarkable as the changes were, the economy remained a socialist economy and, perhaps even more important, its governing political and social ideology was strongly socialist in tone and content. There was plenty of grumbling about petit-bourgeois mentalities and the intrusion of capitalism, but genuine private enterprise was, in fact, of little real consequence except for its great symbolic significance. Writing in the mid-1970s, Bogdan Denitch observed that the "tiny" private sector carried "almost no social and political weight." An altogether new grouping made up mainly of small tradesmen and owners of restaurants and cafés, it had no major functional or lineal connections with "the prewar owning classes" and, in the end, represented nothing more than "fundamentally a thin layer of petit bourgeoisie, which exchanges its relative material prosperity for a pariahlike political status."[54] Yugoslavia had not, as some Westerners hoped and some domestic critics complained, embarked on the path to a true market economy, and it was in no real danger of becoming capitalist.

This is not to suggest, however, that capitalism itself had no role in nourishing the growth of a consumerist orientation. Many times, in fact, Yugoslavs learned about modern capitalist consumerism firsthand, by participating in it themselves while away on their frequent trips abroad. Beginning in the early 1960s, restrictions on foreign travel were relaxed noticeably. Border crossings by Yugoslav citizens jumped dramatically in the mid-1960s and would continue to increase rapidly in most later years.[55] Yugoslavs became keen, resourceful foreign travelers and, importantly, eager shoppers in Western markets.

They also learned about the pleasures of modern consumption by living and working in Western Europe, which was enjoying a burst of postwar affluence and was already thoroughly steeped in a consumer culture of expanding abundance. After the relaxation of official attitudes toward work abroad that began around 1962, large numbers of Yugoslavs experienced life in the consumerist West. So many were living abroad that they became,

---

54. Denitch, *The Legitimation of a Revolution*, 57–58. The percentage employed in this private sector declined from 1966 to 1970 to about 5% of the total nonagricultural workforce. Ibid., 58, citing *Statistički godišnjak Jugoslavije, 1972* (Belgrade, 1972).

55. The figure rose from 449,000 in 1964 to 1,284,000 in the following year, with extraordinarily rapid growth through the remainder of the decade. As a result, in 1970, there were almost 10.7 million border crossings. Growth leveled off to some extent shortly thereafter (and fell in 1971–1972), but by 1976 the number rose again to over 16 million. From 1960 to 1963, there were never more than 300,000 crossings annually. William Zimmerman, *Open Borders, Nonalignment, and the Political Evolution of Yugoslavia* (Princeton, N.J., 1987), 80, citing Vojislav Mićović, *Otvorenost Jugoslavije prema svetu* (Belgrade, 1977), 115.

as William Zimmerman argues, a "seventh republic," that is, an extension of the "political community of Yugoslav citizens who expect services and rights from, and render obligations to, a Yugoslav government."[56] By accepting Zimmerman's definition of the "seventh republic" as part of a *politically* defined community of *Yugoslavs*, that is, of citizens of the state, I am not suggesting that Yugoslavs abroad discarded their various ethnic identities. In some cases, close contacts with nationalistic émigrés, who had often left to avoid the Communists, resulted in strengthening ethno-national sentiments among the *Gastarbeiter* migrants.[57] There are reasons to believe, however, that at least certain aspects of life and work abroad may have had the opposite effect. For the most part, the populations and institutions of the West encountered Yugoslav citizens abroad as precisely that: Yugoslav citizens abroad. Fine distinctions between Croats and Slovenes, Montenegrins and Macedonians, Kosovars and Bosnians were not so salient abroad; these were niceties often lost on the bureaucrats, employers, landlords, and shopkeepers of the West, who most likely treated them as simply Yugoslavs. These common aspects of *Gastarbeiter* life may have made the experience one of those rare factors—like military service, foreign travel more generally, and, I argue, participation in a unifying consumer culture—that tended to minimize ethnic particularities in favor of a concurrently held pan-Yugoslav identity.

From a mere 18,000 in 1960, the number of migrant workers rose to 130,000 in 1965, climbing again to 600,000 by 1970. The figure peaked at 860,000 in 1973 before dropping again to around 700,000 in the last years of the decade.[58] By 1971 there were almost 412,000 Yugoslavs working in West Germany alone.[59] Considering that the population of the entire country in 1971 was approximately 20.5 million, including a large number of young and elderly people, a substantial fraction of the Yugoslav workforce

56. Zimmerman, *Open Borders*, 83.

57. Mark Allan Baskin, "Political Innovation and Policy Implementation in Yugoslavia: The Case of Worker Migration Abroad" (Ph.D. diss., U. of Michigan, 1986). On the apparent significance of the Croatian mass media in maintaining a republic-based (and thus presumptively ethno-national) identity among Croatians abroad, see Franjo Letić, *Društveni život vanjskih migranata* (Zagreb, 1989). Letić finds that the federal government's attempts to organize its citizens abroad on a pan-Yugoslav basis had only limited effects, though such clubs and groups did, by encouraging the expression of those elements common to all the state's citizens, enjoy at least some limited success as a means for allowing migrant workers to maintain a sense of belonging to the Yugoslav "homeland." Ibid., 222.

58. Zimmerman, *Open Borders*, 81, citing Ivo Baučić, "Stanje vanjskih migracija iz Jugoslavije krajem sedamdesetih godina," *Rasprave o migracijama*, no. 57 (1979); and Ivica Nejašmić, "Povratak jugoslavenskih vanjskih migranata i njihovo uključivanje u gospodarski i društveni život zemlje," *Rasprave o migracijama*, no. 73 (1981). Laura D'Andrea Tyson puts the figures even higher, with the 1973 peak at over one million. Tyson, *The Yugoslav Economic System*, 52.

59. Singleton, *Twentieth Century Yugoslavia*, 186, citing *Erfahrungsbericht ausländische Arbeitnehmer 1969 der Bundesaustalt für Arbeit* (Nürnberg, 1970). In 1965 the number of *Gastarbeiter* in the Federal Republic was only 64,060; the figure for 1954 was a paltry 1,801.

obviously had opted for employment abroad. At the beginning, guest workers came disproportionately from the more prosperous areas of the country, but over the course of the 1970s that tendency was corrected, and by 1977–1978 workers from the less-developed regions represented 44 percent of the total.[60] Remittances from these *Gastarbeiter* contributed substantially to the Yugoslav economy, and their changing tastes and lifestyles held enormous implications for Yugoslav culture and politics.[61]

By the mid- to late 1970s, then, Yugoslav citizens had become thoroughly accustomed to rising living standards and ever increasing access to the abundance and choice of modern consumer society. But their expectations for continued prosperity would soon be disappointed, as the economy entered a drastic decline beginning around 1978.

I Can't Believe It's Not Better: The Economic Collapse of the Long Final Decade

The causes for the economic crisis that began in the late 1970s were complex, and although opinions vary as to the weight each should be assigned, critical factors can be identified with some certainty. One trigger, for instance, was the oil crisis of 1979, a shock that was particularly ill-timed for Yugoslavia, since in a number of other respects the country's economy was about to hit the end of its rope. Of perhaps greatest significance was the role of foreign indebtedness, which had been used to help propel the earlier expansion. Yugoslavia's obligations had continued to mount to troubling levels and now began to drag down the performance of the economy as a whole. Moreover, creditors were becoming jittery, more insistent about repayment and anxious over Yugoslavia's long-term prospects after the death of Tito. International lending organizations such as the International Monetary Fund (IMF) pressed for further economic reforms and attempted to impose more of the market on the Yugoslav system, but the country's political leadership remained reluctant to accept most such proposals. Politically it proved almost impossible to make the economy efficient enough to handle the growing crisis: the market in Yugoslavia seemed to have reached its limits.[62] The dinar remained nonconvertible and overvalued, inflation

60. Tyson, *The Yugoslav Economic System,* 64.

61. Remittances grew from $59 million in 1965 to $500 million in 1970, and by the peak of 1973 had risen to $1.2 billion. Singleton, *Twentieth Century Yugoslavia,* 181, citing various sources. Lampe observes that both Western tourists and Yugoslavs returning from work abroad "brought a further infusion of Western popular culture and consumer demand that pressured the Yugoslav Communist regime to respond, a process still unfamiliar to the Soviet bloc." Lampe, *Yugoslavia as History,* 289.

62. Notably, very positive results were achieved with the strong medicine administered by Prime Minister Ante Marković in 1989–1990, but by then the improvement was too little, too late.

raged, and many enterprises found themselves unable to operate profitably and efficiently. Because of its structural weaknesses and inflexibility, the Yugoslav economy proved incapable of responding effectively to pressures from outside.

Caught in the confluence of negative forces, the Good Life in Yugoslavia largely disappeared over the course of the 1980s. Real net personal income per capita peaked in 1978, and after 1979 it began a decline even steeper than the dramatic ascent that had started in the mid-1950s. By 1984–1988, real income had dropped to levels not seen since the mid- to late 1960s.[63] Inflation, which had dragged down the economy since the early 1960s, rose to staggering levels and gnawed away at consumers' buying power from the minute they received their paychecks. Prices rose at an average annual rate of 36 percent in 1980–1983 and by an even more burdensome 63 percent per year in 1984–1985.[64]

The Yugoslav economic miracle had been built in large part on continually expanding opportunities for personal consumption. Now, despite expectations to the contrary, those opportunities evaporated. Personal consumption per capita, which had grown by an annual average of 5.7 percent in 1960–1970 and 4.5 percent in 1979, took a downturn: from 1979 to 1985, consumption fell at an average annual rate of 1.3 percent, with the total decline over that period amounting to 7.7 percent. Unemployment rose to seemingly intolerable levels, and real earnings fell dramatically.[65] In the social sector of the economy, real net personal income per worker fell an average of 4.7 percent per year from 1979 to 1985, for a total decrease of almost 28 percent.[66] In these circumstances, regional disparities in wealth, which had been severe even in the early days of the socialist state, grew even more extreme in many cases.[67]

Given the obvious impact of nationalist politics in Yugoslavia in the 1980s and 1990s, analyses of the Yugoslav breakup have tended to focus on the sources and consequences of virulent ethnic antipathies. This is undoubtedly as it should be but, with some welcome exceptions, notably in the work of Sabrina Ramet, John Lampe, Susan Woodward, and Branka

---

63. See Lenard J. Cohen, *Broken Bonds: The Disintegration of Yugoslavia* (Boulder, Colo., 1993), 46, citing *Statistički godišnjak 1989*.

64. Lampe, *Yugoslavia as History*, 311, citing *Jugoslavija, 1918–1988, Statistički godišnjak* (Belgrade, 1989), 160–166, and *Jugoslavija, 1945–1985* (Belgrade, 1986), 72, 239. Corresponding average annual rates of increase for prior periods were 12% for 1965–1970 and 17.7% for 1970–1979.

65. In the social sector of the economy, real earnings fell by 25% between 1979 and 1985, and continued to decline for most of the remaining years of the federation. Lampe, *Yugoslavia as History*, 293.

66. Ibid., 317, citing Lydall, *Yugoslavia in Crisis*, 41.

67. See the overview in Lampe, *Yugoslavia as History*, 326–334.

Magaš, economic influences have been unduly slighted.[68] Many observers have recognized, of course, that insofar as economic hardships could be identified with a particular republic or region, they tended to make inter-ethnic conflicts more severe. Had Serbia, Kosovo, Bosnia-Herzegovina, and the Krajina region of Croatia been more prosperous, and had residents of these areas not felt themselves to be the victims of unfair economic policies and development priorities, the ethnic hostilities seen there almost certainly would have been slower to emerge and less intense.

But prosperity, or at least relative wealth, was no guarantor of calm, reason, and accommodation: many people in Croatia and, especially, in Slovenia felt exploited by transfers of wealth to the poorer, southern regions of the country and frustrated by the government's unwillingness to introduce further market reforms. Although these two most prosperous republics could better weather the difficulties thanks to their earnings from tourism, industrial production, and exports to the West, they were nonetheless the sites of strong, and early, separatist movements.[69]

The connections between regional economic interests and interethnic hostilities are thus reasonably apparent. What has yet to be closely examined is how the expansive Yugoslav culture of consumption that flowered in the 1960s and 1970s, as a phenomenon that touched the entire country, may itself have contributed to the consolidation and later the dissolution of the federation. These effects are the subject of the final chapter of this volume, which considers how the country's immersion in consumer culture exacerbated the consequences of the downturn and deepened the sense of dissatisfaction that came to pervade Yugoslav society, thereby accelerating the collapse of socialist legitimacy and the rise of inter-republic and interethnic strife. But before moving to the perverse and unwelcome boomerang effect that accompanied the disastrous slide, we need to understand just how it was that Yugoslav society cultivated such a rapid, deep, and thoroughgoing dependence on the pleasures of modern mass consumption. It is to this critical part of the story—the making of market culture and consumer culture—that our account now turns.

---

68. See Ramet, *The Three Yugoslavias*; Branka Magaš, *The Destruction of Yugoslavia: Tracking the Break-up, 1980–92* (New York, 1993); Susan Woodward, *Balkan Tragedy: Chaos and Dissolution after the Cold War* (Washington, D.C., 1995), esp. 47–81.

69. See Jože Pirjevec, *Jugoslavija 1918–1992: nastanek, razvoj ter razpad Karadjordjevićeve in Titove Jugoslavije* (Koper, 1995), 385.

2 Making It

Building a Socialist Brand of Market Culture

This is the way it used to happen: The shopkeeper filled up his stockroom.
Customers bought from him or just walked by. Autumn approached,
but in the stockroom there was still far too much merchandise. And the
shopkeeper also knew that too much of his merchandise was out of date.
He worried about things for two or three days, and on the fourth day
he called the newspaper to get them to send him "someone" quickly.
"Someone" came, and an ad appeared announcing a great sale of the
best merchandise at the lowest prices, saving the day.... "The crowds
are swarming—save me!" This was advertising in the old style of the
fairground hawkers, which is still to be found today.

—*Naš publicitet*, 1955

Told from the perspective of one of socialist Yugoslavia's first professional advertising journals, the vignette related in the epigraph above
tried to capture the way things got done in the bad old days. With this
mordant little tale, brief but full of meaning, the disapproving editors of *Naš
publicitet* ["Our Publicity" or "Our Promotion"] offered their readers (and,
not coincidentally, the clients and potential clients of their parent institution Oglasni Zavod Hrvatske, or OZEHA) a taste of the supposedly backward past of Yugoslav advertising and the sorts of shoddy practices they
were aiming to transcend.[1] It was not a pretty picture. The poor merchant
in question followed no marketing program. He just bought merchandise
and sold it—or not—in a haphazard way, slipping from blissful ignorance
into a panic when things went poorly. Then, in desperation, he resorted to

---

Source for the epigraph: untitled piece, *Naš publicitet* 2, no. 2 (September 1955).
 1. The possessive adjective "*naš*" in the publication's title requires some special attention.
Although its literal meaning is "our" or "ours," in the standard Yugoslav usage encountered
here it ordinarily connotes something that applies to the whole society. Following the dissolution of the federation, the word is now used to signify ethno-national communities, but during the period under consideration in this book it was often used more or less synonymously
with the adjective "Yugoslav." Given the multivalence of both words in the journal's title,
Naš publicitet—literally, "Our Publicity" or "Our Promotion"—might just as properly be understood to mean something more on the order of "Yugoslav Advertising" or "Commercial
Promotion in Yugoslavia." Given the really quite expansive purview of the journal's coverage,
this might indeed be the superior rendering.

an advertisement of the simplest and crudest sort, not much more than an announcement really, and one that relied on exaggerations and unmerited superlatives: a "great" sale of the "best" goods at the "lowest" prices. The appeal was, moreover, deceptive and unfair: while it promised the finest quality, in reality the goods were out of fashion or growing obsolete.

More problematic still, the merchant ultimately proved unable to satisfy his customers' needs, overwhelmed by the "swarming" crowds. There were far too few buyers for long stretches of time, and far too many in an instant. Nothing about these contacts with the market was timed or planned. And to make matters worse, the advertisement was slapped together—certainly not "created," the piece suggested—by the kind of inexpert, mercenary hack who really had no place in a modern, sophisticated, genuinely professional advertising campaign. That "someone" referred to darkly in the piece was almost certainly an *akviziter,* that is, an agent of the newspaper who, as one of the commission-hungry "modern pirates" so disliked by the emerging cadre of creative industry professionals, made his living by selling advertising space to merchants and others for a cut of the expenditure, typically somewhere in the range of 5 to 20 percent of the cost of the advertisement.[2]

With the pointed concluding remark about "advertising in the old style of the fairground hawkers" [*to je bila reklama vašarskog stila*], the anonymous author of the piece succinctly dismissed the previous traditions of doing business. In the first place, the old mode involved the disreputable, primitive *reklama* form of advertising and not the modern, salutary *ekonomska propaganda.*[3] Worse yet, it was undertaken in the simplistic style of market

---

2. See C., "Moderni gusari," *Naš publicitet* 1, no. 1 (August 1954) (the omission of page numbers here, and in following citations, indicates that the journal pages were unnumbered). These *akviziteri* were the bane of the new, aggressively professionalizing trade in the 1950s. Contemporary industry sources are peppered with attacks on them. They were particularly despised by Zagreb's OZEHA bureau. See also, for example, d.m. [Dušan P. Mrvoš?], "Akviziteriade," *Naš publicitet* 1, no. 2 (December 1954); Veljko Klašterka, "Predgovor," in Dušan P. Mrvoš, *Propaganda, reklama, publicitet: teorija i praksa* (Belgrade: OZEHA Zavod za ekonomsku propagandu i publicitet, 1959). Similarly the Belgrade advertising enterprise Savremena privredna propaganda used its journal of the same name to alert clients of its decision to sack its network of *akviziteri.* See also, for example, Zapisnik o stenografskim beleškama sa savjetovanja preduzeća za ekonomsku propagandu Jugoslavije, koji je održan dana 10 februara 1957 godine, Arhiv Jugoslavije, collection Stručno udruženje preduzeća za ekonomsku propagandu i publicitet, AJ-262-1.

3. The translation of the English terms "advertising" and "advertisement" poses peculiar problems in both the Yugoslav languages used in this book. In Serbo-Croatian sources the word "advertisement" was probably most frequently rendered (especially in common parlance) as "*reklama,*" taken from the French "*réclame,*" "advertisement," a term itself derived from the verb "*réclamer,*" "to call for, to ask for." Industry leaders, however, mounted a wholehearted campaign to banish the allegedly primitive *reklama* in both word and deed and replace it with the more dignified and professional "*oglas,*" a word with connotations more akin to "announcement." For the more abstract concept of "advertising," Serbo-Croatian again used "*reklama*" alongside other terms more favored in the field, "*ekonomski publicitet,*" "*oglašivanje,*" "*privredna propaganda,*" "*ekonomska propaganda,*" and sometimes simply "*propaganda.*" The term "*publicitet*" (or "*ekonomski publicitet*") admits of multiple meanings, and was used

hawkers, essentially doing little more than shouting out to customers the qualities of the offered goods, qualities that were most often exaggerated, if not flatly false.

Against that picture of a primitive past saddled with the vices of crude, unfettered, profit-seeking capitalism, *Naš publicitet* offered a rational, conscientious, and crisply professional alternative, a fresh vision of how business could be done and should be done in the aggressively modernizing new Yugoslavia of the mid-1950s. Advertising campaigns conceived in harmony with the guiding principles of the contemporary profession, the review's commentator maintained, represented a radical departure from the past. In contrast to the bad old ways of the bad old days, modern advertisements instead

> draw their arguments from only two vital and truthful sources, namely, the usefulness and advantages of the products and services advertised and the wishes and needs of the buyer-consumer-user. There is no other, third source for the message. The interests of the producer and seller are subordinated to the interests of the customer. Respectable trade brands are developed, and along with them contemporary commercial promotion [*ekonomski publicitet*] on a completely scientific basis. The creation of the message as well as the source and the dissemination of the medium that will carry the message are all precisely planned. The methods, in and of themselves, do not represent anything independently; they are merely a mode of transmission.[4]

Simultaneously an overture to potential clients and an appeal for respect on some deeper, noncommercial level of social and political values, this source neatly captures one of the most important messages sent out by the Yugoslav advertising industry in the early days of its growth and consolidation under self-management socialism.

The promise was unequivocal: the familiar old styles may indeed have prevailed in the unenlightened conditions of primitive capitalism and the backward economy of the interwar kingdom, but the Yugoslav advertising of the future would be something completely different. And fortunately, so the message went, the future was right at hand, thanks, of course, to the

---

sometimes in the stricter sense of "publicity" and at other times as something more or less synonymous with "advertising" or, more generally "promotion." It is important to note—especially in a study of a socialist country—that "*propaganda*" does not carry the strongly negative connotations of artificiality and falsity that it does in English. In Slovenian sources one also quite frequently encounters references to the *reklama*, although here, too, advertising professionals had a decided preference for "*oglas*." For "advertising," Slovenian industry leaders tended to prefer "*oglaševanje*," though one encounters "*ekonomska propaganda*" as well, especially in older sources. Where appropriate, I have included the original usage in the source language with the English translations of these and related terms. The battle against the *reklama* is discussed below in the context of the industry's efforts at professionalization.

4. Untitled piece in *Naš publicitet* 2, no. 2 (September 1955).

commitment and skill of the new industry professionals. As it happened, Yugoslavia's future would indeed be one of zealous, skillful advertising and abundant consumer promise. How that future was created and what the advertising and marketing industry brought to the country along the way are the subjects of this chapter.

Approaching commercial promotion from a Western perspective, and thus inured to the sort of thinking about brands and media appeals and the supremacy of consumer desires that the people behind *Naš publicitet* and its counterparts were proposing, we might at first fail to recognize just how unusual and surprising was this new orientation advocated by what was, in effect, an emergent Yugoslav industry specializing in advertising and marketing services. But in the context of a socialist economic order that otherwise had been largely indifferent to consumer preferences, this new Yugoslav line was indeed radical. Beginning in the mid-1950s, advertising specialists gradually turned Yugoslavia into something without parallel in the world of state socialism: a place where, on a regular basis, ordinary citizens were bombarded with advertising messages. From this time until the dissolution of federal Yugoslavia in 1991, the country's consumers encountered advertisements practically everywhere they went. They started seeing ads in their daily newspapers, in magazines, on the radio, on television, in movie theaters, on the streets, and even in the stores where they shopped, stores that were typically quite well stocked, with help, as explained in the previous chapter, both from a reformist economic policy that valued market mechanisms and the satisfaction of consumer desires and from a hefty infusion of borrowed foreign cash used to boost workers' salaries.

Like so many other things about the country, the mixture of advertisements produced in socialist Yugoslavia was exceptional for its diversity, defying neat categorization. Some ads seemed like throwbacks to the most primitive models of what typically passed for advertising in the Soviet Union. These old-style advertisements might merely announce, for example, that a certain chain of shoe stores was indeed a place where customers could buy shoes, or they might use up an entire page in a mass-market weekly magazine apparently to do no more than just remind readers of the existence of one of the country's textile manufacturers, perhaps bolstering that none-too-shocking claim with photographic documentation of the factory itself.

Especially in the early years, Yugoslav advertising occasionally did, like its Soviet-bloc counterparts, betray a disconnection from the realities of the market that makes it appear strange or even absurdly irrational to observers schooled in the Western logic of advertising. To be sure, some of those intimately involved with the development of the craft in Yugoslavia were painfully aware of these lapses. Along these lines, for example, one industry source recounted with a mixture of amusement and scorn the story of one "notorious" television spot for a domestic manufacturer of industrial compressors, a product for which there could have been, at most, no more than five thousand potential purchasers in the entire country. This was a tiny market, far too small for any broad(ly)cast appeal like a television commercial to make sense. Moreover, there was no assurance that very many of the possible customers would even be reached by the spot, while the manufacturer was saddled with the undue expense of beaming it to a huge audience with millions of absolutely uninterested viewers such as ordinary workers, retirees, and children![5] As early as 1955, advertising professionals were ridiculing the market-blind folly that led to such absurdities as the use of "frenetic advertising posters" pasted up far and wide in what was, at least on the surface, an attempt to promote the sale of highly specialized items such as manometers, or industrial pressure gauges.[6]

Like these fairly extreme cases, a few Yugoslav advertisements provoke the strong suspicion that, occasionally, enterprises were simply engaging in advertising for the sake of advertising, that is, to proclaim the presence of the company in the domestic market more as a matter of prestige than as a function of any real need to sell something, or even as an expression of concern for the concrete commercial implications of their public image. Lest we judge advertisements of this sort too harshly, it is worth noting that Western companies, notwithstanding the more immediate imperatives of the market, quite frequently engage in "image" advertising that is not designed to promote the sale of any goods or services in particular but rather to burnish the public reputation of the company. Some of the ostensibly less-than-rational Yugoslav advertising reviewed here could perhaps be redeemed if interpreted in this way.

On the other hand, given the implications of the larger context of the socialist economy, there are also grounds to incline toward the contrary interpretation, that is, to the inference that what we find in these instances is indeed advertising for the sake of advertising. Neither in the Soviet bloc nor even in the unique conditions of Yugoslav self-management socialism were there any genuinely compelling financial reasons for enterprises to worry about their image: as we have seen, bankruptcy for unprofitability was hardly a real option, and firms would not fail if they came to be held in low esteem by the public.

Another very real possibility (though one that is difficult, if not impossible, to substantiate) is that ads of this sort were placed more or less as favors to friends and business associates in the various media companies. Given the workings of the Yugoslav economy and the critical role of personal connections, this explanation cannot be ruled out. If market exigencies

---

5. Borislav B. Mitrović, *O+P+P=: priručnik za upravljanje propagandom* (Belgrade, 1989), 30. A targeted solicitation and brochure, Mitrović suggested, would have been much wiser.

6. Jovan S. Dimitrijević, "Za pravilnu upotrebu sredstava namenjenih privrednoj propagandi," *Standard* 1, no. 1 (May 1955): 5–6.

did not really matter at the end of the day, then the content and the efficacy of the ads themselves could be of little concern as well.

With time, however, "mistakes" like these came to be treated by advertising and marketing specialists as aberrations and holdovers, part of the unfortunate, "primitive" history of the Yugoslav craft—and, importantly, evidence of the pressing need for more exacting standards, better training, and, yes, *more* advertising of a higher, smarter, more rational sort. And as the industry matured, such crude or seemingly pointless ads did indeed become increasingly rare exceptions. Most Yugoslav advertisements aspired to much higher standards of creativity and efficacy, and many were hardly distinguishable from contemporary analogues from the ad-besotted West.

The specialists who made up the rapidly professionalizing industry that created these ever more sophisticated messages might seem unlikely agents of social change. To begin with, compared to their counterparts in those places where advertising was already firmly established, their numbers were small, especially at first, and their presence in the country's commercial culture more limited. They were, moreover, hampered until the waning days of the socialist system by a political climate that remained leery of, if not openly hostile toward, advertising and the suspect consumerist values associated with it. Yet given socialist Yugoslavia's surprising and rapid transformation into a consumer society, or at the very least into something closely resembling one, we ought to be curious about the mechanisms by which that conversion took place, and the rich record of the birth and growth of consumer culture in Yugoslavia leaves no doubt that the domestic industry of commercial promotion must rank among the prime agents of change.

It is apparent that many of these practitioners were imbued with a thoroughly activist, self-consciously pioneering spirit. They *wanted* to effect a dramatic change in the country's commercial culture, even if they typically maintained, very reassuringly, that Yugoslavia was not, and should not be, a consumer society driven by the same concerns as those that prevailed in the West. They were dedicated to the advancement of their profession, and they worked hard to legitimize its role in the new economic order that the government had inaugurated in 1950, two years after the fateful break with the Soviets. Moving only cautiously and tentatively at first, Yugoslav advertising specialists slowly carved out a niche among the country's business élites. With only the most meager collection of training materials in their own languages at their disposal, and with an atmosphere of grave suspicion retarding the practice of their craft in other parts of the socialist realm, they were forced to look elsewhere for inspiration and practical guidance.

Naturally they looked to the West. Tito's disengagement from the Soviet bloc and the concomitant repositioning of Yugoslavia as "something in-between" had made this resort to capitalist sources a great deal easier, both as a practical matter and as a question of politics and ideas, for the new ideological climate had lifted many of the familiar communist taboos against things Western. Thus freed, advertising specialists did what they could to master the techniques and the theories of advertising that had been developed and refined in the exuberant, alluringly prosperous consumer societies of postwar America and Western Europe. They quickly set about the work of building institutions that would secure for them a safe and respected place in the country's economic order: a host of professional associations, advertising departments within other large commercial enterprises, and, later, independent advertising agencies. As they became more confident and assertive, they began to publish prolifically, leaving behind a detailed record of their problems, concerns, values, and agendas for the future. And, over time, they convinced many business leaders that advertisements were a constant necessity for the domestic Yugoslav market, and not just something to be pressed into service only on occasion, when seeking export sales abroad in countries with more sophisticated business cultures where advertising had long since become de rigueur. Advertisements aimed at domestic consumers consequently became, by the mid-1960s, a prominent part of Yugoslav life. Meanwhile, all these ads and the many products they promoted found quite a receptive audience (detailed in chapter 7). And so, owing in part to the efforts of advertising and marketing specialists in Zagreb, Belgrade, Ljubljana, Sarajevo, and other cities, Yugoslavia became a country consumed with consumption, a curious and decidedly unorthodox experiment in refashioning the dictatorship of the proletariat as a shoppers' paradise.

The profession's rise to prominence must be reconstructed largely from primary sources produced by those who were employed in the industry or who supported it through their academic work, and such sources for the earlier years are fragmentary at best. An intricate institutional history of the industry itself is, of necessity, beyond the scope of this work. But any investigation into the move toward a consumer society in this unusual case does require an effort to determine the main lines of growth within the field and, just as important, to isolate the *ideology* associated with advertising in Yugoslavia in a way that permits us to track the development and the diffusion of these new ways of thinking about business, the economy, and the daily life of ordinary citizen-consumers.

Studies of advertising typically proceed in one of several dominant modes. They may, for example, be tied tightly to the business of commercial promotion and the people who have led that business, as is the case with Stephen Fox's detailed institutional examination of American advertising in the twentieth century.[7] Roland Marchand's analysis of American advertising in the 1920s and 1930s, an indispensable starting point for any consideration of the power of advertising to mirror and mold culture, approaches the role of the industry a bit differently, focusing on the content of the advertisements

---

7. Stephen Fox, *The Mirror Makers: A History of American Advertising and Its Creators* (Urbana, 1997).

themselves. But along the way Marchand acknowledges the critical, culture-creating function of the emergent class of advertising professionals: These "apostles of modernity," he concludes, "brought good news about progress" and held out the promise of an American Dream of progress without pain, advancement without alienation, growth without dehumanization.[8] In a similar vein, James D. Norris takes issue with what he characterizes as the tendency of economic historians to dismiss the significance of advertising; he credits the American profession with the creation of national markets, with the generation of new demands and desires, and, more generally, with the production of a national culture that set a premium on consumption.[9]

Other studies have ventured further and dared to offer more sweeping interpretations of the role of advertising and its creators in shaping the national culture. This is the case, for instance, with the work of T. J. Jackson Lears, who has turned the standard portrayal of American advertising on its head, rejecting explanations that see it primarily as a vehicle for magical, carnivalesque escapism and hedonism, and arguing that the advertising craft in the twentieth century has instead served as a tool for cultivating a *management* ethos of control, discipline, order, efficiency, productivity, and only very measured pleasures.[10] Still other analyses have pointed to the difficulties inherent in assessing the cultural and, for that matter, even the practical economic impact of commercial promotion. Moving along these lines, Michael Schudson parts company both with industry apologists who deny any harmful effects on the broader society and with social critics who treat advertising as an insuperable force sculpting (for the worse, usually) modern culture, attitudes, and behaviors.[11]

Many important questions about the effects of advertising have yet to be answered, of course, but on balance these and other leading historical and sociological analyses confirm its significance as a force with important consequences for the larger culture in which it operates. In particular, they signal the power of advertising to "sell" a specific, that is, capitalist, notion of the Good Life, to present to a mass audience the liberal capitalist experience of modern life in idealized and highly (or unrealistically) appealing terms, and to reinforce the manifold consumerist wants and needs that help sustain the dominant political economy. Finally, and most significant for the present inquiry, these interpretations emphasize the importance of the creators

---

8. Roland Marchand, *Advertising the American Dream: Making Way for Modernity, 1920–1940* (Berkeley, 1985), 1.

9. James D. Norris, *Advertising and the Transformation of American Society, 1865–1920* (New York, 1990).

10. T. J. Jackson Lears, *Fables of Abundance: A Cultural History of Advertising in America* (New York, 1994).

11. Michael Schudson, *Advertising, the Uneasy Persuasion: Its Dubious Impact on American Society* (New York, 1984).

of advertising—among the truest of capitalism's true believers—as critical agents of these processes of cultural reinforcement and cultural change.

Typically, however, studies of the work of the advertising industry in the highly developed West do not contemplate the potential that advertising professionals elsewhere might also be able to remake with their own images a culture that does not take as its starting point the values, attitudes, and business practices of capitalistic production and distribution. Yet something very closely resembling Western-style advertising can function, and indeed has functioned, in places not fully integrated into the world of liberal capitalism, places where the market for consumer goods has been either undeveloped or affirmatively obstructed, and where the dominant political order has not, as in the West, celebrated the values of the market.

Predictably, if to some extent justifiably, the very notion of consumer society has been bound up narrowly with the practices and values of capitalism. For scholars interested in the history of consumption and its deeper social meanings, all these delightfully potent and marvelously irritating manifestations of consumer society in the consumption-driven West are, to be sure, compelling and deserving objects of study. Yet the net effect of the overwhelming concentration on advertising as practiced in the West has been to reinforce this already tight association and channel our gaze toward strong cases that neatly fit the capitalist mold.

With the Yugoslav experience we can begin to see how problematic this view may be when it is applied to advertising. Commercial promotion, seen in the dominant frame, tends to be understood as a device by which capitalist institutions, operating within an already thoroughly capitalist economic structure, beget an even more strongly capitalist culture and an even more unshakably capitalist economy. The standard reading of consumer society as something consummately capitalist thereby deflects our attention away from another, little explored option of interpretation and etiology: the possibility that the *culture* of consumer society, even if we understand that culture as one suffused with styles and values that are thoroughly capitalist, need not necessarily be grounded upon capitalist *economic relations*. The market culture(s) of the developed West may indeed be capitalist at the core, and yet the Yugoslav case suggests that many of the most important cultural features at work are, in fact, highly flexible and portable, and that elements of consumer society may therefore be created in—or transported to—an underlying economic and political system that is not only different from but avowedly antagonistic to capitalism.

Socialist Yugoslavia thus presents us with a departure from the standard fare: a very different social and political terrain on which the culture of the market and the cultural content of consumerism could operate. To be sure, Yugoslav advertising specialists did see themselves, as did their predecessors in America, as pioneers, working hard to establish a new and more efficient way of doing business. But in the uncertain circumstances of Yugoslav socialism, the country's advertising and marketing experts were more than just path-breaking importers and propagators of new, value-free, and politically neutral business techniques. Quite to the contrary: whether or not it was recognized as such by its purveyors, the system of values inherent in the ideology of advertising as it was practiced in Yugoslavia challenged the reigning principles of Yugoslav political life. As it carried the day as a new model for commercial culture, the implicit ideology of customer-oriented, ad-driven business carried with it the potential to erode earlier assumptions about the primacy of the ordinary citizen's role as worker-producer, substituting for those orthodox tenets of socialism a new emphasis on the needs and wishes of the ordinary citizen as consumer. In the West, the work and the message of the apostles of advertising and marketing ultimately rested on an endorsement—indeed, even an enshrinement—of the fundamental values of capitalism, and thus of the governing socioeconomic order. In contrast, the evangelizing efforts of the Yugoslav profession involved, at its heart, something quite subversive.

With the ultimate aim of identifying those critical values embraced and advanced by advertising and its creators, we turn now to a historical outline of the expansion of the Yugoslav advertising and marketing profession during the socialist period. The development of the craft can best be understood with reference to four phases, a temporal framework derived not simply from a narrow consideration of events in the industry but rather from a broader consideration of the workings of consumer culture in the socialist era. We thus encounter (1) a period of suppression in the first five years of Stalinist-style governance and rigid central planning; (2) a phase of slow, gradual, and inconsistent growth of the industry and its influence from 1950 to 1965, after the first gestures toward the market and the loosening of many political strictures; (3) a heyday from 1965 until about 1980, marked by dramatic expansion of the consumer economy in the wake of new and even more significant market reforms; and (4) an unhappy unraveling of the national economy that lasted from around 1980 until the dissolution of the federation in 1991, a period in which the advertising industry remained strong and its messages just as pervasive despite radical reductions in consumer purchasing power. To be sure, the responses of the industry sometimes lagged a bit behind the major transformations of the country's political and economic system (though by promoting consumerism, the advertising profession was, at the same time, contributing to a number of those large-scale changes). Nevertheless, developments in the field did, by and large, correspond to bigger trends in the country's political and economic history.

Dark Victory: The Eclipse of Advertising under Central Planning, 1945–1950

Once Tito and his Communists had consolidated their control over the country in the years immediately following World War II, Yugoslavia embarked on an orthodox path of strictly centralized economic planning and Stalinist political control. The consequences for the country's commercial culture were drastic. Consumer choices (and, accordingly, consumer expectations) were radically limited as the government pursued a familiar socialist program of rapid industrial development, focusing on heavy industry and slighting the consumer sector. The decisive orientation of economic priorities away from consumer items was, moreover, amplified by the sheer scarcity that enveloped Yugoslavia as a consequence of the depredations of the war.

A proper grasp of the unpromising environment from which the Yugoslav advertising and marketing industries emerged also requires an understanding that the country had been extraordinarily poor, and its consumer markets only incompletely and haphazardly developed, even *before* the war. As a result, advertising in the interwar monarchy had only a limited public presence and, significantly, not one that had served as a great impetus to the growth of either domestic Yugoslav manufacturers and sellers or a native advertising specialty. For in the modest economic conditions of the "first" Yugoslavia of 1918–1941, there was very little production of finished consumer goods for the retail market; most manufacturing instead involved semi-finished products, which were then shipped abroad for final processing. These, along with considerable shipments of raw materials, constituted the bulk of Yugoslavia's exports before the Second World War.

Accordingly, most advertising was undertaken to promote foreign products, with rare exceptions. Along these lines Veljko Klašterka, one key industry insider in the early years of socialism, observed that most consumer-oriented manufacturing firms during the interwar period "were the property of various corporations that often served as a cover for foreign capital. These firms imported into Yugoslavia materials for advertising their products that were likewise already in finished form. Only the texts and the appeals were adapted to suit the character of the backward Balkans."[12] Prior to the war, advertising of imported goods consumed something on the order of 90 percent of advertising budgets.[13]

Because of the shortage of contemporary evidence from the first years of communist rule (other than the many primary sources that prove the negative, that is, those that confirm the absence of commercial promotion), it is difficult to assess with complete confidence the attitudes that then prevailed toward prior advertising practices. But in the advertising literature that began to appear in socialist Yugoslavia somewhat later, beginning in the mid-1950s, one encounters an attitude toward prewar practice in the country that is, at best, decidedly ambivalent, and sometimes flatly negative—this

---

12. Klašterka, "Još nešto o inflaciji stručnjaka za reklamu," *Naš publicitet* 4, nos. 3–4 (December 1957): 22.

13. Mrvoš, "Važnost propagande za našu privredu," *Naš publicitet* 1, no. 1 (August 1954).

even though a few of the leaders of the new industry got their early training in precisely that setting. To the extent that interwar practice is discussed, the tone adopted is often fairly dismissive.[14] Along these lines, for example, consider the rather harsh assessment of Dušan P. Mrvoš, one of the prime movers of the Yugoslav advertising industry in its early years. Mrvoš was at the forefront of the later effort to cast advertising work as a highly professionalized, expert specialty. Reflecting on the growth of the craft from its very humble beginnings, he stated bluntly that "one cannot speak about advertising [and here Mrvoš used the favored term of the industry's self-styled progressives, *ekonomska propaganda*] of any serious measure in Yugoslavia prior to 1941."[15] Mrvoš was one of the industry specialists with the most extensive prewar background. With these remarks he was, strictly speaking, addressing the presence of *ekonomska propaganda,* and not the *reklama,* in interwar Yugoslavia. We must therefore be careful not to read his statement as a bald assertion that there was little or no advertising of any sort in Yugoslavia prior to World War II. Mrvoš knew as well as anyone that this was not the case. Rather, this advertising activist sought to underscore the absence of modern, professionalized commercial promotion of the type he sought so tenaciously to encourage through his work with Croatia's OZEHA agency.

In the vast majority of the many trade publications and instructional materials produced by Yugoslav specialists, however, these earlier experiences are simply not addressed at all. As a result, much of that literature has an extraordinarily ahistorical tone, and when the beginnings of the Yugoslav craft are discussed, the treatment is typically cursory and goes back only to 1950 and the shift to self-management. One wonders whether the prewar past was relegated to near invisibility for political reasons, that is, as the result of a more general ideological hostility to the capitalist predecessor regime, or simply because by the 1950s, when the young industry had managed to gain some footing once again in the domestic economy, the methods and techniques of the previous period were deemed outmoded according to new criteria elaborated with reference to the professional standards that prevailed in developed capitalist countries. In this regard, it is noteworthy that Yugoslav trade and instructional materials do occasionally refer, positively, to literature produced prior to 1945 in the developed West and to the prewar practice of advertising there. Most likely, some combination of these two potential causes was involved. In any case, for most of these

---

14. The history of advertising in interwar Yugoslavia has been the subject of sparse scholarly attention. One useful exception is Milan Ristović, "Pogled kroz ogledalo: reklama i istorija," *New Moment,* no. 6 (1996): 102–110. Ristović detects in the advertising of the period a tension between the interest in creating a unified Yugoslav market and the nationalistic "buy Croatian" or "buy Serbian" sentiments that came to the fore in the mid-1930s. On earlier Yugoslav practice, see, for example, "Kako se nekad oglašavalo," *Savremena privredna propaganda* 2, no. 3 (April 1958): 18–19; "In memoriam—Miroslav Feller," *Ideja,* no. 10 (April 1981): 14.

15. Mrvoš, "Važnost propagande za našu privredu."

insiders, it is as if the history of advertising in Yugoslavia itself—or perhaps more precisely the relevant, admissible, *usable* past—begins abruptly in 1945 (or often even later, for although many writers do acknowledge the disappearance of advertising under the "distributive" economy of the immediate postwar period, they typically hasten onward to talk about happier times).

The prewar foundations of the advertising industry, rudimentary as they were, were all but wiped away by the events of the next decade, first by the war itself and then by the dictates of central planning. The military conflict appears to have taken a heavy toll on advertising specialists, and in 1954 Mrvoš observed grimly that "you could no doubt count the remaining expert cadre from prewar Yugoslavia on your fingers."[16]

Even more important than the destruction of the war, however, was the new government's dramatic ideological realignment toward socialism on the command-economy model, a shift that made consumer advertising mostly if not completely superfluous. As a result of the Communists' fervent faith in the promises of a rigidly planned economy, what was left of the country's tiny advertising industry—and with it, advertising itself—largely disappeared from public view during this initial phase. The period is, in fact, noteworthy for the nearly total silence that surrounded the idea of consumer advertising. Not only were consumer advertisements themselves almost entirely absent from the Yugoslav press, but practically nothing on the subject was published. In the rich trade literature that began to develop in the mid-1950s, citations to Yugoslav sources from the immediate postwar years are exceedingly rare, and the works that are referenced deal with advertising only tangentially, if at all.

A sampling of important daily newspapers and mass-circulation magazines from the period confirms the conclusion that commercial advertising was largely absent from the public scene. A consideration of one representative example, the Slovenian popular magazine *Tovariš* [Comrade], is instructive. The periodical began publication in 1945, nominally as a weekly, though at this time it was published irregularly. It carried a mixture of news items, social and political commentary, and a range of features meant more for entertainment and diversion. The first year's issues contain no advertising at all, while only the most limited advertising appears in the pages of the 1946 issues, and these are all small, text-heavy announcements reminiscent of classified ads in Western publications. Moreover, some issues from this volume of the magazine have no advertising at all. By 1950 even this minimal advertising had disappeared, suggestive of a policy strongly discouraging if not prohibiting advertising. (Some evidence suggests, in fact, that at least a few Yugoslav press enterprises in 1948 and 1949 consciously sought

---

16. Ibid.

to eliminate advertisements from their pages.)[17] The picture presented in *Tovariš* speaks clearly, and it is one replicated in other newspapers and magazines elsewhere in the country.

State policy, concerned at the time with industrialization and the stabilization of production, simply was not amenable to the use of consumer advertising to stimulate demand. Reflecting some years later on the industry's modest beginnings and its limited prospects in the immediate postwar period, Zagreb's Veljko Klašterka explained that the country's entire economic system had been conformed to the planning model. As a result, he observed mildly, "at that time there did not prove to be a great need for advertising and commercial promotion."[18] I suspect that we may need to read between the lines here to find an implicit criticism of the government's prior policies, for Klašterka, like his colleagues, was very much an agitator for the growth of advertising and a firm believer in its value to the Yugoslav economy. In 1957, when he offered this assessment of the industry's shaky beginnings, Yugoslavia was not all that far away from its command-economy past, and its system remained a mixed one, with high-level guidance still enjoying a prominent and respected role. In such circumstances, anything other than an oblique attack on the logic of previous policies would likely have been unwise.

As such, pronouncements like this might well be understood as a model of diplomatic understatement, for the true picture of the circumstances then facing the industry—if indeed we can fairly call it an "industry," given its limitations at the time—was a good deal more disheartening. Effectively cordoned off from the domestic economy, advertising during this first period was put largely to those few ends that were considered permissible under orthodox Marxist notions of the place of commercial promotion in a planned economy. It was for the most part confined to the stimulation of tourism and foreign trade.[19]

In this respect, advertising activity during the early, central-planning stage of Yugoslav socialism strongly resembled the patterns of practice seen elsewhere in the socialist world even much later. Tourism was, not surprisingly, of only minor importance during the immediate postwar years. The destruction and the enduring economic hardships caused by the fighting had dramatically limited opportunities for foreign travel, while the chill in East-West relations diminished the appeal of Yugoslavia abroad. Although there is evidence of some efforts to develop the advertising of tourism during this period, most of the limited attention paid to advertising was in connection with exports, which also held the promise of badly needed hard-currency earnings. According

---

17. *Drugo jugoslavensko savjetovanje propagandista* [Proceedings of the Second Yugoslav Conference of Advertising Specialists], Zagreb, 22–23 February 1963 (Zagreb, 1963), 46.

18. Klašterka, "Još nešto o inflaciji stručnjaka za reklamu," 22.

19. See Mrvoš, "Važnost propagande za našu privredu."

to one industry source, the promotion of exports in this early period was certainly the most significant if not the only area in which there was a genuine perceived need for advertising.[20] Yet even within these circumscribed "safe zones," the advertising industry of the new Yugoslavia did not seem to be off to a particularly promising start. Lacking resources, training, and clients with any serious demand for its services, the profession lagged far behind Western standards of creativity and efficacy. Retailing, viewed at the time as mainly a question of distributing the goods that planners had decided were needed, remained similarly undeveloped, conducted for the most part along traditional lines and certainly without heavy reliance on advertising.[21]

The big problem for the industry was that the state planners who dictated the new economic order saw so little need for it. Advertising seemed doomed to irrelevance. Once the advertising specialty began its rise to prominence, its leaders would remember these as particularly bleak times:

> As regards advertising as a work activity, *it did not exist*. There were no economic motivations for its existence and it did not fit into the concept of the new social and economic order. The foundations of advertising activity that had been created in the prewar Yugoslavia were in ruins. The organizational forms of advertising work, that is, bureaus [*zavodi*] and agencies, did not exist. The cadres that had developed in this field of economic activity, insofar as they had not perished in the war or had not compromised themselves in some way, were to a greater or lesser extent incorporated into so-called political and ideological propaganda. They were involved in the technical work of this propaganda.[22]

These were dark days for advertising—so dark, in fact, that advertising and those who practiced it became almost invisible. If Yugoslavia in 1941 had remained at a great remove from the perils and pleasures of consumer society, it was even farther away by 1950.

This is not to say that advertising for domestic audiences disappeared from public view during these first socialist years. There were, to be sure, still a few advertisements to be seen. And several other uses of advertising were deemed sufficiently harmonious with the ideological dictates of the

20. M. [Dušan P. Mrvoš?], "Deset godina OZEHA," *Naš publicitet* 1, no. 2 (December 1954).

21. For comparisons to the Soviet retailing experience, see Julie Hessler, *A Social History of Soviet Trade: Trade Policy, Retail Practices, and Consumption, 1917–1953* (Princeton, N.J., 2004); Hessler, "A Postwar Perestroika? Toward a History of Private Enterprise in the USSR," *Slavic Review* 57, no. 3 (fall 1998): 516–542; Amy E. Randall, *The Soviet Dream World of Retail Trade and Consumption in the 1930s* (Basingstoke, England, 2008); Randall, "Legitimizing Soviet Trade: Gender and the Feminization of the Retail Workforce in the Soviet 1930s," *Journal of Social History* 37, no. 4 (summer 2004): 965–990; Marjorie L. Hilton, "Retailing the Revolution: The State Department Store (GUM) and Soviet Society in the 1920s," *Journal of Social History* 37, no. 4 (summer 2004): 939–964.

22. Dragutin Vračar, *Privredna propaganda* (Skopje, 1974), 126–127 (emphasis added).

new system. One was the effort to structure demand in conformity with policy preferences and, perhaps even more important, with the limitations of domestic production. Thus there was some narrow use of advertising in order to induce consumers to use new products that were being produced pursuant to the state's plan, especially surrogates for those that were in short supply or available only by import.[23]

Another politically acceptable orientation of domestic advertising was more closely akin to the explicitly propagandistic services ("propagandistic," that is, in the Western, noncommercial sense of the term) into which the remnants of the prewar advertising industry had been impressed. Advertisements of this type were designed not so much to sell anything as to showcase the "economic achievements" of the new socialist economy, and, accordingly, "every success that was achieved in this field was an outstanding point in the struggle for the affirmation of the new, socialist society."[24] Here it is not hard to detect a suggestion of ironic distance, one that hints at a sense of superiority bordering on dismissiveness.

Even at the remove of only a decade or so, the image that emerges from the ad-industry sources quite obviously betrays a judgment that "advertising practice" in the infancy of Yugoslav socialism scarcely merited the name. Those sources recall, for instance, that "the production successes of individual enterprises were underscored using all forms of public communication, especially the newspapers and radio. There were announcements about the fulfillment of plan requirements, about taking over the production of some product that until then had not been manufactured or had only been imported, and the like."[25] Promotional work of this type was clearly a far cry from what predominated in the West, and it certainly was not about to spark the development of a rich and varied consumer culture.

Even if they had been interested in launching some restoration of the arts of commercial promotion during the first postwar years, Yugoslav specialists would have been hard pressed to do so. To the very limited extent that advertisements for consumer items targeted at domestic audiences did appear, they were typically the products of advertising departments within media outlets, for example, in large, state-run newspaper publishing houses. This sort of institutional setting, particularly in the quasi-Stalinist political environment of the times, allowed very little freedom of professional activity. Usually what was done was what was decreed from above. A few semi-autonomous professional institutions such as Interpublic—not really independent "agencies" in the strict sense of the word—did indeed exist during this period, but their work and influence were quite curtailed. Both

---

23. Ibid.
24. Ibid.
25. Ibid.

advertising budgets and the number of firms that bought advertising remained, moreover, minimal.[26]

Nevertheless, an important if small pool of advertising expertise did begin to develop as the result of the work done at various sites around the country, especially within a few key institutions.[27] Most notable among the new enterprises was OZEHA, the Advertising Bureau of Croatia. Although OZEHA would later rise to a prominent position within the industry, its circumstances during this initial postwar period were extraordinarily modest. However inauspicious those beginnings may have been, those associated with the organization would later take great pride in its pioneering work and the fact that it was the first institution of its kind to appear in socialist Yugoslavia. Thus we read in one representative promotional piece, published in the group's journal to celebrate ten years of its existence, an account of its founding on "just the third day" after the liberation of Zagreb.[28] (Like other similar self-representations in OZEHA's publications, this insistence on the agency's pedigree seems designed not just to emphasize its experience in the field but also to underscore that it had been a reliable partner for the new communist government from the very beginning.) Although it ultimately came to be known simply by its phoneticized acronym OZEHA, the organization was originally constituted as the *Oglasni Zavod Hrvatske*, that is, the Advertising Bureau of Croatia. This was a fairly grand name for what was, in reality, a tiny group of holdovers—four office employees and one worker who put up posters—from the old Interreklama company. Among the members of this little core cell was Dušan P. Mrvoš, who, as the most senior and experienced member of the organization, would go on to become a dominant figure in the early history of Yugoslav advertising.[29]

In the beginning the new bureau's work had very little to do with advertising per se. It began by putting up posters with the announcements and decrees of the Komanda grada Zagreba, the partisan military command of the city.[30] Plastering the city with the authorities' posters would occupy the bulk of their time in these earliest days.

---

26. *Drugo Jugoslavensko savjetovanje propagandista,* 51.

27. On the growth of Ljubljana's Jugoreklam organization, founded in April 1948, see Edo Vouk, "25 let izkušenj in novih idej," *Bilten: Glasilo Društva ekonomskih propgandistov Slovenije,* no. 17 (1973): 14–15 [hereafter, *Bilten DEPS*]. From very modest beginnings, Jugoreklam would grow over the next quarter-century into a large enterprise employing more than one hundred workers, with branch offices in Belgrade, Zagreb, and Velenje, and an impressive list of major industrial clients.

28. "Već treći dan," *Naš publicitet* 2, no. 2 (September 1955).

29. For more on the history of OZEHA and its precursors in Croatia, see M., "Deset godina OZEHA"; "Stasanje naše struke i društva," *Ideja,* no. 2 (February 1978): 7–14. Mrvoš began work with the Zagreb office of Rudolf Mosse in 1925, and by 1937 he had become the director of Publicitas, then the leading Zagreb advertising firm. Ibid., 9.

30. "Već treći dan."

Before long, however, OZEHA moved into newspaper, film, and radio work, although, as explained above, there was almost no place in the new economic order for consumer-oriented advertising, and consequently those services, too, remained mostly politically propagandistic in nature. Gradually OZEHA was drawn into projects that more closely resembled the advertising and marketing activities that would later form the focus of its operations. In 1947, for example, the agency was heavily involved in the promotion that surrounded the Zagreb Trade Fair, an important fixture of the country's international business relations that had been resurrected from its wartime suspension the year before. In the same year, 1947, OZEHA was "fused" with a sister propaganda organization with the wonderfully stereotypical name Olikprop [from Odjeljenje za likovnu propagandu, or Department for Visual Propaganda]. But that marriage was short-lived, and soon OZEHA again became a free-standing organization. For most of its existence it does appear to have functioned more or less autonomously, although it sometimes did so as part of larger formal structures, as in 1946, when it was incorporated into the larger media enterprise *Narodna štampa* [National Press].

OZEHA was particularly important because it was so unusual and operated with so little competition. The bureau also appears to have developed very close ties to government authorities through its work in disseminating official announcements, something that may have helped it build and maintain a privileged position. Among such contacts, for instance, was a course presented by OZEHA for employees of various export companies under the sponsorship of the Ministry for Import and Export.

Because OZEHA was comparatively quite large and for the most part unrivaled, it also became uniquely prominent and thus exerted a disproportionate influence over the development of the advertising specialty in these earliest years (and to some extent even thereafter). As the bureau's official journal put it, OZEHA had "frequently and unintentionally functioned as the regulator of the profession itself."[31] There may be some reason to look skeptically at this pronouncement, coming as it does from an in-house source with the aim of impressing potential clients. But while the claim may exaggerate slightly OZEHA's importance, it is nonetheless clear that the organization's role was a seminal one, and OZEHA director Veljko Klašterka was surely correct in observing, as he did later, that the one-of-a-kind bureau served as "some sort of unofficial center" for the emerging guild of advertising specialists and provided the impetus for the establishment of professional organizations.[32] It enjoyed a steady growth in revenues as well. In 1946 the bureau's receipts totaled 1.2 million dinars; in 1947, 8.5 million dinars; in 1948, 26 million dinars; and in 1949, 43 million dinars.[33]

31. M., "Deset godina OZEHA."
32. Klašterka, "Predgovor," in Mrvoš, *Propaganda, reklama, publicitet*, 4.
33. "Već treći dan."

Yet OZEHA is really more important for what it would become than for what it actually represented during this initial period. Its work remained quite limited in both practical and ideological terms, and ultimately it makes more sense to interpret the bureau's earliest activities as part and parcel of the overall suppression of advertising activity that was the order of the day. Even in the case of OZEHA, the most prominent "advertising" institution in these first years, what stands out is just how little advertising work was taking place and how unimportant Western notions of market communication had become.

For this first phase, then, it would be fruitless to try to isolate any pronounced ideology of market culture inherent in the work of Yugoslav commercial advertising. The field was too circumscribed, and there was too little advertising aimed at consumers in Yugoslavia. We can, however, with justification, read the very absence of consumer advertising as indicative of a climate of suspicion and hostility. This lingering atmosphere of distrust proved a central element of the broader sociopolitical context in which the young industry emerged. Even later, when a large and activist-minded cadre of advertising and marketing professionals began to construct a new, more unapologetically consumer-centered ideology, these misgivings would continue to rein in their activities.

Attention, Interest, Desire, Action: The Making of a New Yugoslav Industry, 1950–1965

Only after the initial steps toward the development of a distinctively Yugoslav, market-oriented brand of "self-management" socialism did a real domestic advertising industry begin to develop, and then, at first, only rather tentatively and sporadically. Timid as they were, the initiatives toward market reform nonetheless made advertising suddenly much more *permissible,* removing some of the capitalist taint that had contributed to the suppression of advertising in previous years. Moreover, they allowed those who hoped to see a larger role for advertising in the country's economic life to argue that advertising had become, in fact, something *necessary* to the future development of Yugoslav socialism. Markets, they would argue, functioned best when advertising helped consumers get the products they needed and wanted. Free to promote their craft as never before, the practitioners of advertising set about creating demand for their work.

Where there had been almost nothing of the sort before, advertising for consumer goods and services now began to crop up all over the country. Advertisements became more common in mass-circulation magazines and newspapers, on the radio, in cinemas, and, toward the end of this second period, on television. Outdoor advertising such as posters, billboards, and painted exterior walls remained a favored form, and these methods were now put to use much more often in the service of commercial promotion. Neon signs became an increasingly familiar sight. In an imitation of a technique quite common in the West, overhead advertising placards proliferated in Zagreb's streetcars. And businesses paid much more attention to in-store advertising, merchandising techniques, and the promotional potential of packaging design.

Along with the rapid expansion of advertising came a similar growth in the number and variety of media outlets that served as vehicles for those messages to Yugoslav consumers. Whereas in 1950 the Yugoslav media landscape remained much like that of 1945, the picture was markedly different by 1965. In the quite modest media market of 1950, there had been only ten major weekly periodicals, with a combined circulation of approximately 472,500. Those numbers had swelled by 1965 to thirty-nine weekly publications with a combined circulation of almost 3.4 million copies.[34]

The expansion was all the more noteworthy for its tendency to shift the orientation of the Yugoslav media away from "hard news" and political coverage toward entertainment and what would elsewhere be called "lifestyles" features, some of them directly connected with the emerging consumer culture. Among the new mass-circulation periodicals established during this period were those devoted to automobiles (*Moto revija*), film, television, and other entertainment (*Arena, Antena, Filmski svet, Studio, TV novosti*), and sports (*Fudbal*), along with a number of other publications mixing news, features, educational items, and various diversions, including erotica (*Čik, Ilustrovana politika, NIN, Politikin zabavnik, Svet, Svijet, Tovariš, Vjesnik u srijedu*). Most of these major publications were distributed in all areas of the country and had for the most part a "Yugoslav character" rather than any particular regional or ethnic flavor.[35] As such, they contributed to some degree to a homogenization of the Yugoslav consumer market, lending important elements of unity to the country's mass culture. And, critically, advertising became an increasingly prominent feature of magazines of this popular, widely distributed type.

The latter part of this fifteen-year period saw, furthermore, the beginnings of a vastly expanded role of the broadcast media. It was during this time that television arrived in Yugoslavia and, with it, the first efforts to use the new medium as a vehicle for advertising.[36] The number of television subscribers in Yugoslavia grew from 61,538 in 1961 to an estimated 770,000–800,000 in 1966. By 1966, 72 percent of Yugoslav territory could

---

34. Živorad K. Stoković, *Štampa naroda i narodnosti u SFRJ 1945–1973: grada za istoriju štampe* (Belgrade, 1975), 188.

35. Ibid., 187.

36. On the development of television advertisements for Slovenian markets, see Jana Novak, "Razvoj slovenskega televizijskega oglaševanja v obdobju 1960–1980" (*diploma* thesis, University of Ljubljana, Faculty of Economics, 1997). The electronic media quickly became a significant element of the overall mixture of advertising strategies.

receive television broadcasts, for a theoretical viewership of some 16 million persons. For the same period the growth in the number of radio subscribers was, though more modest in proportion, nonetheless impressive: from over 1.8 million subscribers in 1961 to approximately 3 million by 1966. By 1966 the Yugoslav average was one radio receiver for every seven citizens, and in Slovenia and the Vojvodina the figures were approaching the European average, with one set for every four people.[37]

When describing the sudden spread of advertising across Yugoslavia, however, it is important not to overstate the case. While advertising during this period did indeed increase dramatically with respect to previous years, it remained rather modest compared to the phenomena seen all over the developed West. Most newspapers and magazines from this period, for example, come across as remarkably short on advertising when viewed against Western analogues. Thus, as late as 1956, OZEHA's journal could note (quite accurately) that "if we leaf through any leading daily newspaper from Belgrade, Zagreb, or Ljubljana, we will find in them advertisements for special occasions [*prigodni oglasi*] that announce competitions, auctions, or new editions of books. In addition we will encounter a 'classified ad section' [*mali oglasnik*], well developed or not so well developed, for articles to be bought and sold, employment, the exchange of housing, and other similar announcements of a personal interest. In general, there are no standard or serial advertisements."[38] The term "serial" advertisements here apparently refers to those running as part of a promotional campaign and appearing more than once, in contrast to the one-time "announcements" that dominated the advertising content of most newspapers. Surveying the situation, the writer asked with evident dismay, "Why don't our newspapers have advertisements?" The problem appeared to stem from certain legal regulations that required an unfavorable accounting treatment of advertising expenses, from a general lack of advertising expertise among the personnel of press enterprises and, most important, from unrealistically high prices for advertising space, something that, in the author's view, attested to a failure of the newspaper business to take proper account of the imperatives of the market.[39] As examples like these suggest, even at this early stage Yugoslav advertising activists were attempting to use the new legitimacy of the market to reinforce the legitimacy of their craft and build constituencies for their work.

The state of advertising practice was rather different in a number of the country's mass-market magazines, especially near the end of the period, in

37. These figures are reported in Matjaž Deržaj, "Posredniki propagandnih sporočil in njihova realna vrednost," *Bilten DEPS*, no. 1 (October 1967): 14–23.

38. d.m. [Dušan Mrvoš?], "Zašto naši listovi nemaju oglasa?" *Naš publicitet* 3, no. 2 (September 1956).

39. Ibid.

the mid-1960s. The number of advertisements appearing in *Tovariš,* for example, increased substantially. Advertising content in the magazine was still minimal in 1955, but by 1960 it was much more noticeable. At this point, however, the advertisements that did run in the magazine were not yet thoroughly commercial: full-page consumer ads for products such as Argo soup and Radion laundry detergent were interspersed among decidedly non-commercial placements for large enterprises like banks and import-export companies. In a mass-market magazine that covered news, film, entertainment, celebrities, fashion, popular music, cooking, and fiction, this sort of advertising mix surely was not what the pioneers in the field were hoping for. Things were indeed somewhat better from the industry's point of view by 1965, but even as this period drew to a close the level of print advertising in *Tovariš* and other similar publications such as the popular Croatian women's magazine *Svijet* [World] did not approach that seen in the West.

Television advertising, though certainly a prominent part of Yugoslav programming, nevertheless remained relatively limited, especially if viewed against the less tightly regulated American system of television broadcasting. Rather than breaking into the main programming, television ads were typically run in a unified block between other shows. American companies by this time were already worried that ad-saturated television audiences would walk away or otherwise tune out while commercials briefly interrupted the shows they were watching. Yugoslav advertisers, in contrast, were counting on a public that was eager to consume more and very interested in new products—and, moreover, simply attracted by the unfamiliar phenomenon of television advertising, which for a time could take advantage of its sheer novelty value. Thus they hoped that audiences would be willing to stay seated in front of the screen for an even longer period.

The country's advertising practices during the period were, in classic Yugoslav style, neither fully Eastern nor fully Western. Yugoslavia remained, in the phrase that became an axiom across the country, *"nešto između,"* "something in-between."[40] That mixed quality was manifest in the structure of the country's nascent advertising industry as well. On the one hand, this period saw a rapid increase in the number of people and organizations engaged in advertising work. It was, of course, easy enough to achieve a dramatic rate of expansion given that the starting points had been so modest,

40. Reporting on the state of Yugoslavia's advertising industry in 1963, the Croatian Advertising Association estimated that the total ad space purchased annually in the most important daily and specialty periodicals cost 2.4 billion dinars. Half of this amount, however, went for advertising space used for something other than the consumer market, that is, for employment ads, announcements of competitions, personal announcements, and the like. More exact figures for advertising expenditures in the country's various radio and television stations ran to 1.2 billion dinars, or roughly the same amount spent in the most important press outlets. *Drugo Jugoslavensko savjetovanje propagandista,* 49. Yugoslav advertising expenditures were, moreover, far in excess of those in other socialist countries. For comparative data on advertising outlays, see Hanson, *Advertising and Socialism.*

but, even so, the absolute growth was impressive on its own terms. By 1955, just five years after the inauguration of the first market reforms under the self-management system, a number of new advertising enterprises had already been established.[41] OZEHA and Interpublic quickly became the country's largest institutions devoted specifically to advertising, and they were joined by smaller organizations such as Jugoreklam.[42] OZEHA, which as one of the earliest entrants into the industry had the advantage of establishing its network of clients at a time when there were very few similar, competing organizations, had very quickly exploited its dominant position and embarked on a program of expansion into other major Yugoslav cities. By 1957 it had opened offices in Belgrade, Sarajevo, Skopje, Rijeka, Split, and Banja Luka. Interpublic had a number of branch offices during this period as well. By the mid-1950s the increase in advertising activity had been so dramatic that industry leaders could report, with evident satisfaction, that "our bureaus [*zavodi*] have joined the circle of modern and serious institutions of European rank."[43]

This multiplication of advertising organizations was accompanied by substantial growth within them as well. OZEHA, for example, had by 1954 swelled to over one hundred employees.[44] Its revenues, which in 1949 had totaled 43 million dinars, underwent what can only be called explosive growth. By 1952 the bureau's receipts would reach 98 million dinars, and in 1954 that number would more than triple, rising to 340 million dinars.[45] Archival records including OZEHA's reports show that the trajectory of expansion continued in the following years, with receipts increasing to 353 million dinars in 1956, 410 million dinars in 1957, and 443 million dinars in 1958.[46]

41. V. Desantolo, "Uz prvi broj časopisa Standard," *Standard* 1, no. 1 (May 1955): 1–2, at 1.

42. Surviving sources offer a strong enough sense of the ideas, styles, and values that prevailed among the largest enterprises, but they only hint at the activities of smaller, insecurely established advertising operations. Along these lines, for example, see the coverage of a proposal by several young Belgrade artists, painters, and sculptors to launch their own *atelier* to compete with the dominant larger firms. "Pred stvaranje umetničkog ateljea za savremenu propagandu i reklamu," *Savremena privredna propaganda* 1, no. 1 (August 1957): 14.

43. Mrvoš, "Zadaci i metode savremenog zavoda," *Naš publicitet* 1, no. 2 (December 1954).

44. M., "Deset godina OZEHA."

45. "Već treći dan." The official exchange rate in 1954, derived from gold-parity prices, was 632 dinars to one U.S. dollar; as the result of the inflation that continually plagued the Yugoslav economy, that rate had slid to 750 dinars/dollar by 1961, and by mid-1965, to 1250 dinars/dollar. Biljana Stojanović, "Exchange Rate Regimes of the Dinar, 1945–1990: An Assessment of Appropriateness and Efficiency," in *Workshops—The Proceedings of OeNB Workshops,* The Experience of Exchange Rate Regimes in Southeastern Europe, *Proceedings of the Second Conference of the South-Eastern European Monetary History Network,* 13 April 2007, no. 13 (2008): 202.

46. Letter from Velimir Kovačić and Veljko Klašterka of OZEHA to the Udruženje preduzeća za ekonomsku propagandu i publicitet Jugoslavije, 14 August 1959. Arhiv Jugoslavije, collection Stručno udruženje preduzeća za ekonomsku propagandu i publicitet, AJ-262-3.

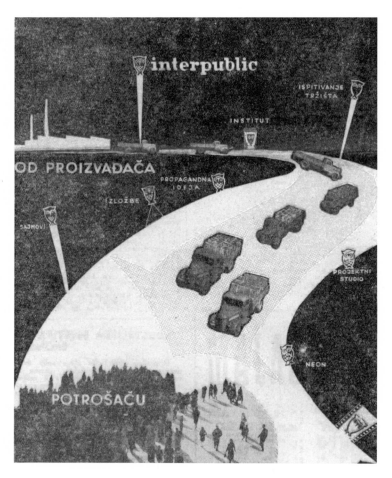

Figure 1. Advertisement for the Interpublic advertising enterprise, 1956. "The function of advertising [*ekonomska propaganda*] in the advancement and expansion of the distribution of goods [*plasman robe*] from the producer to the consumer." The details in the image are labeled as follows: From the Producer, Interpublic, the Institute, Market Research, the Advertising Idea, the Project Studio, Displays, Exhibitions, Neon, To the Consumer. *Interpublic: List za pitanje ekonomske propagande, industrijske estetike i psihologije rada* 1, no. 1 (August 1956): 2.

Figure 2. Self-promotion by Zagreb's OZEHA advertising
agency, ca. 1970. The neon signs read: Advertising (*ekonomski
publicitet*), Market Research, Advertising Plans, Press, Neon,
Displays, Slides, Announcements, Postering and Billboards
[*plakatiranje*], Television, Packaging. *Naš publicitet*, unnumbered
(n.d. [ca. 1970]): 19.

Not surprisingly, the ongoing expansion of advertising activity in Yugoslavia was a frequent theme of the industry publications and of related educational literature produced during this period. While those sources document a serious dissatisfaction with the comparatively underdeveloped state of the craft, they nevertheless communicate a real sense of excitement and promise. Among advertising and marketing specialists there was the hope that they would indeed prove to be pioneers: participants in a remarkable boom that would only become more noteworthy—and more important for the country's economy—as time passed. And even by the mid- to late 1950s, the changes were so dramatic that industry insiders were already commenting on, and arguing over, the noticeable new "inflation of advertising experts."[47]

With a few notable exceptions such as the independent enterprises OZEHA, Interpublic, and Reklamservis, the first organizations engaged primarily in the practice of advertising tended to develop as internal units created by, and subordinated to the broader commercial purposes of, larger enterprises, particularly those concerned with international trade and what socialist parlance called "public information." Media outlets were, in particular, a prime area for development along these lines. By 1963 many publishing enterprises across the country had organized their own separate advertising departments, with staffs ranging from three to twenty-seven persons; these in-house departments functioned, in effect, as small advertising agencies.[48] At the same time practically all of Yugoslavia's largest business establishments had their own advertising departments, and many smaller enterprises had at least a staff representative responsible for advertising.[49] In heavily industrialized Slovenia, for example, by 1965 there were advertising departments within the management structures of many important manufacturers such as Litostroj (heavy industrial equipment), Iskra (electrical and electronic equipment), and TAM (automobiles), and similar departments existed in the offices of retail chains such as the large Metalka group of stores.

This second phase of the industry's development was also a time in which advertising specialists working in various enterprises and locales began to come together with the specific mission of establishing their craft as a recognized profession. To that end, they began forming a number of important regional and national professional organizations. In October 1954, for example, representatives of a number of advertising institutions met in

---

47. Klašterka, "Još nešto o inflaciji stručnjaka za reklamu," 22.

48. *Drugo Jugoslavensko savjetovanje propagandista*, 51. All the country's "billionaires," i.e., enterprises with a gross annual product of one billion dinars or more, reportedly had such internal advertising departments. Ibid.

49. Ibid., 9. See also Izveštaj Upravnog odbora o istorijijatu [sic] osnivanja Udruženja preduzeća za ekonomsku propagandu i publicitet Jugoslavije. Undated; context allows the document, which details the history of efforts to establish a pan-Yugoslav association, to be dated to late 1957 or early 1958. Arhiv Jugoslavije, collection Stručno udruženje preduzeća za ekonomsku propagandu i publicitet, AJ-262-1.

Belgrade to work toward creating an association of such groups.[50] In February 1960 industry leaders and others from around the country convened for the first Yugoslav Conference of Advertising Specialists (Jugoslavensko savjetovanje propagandista). The second such national conference followed in Zagreb three years later. Efforts among Zagreb's practitioners to establish a professional society intensified after 1956, and in 1958 the Croatian Advertising Association (Udruženje ekonomskih propagandista Hrvatske) was officially recognized. This republic-level group, the first of its kind in the country, would play a leading role in the professionalization of the field.[51] Meanwhile, specialists in Belgrade took the initiative in establishing a Serbian Advertising Association (Udruženje ekonomskih propagandista Srbije) in 1960–1961. A Slovenian Advertising Association (Društvo ekonomskih propagandistov Slovenije) followed in 1963, and that group convened its own major conference in March 1964.[52] A similar group for Bosnia-Herzegovina was constituted in 1964.

Efforts to coordinate activities across the country, however, did not progress quite as smoothly. Holdings in the federal-level archives for what was once Yugoslavia document that, beginning in 1957, advertising specialists did initiate a countrywide Association of Advertising Enterprises of the FNRY [Udruženje preduzeća za ekonomsku propagandu i publicitet FNRJ].[53] By the beginning of 1958 at least sixteen institutions had joined the Association, with work sites distributed around Yugoslavia in a way that suggests both the spread of interest in advertising and the continuing importance of the major business centers.

Almost as soon as it was formed, however, the Association of Advertising Enterprises ran into serious organizational difficulties. OZEHA, which had taken a leading role early on, quarreled with the Association and some of its constituent enterprises over a variety of issues, most notably the choice of a president for the managing committee, and by 1958 the firm was not listed in the membership rolls after refusing to pay its membership dues for 1957 and 1958.[54] For its part, the Association took OZEHA to task and acted to exclude the Zagreb enterprise from further organizational activities. In a

50. Mrvoš, "Zadaci i metode savremenog zavoda," *Naš publicitet* 1, no. 2 (December 1954).

51. See "Osnovano je Udruženje ekonomskih propagndista NRH," *Privredni vjesnik*, 13 June 1959.

52. See *Zapiski s posvetovanja ekonomskih propagandistov Slovenije, od 20. do 22. marca 1964* (Ljubljana, 1964).

53. See, especially, Arhiv Jugoslavije, collection Stručno udruženje preduzeća za ekonomsku propagandu i publicitet, AJ-262-1, AJ-262-2, and AJ-262-3.

54. See, for example, the letter from Veljko Klašterka of OZEHA to the Udruženje preduzeća za ekonomsku propagandu i publicitet Jugoslavije, dated 24 February 1958; Veljko Klašterka and Velimir Kovačić, Promemoria OZEHA po pitanju Udruženja preduzeća za ekonomsku propagandu i publicitet Jugoslavije, sent to Zavod Primenjenih Umetnosti, Belgrade, 5 April 1958; letter from V. Konstantinović, president, and M. Stefanović, secretary, of the Inicijativni odbor, Udruženje preduzeća za ekonomsku propagandu i publicitet, to OZEHA, dated 24 March

Table 2.1 Association of Advertising Enterprises of the FNRY, members and revenues, 1958

Member organization	Home office	Projected gross revenues in dinars (*brutopromet*) (in millions)
Interpublic	Zagreb	440
OZEBIH	Sarajevo	320
Forum	Belgrade	240
Dekorbiro	Skopje	130
Exportprojekt	Ljubljana	100
Zavod primenjenih umetnosti	Belgrade	80
Jugoreklam	Novi Sad	50
Agencija MI	Maribor	46.5
Biro za unapredjenje trgovinske mreže	Belgrade	45
Zagrebreklam	Zagreb	45
Interreklam	Belgrade	40
Prospekt	Zagreb	38
ABC	Zagreb	36
Reklamtabor	Maribor	35
Jugoreklam	Belgrade	20
Publicitet	Split	20

Source: Predlog budžeta za 1958. godinu Udruženja preduzeća za ekonomsku propagandu i publicitet FNRJ. Arhiv Jugoslavije, collection Stručno udruženje preduzeća za ekonomsku propagandu i publicitet, AJ-262-1. In other documents of the Association, the Biro za unapredjenje trgovinske mreže is identified by a different name, as the Biro za organizaciju i unapredjene trgovinske mreže. See, for example, the office's undated response to the organizational letter of 29 March 1957, sent by OZEHA's Veljko Klašterka on behalf of the Association. Arhiv Jugoslavije, collection Stručno udruženje preduzeća za ekonomsku propagandu i publicitet, AJ-262-1.

letter of 12 March 1958, preserved in the Association's records, the officers of the group told OZEHA in no uncertain terms that "the isolated situation of your firm is the consequence of a position that you took on your own, and voluntarily."[55] At the planned founding assembly for the group, they wrote, only "those founding members who have fulfilled their obligations to the Association will participate." At this point, at least, the pioneering industry giant appeared to have overplayed its hand.

1958. Arhiv Jugoslavije, collection Stručno udruženje preduzeća za ekonomsku propagandu i publicitet, AJ-262-3.

55. Letter from V. Konstantinović, president, and M. Stefanović, secretary, Udruženje preduzeća za ekonomsku propagandu i publicitet, to Dušan Mrvoš, dated 12 March 1958. Arhiv Jugoslavije, collection Stručno udruženje preduzeća za ekonomsku propagandu i publicitet, AJ-262-3.

Svijet

15. V 1966.

10

1,50 ND
(150 SD)

3. Images of choice and plenty. Cover of *Svijet*, 15 May 1966.

Socialist advertising or advertising in socialism? Yugoslav consumer culture in the pages of *Svijet*.

4. "Use Vital Oil," *Svijet* no. 4, April 1962, back cover.

5. "In every hour of the sun," Di cosmetics, *Svijet* no. 14, 15 July 1970, inside front cover.

7. "Gorenje makes them happy," Gorenje appliances, *Svijet* no. 26, 18 December 1969, 54. Courtesy of Gorenje, d.d.

6. "Just the way you imagine it—a comfortable home," Oriolik furniture, *Svijet* no. 3, 11 February 1970, 52.

**Taking care of socialism's dirty laundry? "Every month a new detergent."
Full- and half-page magazine ads.**

8. "It doesn't matter what kind of washing machine you own," Net efekt detergent, *Svijet*, 11 February 1970, 41.

9. "For your laundry," Tajm detergent, *Svijet*, September 1962, back cover.

11. "New!—3 Advantages for your laundry," Biomat detergent, *Svijet*, 9 October 1968, 57.

10. "Clothes that have been Melizated are clothes that are nicer!" Mixal detergent, *Svijet*, 12 August 1970, 38. The term "Melizated" [*melizirano*] was apparently a completely new ad-speak coinage, invented to conjure up the purported softening and brightening properties of the detergent.

"Our special, socialist content"—What was really being sold in Yugoslav advertising? Images from *Svijet* and *Start*.

12. "With our newest models you will achieve extraordinary comfort, an attractive figure, and a true-to-life form," Lisca lingerie, *Svijet* no. 13, 19 June 1968, 2.

13. "Brigitte Bardot—the Lipstick of Success," Krka cosmetics, *Svijet* no. 17, 14 August 1968, 42.

15. "Million Look—The Shirt with All the Advantages," Domača Tvornica Rublja, *Svijet* no. 1, 1 January 1968, 54.

14. "The Legend Lives," Levi's jeans, *Start* no. 399, 5 May 1984, 2.

Sodobna proizvodnja -
iz sodobne tovarne -
za sodobni dom za vaš dom

gorenje

16. "Contemporary products—From a contemporary factory—For the contemporary home—
For your home." Full-page ad for Gorenje appliances in the home-improvement magazine
Naš dom, December 1969, inside front cover. Courtesy of Gorenje, d.d.

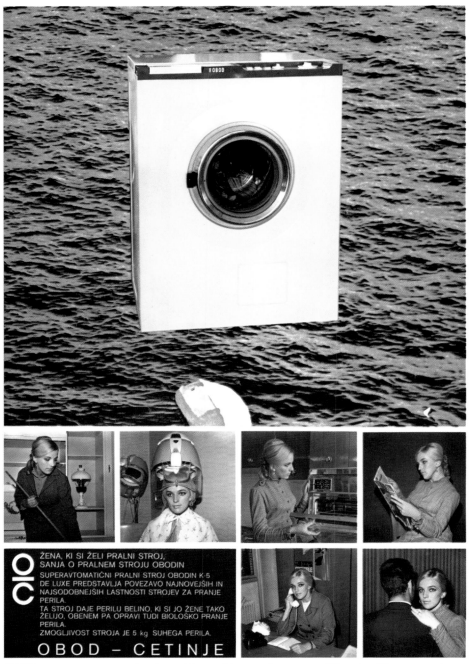

17. What women want so much—the washing machine as an instrument of liberation. "The woman who wants a washing machine dreams about the Obod washing machine. The super-automatic Obod K-5 De Luxe washing machine combines the newest and most modern qualities of machines for washing laundry. This machine gives laundry the whiteness that women want so much, and at the same time it can also handle washing with biological methods." Full-page ad for Obod washing machines in *Naš dom*, December 1969, 51.

18. Selling style and sex appeal. "Castor Končar super-automatic washing machines—Super-automatic dishwashers" Full-page ad for Castor-Rade Končar appliances in *Naš dom*, December 1969, inside back cover.

19. The joy of laundry—"Ask the woman who already has one." Full-page ad for Gorenje washing machines in *Svijet* no. 15, 29 July 1970, 34. Courtesy of Gorenje, d.d.

Meanwhile, a number of the smaller firms found the group's dues too burdensome and threatened to withdraw.[56] Partly as a result of such disagreements, the coordinating work of the Association would founder, and a fully functional pan-Yugoslav association of advertising institutions would not be formed until 1973.[57] The proliferation of enterprises and interests on the ground, it seemed, made cooperation difficult, even as many leaders in the field of commercial promotion felt that such alliances were critical to the advancement—and defense—of their work.

Despite all the burgeoning institutional development, the organizational forms of advertising practice still did not closely correspond to Western models. Even toward the end of this period comparatively few organizations offered a full range of services, and few had an institutional existence independent of some larger public media combine or "socially owned" commercial enterprise. Moreover, advertising professionals could not be certain of their creative freedom. Because the management of such major enterprises was almost invariably involved in Communist Party activities, prevailing attitudes about the proper role of advertising and the permissible limits of its use in conditions of "self-management socialism" tended, in practice, to filter down from on high, even in the absence of explicit political restrictions on the content and use of advertising.

Partly because of this lingering tendency of some in the country's political and economic élite to look with real skepticism at advertising and marketing work, careers in the field remained to some extent the province of risk takers. The archival transcripts of early efforts to establish a pan-Yugoslav trade association, for example, make it clear that advertising work found many detractors, even in the business community. With such problems in mind, Velimir Šoć, the director of Sarajevo's OZEBIH, opened one organizational meeting in 1957 with complaints about what he called the persistence of "drastic examples" of hostility toward the field, lamenting that "even today...the largest graphics enterprise in Belgrade will not permit our people to come through their door because, in their opinion, we are people who want to get money in an easy way and because they think that it is not necessary, and should not be permitted, for us to engage in that activity."[58] Even toward the end of this first significant period of expansion, advertising remained a suspect, uncertain calling. One specialist from Croatia, Ante Batarelo, recalled that when an autonomous Advertising Service was formed

---

56. See, for example, the letter from Split's Publicitet agency to the Association, dated 18 May 1959. Arhiv Jugoslavije, collection Stručno udruženje preduzeća za ekonomsku propagandu i publicitet, AJ-262-1.

57. See "Stasanje naše struke i društva," *Ideja*, no. 2 (February 1978): 7–14, at 11.

58. Velimir Šoć, quoted in Zapisnik o stenografskim beleškama sa savjetovanja preduzeća za ekonomsku propagandu Jugoslavije, koji je održan dana 10 februara 1957 godine, p. 1. Arhiv Jugoslavije, collection Stručno udruženje preduzeća za ekonomsku propagandu i publicitet, AJ-262-1.

on his initiative as part of the operations of the Zagreb daily *Vjesnik,* no one was so naïve as to apply for a position with such dubious prospects. In the end Batarelo took the job himself, leaving his safe post as the newspaper's Director of Sales in the belief that "this is a profession that has a future" but acknowledging that "to others this may have seemed more of an adventurist move than it did to me."[59]

With the emergence of advertising as a distinct profession (or at least as a type of work with earnest aspirations to that status), there also appeared the first efforts to develop a trade literature that would support and encourage the further development of advertising and marketing practice. Leaders in the field began writing and publishing energetically in an effort to explain to an uninformed audience just what advertising and marketing were (or should be), how they were practiced, and what promises they held for producers, sellers, and consumers. With all this came the first clear evidence of an important process that is analyzed in more detail in the following chapter: the industry's persistent attempts to justify its place—and claim an even larger role—in Yugoslav society.

Progress was slow in the beginning. The first industry publications were themselves fairly modest and isolated efforts. In 1956, for example, the Zagreb office of Interpublic produced a would-be trade journal that staked out an aggressive claim as a "Journal for Advertising, Industrial Aesthetics, and Labor Psychology," but the self-titled *Interpublic* proved an ephemeral thing.[60] One notable exception to the otherwise spotty pattern was the journal *Naš publicitet,* launched in August 1954 by the Zagreb-based OZEHA bureau. The magazine, which was issued through 1957 (with a brief resurrection in 1970–1971 on the occasion of the agency's twenty-fifth anniversary), turned out to be in many ways a not-so-veiled effort to promote the services offered by its publisher. But the review had much broader horizons as well, and along the way it managed to offer a thorough overview of the state of the industry around the country, a surprisingly sophisticated set of prescriptions for raising technical standards, and a consistent appeal for the recognition of advertising as an indispensable tool for economic development and the modernization of Yugoslav society.

Although Zagreb had clearly emerged as the creative center of the country's advertising industry, Belgrade's specialists were not without their contributions. Some put out their own little magazine, *Standard,* in 1955. Although its influence is questionable at best—the periodical appears to have folded almost immediately, reappearing briefly in 1968—*Standard* nonetheless offers a revealing glimpse of how advertising was viewed in the country's

---

59. Stasanje naše struke i društva," 12.

60. See *Interpublic: List za pitanje ekonomske propagande, industrijske estetike i psihologije rada* 1, no. 1 (August 1956).

center of political power in the years just after the first moves toward the market.[61]

Shortly thereafter, in August 1957, the Belgrade advertising organization Jugoreklam helped launch the journal, *Savremena privredna propaganda* [Contemporary advertising]. Though it was also to be short-lived, it, too, provides a useful window onto the state of contemporary thought and practice. In the magazine's first issue, for example, one contributor observed that Yugoslav advertisers had their work cut out for them, for "among the majority of our businesspeople there has taken root the attitude that any advertisement of a product is completely unnecessary, because 'the goods speak for themselves.'"[62] Moreover, the writer maintained, much of the advertising that did appear was so clumsy or tasteless that Yugoslav audiences tended to dismiss all advertising as a result. There was much work to be done.

Over the course of its brief run, *Savremena privredna propaganda* offered its readers observations on the generally backward technical state of the advertising in Yugoslavia and briefed them on the efforts of the fledgling industry to correct those deficits. The content of the periodical continually revealed its upstart quality, reflecting, one suspects, some degree of resentment that the capital had been eclipsed by Zagreb, where a number of advertising specialists with pedigrees from the shady days of unfettered capitalist enterprise were now more or less running the show. In particular, there were occasional upwellings of rather bitter resentment toward the dominant position that Zagreb's OZEHA enjoyed. Thus the new Belgrade review decried alleged efforts to turn the advertising industry into an élite "cartel,"[63] complained about the pretensions of the industry's self-appointed "experts," and predicted that the better-known firms, with their "extremely tasteless advertising paraphernalia," might soon be overtaken by smaller and lesser-known but better-organized competitors.[64]

The dispute got ugly at times. OZEHA, for its part, called for a set of professional standards, imposed as a requirement for membership in some future associations of advertising specialists and of advertising enterprises, that would effectively "separate the dilettantes from the artists." The absence of such a dividing line, the journal suggested, "is costing our economy millions and millions in foolishly spent money [for advertising]."[65] In contrast,

61. See *Standard* 2, nos. 2–3 (1968).

62. Ž. I., "Savremena privredna propaganda," *Savremena privredna propaganda* 1, no. 1 (August 1957): 3–4, at 3.

63. "Mi ostajemo konsekventni," *Savremena privredna propaganda* 1, no. 3 (October 1957): 8. For more on the rivalry with OZEHA, see, for example, "Ua, Espepe!," *Savremena privredna propaganda* 2, no. 2 (1958): 28; for the Zagreb group's position, see, for example, Velimir Kovačić, "Djelatnost zavoda za ekonomsku propagandu i publicitet," *Naš publicitet* 4, no. 2 (1957): 18–19; N. Vučetin, "O inflaciji stručnjaka za reklamu ili o liku jednog našeg časopisa," *Naš publicitet* 4, nos. 3–4 (December 1957): 20–21.

64. Ž. I., "Savremena privredna propaganda," 3.

65. Vučetin, "O inflaciji stručnjaka za reklamu ili o liku jednog našeg časopisa," 21.

Savremena privredna propaganda strove for a more inclusive understanding of what constituted the advertising profession, including the recognition of advertising *servisi,* that is, small organizations with minimal staffs that could not offer the more complete range of promotional services provided by the industry leaders.

Like those *servisi,* the Belgrade review seems to have struggled throughout its existence to find a place in the new commercial landscape. In 1958 it was discontinued, giving way to a successor whose title, *Pregled medjunarodnih sajmova* (Overview of international expositions) suggests not only what turned out to be a drastically curtailed scope of coverage but also a much more conservative editorial posture, one oriented toward more traditional techniques of promoting international trade that by this time had already become familiar in other socialist countries.

More substantial steps toward the creation of a comprehensive and systematized professional canon came in 1958, when Josip Sudar published the country's first and, ultimately, best-known advertising textbook, *Ekonomska propaganda u teoriji i praksi* [Advertising in theory and practice].[66] Sudar's work was followed a year later by another landmark textbook penned by Dušan Mrvoš, the driving force behind OZEHA and a man who was intimately involved with the advertising industry in Yugoslavia since the 1920s, when he began working in the Zagreb branch office of a large foreign firm. The Mrvoš book, *Propaganda reklama publicitet: teorija i praksa* [Propaganda, advertising, publicity: Theory and practice] was, like Sudar's work, an impressive accomplishment, running to more than five hundred pages and offering a comprehensive and in most respects quite up-to-date overview of advertising practice.[67]

For the young guild, both works served as something akin to holy writ. Mrvoš was an especially engaging writer and a dynamic advocate for his cause—and for him, as for a number of other early leaders in the field, advertising genuinely was a *cause*—but his work was cut short by his death in the same year as the publication of his book. With the master promoter no longer around to move his ideas, the Mrvoš text appears to have met with somewhat less enduring success than that of his counterpart Sudar, which went through several more editions and saw heavy use in the schooling of industry professionals throughout the entire socialist period.

From the very beginning, Western ways of thinking about advertising and marketing heavily influenced the Yugoslav craft.[68] Much more than mere

---

66. Josip Sudar, *Ekonomska propaganda u teoriji i praksi* (Zagreb, 1958). See also Sudar, *Promotivne aktivnosti udruženog rada na tržištu* (Zagreb, 1984 [1979]), an updated and expanded version of the author's original work.

67. Dušan Mrvoš, *Propaganda reklama publicitet: teorija i praksa* (Belgrade, 1959).

68. Occasionally, however, the Yugoslav advertising pioneers looked to the experience of socialist states, too. See, for example, a letter sent to Dušan Mrvoš by an unidentified writer (signature illegible, but it appears to be that of Mile Stefanović, secretary of the Udruženje),

technical knowledge was transferred, however, although there was plenty of that as well. Rather, Western presentations of the role of commercial promotion taught Yugoslavs how to do business and, more important, taught them a new conception of the nature of the relationship between consumers and the producers and sellers who hoped to do business with them. This transfer of ideas is abundantly clear, for example, in both the Sudar and Mrvoš volumes and throughout the rest of the trade literature published during the 1950s. For example, on the question of how to structure advertising practice within the constraints imposed by Yugoslav commercial organization, it is obvious that Western models and Western literature exerted a strong influence on Yugoslav thinking.[69] Along these lines, one typical contribution to *Naš publicitet* looked to the English experience for evidence of the advantages offered by freestanding institutions specialized in the practice of advertising. Many aspects of this "agency system," it was suggested, might successfully be imported to Yugoslavia.[70] In much the same way, advertising specialists also explicitly invoked Western models of retail display,[71] packaging,[72] and customer service.[73]

Although they were undeniably proud of their own accomplishments at home, it was really the images of the West that captured the gaze of these earliest promoters of a new market culture. The 1959 textbook by Mrvoš, for example, came richly illustrated with examples of advertisements used in America, England, and elsewhere in Western Europe, with especially keen attention to West Germany. There newcomers to the field saw the techniques that had been used to sell the consumer abundance of the developed West: Gruen watches, Coca-Cola, Douglas aircraft, Dr. Oetker baking powder, Continental and Goodyear tires, Persil and Blue Dew laundry detergent, Buick, Ford, Jeep, Mercedes-Benz, and more. Readers were shown, among many other examples of the art, public relations materials from the American Meat Institute and a self-promoting advertisement by the British

---

13 March 1958, requesting copies of "the lectures that you brought back from Czechoslovakia" by Soviet and GDR practitioners. Arhiv Jugoslavije, collection Stručno udruženje preduzeća za ekonomsku propagandu i publicitet, AJ-262-3. The papers in question are almost certainly presentations from the 1957 Prague conference of socialist advertising specialists, discussed later in this book. The contemporaneous internal serial numbering of the letter (no. 328) suggests that it came from the offices of the Udruženje.

69. See, for example, Čedo Dinter, *Ekonomsko-propagandna služba u poduzeću* (Zagreb, 1961). Dinter's work draws liberally on ideas from key Western sources such as the American Marketing Association and the leading advertising literature.

70. "Prednosti suradnje sa zavodima za ekonomsku propagandu i publicitet," *Naš publicitet* 4, no. 1 (1957): 13.

71. For example, "Čemu služi izlog," *Savremena privredna propaganda* 1, no. 3 (October 1957): 10.

72. See the trade journals *Ambalaža* [Package] and *Savremeno pakovanje* [Contemporary packaging], both published in Serbia, which first appeared in 1954 and 1960, respectively.

73. Mihailo Trifunović, "Odnos prema kupcu kao vid dobre reklame," *Savremena privredna propaganda* 1, no. 3 (October 1957): 13–14.

magazine *Woman's Own* that trumpeted its power to reach the critical market of female consumers with its weekly sales of almost 1.8 million copies. They learned about the value of market research with reference to how the Gillette Company approached the subject (and since the phonetic rendering *žilet* had become a more or less generic name for safety razors and blades in parts of Yugoslavia, they had all the more reason to respect the company's insights). In another of many admiring nods to the power of the Western brands, Mrvoš cited the famous RCA trademark that had become, as he said, "known all over the world as much for the dog as for the idea of fidelity."[74] (True enough, for the image reprinted in the text is instantly familiar to English-speaking readers of a certain age, even though this particular *cane* is listening intently, head cocked, to "*La voce del padrone.*")

Throughout these earliest sources, the array of visual images offered up was one deeply imprinted by Western styles and tastes: thus we find attractive soup packages, clever posters for Philips electric razors, graphic advertisements for Dermaplast bandages and Pirelli tires, vibrant stripes on the packages of chocolate Easter eggs, and the distinctive labels used on Birds Eye frozen foods. To suggest the shimmering future of illuminated signs, these collections presented that most classic of neon sights, the flash and dazzle of the Las Vegas strip, along with a city streetscape marked by the familiar Walgreens drugstore logo, burning bright in the shadows of the night. As one writer put it, neon had the power to convert "an uninterested passer-by into a passive observer, and a passive observer into an actively interested buyer." To drive home the point, there were photos of America's Horseshoe, Lucky Strike, and Golden Nugget casinos.[75]

While industry leaders did offer plentiful examples of successful advertising produced in Yugoslavia itself, it was Western styles and techniques that clearly garnered the most attention and respect as potential models for the domestic trade. (Archival records of business associations in these early years suggest that much the same held true for retailing as well.)[76] They were drawn in by the dynamism of advertising in its classic forms and by the adventure of the way it was practiced, and they were eager to see just how much of that romance could be replicated at home. Mrvoš and his colleagues, for example, frequently spiced their work with anecdotes from Western practice, often drawn from popular accounts of advertising, marketing, and design work with titles such as *How I Learned the Secrets of Success in Advertising* and *Never Leave Well Enough Alone*. In much the same vein, a writer for *Savremena privredna propaganda* reported, in

---

74. Mrvoš, *Propaganda reklama publicitet*, 40.

75. T. K., "Uloga, značaj i prednosti neonske reklame: neonska reklama—savremeni način reklamiranja," *Savremena privredna propaganda* 1, no. 3 (October 1957): 7.

76. See, for example, the requests for various Western business films and books documented during this period in the files of the country's Association of Chamber of Commerce [Savez Trgovinskih Komora]. Arhiv Jugoslavije, collection Savez Trgovinskih Komora. AJ-STK-087.

1957, on the "seven principles of modern propaganda," a set of quasi-academic insights into the popular mechanics of persuasion that were reportedly grounded in the findings of solid public opinion research undertaken by those more advanced, reliably scientific Americans: "name-calling," "glittering generalities," "transfer" of virtues and attributes to one's product, "testimonials," representing the interests of "plain folks," "stacking the cards" against counterarguments, and calling on consumers to "jump on the bandwagon."[77] Although the piece did acknowledge that the use of some of these techniques would almost inevitably result in unfair advertising, it ultimately concluded that quite a lot in the "seven principles" could be exploited for use in Yugoslavia, and that familiarity with them would surely prove of great benefit to the country's advertising specialists.

Yugoslav specialists in this period often voiced some concerns about the excesses of Western advertising, but those doubts already seemed to be outweighed by their envy of its successes, as we see, for example, in another commentator's reflections on the state of the art in the same year, 1957: "Perhaps the rule of certain Western 'businessmen,' according to which half their earnings [*zarada*] goes for good advertising, is overdoing it. But thanks precisely to that sort of advertising, their products are in great demand here in Yugoslavia and, unfortunately for our manufacturers, they persistently tend to force out domestic products of the same sort and of even better quality."[78] Notwithstanding a few such quibbles about possible abuses, the West was understood as having created something of extraordinary utility to business. It was, consequently, a repository of valuable lessons for Yugoslavia. Along these lines, for example, one of *Savremena privredna propaganda*'s reports on professional standards abroad pointed to the success of the milk industry's advertising campaign in Britain with obvious approval,[79] while another article praised the achievements of the French advertising firm Technes and its slogans "you buy with your eyes" and "beauty pays."[80]

Moreover, the West served not only as a font of practical models but also the most reliable source of theoretical underpinnings for the modern practice of advertising. Thus both Sudar and Mrvoš made liberal reference in their textbooks to scholarly and practical literature published in the West. In establishing the meaning of key disciplinary terms such as *ekonomska propaganda, publicitet, propaganda,* and *reklama,* they and other writers

---

77. V. M., "Kako se treba obraćati javnom mnenju," *Savremena privredna propaganda* 1, no. 3 (October 1957): 4–6. These techniques have been the subject of a sustained and harsh critique in the West as the "seven devices of propaganda." See J. Michael Sproule, "Authorship and Origins of the Seven Propaganda Devices: A Research Note," *Rhetoric & Public Affairs* 4, no. 1 (spring 2001): 135–143.

78. Ž.I., "Savremena privredna propaganda," 3.

79. "Reklama mleka u Velikoj Britaniji," *Savremena privredna propaganda* 2, no. 2 (1958): 15–16.

80. Cf. "Francuska industriska reklama," *Savremena privredna propaganda* 2, no. 3 (April 1958): 21.

elaborated the emerging Yugoslav professional lexicon with explicit reference to Western definitions and understandings.[81] Even at this comparatively early stage, Western ways of thinking about advertising and marketing had begun to leave a deep imprint in the mentality of the Yugoslav profession.

Anyone who has spent even a little time with the industry literature produced in the West will recognize its pronounced fondness for catchy, memorable formulations that can be used to communicate in a succinct fashion (some would call it glib) the essential ideas behind the often elaborate, psychology-laden theory. Drawn to the achievements of capitalist advertising, Yugoslav industry specialists latched onto these formulas and to the highly schematic and programmatic way of talking about advertising, retailing, and marketing that dominated industry discourse in the West. At times some effort was made to modify these intellectual products for the domestic market, but more often the standard pedagogical schemes of the West became the standard pedagogical schemes of Yugoslavia. Like many others, Dušan Mrvoš schooled his readers in AIDA, the progression from *Attention* through *Interest* to *Desire* and, ultimately, *Action*—one of the most familiar Western formulations of how advertising is supposed to work.[82] As it would in the West, AIDA remained a standard of the Yugoslav industry's educational repertoire. And if Western sources sometimes steered the Yugoslavs toward a highly theorized approach to advertising, that tendency was even more pronounced when it came to the reception of the concept of marketing, although this more academic bent remained in constant tension with the practical exigencies of the craft.

This professional familiarity with foreign styles of doing business sometimes translated into more immediate, personal contacts with the West as well, as happened when Yugoslavs mixed with colleagues from the capitalist world at international advertising and marketing gatherings. Trade exhibitions were also an important conduit for Western ideas and styles, and another point of contact between the Western leaders of the field and their eager Yugoslav counterparts. By the mid-1950s, for example, OZEHA designers had mounted the Yugoslav pavilions for trade shows in Utrecht, Paris, Milan, Vienna, Brussels, Trieste, Stockholm, Alexandria, and Smyrna,

---

81. See, for example, Čedomil Dinter, "Stručna terminologija," *Naš publicitet* 4, nos. 3–4 (December 1957): 23–24 (with reference to the advertising texts of West German specialist Rudolf Seyffert); Dinter, "Stručna terminologija," *Naš publicitet* 4, no. 2 (1957): 20–21 (with reference to Seyffert and a host of English-language advertising and marketing handbooks, textbooks, and periodicals). Mrvoš appended to his textbook an afterword in which he warned readers that capitalist literature, while it "extends to us many interesting and very instructive solutions," was not entirely appropriate for "our reality." Mrvoš, *Propaganda reklama publicitet,* 501. Notwithstanding this disclaimer, which is perhaps the product of the less than welcoming political climate that advertising still faced at the time, the book is heavily influenced by Western literature and Western practice.

82. Mrvoš, *Propaganda reklama publicitet,* 229–232.

as well as Prague and Leipzig.[83] Elaborately staged East-West encounters, the trade fairs of the Cold War era proved to be fascinating arenas for competition[84] and, less obviously, for exchange between the two dominant socioeconomic paradigms, as happened, for example, in 1957 when U.S. commercial and political interests joined forces to bring a sample of the American shoppers' paradise to Yugoslavia through the well-attended Supermarket USA exhibition at the Zagreb International Trade Fair.[85] This amazing show of American prosperity was not simply meant to impress the Yugoslavs and build bridges to this unusual communist society; it also represented, as Shane Hamilton notes, "an all-out effort to embarrass the Soviets."[86]

The broader geopolitical context of these meetings had special implications for Yugoslavia: no matter where they took place, such expositions could be used to foster the idea of Yugoslav exceptionalism and to sell the merits of a system that was seen as nestled comfortably between the East and the West. But the flow of images and ideas went both ways. These contacts with the world beyond socialism left the Yugoslav practitioners keenly aware of how much catching up would be necessary if they were to meet Western standards.[87]

Even in these early years, then, Yugoslav practice was edging closer to European and American models and, more important, to an understanding of the buyer-seller relationship and consumer sovereignty that had been elaborated in, and was imbued with the spirit of, business practice in developed capitalist lands. The stage was set for major change.

Nothing Succeeds Like Success: The Consolidation of the Industry's Gains, 1965–1980

Following the more dramatic and thoroughgoing market reforms initiated in 1965, Yugoslav advertising came into its own. For the Yugoslav economy, this was a time of rapid expansion. For ordinary Yugoslavs, whose salaries and real purchasing power rose substantially, it was a time of new wealth, new experiences, new desires, and new dreams. And for the expanding

---

83. "Već treći dan."

84. See Ottó Gécser and Dávid Kitzinger, "Fairy Sales: The Budapest International Fairs as Virtual Shopping Tours," *Cultural Studies* 16, no. 1 (2002): 145–164.

85. See Shane Hamilton, "Supermarket USA Confronts State Socialism: Airlifting the Technopolitics of Industrial Food Distribution into Cold War Yugoslavia," in *Cold War Kitchen: Americanization, Technology, and European Users*, ed. Ruth Oldenziel and Karin Zachmann, 137–159 (Cambridge, Mass., 2009).

86. Ibid., 138.

87. For more on the significance of international fairs for the development of the Yugoslav advertising industry, see, for example, Čedomir Đomba, "FNR Jugoslavija na inostranim sajmovima 1957–1958," *Naš publicitet* 4, nos. 3–4 (December 1957): 1–2; Stefan Askanas, "Medunarodni Poznanjski sajam," *Naš publicitet* 4, nos. 3–4 (December 1957): 4.

commercial promotion industry, it was a time of growth, even more rapid institutional consolidation, professionalization, creative maturity, and increased legitimacy. Perhaps most important, it was also an era in which those who made their living in advertising, retailing, and marketing felt emboldened to propagate even more aggressively their vision of how business ought to be conducted, a vision that they said was in essential harmony with the country's optimistic new orientation toward the market and consumer satisfaction. The new round of reforms was thus treated as something that required an even greater reliance on advertising and marketing.[88]

Significantly, however, this was also a time when criticisms of commercial promotion and its potentially damaging effects on society intensified dramatically. As explored in detail in subsequent chapters, the industry's new success and prominence called forth a wave of serious concern and outright opposition. In conjunction with the purges of "liberalism" in the early 1970s, advertising and marketing work became a more frequent target of communist suspicion and scorn. The worst of the backlash, part of a much larger reaction against the alleged excesses of the market, proved only temporary, but it nevertheless had the effect of causing many businesses and even some media enterprises to shy away from advertising. As a result, the quantity of advertising in many leading publications was, for a time, drastically reduced, causing substantial difficulties for some publishing companies. The years around 1972–1974 represented, for advertising and marketing professionals, a very unsettling reversal in a larger pattern of expansion and success. The threat to the industry's continued growth appeared, at least for a while, quite real. In the darkest hours of this strained interlude, the new hostility toward advertising caused some industry leaders to fear for the fate of their craft in socialist Yugoslavia.

Yet the broader trend toward expansion continued. As we have seen, the previous period from 1950 to 1965 had witnessed a noteworthy rise in the presence of advertising in the Yugoslav mass media and elsewhere.[89] But whereas the earlier penetration of advertising into the country's business and media culture had been spotty, commercial appeals now became a much more frequent feature of daily life. Television advertising grew even more common and important, and advertising broadcasts managed to retain a fairly high level of viewership. Promotions on the small screen spread to new parts of the country as well. For example, Sarajevo's broadcasting enterprise, which for the previous two years had been carrying the advertising

---

88. See, for example, Radmilo Dimitrijević, "Ekonomska propaganda i privredna reforma," *Propaganda* 1, no. 2 (December 1967): 5–8.

89. The expansion of the mass-market media continued as well. In this period several new, widely circulated publications appeared, including, for example, *Tempo* (sports) and *Stop* and *Radio TV revija* (entertainment).

programming produced by TV Zagreb, began running its own commercials starting in 1969.[90]

Among advertising specialists, however, there remained a perception that Yugoslav broadcasters had yet to determine the right way to handle television spots. One prominent commentator cited the fairly common problem of overly long blocks of advertisements between, or sometimes in the middle of, regular programming. Pauses of ten and fifteen minutes for advertising in the middle of a sports event (e.g., between the periods of a soccer match) were, *Ideja*'s Čedo Dinter suggested, nothing more than a "graveyard for commercials."[91]

Meanwhile, in the popular press, advertising became an increasingly familiar sight, and a standard feature of many print media. Daily newspapers continued to run comparatively little advertising; most of the more radical changes occurred elsewhere. But these other outlets, even the ones most open to commercial promotion, were not crammed full of ads as were their contemporaneous Western counterparts. As late as 1979 and 1980, for example, advertising other than small, textual classified ads [*mali oglasi*] would occupy only a small percentage of the important Belgrade daily *Večernje novosti* [The evening news], a paper with one of the highest circulation figures in the country. Advertising was, at the time, only somewhat more prominent in the popular Serbian news and features magazine *NIN: Nedeljne informativne novine* [NIN: Weekly informative news], although that periodical often did feature full-color, full-page advertisements on its back covers.

Nevertheless, over the course of this period, it became quite common for many mass-circulation magazines to include a dozen or more full pages of advertising, executed both in traditional black and white and in color. The tendency was strongest in those magazines whose subject matter was most closely tied to the new consumer economy: women's periodicals, fashion reviews, and home-and-garden magazines. This, of course, is not particularly surprising. What *is* surprising, however, is just how much advertising was included in these periodicals. From the mid-1960s on, for example, the leading Croatian women's journal *Svijet* increasingly included advertising—

---

90. "Ekonomska propaganda na malom ekranu i u BiH," *Propaganda* 2, no. 3 (March 1968): 68.

91. Čedo Dinter, "TV-EPP može postati bolji. Kako?" *Ideja*, no. 4 (November 1978): 10–14, at 11. The author further noted that even commercial programming in the more welcome and familiar time slots, such as that which aired immediately before and after evening news shows, showed some drop-off in audience attention. RTV Ljubljana's research for an apparently typical evening in May 1977 indicated, for example, that the number of poll respondents who had watched the five-minute commercial block after the news broadcast fell by 16 percentage points, or almost one-third of the audience of the news show (52%). The broadcaster regained the lost audience with the show that followed, *Josip Broz Tito—The Struggle and the Development of the Communist Party of Yugoslavia*. Ibid., 11–12. It is difficult, of course, to determine exactly how such figures should be interpreted, for over two-thirds of the audience for the two main shows was, in fact, tuned in for the advertising segment.

much of it in full-page format and in color—from a wide range of consumer goods manufacturers and sellers. Typical issues from the late 1960s and early 1970s might include as many as a dozen pages of advertising out of a total of fifty to sixty. Similar patterns could be found in other consumer-oriented, mass-market reviews.

The tendency toward an increasing saturation with advertising content was especially evident in publications targeted at the home.[92] To cite one representative instance, the April 1976 issue of *Naš dom* (Our home), advertising took up twenty of the magazine's fifty-six pages, and this figure does not include the many pages of features on various furniture items and other consumer products that might fairly be treated as an indirect form of commercial promotion. The "product placement" in such coverage strongly suggests that the staff of periodicals of this type saw the celebration and promotion of new consumption opportunities as an important purpose of their work, while the continual attention to the new offerings of various Yugoslav firms is likely an indication of cozy relationships between the staffers of these mass-market magazines and the manufacturers whose goods they covered.[93]

Moreover, much of the advertising in these publications came, as in *Svijet* and *Naš dom,* in the form of full-color, full-page layouts, some quite professionally executed. In its quantity and quality—and especially in the distinctive sense that many Yugoslav manufacturers and retailers were not just going through the motions but truly were trying to attract customers to their products and their stores—the advertising in consumer-oriented Yugoslav magazines was, by all indications, something only rarely, if ever, encountered elsewhere in the socialist world. The question of Yugoslavia's distinctiveness in this respect is one that demands further research with a broad comparative scope, but my own work along these lines thus far suggests that

92. On the importance of the home as a site of socialist competition with the West, see Greg Castillo, *Cold War on the Home Front: The Soft Power of Midcentury Design* (Minneapolis, 2010); Susan E. Reid, "Cold War in the Kitchen: Gender and the De-Stalinization of Consumer Taste in the Soviet Union under Khrushchev," *Slavic Review* 61, no. 2 (2002): 211–252; Reid, "The Khrushchev Kitchen: Domesticating the Scientific-Technological Revolution," *Journal of Contemporary History* 40, no. 2 (2005): 289–316; Krisztina Fehérváry, "American Kitchens, Luxury Bathrooms, and the Search for a 'Normal' Life in Postsocialist Hungary," *Ethnos* 67, no. 3 (November 2002): 369–400; Fehérváry, "In Search of the Normal: Material Culture and Middle-Class Fashioning in a Hungarian Steel Town, 1950–1997" (Ph.D. diss., University of Chicago, 2005).

93. A representative sample of issues of *Naš dom* from other years yields similar results. For April 1968, ads took up almost one-third of the forty-eight pages; in February 1969, approximately one-fourth of the forty-four pages; September 1977, approximately one-fourth of the eighty pages. In 1967, the first year of publication, there was usually somewhat less advertising, with ads typically accounting for only one-tenth to one-fifth of the pages. *Naš dom* was very widely circulated. In 1973, for example, it was the periodical with the second-highest circulation figures in Slovenia; its 102,000 copies surpassed even the average daily circulation of the main Ljubljana daily. "Pregled poprečnih naklad časopisov in revij v obdobju I.-X. 1973," *Bilten DEPS*, nos. 18–19 (1973–1974): 35. A Serbo-Croatian edition was published as well.

Yugoslav advertising did in many ways represent a truly radical departure from the way things were done in most other places across Eastern Europe and the Soviet Union.

As for the ads themselves, they still ran the gamut of technique and creativity. Some Yugoslav advertisements remained quite primitive, whereas others seemed much like the products of some experienced Western advertising design firm. Most probably fell short of the highest technical and creative standards. Generally, however, the tendency over the course of the period was toward a slow but steady improvement in what the professional activists recognized as quality, and so toward the end of the 1970s many Yugoslav advertisements had a decidedly Western look. In both style and content, domestic advertisements frequently emulated Western models. If they did not go so far as to offer the escapism that Elémer Hankiss has called "the toothpaste of immortality," they were quite literally, as seen in one appeal for the Krka enterprise's Brigitte Bardot cosmetics, purveyors of "the lipstick of success" (Figure 13). And sometimes the advertisements were literally for Western brands themselves, especially for the variety of well-known European and American products made under license in Yugoslav factories. The pages of Yugoslav mass-circulation magazines during these years therefore include many sophisticated ads for products such as Marlboro and Milde Sorte cigarettes, Braun electric razors (made by Slovenia's Iskra), Maggi soups (under license to Croatia's Podravka), Nestlé chocolates (by Croatia's Zvečevo), and Helena Rubinstein cosmetics (from the Croatian company Saponia).

Outright competition between domestic brands also set Yugoslav business apart from production and sales elsewhere in the socialist world, and advertising was a key element of that more competitive environment. Thus, in just one of innumerable examples of head-to-head rivalry through advertising, the December 1969 issue of *Naš dom* included full-page, full-color advertisements for modern washing machines produced by no fewer than three different Yugoslav companies: Slovenia's Gorenje, Montenegro's Obod, and Croatia's Castor-Rade Končar. Like so much of what appeared in the popular media of the time, these advertisements are extraordinarily revealing about the new orientation of Yugoslav advertising and Yugoslav consumer culture.

Gorenje's ad, prominently positioned on the inside front cover, shows a group of handsomely dressed children playing in front of an oven range, washing machine, and refrigerator, all plunked down in an incongruous but attention-grabbing setting: a sunny, leaf-strewn clearing among birch trees. Two small girls are happily playing with pots and pans on a toy stove, shown to the magazine's readers, as it were, in training for their future roles, while a young boy stands off to the side, hands in pockets, looking more than a little detached from it all. The vision is one of reassuring prosperity, idyllic order, domestic and familial contentment, children being raised the "right" way, clear gender functions, and, not least of all, comforting tradition blended with a confident sense of progress and modernity: Gorenje's message promises, as the text puts it, "Contemporary products—From a contemporary factory—For the contemporary home—For your home."

The modernity invoked here is a major motif of Yugoslav advertising throughout the socialist period, and it also proves central to the ad for the Obod company, which takes up the common Western theme of the modern household appliance as a boon to womankind. The washing machine advertised here is the product of a factory in Cetinje, the sleepy little backwater that was the old Ottoman-era capital of Montenegro. As such, it comes from a part of the country that Yugoslavs themselves often liked to think of, with some orientalist condescension but also no small amount of admiration, as a notoriously wild and primitive place. This particular Montenegrin enterprise, however, was sending out a powerful message about socialist modernity. Like the other ads considered here—and like so many of the thousands of socialist-era advertisements I have reviewed—it traffics in strong gender images and participates in an evolving discourse about gender roles that formed a central problematic for the peoples and governments of socialist Europe. Those societies found themselves in a difficult situation. On the one hand, their public cultures were infused with Marxist egalitarianism, and their policies toward gender equality were shaped by the sheer demand for women's productive labor—and the need for women's income to help support families. On the other hand, they often saw the persistence of what were often highly traditional and, in some parts of Eastern Europe and the Balkans, even unapologetically patriarchal attitudes toward women's roles.

The Obod ad strides boldly into those contradictions, offering its viewers not simply the machine itself but also all that the machine promises the new Yugoslav working woman. In the ad copy, potential customers are told that this is the model that "the woman who wants a washing machine dreams about." This washer, the firm promises, "gives laundry the whiteness that women want so much." But the bland text of the advertisement is less important than the carefully constructed visual elements. As in each of the ads, the appliance is shown utterly disengaged from its normal setting in the home, the actual site of housework. In the Obod advertisement, we find the machine floating over the surface of a beautiful and calm blue sea. Like the sunny birch grove of the Gorenje appliances, this seems a bizarre and incongruous pairing, but it actually makes sense: here was a message that people who lived in Yugoslavia would likely have recognized immediately as a visual evocation of the Adriatic seacoast. The placement of the machine thus conjures up the quintessential Yugoslav imagery of free time, leisure, and enjoyment.

The visual elements of the Obod ad are also clearly designed to amplify its gender-specific textual messages with suggestions that the product holds even greater promise for women. In a series of small photographic panels, we see the lucky purchaser going about her day (or perhaps she is the recipient—in that respect the ad cleverly plays to both sides of the gender divide). She is young, blonde, stylish, and modern. She is traditionally feminine-looking, and her makeup is always perfect, but she is also clearly moving beyond the older, more limited conceptions of women's traditional roles. With this appliance, she is liberated from the drudgery of laundry, and, as a result, she is enjoying time to have her hair styled, to contribute productively to the economy by working in a modern office, to do some pleasure reading (doing so, significantly, as a *consumer*—she is looking through *Naš dom*, the very magazine in which the ad appears!), and, at the end of the day, to wind up dancing serenely in the arms of her man. Two other photos make it clear that she will also have time to get a little cooking and cleaning done along the way. This appliance, then, clearly offers her liberation *within* her role as a modern Yugoslav woman, not emancipation *from* that role. Much of the traditional is preserved even as the modern is added, and though her lot is made easier with the addition of the super-automatic washing machine, the new Yugoslav working woman still ends up having to do it all.

Like the other two advertisements, the appeal for Castor-Rade Končar's equally super-automatic washing machines is also supremely responsive to the gendered division of labor that persisted in nominally egalitarian social-ist societies at least as tenaciously as it did in the West, if not more so. But this ad tries a somewhat different approach, one more obviously geared to the purchasing power of men: it features an attractive, modishly dressed young woman, looking like anything but a stereotypically frumpy housewife as she leans up against the machine from behind and looks up alluringly, one shapely leg splayed out to the side for a nicer view. One finger—all she needs—is poised on the button that makes it all happen.

Notwithstanding the common reassurances that advertising in Yugoslavia was tailored to the specific circumstances and values of the socialist society, these advertisements, like many others that appeared in the years before and afterward, are strongly suggestive of circumstances and values rather more like those that prevailed in the West. The images seen here are, of course, *advertising* images, and, as such, they are not necessarily true representa-tions of reality, of Yugoslav life *as lived*. Yet they are indisputably reflective of what the creators of Yugoslav advertising believed to be the very real aspirations of ordinary consumers. That reality—the reality of encouraging accomplishments today paired with dreams and hopes for a richer, more fashionable, more comfortable tomorrow—was at once the target and the creation of the new Yugoslav advertising, and during these years it took on an increasingly Western aspect.

Reflecting later on the radical expansion of opportunities for shoppers and those who courted them in this halcyon era, Jure Apih has emphasized that, at the time, the new orientation was felt to represent a decisive shift toward Western values and away from a limited, modest way of life that had come to be identified with state socialism:

In the second half of the 1960s... it seemed that a new wind had begun to sweep in. After a decade of consumer [rationing] points and controlled supply, goods meant for a more joyful life started to arrive on store shelves and even in the display windows of the state stores. Cosmetics and fashionable apparel, radios and televisions, mopeds and even small automobiles. The magic word that was supposed to solve all the problems that had heaped up and, at the same time, separate us definitively from our Eastern patrons and brothers who overnight had turned out to be ugly and rotten—that magic word was "the market."[94]

Apih, who over the course of his career became probably the most prominent of Slovenian advertising and marketing specialists, and indeed one of the leading figures in the field throughout Yugoslavia, remembered this as a momentous reorientation. Although he pointed first to outward manifestations, that is, to the very obvious change in lifestyles that accompanied the government's more experimental policies, Apih ultimately viewed these years as more than just a time for new tastes, clothes, and diversions. For this well-connected businessman, the thoroughgoing consumerist spirit of the late 1960s was part of a much more radical embrace of the market that hinted at a fundamental departure from socialism.

This reversal, Apih indicated, opened the way for new ideas, new members of the élite, new attitudes toward advertising and marketing, and a new understanding of what it meant to do business: "Only the kind of work that will be confirmed by the market is to be recognized by the society: this was the idea that turned the state and its future upside down. Different things and different people became important. People started to decide, argue over, and *even think about things differently*. Directors, traveling sales representatives, and the heads of advertising services entered the scene."[95] For a while, Apih suggested, this excited rush to the market almost overshadowed the communist character of the system, although the expansive spirit was tamped down to some extent as part of the authorities' stern reckoning with "liberalism" that took place in the early 1970s.

If the forms and content of Yugoslav advertising were becoming much more Western, the business of advertising was drifting more quickly toward Western models as well. In an extension of prior developments, the period was marked by a keen interest in the "agency" system developed in the West,[96] and organizational models from Europe and America evidently exerted a strong influence on the structure of the many new advertising organizations that were formed.[97] Yet the great majority of advertising specialists

---

94. Jure Apih, *Oglašanja v A-duru* (Ljubljana: Slon, 1996), 5.
95. Ibid., 5–6 (emphasis added).
96. See, for example, Marjan Serdarušić, "Agencijo, a što sada!" *Ideja*, no. 3 (December 1972): 16–17.
97. Among the most significant of these was the Croatian enterprise Apel [Appeal]. Founded in 1968, it experienced rapid growth over the course of the next decade and, for a time, pub-

continued to work "in-house," that is, within large commercial enterprises like manufacturers, retailers, and media organizations, rather than as employees of independent organizations devoted specifically to advertising.

As before, the centers of advertising activity were, especially at the beginning of the period, Zagreb and Belgrade, the country's two largest cities and the capitals of the republics organized around its two dominant ethnonational groups. In the mid-1970s Zagreb was still home to the three largest advertising enterprises in the country.[98] At the same time professional interest in advertising was beginning to diffuse outward to other smaller cities and regional centers. Slovenian advertising and marketing activity, for example, quickly started to catch up with trends in Zagreb and Belgrade, anticipating an even more impressive development of the industry there in future years. Even Slovenia's second-largest city, Maribor, a town with a small population but an important strategic location near the Austrian border and the city of Graz, had its own Association of Advertisers (Društvo ekonomskih propagandistov) by 1978. There were signs of increased institutional strength from Bosnia-Herzegovina as well, as, for example, in the work of Sarajevo's OZEBIH bureau, but in general specialists from that republic had a much lower public profile than their counterparts in Croatia, Serbia, and Slovenia. While the Montenegrin guild had formed its own association in 1967, professionals in Macedonia, the laggard republic in terms of advertising and marketing activity, would wait until the late 1980s to form their group, the last of the republic-level trade organizations.

The institutional consolidation and organizational activities that had been inaugurated by the pioneers of the previous period now continued at an even more intense pace. A pan-Yugoslav professional association, the Advertising Federation of Yugoslavia (Savez ekonomskih propagandista Jugoslavije) was finally established in 1973.[99] Paralleling these developments was the proliferation of professional conferences and training seminars held in Yugoslavia itself, where Western experts arrived to share the benefit of their decades of experience and where Yugoslav specialists proclaimed the importance of advertising and marketing for the continued success of self-management, traded insights into the latest methods of consumer persuasion

---

lished its own professional journal, *Apel*. On the history of the organization, see "Prvih deset godina Apela," *Ideja*, no. 3 (December 1978): 30–31. From 1969 to 1997 the revenues of the enterprise increased twelvefold, while its workforce quadrupled. Ibid. Some of this growth is likely attributable to Apel's integration, during this period, into the much larger Podravka manufacturing enterprise.

98. "Zagrebačke agencije pred integracijom," *Ideja*, no. 1 (October 1975): 1.

99. The delay seems to have been caused at least in part by some internecine squabbling among industry leaders from the various republics. On the "blockage" that afflicted the organizational consolidation of the field from 1965 through 1971, see Žozef Lončar, "Pismo glavnog urednika," *Privredna propaganda* 3, no. 14 (December 1971): 15–16. See also Marijan Serdarušić, "Tvrdoglava nada," *Ideja*, no. 6 (1973): 5; M. S., "Kako je osnovan SEPJ?" *Ideja*, no. 6 (1973): 6–7.

and marketing research, and promoted their vision of the sovereignty of the consumer in the country's commercial affairs.[100]

Even though the Yugoslav guild had now grown to quite a respectable size,[101] its members were still troubled by the idea that professional training was inadequate and that the needs of the profession had not been properly acknowledged by the state-run educational system. A hunger for the legitimacy that would come from the state's imprimatur (and financial support) was apparent. Along these lines, one overview of the development of the discipline in Croatia noted that the call for a special advertising school at the university level, a proposal that had been floated by some of the Zagreb visionaries as early as the 1950s, was still nothing more than wishful thinking.[102] Government authorities did, however, devote significant attention to the development of the industry. The Federal Economic Council [*Savezna privredna komora*], a state organ charged with the oversight of federal economic policy and the policies of the various republics, had by 1967 established its own Bureau for Advertising, and representatives of governmental institutions were frequent participants at conferences and other professional gatherings.

Along with all this professional and organizational ferment came a noticeable increase in the volume and scope of marketing and advertising publications. A host of new textbooks, handbooks, and other instructional materials appeared, and after a curious lull following the discontinuation of *Naš publicitet* and *Savremena privredna propaganda* in 1958, new and vital trade reviews arose to fill the gap. The period thus saw a real maturation of the country's professional press,[103] although the multiplication of the

---

100. See, for example, *Zbornik referata sa II međunarodnog simpozijuma privrednih propaganda* (Belgrade, n.d.). Papers presented at the Second International Advertising Symposium, Bled, 2–7 November 1969.

101. As of 1971, for example, there were 1,048 people employed in various bureaus, agencies, and other enterprises engaged in advertising. This figure, however, does not include those working "in-house" for producers and media enterprises. Accounting for these, the number of advertising specialists was probably three thousand to four thousand. Aleksandar Spasić, interviewed in "Naš sagovornik," *Privredna propaganda* 3, nos. 17–18 (September 1972): 76–79, at 77.

102. "Stasanje naše struke i društva," *Ideja*, no. 2 (February 1978): 7–14, at 11.

103. The most important periodicals that first appeared during this period included *Propaganda*, the journal of the Yugoslav Advertising Association, published from 1967 to 1970; *Bilten*, the organ of the Slovenian Advertising Association, published (with its successor *MEDIJ: glasilo Društva ekonomskih propagandistov Slovenije*), from 1967 to 1974; *Privredna propaganda*, the organ of the Belgrade advertising firm Ekonomska propaganda, published from 1969 to 1976; *Marketing*, the journal of the Yugoslav Marketing Association, published continuously since 1970; *Kreativne komunikacije*, published by the marketing agency of the main Zagreb daily, *Vjesnik*, from 1972 to 1983; and *Ideja*, the journal of the Croatian Advertising Association, published from 1972 to 1981 and resurrected in 1988 (an earlier version of the review was published from 1961 to 1965). A wealth of evidence concerning Yugoslav consumer culture is also found in *Supermarket: časopis za praksu suvremene trgovine*, published in Zagreb from 1976 to 1991 and then renamed *Suvremena trgovina*. For each of these periodicals, I have reviewed the entire publication run during the socialist period, with the ex-

specialty journals did prompt some debate over whether all this promotion of promotion was really necessary.[104] Whereas the trade journals of the prior period had been extremely limited in both their number and scope of coverage, the industry's new literature was marked by its greater breadth and diversity. Many of the new trade reviews also proved more durable than their predecessors in the 1950s. Better staffed and apparently better funded, they were published much more frequently and regularly, and they offered readers increasingly detailed and sophisticated coverage of developments both at home and abroad.

A survey of this rich new professional literature leaves little doubt about where Yugoslav advertising and marketing were headed. If Western models and ideas had already heavily influenced the field in the period before 1965, that tendency only grew stronger in this new time of expanded opportunities. Even as early as 1967 one contributor to the Slovenian Advertising Association's professional journal would observe that, in Yugoslavia, "advertising is acquiring an ever more Western definition."[105] But he concluded that there was still a long way to go: the work undertaken in Yugoslavia continued to show elements both of simple East European practice, which viewed advertising primarily as an unnecessary burden, and of more advanced Western approaches, with their sensitivity to economics, to the complexity of the marketing mix, and, above all, to the "unceasing battle to place product in the marketplace." As such, Yugoslav advertising was "still, unfortunately, a conglomeration of both influences."[106]

Beginning shortly after 1965, however, that mixture would start to become considerably more Western and considerably less socialist. The inflow of Western thought about marketing and advertising continued, except that what was once a steady but slow trickle now became a torrent. Western ideas poured in, and in the publications of the industry's leaders, Western ideas poured out again. Continuing a practice started in the previous period, Yugoslav industry publications devoted considerable analysis to industry developments abroad[107] and frequently reprinted new and important contributions to the Western professional literature or published the observations

---

ception of a few individual issues missing from collections in Belgrade, Zagreb, and Ljubljana, where I conducted my research. The given dates of publication are based on the best available bibliographical resources.

104. "Umesto otvorenog pisma," *Propaganda* 3, nos. 7/8 (July–November 1969): 15–18.

105. [Anton] Kočevar, "Ekonomska propaganda v novih razmerah," *Bilten DEPS*, no. 1 (October 1967): 11–13, at 11. Tellingly, the source to which this Slovenian writer looked for confirmation of his conclusion about the Westernization of Yugoslav advertising was Roger Barton's massive *Advertising Handbook*, an important work published originally in 1950 and made available in a Serbo-Croatian edition in 1964.

106. Ibid., 13.

107. See, for example, M. Graf, "Problem marketinga u Engleskoj," *Propaganda* 2, no. 3 (March 1968): 21–24.

of guest commentators from capitalist countries.[108] They followed trends in the West carefully, reproducing examples of successful and admired foreign campaigns and explaining the techniques used, obviously for possible replication in the domestic market. Thus the trade journals remarked, for example, on the fashionable concept of "know-how" as used in electronics industry ad campaigns[109] and on a clever ad by Mercedes-Benz that juxtaposed a page crammed with four thousand words of text "for the technically minded" with one simple photograph "for the rest of us."[110] This sample of foreign output might have had particular appeal to Yugoslav readers: in the early years of the industry's development, the country's advertising leaders had decried the tendency to load up advertisements with text at the expense of eye-catching visuals and simple, attractive messages. Such examples of the Yugoslav industry's fascination with foreign advertising are, to put it mildly, plentiful. They spill out from the pages of the trade literature in issue after issue, year after year.[111]

Occasionally some mild objection would be made, for example, to the "excessively forced use of sex in German advertising" as reported by the Munich magazine *Werben und Verkaufen* [Advertising and selling] (and dutifully documented for the consideration of the largely male Yugoslav readership with four examples of such ads, all featuring half-naked or suggestively dressed women).[112] But such reservations were noteworthy primarily for their exceptional quality.

In their pursuit of creative quality, Yugoslav advertising leaders showed an unmistakable enthusiasm for the competitive awards system that had captured so much attention in the developed capitalist world. They followed Western jury prizes with great care and reported on them in piece after approving piece, often reproducing the winning creations in Yugoslav publications.[113] Meanwhile they set about duplicating the system of awards and festivals at home.

A similar keenness for Western modes appears in the educational literature that appeared during this period. In just one chapter on "advertising and psychology," for example, the updated 1971 edition of Josip Sudar's classic

---

108. See, for example, Neville Darby, "S potrošačeva gledišta: kako djeluje EP," *Ideja*, no. 3 (July 1978): 24–29. Darby was the director of research of the London office of Ogilvy Benson & Mather.

109. "Važno je zvati se 'know-how,'" *Kreativne komunikacije*, no. 3 (September 1972): 29.

110. "Svjetska scena," *Ideja*, no. 6 (1973): 39.

111. See, for example, "Oglasi uspjeha," *Kreativne komunikacije*, no. 6 (January 1973): 31.

112. "Izlog seksi-oglasa," *Kreativne komunikacije*, no. 5 (December 1972): 37.

113. Instances of this abound. See, for example, Mihaela Zamolo, "Naš tiho umirući plakat," *Ideja*, no. 6 (1973): 26–28 (complaining that Yugoslavia was one of the few countries that offered no award for poster and billboard advertising, and showing readers two award-winning British billboards). For an atypically skeptical report on the "flood" of awards, see Goroslav Keller, "Mnogo 'zlata' za malo dobrog dizajna," *Kreativne komunikacije*, no. 4 (October 1972): 17–19.

textbook acquainted readers with full-page reproductions of a wide variety of Western consumer advertising for such successful brands as Coca-Cola, Lux dishwashing liquid, General Tire, Kraft foods, Quaker Oats, Mutual of New York, Bayer Aspirin, Pepto-Bismol, Shower to Shower powder, Morton Salt, Volkswagen, and Renault. It is clear (and telling) that advertisements for luxury items had not been deemed off limits as potential models for the psychological appeals of Yugoslav ads: Sudar offered examples of advertising by Martini vermouth, Cointreau, Philips Electronics, General Electric central air conditioning, and even Rolex watches, to name just a few.[114] This sort of openness to and admiration for the advertising of the highly commercialized West was no aberration. It was, indeed, a recurring and important feature of many other such works as well.[115]

The tendency to simply reproduce the unmediated opinions of Western advertising and marketing experts, already a significant characteristic of the germinal period from 1950 to 1965, now grew even stronger. Yugoslavia's professional press had certainly not attempted to seal out any possible contamination by Western ideas, and in they came. The organ of Belgrade's Ekonomska Propaganda advertising firm, for example, thus published a speech by the president of General Motors to American advertisers on the topic "Who is and where is the consumer?"[116] In another issue, the journal reprinted an article from the French commercial review *Vendre* [To sell] on the "revolution in packaging" and the new popularity of shopping bags printed with advertising messages for products and stores.[117] (Although many stores, following the standard practice in Eastern Europe, still relied on customers to bring something to carry home their purchases in, promotional bags of this sort became an increasingly common sight in Yugoslavia. Critically, these bags gave customers the opportunity to display their buying habits long after the sales transaction was over, especially since the bags could be reused on other shopping outings.)

The transmission of reports on foreign know-how was continuous, and the flow of ideas so rich and abundant that it is impossible to do it justice with the few samplings that must suffice here. But the Yugoslavs were clearly fascinated with Western success and eager to emulate it if they could. In 1972, for example, the marketing and advertising director for Denmark's leading brewery explained "how Tuborg conquered the world."[118] Similarly

---

114. Sudar, *Ekonomska propaganda*, 31–74.

115. See, for example, Bogomir Deželak, *Marketing* (Maribor, 1971); Deželak, *Ekonomska propaganda* (Maribor, 1973 [1966]; Bogdan Novković, *Tehnika privredne propagande* (Belgrade, 1973); Franc Lorbek, *Osnove komuniciranja v marketingu* (Ljubljana, 1979).

116. Edward N. Cole, "Ko je i gde je potrošač?" *Privredna propaganda* 2, no. 9 (1970): 33–35.

117. Maurice Pariat, "Renensansa jednog propagandnog medijuma," *Privredna propaganda* 1, no. 1 (February 1969): 62–63.

118. Flemming Jörgensen, "Kako je Tuborg osvojio svet," *Privredna propaganda* 3, nos. 17–18 (September 1972): 19–22.

the West German marketing specialist Christian Vogel contributed a long piece to Zagreb's *Kreativne komunikacije* sharing his views on the proper ways to create and shape a corporate "image."[119] In the same vein, the journal reprinted an opinion piece in which the editor of Munich's *Werben und Verkaufen* argued that the growing consumer protection movement made it all the more imperative for marketing specialists to live up to their ideals of treating consumers as *partners*.[120] The journal of the Slovenian Advertising Association, *Bilten* [Bulletin], was especially keen to keep its readers abreast of developments abroad, running the regular columns "From Foreign Practice" and "From Foreign Literature" that channeled a steady stream of information about Western developments and, in so doing, helped propagate a new understanding of the very nature of business.[121] In just one of many such instances, *Bilten* reprinted a collection of twenty maxims about the practice handed down from the giant advertising firm of David Ogilvy. "Be courageous," the Ogilvy agency told its representatives (and now, indirectly, Yugoslav ad specialists), "people die from boredom, but not from too much work. The more you work, the more you develop your capacity for work.... Always keep your eye on the market.... Learn to be a good businessman. You have to know how to sell your idea or position. A great idea means nothing if it is not sold." Ogilvy's secrets to success, of course, were originally meant for workers in-house, but as *Bilten* pointed out for its readers, "this advice can no doubt directly benefit our work as well."[122]

During this period it also became even easier for Yugoslav specialists to exchange ideas with their Western counterparts at conferences, educational programs, and festivals, on business trips, and in other face-to-face encounters. The trade journals and newsletters of the time are packed with reports on advertising conferences, marketing seminars, awards presentations, film festivals, and other professional gatherings in the West.[123] Another favored form for introducing audiences to the ideas of Western specialists in the trade journals was the interview, which, editors willing, allowed ideas from the capitalist world to be introduced verbatim, straight from the source, without the need for the apologetic introductory invocations of socialist values that marked so much of the domestic literature.[124]

---

119. Christian Vogel, "Kako stvaram image poduzeća?" *Kreativne komunikacije*, no. 4 (October 1972): 22–24.

120. Claus Schuldes, "Bauk 'konzumerizma,'" *Kreativne komunikacije*, no. 6 (January 1973): 21–23.

121. See *Bilten DEPS*, 1968–1974.

122. "Dvajset nasvetov propagandne agencije D. Ogilvy," *Bilten DEPS*, nos. 15–16 (n.d. [ca. 1972–1973]): 33–35.

123. See, for example, Iskra Mikačić, "Sjećanje na sutra," *Kreativne komunkacije*, no. 3 (September 1972): 21–22. Report on the Nineteenth International Advertising Film Festival, Venice, 1972.

124. See, for example, "Diagnoza 'smrti' marke na tržištu," *Kreativne komunikacije*, no. 1 (1972): 14–17 (interview with American marketing motivation specialist Louis Cheskin,

The decided lack of attention paid to socialist practice during this period is particularly telling. Soviet-bloc commercial styles had long since become uninteresting to the country's advertising and marketing leaders. Instead, Western—and often specifically American—ways of thinking about business were steadily spreading. Examples of this shift are too numerous to list, but one especially revealing instance can be found in the collection of managers' reflections on the imagined qualities of "the ideal salesman" gathered at a panel discussion organized by the American marketing magazine *Sales Management* and then translated for a Yugoslav audience in 1972. Reprinted with little editorializing in *Kreativne komunikacije*, the magazine of Zagreb's Vjesnik Agency for Marketing, these observations are noteworthy for the heavy emphasis placed on aggressiveness, competition, and entrepreneurial spirit. The perfect salesman, readers were told, was:

Someone who is competitive, a little bit selfish, and loves recognition.
He knows how to lead. Maybe he was the captain of a football team or active in a drama group at school.
Internal power and strength must be obvious.
This has to be someone who is hungry.
He has to be a special individual who distinguishes himself from other, ordinary people.
A very disciplined person, one who possesses the capacity to plan his life.
He is in a position to do everything well, without regard to how he is employed.
Someone who will be in a position to grow together with his company.
Well trained, a good conversationalist, intelligent.
He has to be a little crazy. All salespeople are crazy. I know I am, too.
Someone who resembles me completely.[125]

Coming as they do from a country known and admired among Yugoslavs for its business acumen and can-do spirit, these American desiderata suggest the transfer of a new and stunningly un-socialist notion of commercial success, a notion grounded above all in a concern for what it takes to compete successfully in the marketplace.

The importation of capitalist understandings continued apace in other ways as well. The predilection for neat (and unmistakably Western) formulations, schematics, and acronyms, already firmly rooted in the first phase of the industry's expansion, became even more noticeable. AIDA (Attention, Interest, Desire, Action) was joined by DAGMAR (Defining Advertising

---

author of *Secrets of Marketing Success);* "Svatko ima propaganda kakvu zaslužuje," *Ideja,* no. 4 (1973): 26–27 (interview with American television advertising expert Bruce Stauderman); "Tražim suradnike bolje od sebe," *Ideja,* no. 4 (1973): 24–25 (interview with Eric Padt, secretary of the European Division of the International Advertising Association).

125. "Idealni prodavač," *Kreativne komunikacije,* no. 4 (October 1972): 41.

Goals for Measuring Advertising Results) as the Yugoslav trade literature filled up with a ponderous quasi-scientific apparatus largely borrowed from American and European models: flow charts, organizational diagrams, business theories, and all manner of psychological explanations.[126] Influenced by Western styles, Yugoslav industry leaders worked up inventive formulations of their own.[127] In stressing the need for a planned, programmed approach to advertising practice, for example, Sudar's seminal textbook summed it all up for students with the handy homegrown mnemonic "ISKRA" ["SPARK"]. In this scheme, success could be ensured by developing an advertising campaign through a series of rational and carefully thought-out steps: market research (*istraživanje tržišta*); advertising strategy (*strategija ekonomske propagande*); concept, creation of the plan, and message (*koncepcija, kreacija plana i poruka*); execution (*realizacija*); and analysis (*analiza*).[128]

It is tempting to dismiss this deluge of diagrams, acronyms, and formulas as overly clever (or not clever enough) attempts to lend intellectual credibility to a discipline still profoundly uneasy about its second-class status. Without a doubt, all this attention to theory and process does reflect a lack of confidence (one that has plagued advertising and marketing in the West, too). Yet there is more at work in schemes like these than may be apparent at first glance. Understood in their larger political and ideological context, they appear as yet another example of the eagerness of the new Yugoslav industry to take advantage of the wisdom of the "lands of developed capitalism." What we see here is the importation of systematized, formulaic, and decidedly Western ways of thinking and talking about business. What came to Yugoslavia in devices like these was a mind-set that took business on internationally standardized terms, an approach to economic matters indelibly stamped by capitalist understandings of the supreme virtues of the market.

Real change was afoot, and many industry leaders sensed it. They recognized, moreover, that their own work was one of the most important instruments of that change. As one wrote, "it is indisputable that more modern understandings of marketing and advertising were, for a relatively long time, the 'clever gadget' used by only a few enterprises, but their expansion in commerce and in the marketplace has started to 'infect' [*djelovati zarazno*] the others to an ever increasing degree, and to *gradually control their way of looking at things*."[129]

---

126. Josip Šintić, "DAGMAR u teoriji i praksi EP," *Ideja*, no. 3 (July 1978): 17–23. That DAGMAR had been promulgated as an official theory of the largest advertising association in the world, the Association of National Advertisers, the writer said, "has given this model the greatest possible authority in our discipline." Ibid., 18.

127. See, for example, Dunja Hebrang and Miodrag Hitrec, "Znate li proces komuniciranja," *Ideja*, no. 6 (1973): 33–34.

128. See Sudar, *Ekonomska propaganda*, 15–16.

129. "Stasanje naše struke i društva," *Ideja*, no. 2 (February 1978): 7–14, at 10 (emphasis added).

Yugoslavia was indeed infected. But it is impossible to know whether the introduction of these foreign elements into the lifeblood of the country's economy would have, on its own, proved healthful or harmful, for just as the new orientation toward marketing and advertising was taking hold, the economy was beset by other troubles and collapsed into a malaise from which it would never recover.

It Keeps Going and Going and Going: Economic Scarcity, Advertising Abundance, and the End of the Yugoslav Dream, 1980-1991

The period from 1980 until the dissolution of the Yugoslav federation in 1991 saw the further expansion of an increasingly professionalized, sophisticated, and influential advertising and marketing industry, one that now regularly blanketed ordinary Yugoslavs with advertisements in print, on the radio, and on television. Institutionally the craft of commercial promotion was by this point quite healthy. Its members had finally realized some of their aspirations to professional status and managed to secure for themselves a relatively stable and well-respected place among the country's business élites. Success on this last count was never total, however, and the guild still seemed to be laboring against perceptions of inferiority.

Notwithstanding the continued progress on a number of fronts, the industry during this final period faced an enduring problem, one almost certainly worse than the uncertainties and political pressures of prior years. By 1980 the country had slipped into a fatal downward economic spiral, and this unwelcome and largely unexpected turn of events made the work of commercial promotion all the more difficult and, in turn, made the social consequences of advertising and consumer culture all the more problematic. For the men (and women—now their numbers were growing) whose activities had made them not just promoters of individual consumer products and services but also purveyors of a grand vision of expansive and expanding prosperity, the day-to-day effort to sell their clients' offerings to the public now became more of a challenge, as many ordinary citizens were much less able to afford the abundance that had, not long before, seemed to be one of the defining characteristics of Yugoslav socialism.

Now the once beautiful Yugoslav Dream started to fade away. It was during this last phase in the history of the socialist federation that a large and widening gap opened up between the realistic prospects of the consumer(ist) masses and the vision of prosperity and progress that had become a central feature of the country's consumer culture. The motivating force of a consumer culture grounded in abundance depends, in no small part, on the perception that the Good Life is, when all is said and done, *attainable*. Consumers will likely tolerate an awareness of some disparity between their own more modest circumstances and the proffered images of comfort, wealth, and sophistication. If, however, advertising is to spur on potential buyers to action—if it is to induce them to do what is required to make the purchase, even at the cost of sacrifices in other areas—then the visions "sold" to consumers need to be more than just empty dreams and escapist diversions. Instead, the gap between present realities and future consumerist satisfaction ought to appear bridgeable.

The downturn in the Yugoslav economy was so severe, and the reduction of living standards so drastic, that for many, if not most, Yugoslav citizens, the old vision of the Good Life would no longer seem attainable, or at least not attainable any time soon. The sudden disappearance of prosperity, however, would not have been possible to detect readily from a review of Yugoslav advertising itself during the 1980s. The most obvious visual manifestations of consumer culture, that is, advertisements, commercials, and retail displays, remained remarkably constant in their affirmation of the potential for better living through spending. Consumer outlays had to be curtailed, but the ads competing for the now scarcer dinars certainly did not disappear. If anything, the increased technical and creative sophistication of Yugoslav advertising work resulted in the presentation of a market culture that, at least in its outward, visible aspects, communicated even more reliably the messages of modernity, comfort, progress, and abundance, with the occasional little luxury thrown in for good measure in order to make the sense of consumption-as-reward sweeter still. There were some occasional exceptions. Shortages now began to plague the Yugoslav economy from time to time, leaving embarrassing gaps on store shelves where, for example, coffee or laundry detergent ought to have been. This sort of unpleasantness evoked the Soviet experience of shopping, something many Yugoslavs thought they had been spared. In the main, however, advertising in Yugoslavia in these last years still offered consumers a vision of the Good Life that held out the promise of the same abundance to which they had become so accustomed during the fat years of the 1960s and 1970s.

While the Yugoslav economy was slowly—or not so slowly—crumbling around them, the country's advertising and marketing specialists continued to practice, refine, and aggressively promote their craft, much as they had done in previous years. They published energetically, drawing heavily on insights from practice in the West. They flocked to all manner of professional conferences and training seminars both in Yugoslavia and abroad. They kept on traveling abroad when they could and came back full of new observations and ideas about how to do business and, in the process, perhaps save the Yugoslav economy.[130] They cultivated their extensive contacts with foreigners involved in the same line of work, and they so successfully built the image of Yugoslavia as a promising and dynamic site of advertising activity that they were able to convince the International Advertising

130. See, for example, Dane Urbanc, "Slovenski propagandisti v Ameriki!" *MM: marketing magazin*, no. 1 (May 1981): 7.

Association to hold its conference in Belgrade in 1983.[131] They pursued, as they had in the past, the elusive goals of professionalization and respectability, and they continued to encourage technical and creative sophistication with a now wholehearted embrace of their Western counterparts' practice of holding regular awards ceremonies, competitions, and festivals intended to recognize outstanding achievement. They shielded their work against a continuing stream of sometimes quite bitter social criticism, and at the same time they strengthened their ties to the powerful élites who managed the country's media institutions and business enterprises. They tried to take full advantage of the ongoing growth of the Yugoslav mass media.[132] They expanded their offices, created new agencies, and opened branch offices of existing ones across the country. And they multiplied: one 1988 industry source referenced approximately three thousand registered "*propagandisti.*"[133]

Superficially, at least, the business of commercial promotion in Yugoslavia therefore looked quite healthy in these final years. The pioneer spirit of earlier times, and the tone of defensiveness and insecurity that had once surfaced quite frequently in the trade literature, now abated somewhat, giving way to a more self-confident, comfortable, sophisticated, proud, and sometimes even bold and unapologetic manner of self-representation.

The focus here on the elements of continuity and progress in the work of Yugoslav advertising and marketing specialists is not meant to suggest that the industry was oblivious to the implications of the economic collapse for their products, their clients, and the place of their work in the larger scheme of self-management socialism. This was by no means the case. It was obvious to many in the field that, now more than ever, they were vulnerable to the old charge that they were seeking "to sell people things they don't need for money they don't have."[134] The trade literature is, in fact, replete with references to what industry leaders saw as their profession's crucial role in the effort to return the economy to its proper course. "Stabilization" and management of "the crisis" were the watchwords of the times, and the *propagandisti* viewed themselves and their work as essential to any recovery. They had, moreover, direct personal experience of the economic crisis through their regular dealings with enterprise managers.

---

131. For coverage of the conference, see, for example, Jure Apih, "Bila je svetovna konferenca propagandistov v Beogradu," *MM: marketing magazin*, no. 26 (June 1983): 1; other pieces in the same issue address the conference as well.

132. A useful overview of the growth of the Yugoslav mass media is provided in Slavko Splichal and France Vreg, *Množično komuniciranje in razvoj demokracije* (Ljubljana, 1986), see, esp., 71–126.

133. Mitrović, *O+P+P=: priručnik za upravljanje propagandom*, 26. There were still far fewer who specialized in marketing per se.

134. The phrase is from Dragan Tkalac, conference address in *Zbornik predavanja sa seminara vizuelne komunikacije* [Proceedings of the conference "Visual Communication and Advertising," Zagreb, 1975], ed. Mario Hladnik (Zagreb: Društvo ekonomskih propagandista Hrvatske, 1976), 53–59, at 53.

The decline did pose some special new dangers. Advertising, which was never fully accepted in the country's business culture, now seemed especially vulnerable as the kind of discretionary business expense that could be slated for dramatic reductions in a period of mandatory belt tightening. The new, leaner times also made it more difficult to support the wide range of professional activities that had flourished in the previous years. For example, the Zagreb trade journal *Kreativne komunikacije,* which since its inauguration in 1972 had been an especially lively voice not just for its parent enterprise but also for the industry as a whole, discontinued publication in 1983. *Ideja,* the journal of the Croatian professional society, met a similar fate, first cutting the size of its issues in half in 1979 and then ceasing publication entirely in 1981. (It would be resurrected, however, in 1988.)

Yet for all these losses to the industry, the message of the advertisements it produced tended, to a surprising extent, to remain much the same, dangling ever more of the Good Life in front of consumers who could afford less of it with each passing week. Yugoslavia's people were becoming poorer, but, if anything, the country's market culture was growing ever richer and more varied. Thus, for example, Levi's jeans, one of the vanguard brands of the increasingly aggressive, transnational consumerism promoted by the West following World War II, came to Yugoslavia under license in 1983. The arrival of this cultural icon was touted with a slick ad campaign, undertaken by Zagreb's Vjesnik Agency for Marketing, using the slogan "The Legend Lives"[135] (Figure 14).

Despite occasional instances when the more repressive side of the Yugoslav system shone through, the country's advertisers during this final period seemed emboldened to link consumerism with ideas about progress, modernity, and the Good Life, and they did so in a style even more markedly influenced by Western practices than had been the case in the past. By the early 1980s a reliance on Western concepts of good advertising and Western models of professionalism, already strong in previous years, found an unshakeable place in industry circles. Thus Belgrade's Mark-Plan Center for Marketing, in a trade-review advertisement for its services, promised potential clients that its work would be virtually indistinguishable from that of the large, well-known powerhouse firms of advertising in the capitalist world. If Mark-Plan was not quite an established international heavyweight, the advertisement promised, it was certainly the next best thing:

> We aren't McCann-Erickson, but...we have the same philosophy of a professional approach to the problems of clients and the same technology of work. Nor do we always see a business problem and the way of solving it as our client does—instead we study it critically. And our work motto is: be creative—do

---

135. "Legend je oživjela: Levi's," *Kreativne komunikacije,* no. 67 (1983): 24. The jeans were first manufactured in the northern Croatian town of Novi Marof by a unit of the large Yugoslav textile company Varteks.

research, make a diagnosis, give therapy, follow up, correct, conduct a post-therapeutic check of conditions, realize the goals of sales and sales policy!...If we don't know something, we know who knows.[136]

This effort to appropriate some of the cachet of the leading forces of capitalist advertising was not, it should be noted, an isolated incident. In the next issue of the journal, a follow-up message from Mark-Plan equated the firm's approach with the principles (and the successes) of yet another of the Western giants, the venerable Chicago-based Leo Burnett agency.[137] This sort of explicit invocation of foreign—and enthusiastically capitalist—models of success reveals just how deeply Western business practices and, perhaps even more important, Western thought about what "business" required had influenced the ideas and the work of Yugoslavia's commercial promotion specialists.

Visually as well, advertising in Yugoslavia's final decade was coming to resemble its analogues in the capitalist world even more closely, and the same held true, in large part, for the content of the advertising messages. Moreover, those who produced advertising tended to become even more ardent missionaries of the market, arguing that market mechanisms and the orientation toward consumer sovereignty that formed the foundation for their work could be the country's economic salvation. This line was perhaps most evident in the activist stance adopted by Ljubljana's Studio Marketing agency, an outgrowth of the large media enterprise that published, among other things, the main Slovenian daily newspaper *Delo*.

The work of Studio Marketing and rival Slovenian agencies reflects a critical shift in the practice of commercial promotion in Yugoslavia. Over the course of the 1980s Ljubljana largely eclipsed Zagreb and Belgrade as the center of gravity and creative dynamism in the country's advertising and marketing industry. Moreover, Slovenian specialists in the field, like a number of their fellows in the republic's manufacturing and commercial élites, came to see themselves as clearly more oriented toward a Western understanding of "business" than many of their counterparts elsewhere in the country.

The change was evident in the numbers, too. By the early 1980s Slovenia—despite its comparatively small population—had moved far ahead of other Yugoslav republics in the amounts spent on advertising. In 1977 Croatian expenditures had edged out those in Slovenia, 990 million dinars to 984 million; Serbia was in third place, spending (without its two autonomous provinces) only 524 million dinars. Slovenia moved ahead in the following year, and by 1982 its expenditures for advertising had almost doubled to 1.9 billion dinars, a figure that far outstripped the amount spent in Croatia, 1.36 billion

---

136. *MM: marketing magazin*, no. 20 (December 1982): 4.
137. Ibid., nos. 21/22 (February 1983): 6.

dinars. Serbia proper again lagged well behind both in terms of rate of growth and absolute expenditures, which totaled 756 million dinars in 1982.[138]

During these last years Studio Marketing became perhaps the single most sophisticated and enterprising advertising agency in Yugoslavia, and it certainly served as one of the most aggressive proponents of the marketing orientation. The agency's leaders, and its director Jure Apih in particular, used the house journal *MM: marketing magazin* as a platform to call for a thoroughgoing reorientation of Yugoslav policy along more consumerist lines. Although it was based in Ljubljana, Studio Marketing's ambit was truly Yugoslav: the firm therefore sought to make its case (and build its image) outside Slovenia as well, with a parallel Serbo-Croatian edition of *MM* published regularly and occasional issues in the major European languages.

The positions that Apih and his cohorts at Studio Marketing staked out represent the most notable departure from the general pattern of the industry's concerted efforts to maintain that advertising and marketing were fully in accordance with self-management socialism. That pattern had been clearest, of course, in the earliest years of the development of the field. In the work of Studio Marketing during the 1980s, by contrast, we can see the deference to socialist ideology begin to break down. The agency and its leaders were certainly not expressly antisocialist. Rather, they simply seem to have abandoned much of the pretense that they really cared about preserving socialist economics and harmonizing the work of commercial promotion with socialist political values.

As the economy worsened, the self-management system was, in general, becoming noticeably less sacrosanct. But nowhere in Yugoslavia was the impatience with the orthodoxies of self-management socialism stronger than in Slovenia, the part of the country where manufacturing and exports were most important to the economy and where the high standard of living had allowed the population to participate most fully in the consumerist pleasures of the two preceding decades.[139] Naturally enough, Slovenian advertising and marketing specialists were among the most prominent and influential of those leading a new challenge to what they understood as the lingering inefficiencies of socialism, calling for a new and less equivocal acceptance of market mechanisms and, in the process, celebrating the underlying logic of the market. The Slovenes were certainly not alone in this campaign. Something along the same lines was occasionally to be found in the work of advertising and marketing specialists in other parts of the country as well.[140] But Slovenian leadership on this front was remarkable, and remarkably important.

---

138. Ibid., no. 17 (1982); and no. 26 (1983), cited in Sudar, *Promotivne aktivnosti*, 89.

139. Susan Woodward, in *Balkan Tragedy*, explores the roots and consequences of Slovenian frustration with the management of the Yugoslav economy.

140. In the revived Croatian journal *Ideja*, for example, see "U slijepoj ulici polutržišne privrede," *Ideja*, no. 1 (fall 1988): 34–38; cf. the pro-market pronouncements of historian

Confounded by the inefficiencies and contradictions of the Yugoslav economic system, *MM* and the moving forces behind Studio Marketing sometimes adopted an astonishingly impatient tone. We find, for example, one *MM* contributor using his review of a new edition of a book by Fedor Rocco, the country's leading authority on marketing, to complain that the Yugoslav approach remained, after so much time and investment, hopelessly backward: "In 1971 we were twenty years behind the United States," the reviewer groused, "but now it's already a third of a century."[141] Sentiments like these, and there were many, attest to a real and spreading discontent with the existing system. The challenges had become more explicit, more uncompromising.

During the preceding periods in the industry's development, political sensitivities not infrequently had led advertising and marketing specialists to distance themselves and their work from the practice of the West. Pride sometimes seems to have been involved as well, as the common insistence on the value of Western knowledge occasionally rankled some leaders of the Yugoslav field. In this spirit Žozef Lončar, the editor of Belgrade's *Privredna propaganda*, had urged Yugoslav industry specialists in 1972 to try something other than the habitual imitation of styles and practices perfected elsewhere: "Let's stop discovering America!" Lončar exhorted his colleagues. "When it was necessary, Columbus did that."[142]

But in the final period of the industry's development in socialist Yugoslavia, such sentiments seem to have been on the wane. In their stead, leaders of the profession began to advocate more openly a vision that acknowledged commercial promotion in Yugoslavia, both in function and in norm, as part and parcel of a globally valid paradigm of advertising, marketing, and retailing—one that may have had its origins in the West but was just as suitable for Yugoslav use.

Audacious as it was, this new stance represents in some ways just a more frank expression of values that, as described in the subsections above with reference to both the periods 1950–1965 and 1965–1980, had long been implicit in the industry's work. But there was more at work here, and more at stake: by coming into the open as it did, and by emerging most clearly in Slovenia, where it could be coupled with and amplify an incubating separatism, the industry's new willingness to promote the values of the market hardened the mounting challenges to the Yugoslav status quo. In this way, it

---

(and communist official) Dušan Bilandžić, "Tržište: jedini lijek za oboljeli socijalizam," *Ideja*, no. 1 (fall 1988): 6–7.

141. Miro Kline, "30 let zaostanka," *MM: marketing magazin*, no. 20 (December 1982): 3, 6 [review of Fedor Rocco, *Teorija in praksa raziskovanja marketinga*]. The reviewer complained that the book, previously published in 1971 and 1976, had been updated only to a small extent from prior editions. For a contrary assessment, see Vlado Pekle, "Z obratno pošto," *MM: marketing magazin* (Slovenian edition), nos. 24/25 (April/May 1983): 5–6.

142. Žozef Lončar, "Pismo odgovornog urednika," *Privredna propaganda* 3, nos. 17–18 (September 1972): 3–4, at 4.

contributed to the centrifugal forces that undermined support for the socialist government and ultimately brought about the dissolution of the federation.

The creation of a vital commercial culture rooted in ideas of the importance of market values and "business sense" thus proved critical to the fate of the Yugoslav experiment. Once, that business culture had served to undergird the stability of the regime, indeed even to help unify Yugoslav society through the creation of an integrated, functional national market. With time, however, and especially in the crisis years of the 1980s, it worked in the other direction. As the market culture that was propagated in advertisements and the media fueled frustration by continuing to emphasize alluring but now less attainable images of abundance, the intensified pro-market mentality of the commercial elites ate away at any remaining patience for the socialist status quo, while at the same time local business communities in the more prosperous and liberal centers of economic activity came to see themselves as being dragged down by a federal structure that, they believed, stifled innovation, taxed success, and subsidized complacency. The idea of consumer sovereignty unleashed forces that, in the end, could not be contained.

In astonishingly short order, market culture in Yugoslavia had begun to function, to a significant extent, independently of the specifics of the country's economic performance. It had become, in essence, "a machine that would go of itself." When economic progress ground to a halt, this new cultural engine managed to grind on without it, generating many of the same messages, desires, tastes, and needs as in earlier, happier times. Now, however, the consequences were strikingly different. As we will see in the concluding sections of this account, a grave disillusionment with the end of the Yugoslav Dream was one of the important factors that led to a growing rejection of continued communist rule and a widespread popular openness to ethno-national "solutions" to the country's many problems. Yugoslavia's widely shared culture of consumption, which for a time had stabilized the existing order, would now help bring it down.

3 Selling It

Legitimizing the Appeal of Market Culture

> Advertising [*ekonomski publicitet*] is something completely new in the
> socialist economy. Up until now, this topic has been addressed only to
> a relatively small extent in this country. We cannot transfer and take
> advantage of certain experiences of the Western countries, which
> have gone considerably further ahead in the field of advertising, because
> we are aware that these are a reflection of the capitalist economy.
> —Dušan P. Mrvoš, *Propaganda, reklama, publicitet*

> It is increasingly accepted that advertising works over the long term,
> and...for it to be successful, it must be in harmony with the accepted
> system of values and understandings in the given society.
> —Momčilo Milisavljević, "Društveno-ekonomska
> uloga ekonomske propagande"

Yugoslavia's departure from Stalinism opened the door to new attitudes toward commercial promotion, but those in positions of authority typically did not treat advertising and marketing as "natural" elements of the country's commercial life. The atmosphere of official skepticism and even outright hostility did not disappear overnight. Rather, advertising and marketing activities—and, at times, even the very concepts themselves—had to be naturalized. To accomplish this, a small dedicated cadre of specialists mounted an aggressive campaign aimed at securing their creative autonomy, building an industry, and winning a place for themselves as respected professionals alongside other members of the country's economic elites. This chapter examines that struggle to legitimize commercial promotion, to transform it from a seemingly useless relic of a spurned capitalist past into a necessity of modern, rational, socialist production and distribution.

Sources for the epigraphs: Dušan P. Mrvoš, *Propaganda, reklama, publicitet: teorija i praksa* (Belgrade: OZEHA Zavod za ekonomsku propagandu i publicitet, 1959), 9; Momčilo Milisavljević, "Društveno-ekonomska uloga ekonomske propagande" [abridged version of address to the Conference of Radio-Television Centers and Subscribers, Dubrovnik, 6 November 1975], *Ideja*, no. 3 (December 1975): 4–6, at 5.

These efforts to sway political and public opinion are highly instructive. In the first place, they speak volumes about the nature and extent of the opposition that advertisers faced as they tried to secure a place for their craft. The tone of the trade sources and the kinds of arguments presented there, furthermore, reveal how those in the maturing industry perceived the limitations on their creative freedom, how they assessed their strengths and vulnerabilities, how they defined an agenda for the future of their profession, and how they maneuvered to establish their own, business-oriented values as legitimate within Yugoslav society. Because the barriers they met were often more a matter of a hostile political climate rather than any restrictive regulations or other overt official strictures, interpreting the industry literature sometimes becomes an exercise in reading between the lines—a task familiar to historians of communism—to determine just what it was that the advertising specialists experienced as hindrances to their work.

Their long push for acceptance offers, moreover, an important illustration of the ways in which advertising and marketing, practices that might appear to be tightly or even inseparably linked to Western-style capitalism, could nevertheless be harmonized—in theory if not necessarily in practice—with the ideological imperatives of Marxist-Leninist governance.

Finally, and more generally, there are definite parallels between some parts of the Yugoslav story and the sustained struggle of capitalist advertising professionals to justify their work as nothing less than an affirmative social good, and at the same time as nothing more, as the idea was expressed in the slogan of industry giant McCann-Erickson, than "Truth Well Told." That deft little formulation manages to capture an important part of the ethos of the advertising and marketing specialists of socialist Yugoslavia: like their counterparts at the unapologetically capitalist McCann-Erickson firm, the often quite apologetic Yugoslavs continually characterized their work as both artful (the creations of highly skilled professionals) and truthful (informative, not deceptive). Yet the socialist environment did make a real difference, and in the end the Yugoslav industry's efforts at self-legitimization underscore certain key distinctions between the brand of market culture that gradually developed in Yugoslavia and the more familiar and more thoroughly studied circumstances that nurtured the growth of advertising and marketing in the West.

Truth Half Told: Finding the Perfect Pitch for Commercial Promotion in a Socialist System

Members of the country's steadily growing advertising and marketing institutions couched their work in soothing terms, as a benign, value-neutral, even apolitical endeavor, but in reality the political context inevitably stamped that work. In Yugoslavia, as elsewhere, consumerism found no shortage of critics. In some circles there arose fierce resistance to the perceived social dangers of unbridled consumer desire, and even at the time of their greatest breakthroughs, representatives of the industry were clearly feeling the bite of what had become, across the country, an open, sustained conflict over the proper role of advertising and marketing. By 1973, for example, the Zagreb-based trade journal *Ideja* could cite a "broad social debate about advertising" that brought those working in the field face to face with "an astonishing confusion, and even fear" concerning the nature and consequences of commercial promotion.[1] In such circumstances the advertising and marketing industry was obliged to sell the Yugoslav people much more than the rapidly expanding array of products its clients were offering their customers. Advertising and marketing specialists also needed to sell the public—and, just as important, politicians and even business leaders—on the notion that their services were useful, beneficial, necessary, and fully consistent with the values of Yugoslavia's socialist society.

To those who have observed how disputes over consumption have unfolded in other more customary (that is, capitalist) settings, some of the arguments advanced for and against the elevation of consumerist priorities in Yugoslavia will likely seem familiar. In the specific circumstances of Yugoslav socialism, however, these controversies played out in a highly unusual fashion. The complicated, unwieldy economic and political system that resulted from the turn to self-management left its own distinctive marks on the national debate over advertising and marketing, shaping it in ways that make this case especially instructive for scholars interested in the global reach of market culture. Opponents of consumerism had uncommon powers to constrain its influence, while advocates of an orientation that would be more frankly grounded in consumer desire enjoyed an intellectual and practical freedom rare in a Marxist-Leninist polity.

With time, the business of commercial promotion managed to establish a solid structure across the country: as of 1988 Yugoslavia had almost one hundred marketing and advertising agency offices, not including the numerous internal marketing and advertising units within the country's many radio and television institutions and publishing houses.[2] Still, despite its institutional security, the industry could never afford to abandon its defensive posture completely.

But the *propagandisti* were not just reacting. They were constantly creating as well: creating wants, creating values, creating *culture*. To understand how this happened—how and why Yugoslavia saw such an unusual efflorescence of market culture—we first need to focus on the processes of contestation and legitimation that proved critical to the generation of new

---

1. "Otvorena pitanja ekonomske propagande," *Ideja*, no. 4 (September 1973): 13.
2. Mitrović, *O+P+P=: priručnik za upravljanje propagandom*, 299–315.

desires and new perceived needs among the country's shoppers—and no less important, critical to the ideological justification of those wishes and needs as well. To this end, the examination now turns to the wide array of arguments advanced in favor of a new, prominent place for commercial promotion, arguments crafted by those who in studies of consumption and market culture have typically been treated, either despite all their considerable influence or precisely because of it, as "the intellectual savages of the commercial world—advertisers, marketers, packagers, and the media."[3] It is a story of dogged perseverance in the face of powerful resistance, perseverance born of a sincere belief that a strong new emphasis on consumer desires would serve the best interests of the economy. It is, furthermore, at least in certain passages, a story of surprising willingness to work against the prevailing Marxist skepticism toward advertising and marketing. In the end, however, it is also inescapably a story of the clever package and the artful dodge, one in which ideologies were obscured, values concealed, influences disowned, and agendas acknowledged only partially, if at all—a story, as it were, of Truth *Half* Told.

As this twist on the McCann-Erickson slogan suggests, some skepticism toward the claims and postures of these marketing and advertising specialists will likely be apparent in the analysis that follows. But the paramount concerns here are cause and consequence, mechanism and meaning, and the point is not to judge whether the advertising and marketing mavens were *accurately* describing the benefits of their work. Instead, the weight given to the arguments made in the trade is a natural consequence of a quite different interest in determining whether, and how, socialist values might be reconciled with the various forms of modern commercial advertising, which usually has been at least superficially capitalist in its outward manifestations (and, many claim, deeply capitalist in its embedded ideology).

The concern for the rhetoric behind the growth of Yugoslav commercial promotion thus constitutes an acknowledgment of the larger historical importance of the advertisers' campaign for acceptance and, with an eye to questions of origins and effects, a recognition of the skill with which industry representatives pleaded their case. Indeed, a chief conclusion here is that in preparing the social and political terrain for what they hoped would be a radical expansion of their craft, these industry advocates were forced by the Yugoslav political climate to intellectualize the presentation of their work to an extent rarely seen elsewhere—rarely seen, I believe, because rarely needed. Craving respect, they consistently portrayed themselves as master practitioners of serious, intellectually demanding disciplines.

---

3. Ben Fine and Ellen Leopold, *The World of Consumption* (London, 1993), 255.

Making the Sale: Advertising, Marketing, and the Rhetoric of Legitimacy

Starting from extraordinarily modest beginnings, specialists in the arts of commercial promotion gradually claimed a place in socialist Yugoslavia for their craft. More precisely, they *reclaimed* a place for their work, because consumer advertising and those who engaged in it had, as we have seen, all but disappeared during the hard years from 1945 to 1950. Beginning in the 1950s, when the first treatises and articles began appearing in significant numbers, groups of industry activists worked with determination to drive home the message that advertising and marketing were not just a collection of simple skills and tricks. Over time, they made real headway in building the legitimacy of their profession in the eyes of policy makers and others in positions of authority in government and commerce (and, less directly, in the eyes of the broader public as well, though there is good reason to conclude that public opinion about advertising was shaped much more immediately by advertisements themselves than by any rationale the industry offered in defense of its activities). Representatives of various government institutions, typically friendly or at least not overtly hostile, were frequently placed on the speakers' roster at advertising and marketing conferences. This was most likely done not merely to acquaint the industry audience with the latest views of those "inside" the structures of government and party power but also (and perhaps more important) as part of a strategy to secure and, at the same time, display conspicuously the authorities' seal of approval—to communicate that there did indeed exist good party functionaries who were supportive of, even enthusiastic about, the expanding role of advertising and marketing in Yugoslav society.

Given the promoters' relentless campaign to impart a measure of conceptual *gravitas* to their work, the analysis of the industry's arguments and the ways in which its ideas spread becomes fundamentally a task of establishing the connections between the more familiar narratives of Yugoslavia's unsettled political and economic history and a fragment, albeit an unusual one, of the history of ideas in Europe. For in a number of ways the importation of advertising and marketing ideology to Yugoslavia may best be understood as part of a broader transfer to the Continent of American (and to some extent British) understandings of business-consumer relations. Whether or not we might ultimately conclude that the works studied are the insubstantial products of a band of "intellectual savages," there were plenty of ideas in them, and they do indeed reflect a larger process of conceptual and cultural importation, modification, and dissemination. High intellectual history this is not, but our proper concern here is not so much the sophistication of the industry's intellectual defense but rather the *influence* of its argumentation, and this was a campaign with considerable influence.

The struggle to carve out a niche for advertising and marketing came into public view in the mid- to late 1950s, when leading industry figures in

Belgrade and Zagreb launched the first specialty publications and arranged for the printing of the first comprehensive manuals for training a new cadre. The campaign got off to a slow start. As late as 1958 Mirko Sagrak, the organizer of an after-hours course in advertising and publicity (*ekonomska propaganda*) at one of Zagreb's "Workers' Universities" for professional and technical training, could complain with some justification about the lack of appropriate educational literature for his students:

> As far as I know not a single work about advertising has been published in our country from the Liberation until today, either in the original or in translation. Leaving aside several articles in our specialist journals, there is no material in our language [Serbo-Croatian] that could serve as literature either for students in seminars or for lecturers. What little that has been published in the field of advertising is concerned in most cases with tourism, and to a somewhat lesser extent with hotel management [*ugostiteljstvo*] and trade [*trgovina*].[4]

In truth, the situation was perhaps not quite as dire as this frustrated advertising instructor indicated. As explained in the previous chapter, a small but lively domestic literature on advertising had indeed already developed by 1958, most notably through the efforts of the trade groups in Zagreb and Belgrade that published the journals *Naš publicitet* and *Savremena privredna propaganda*. Yet, as Sagrak suggested, little of that material was of the practical, instructional nature most useful to novices. And discussion of advertising up to that point had indeed remained disproportionately focused on tourism and the export trade, probably because those activities involved "safe" presentations directed at foreigners and thus did not raise concerns about the possible noxious effects of advertising on the citizens of a socialist society.

But these earliest instances of Yugoslav professional activism were nevertheless formative and important. Into the ideological clearing that they created there followed a new wave of institution building that yielded a wide-ranging body of trade literature during the next decade, including a healthy selection of Western works in translation and, later still, an explosion of publishing activity in the 1970s and 1980s. The abortive professional journals of the 1950s and 1960s, many of which were, as we have seen, the self-promoting house organs of individual advertising agencies, gave way to better-funded, broader-based, more comprehensive, and (sometimes) more enduring reviews that often sought to transcend the concerns of a particular institution and to represent the emerging profession.

As an indicator of the broader sociopolitical context in which the campaign to legitimize advertising and marketing went forward, the rhetoric used to defend the industry in this Yugoslav specialty literature warrants

---

4. Mirko Sagrak, *Ekonomska propaganda: programi* (Zagreb, 1958), 17.

especially close consideration. In one important way, the Yugoslav sources prove just as significant for what is missing as they do for the arguments chosen. The increasingly rich scholarship on consumer culture in the West, and especially in the United States, highlights the distinctive tendency of advertising specialists to speak frankly, even proudly, about the capacity of their work to transport ordinary consumers (even if only fleetingly) beyond the humdrum of the workaday world and into an imaginary domain of higher social status, more leisure, lasting youth and beauty, and vastly expanded purchasing power. Such grand claims and aspirations are conspicuously absent from the discourse of the Yugoslav specialists. Although they were often well versed in the Western advertising and marketing canon, industry proponents tended to shy away from acknowledging their role as merchants of fantasy and wish-fulfillment, builders of the democratized "dream worlds" of escape, luxury, and exoticism that Rosalind Williams has described in her critical analysis of consumerism in French society at the end of the nineteenth century.[5]

In the West the engineers of consumer culture often spoke openly about their role as vendors of the ideal and the unreal. William Leach, for example, relates how one American speaker at a convention of retail display workers in 1923 told her audience, in no uncertain terms, to embrace their calling:

> Sell them their dreams. Sell them what they longed for and hoped for and almost despaired of having. Sell them hats by splashing sunlight across them. Sell them dreams—dreams of country clubs and proms and visions of what might happen if only. After all, people don't buy things to have things. They buy things to work for them. They buy hope—hope of what your merchandise will do for them. Sell them this hope and you won't have to worry about selling them goods.[6]

Such unabashed appeals to the transformative power of shopping and buying are found almost nowhere in the record left behind by the Yugoslav industry. It is virtually unthinkable that a Yugoslav advertising or marketing specialist would have stated for public consumption, as did one American writer in the formative years of modern advertising in the West, that "the people are seeking to escape from themselves. They want to live in a more exciting world."[7] The diagnosis might have been just as true of Yugoslav

---

5. See Rosalind H. Williams, *Dream Worlds: Mass Consumption in Late Nineteenth-Century France* (Berkeley, 1982), 58–106.

6. Helen Landon Cass, *Philadelphia Retail Ledger*, 6 June 1923, 6, quoted in William Leach, *Land of Desire: Merchants, Power, and the Rise of a New American Culture* (New York, 1993), 298.

7. *Advertising and Selling* (8 September 1926), 27, quoted in Marchand, *Advertising the American Dream*, xvii.

consumers, of course. But the marked absence of appeals to liberation from the quotidian suggests that such rhetoric was deemed out of bounds.

Also largely unacknowledged in the self-representation of the Yugoslav industry specialists is the potential that their work could (re)awaken a concern for social status and reinforce class divisions in a society that was supposed to be uncompromisingly egalitarian. The issue did sometimes arise, usually in response to criticism from without, but it was typically handled with quick, superficial denials that appealed to the democratic values of socialism that were said to undergird Yugoslav advertising practice. Western advertising, in contrast, had grown comfortable with its role as a purveyor of status. Indeed, that process was long since consolidated by the time the postwar Yugoslav industry began taking its first tentative steps. As James D. Norris concludes in his study of commercial culture in the United States during the late nineteenth and early twentieth centuries, American advertising "sold the concept of consumption as the means to achieve social status."[8]

In their daily communications with consumers, the creators of Yugoslav advertising, just like their Western counterparts, sometimes really did work as dream weavers, trafficking in similar emotional appeals. But in their talk *about* advertising and marketing, in their long conversation with those who held the reins of political and economic power in the country, they steered clear of any mention of dreams and hopes and flights of fancy. Instead, their rhetoric bent to the imperatives of socialist politics: it remained cool, rational, and circumspect, marked by its claims to offer straightforward, practical, and, above all, reliable information to meet consumers' real needs.

Trust the Professionals: Standards, Image, and the Needs of the People

One recurring motif in the Yugoslav industry literature, especially early on, was a pronounced guild mentality, a stance that was simultaneously defensive and energetically self-promoting, characterized by concerns about image and quality control and by anxiety over the pressing need for the professionalization of the craft. In this respect Yugoslav advertising specialists were participating, albeit with some delay, in a much larger process that originated in the United States and Europe, where workers in the infant industries of commercial promotion also had struggled to secure their positions.

Faced with their own crisis of legitimacy, advertising workers in the developed capitalist countries had fretted about their inferior status almost from the beginning, and in the first half of the twentieth century they had

---

8. Norris, *Advertising and the Transformation of American Society, 1865–1920*, 168.

embarked on a wholehearted campaign for professionalization, an effort that was intended as much to raise their status in the eyes of clients and other businesspeople and professionals as it was to codify and enforce standards of quality and conduct. American advertisers, for example, formed an Advertising Association in 1926 to "promote public confidence in advertising and advertised goods through the correction or suppression of abuses."[9]

The precise "cure" needed was uncertain, however, and the move toward professional standards could take a variety of forms. In his classic study of the trade, Roland Marchand notes that advertising leaders in the United States, frustrated with the lack of respect granted to their work, developed two alternative paradigms of professionalism. The first stressed the need for serious professional training, public service, and "cultural uplift"; the second sought to win legitimacy by emphasizing "the narrower professionalism of the 'real pro' who loyally supplied his client with practical expertise."[10] At least in their public pronouncements, Yugoslav advertising specialists seemed emphatically to favor the first of these two models, although it remains unclear how they represented themselves in private communications with clients. There is good reason to suspect the Yugoslavs' public preference for the "professional standards" model is largely the product of a political climate that, initially at least, devalued business as such and the competitive skills associated with it.

Even in the sites of advertising's greatest successes, the struggle for acceptance has been a long one. The industry's history has been, since its earliest episodes, continually plagued by the idea that this was a business that needed fixing, and fast. In this connection, T. J. Jackson Lears dates the American ad agents' quest for legitimacy back to the earliest years of their work in urban centers during the 1850s and 1860s. For advertising specialists, Lears concludes, the perceived deficits in status were especially urgent: these men "partook of the Barnumesque aura surrounding all publicity enterprises," and their "stock-in-trade epitomized the insubstantiality and elasticity of value in a commodity civilization."[11]

It was precisely this deeply ingrained public perception of the potential for abuse, if not outright charlatanry, that the Yugoslav innovators inherited from those who had made capitalist advertising such a noteworthy but also notorious phenomenon. As such, the effort to legitimize Yugoslav advertising was not just hindered by opposition generated domestically but was also burdened from the beginning by the less than spotless record advertising and its creators had already racked up in the West. Understandably, then, Yugoslav

---

9. Unidentified industry publication quoted in William Leiss, Stephen Kline, and Sut Jhally, *Social Communication in Advertising: Persons, Products, and Images of Well-Being* (New York, 1986), 136.

10. Marchand, *Advertising the American Dream*, 25–26, and, more generally, 25–51.

11. Lears, *Fables of Abundance*, 89.

advertising and marketing specialists often talked about their work with distinct undertones of wariness and uncertainty about the future. Sources from the 1950s and 1960s in particular, but even those from later years when the field was more secure, bemoan the sorry state of public awareness about the benefits of advertising and its "true nature" as an engine of national economic well-being.[12]

Especially strong was the idea that the Yugoslav educational system slighted advertising at both the secondary and the university levels, leaving the profession sadly limited in numbers, geographic range, and influence. As a result, it was suggested, Yugoslav enterprises were robbed of the tools they required to respond effectively to the needs of potential buyers, dragging down the entire economy in the process. Well into the 1970s the trade literature was still replete with references to the lamentable, backward state of professional standards and training. There was plenty of blame to spread around: industry writers also inveighed against the rampant dilettantism they saw in Yugoslav business, where too many enterprise managers apparently thought they could do without the services of advertising and marketing specialists and simply cobble together promotional campaigns on their own.

Those who usually made such arguments were, of course, more than impartial reporters on trends in advertising and marketing. Much of the specialty literature evidenced a genuine concern for the success of the craft and for its prospects in a not always welcoming socialist milieu, but there was also an inescapable element of self-promotion. The people framing these presentations had a great stake in enhancing their images as expert, successful, and well-connected professionals in order to drum up new business and to assure existing clients that they were receiving first-rate services. Obviously, then, all the concentration on professionalism amounted to more than just a high-minded insistence on ethics.

There were strong suggestions of the defense—or creation—of disciplinary and professional boundaries. Just what did it take, for example, to design the packaging of a consumer product? Who had the qualifications to do so? Should only those deemed "qualified" be permitted to create packages? And would advertising enterprises be permitted to undertake this kind of work? The correspondence preserved in the files of the Association of Advertising Enterprises shows that in the late 1950s and early 1960s questions like these were on the minds of many of the new industry's leaders, sparking a number of interpersonal and inter-firm disputes, some of them quite bitter.[13] In much the same spirit, the archives show that one principal

---

12. For a particularly clear example, see Mihovil Skobe, "U obranu ekonomskog publiciteta i propagande," *Naš publicitet* 4, no. 2 (1957): 4–6.

13. See, for example, letter from Žarko Topolčić, head of the Biro za ambalažu pri Trgovinskoj Komori NRH, to Zagreb's Interpublic office, 19 April 1957. In 1959 the state authorities

representative of the Zagreb agency OZEHA was arguing forcefully against the admission of "fairs and graphic-arts collectives" to the new professional association. Such groups confined their promotional activities to exercises in applied art, and that sort of work, Velimir Kovačić insisted in 1957, was not the primary calling of true advertising institutions. As such, he believed, these enterprises had no place in the new Association.[14]

This pronounced emphasis on professional gatekeeping and standards of quality parallels similar trends seen in the history of many other fields and many other places. Alfred D. Chandler's monumental study of business managers in various U.S. industries in the late nineteenth and early twentieth centuries credits professionalization with promoting efficiency, cooperation among enterprises, and the creation of a common outlook on business matters,[15] all outcomes that concern us here in connection with the Yugoslav case. Absent from Chandler's interpretation, however, is any overriding sense that the movement for managerial professionalization in the particular branches of industry that he studied served a major *defensive* role, that is, as a process of remedial accreditation by which people employed in these fields could shore up the perceived vulnerabilities in their social status.

The situation for the field of advertising has been quite different. For advertising workers in America, Yugoslavia, and elsewhere in both the socialist and capitalist worlds, a self-protective posture has proved to be a near constant.

Notwithstanding some of these common dilemmas, certain aspects of the Yugoslav campaign for professionalization were clearly linked to the distinctive political context and the unstable terrain on which the country's commercial promotion specialists found themselves. There was, for example, a pronounced tendency to identify advertising's purportedly bad values and harmful manifestations with advertising as it was known in capitalist countries, or with the crude, amateurish, and unenlightened practices of half-trained or self-trained advertising dilettantes (practices that were exacerbated, it was hinted, by the effective suppression of advertising in the immediate postwar period). Zagreb's OZEHA, with its roots reaching back

sought to clarify the matter with the issuance of a statement confirming that the design and printing of packaging, labels, brochures, forms, and promotional books were properly a part of the work of an advertising enterprise. Communication from Josip Garvan, pomoćnik Državnog Sekretarijata za poslove robnog prometa FNRJ, to the Udruženje preduzeća za ekonomsku propagandu i publicitet, 7 February 1959. Arhiv Jugoslavije, collection Stručno udruženje preduzeća za ekonomsku propagandu i publicitet, AJ-262-3.

14. Velimir Kovačić, quoted in meeting transcript, Stenografski zapisnik 6 sastanka preduzeća za ekonomsku propagandu i publicitet FNRJ koji je održan na Bledu 30-VIII-1957 god., 12–13. Arhiv Jugoslavije, collection Stručno udruženje preduzeća za ekonomsku propagandu i publicitet, AJ-262-1. The OZEHA representative was calling for the exclusion of one member institution, Belgrade's Zavod primenjenih umetnosti [Institute for the Applied Arts].

15. Alfred D. Chandler Jr., *The Visible Hand: The Managerial Revolution in American Business* (Cambridge, Mass., 1977); see, esp., 130–133, 464–468.

to the interwar years and perhaps the strongest tradition of professional expertise, was particularly strident in denouncing "dilettantism." Its leaders frequently belittled the crude advertisements of the command-economy period. As one wrote: "Messages that just scream out 'we want to sell!' aren't worth anything, because all the rest are also screaming more or less the same thing, mercilessly squandering the budget of the enterprise [*kolektiv*]."[16] What was required, OZEHA's leaders and other authors insisted, was genuinely creative advertising undertaken by experts.

Tellingly, however, the unwholesome side of advertising was not identified with the capitalist experience per se. On the contrary, Yugoslav specialists repeatedly voiced their confidence that much of value could be gleaned from the highly developed practices of the West. One early source, for example, looked expressly to the practices of England, the United States, and France for models of how to do things "when it is desired that advertising be in the hands of the right people—experts." The writer noted with approval that "this work was already, several decades earlier, assumed by highly educated specialists" [*naučnici*, a word that ordinarily means "scientists" or "scholars"].[17] Other contributors rankled at the idea that "advertising is not a skilled craft [*zanat*]" and that "anyone can take care of it."[18]

Those who spoke for the interests of the trade also implied that, at least with regard to advertising, Yugoslavia's constrained and underdeveloped economy in the decades before the Communists assumed power had allowed businesses and their customers to experience only the darker side of capitalist development. If politicians, businesspeople, and ordinary citizens in Yugoslavia had previously developed a strong negative image of advertising, the industry advocates reasoned, these audiences had arrived at such dim views either because much of what they had encountered in the days before socialism was the old, primitive, unprofessional sort of advertising with all its defects, or because they were disproportionately familiar with examples of "bad" Western advertising—that is, with extreme, but fairly uncommon and hence overly publicized, cases of abuse.[19]

---

16. Dušan P. Mrvoš, "Važnost propagande za našu privredu," *Naš publicitet* 1 (August 1954). Compare, in the same issue, Vitasović, "O ekonomičnosti propagande."

17. "Ko treba da vodi reklamu," *Savremena privredna propaganda* 2 (April 1958): 28–29, at 28. For a sense of the great esteem accorded Western advertising, notwithstanding the rhetoric about possible abuses, see, in the same issue of this industry journal, "Francuska industriska reklama," 21; see also B. Novković, "Rad i organizacija preduzeća za privrednu propagandu J. Walter Thomson [*sic*] Co. u Beču," *Propaganda* 2 (March 1968): 13–14. Specialists associated with other aspects of consumerism in Yugoslavia showed the same keen interest in the West. See, for example, the favorable report, with photographs, on a "typical Swiss supermarket": "Švicarski supermarket: mnoštvo usluga," *Supermarket: časopis za praksu suvremene trgovine* 1 (May 1976): 15–17.

18. "Štete od nestručnjaka i samozvanih stručnjaka," *Savremena privredna propaganda* 2 (April 1958): 6.

19. For a critical industry view of Western advertising, see "Propaganda i ekonomski publicitet," *Naš publicitet* 2 (September 1955).

In this view, earlier advertising often had been an instrument of destructive, profit-driven competition, too ready to mislead, seduce, or slander in order to make the sale and drive competitors out of the market. Now, however, the industry proposed something new and decidedly different: a fusion of socialist values with the positive aspects of the impressive business practices perfected in the lands of "developed capitalism." Against the image of the bad old days of deceptive or ineffective sales pitches and crude appeals based largely on guesswork, the Yugoslav guild promised a future of serious, responsible, socially conscious professionalism that would benefit all participants in the Yugoslav economy: producers, workers, and consumers.

In that endeavor, reliance on the idea that modern commercial promotion rested on a sophisticated academic infrastructure proved critical. In their quest to build legitimacy, the new Yugoslav advertising and marketing professionals showed much the same taste for impressive theorization as did their colleagues in the West. As explained in the preceding chapter, they turned out to be at least as smitten with grand conceptual formulations that depict promotional work within economic and psychological "systems" approaches (and in so doing, some say, veil what is quite often an assemblage of ad hoc responses to unforeseen new problems, with little of the detailed market information and painstaking planning such theories presuppose). For practitioners in both settings, one path to security and esteem was to invoke such ideas in order to intellectualize the work of advertising and marketing, thereby cordoning off these practices as expert knowledge possessed only by those with advanced and highly specialized training. Representative of such sentiments was one early writer's insistence that "advertising be approached with complete attention, and [that] the very delicate mission which advertising fulfills be entrusted to top-quality experts who recognize that however capricious the laws of the market may be, the desires of the enormous masses of consumers are more capricious still."[20]

There were, however, certain inherent contradictions in this expert-oriented stance, tensions that were exacerbated by the communist political system's overarching concern for the interests of the common people. Advertising and marketing could claim to be elite disciplines offering (and requiring) special expertise in the service of the Yugoslav economy, but the day-to-day business of commercial promotion inevitably involved simple, direct communications with ordinary consumers and, moreover, relied on the trust and goodwill of business enterprise managers who lacked the supposedly indispensable expert knowledge of the advertising and marketing specialists. To win the confidence of those target audiences and to convince Yugoslav politicians to entrust them with such a constant and conspicuous

---

20. V. M., "Dobra reklama—uslov za uspeh," *Savremena privredna propaganda* 1 (August 1957): 6.

presence in the country's mass media, the industry's representatives also needed a complementary, more uncomplicated formulation of the nature of their work. Their language thus wavered between the imposingly intellectualized and the reassuringly practical. In either case, the power of advertising and marketing was seen as real and reliable, but its nature was inconstant: at times quite arcane, at times wonderfully straightforward.

The public's interaction with advertising clearly came through the simpler, more accessible side of commercial promotion highlighted in the industry's self-portrayals. Adopting a measured, unprovocative, matter-of-fact tone, advertising specialists continually stressed the innocent, informative quality of their work. The early trade literature especially tended to underscore advertising's capacity to help consumers:

> Our working person accepts advertising because he instinctively feels that it is useful to him. Every day we read in the daily press that this or that device is being produced, but the stores have neither brochures nor user instructions, nor is it announced in the newspapers that the product has already appeared on the market. This means that the working person feels that as a buyer, he is being ignored, or that no one is taking account of his wishes sufficiently."[21]

For all these ills, the specialists proposed a remedy: *informative* advertising.

The emphasis on commercial promotion as a harmless conduit for information and education was especially strong in the early years of the craft's development, but it lasted throughout the socialist period, formulated in increasingly sophisticated terms. Thus one industry leader reminded a gathering of his colleagues in 1975 that "we are, above all, professional communicators of the economic subsystem of the society, with the duty of transmitting economic information—primarily, information for consumers."[22] At another conference the same year, attended by both Yugoslav and Western representatives, the keynote speaker sounded much the same theme, stressing that "advertising [*ekonomska propaganda*]...in the conditions of a socialist self-management society must occupy a position *for the benefit of the individual/consumer,* and thus assume the role of a *useful carrier of information* between producers and consumers."[23]

If information was supposedly the primary product of Yugoslav advertising, its most basic goal was said to be helping consumers satisfy their needs. Once again, the industry's rhetoric clearly betrayed a certain defensiveness.

---

21. Editors, "Što je za nas najvažnije u 1957. godine?" *Naš publicitet* 4, no. 1 (1957): 2, 8, at 2.

22. Ante Batarelo, "Uvodna riječ," in *Mediji komuniciranja s tržištem danas i sutra: referati s međunarodnog simpozija ekonomske propagande '75,* ed. Mario Hladnik (Zagreb, 1975), 11–13, at 11.

23. Mario Hladnik, "Predgovor," in *Zbornik predavanja sa seminara vizuelne komunikacije,* 3–4, at 4 (emphasis added).

As explored in later chapters, critics across Yugoslavia continually attacked advertising as a manufacturer of artificial needs and unwelcome, socially harmful desires. The industry's appeals for legitimacy acknowledged those misgivings and attempted to put them to rest. Thus, for example, in 1975, when the country was already thoroughly immersed in advertising, one business psychologist from the Croatian Center for Marketing Research [*Centar za istraživanje marketinga, CEMA*] expressed to a group of fellow trade specialists his dismay at the climate of disapproval:

> Very often they accuse us of participating in the creation of false human values or systems, of imposing on people needs and products that they do not need. It is a fact that today we encounter ever more frequently the opinion, as people say, that "advertising has become more than an unwelcome annoyance," that our work consists of attempts…to sell people things they don't need for money they don't have.[24]

To counter such accusations, Yugoslav advertising leaders repeatedly reassured the public that their work did indeed serve genuine, self-evident human needs and was, moreover, entirely consistent with the country's socialist values.[25]

In the early industry literature, in particular, this emphasis on consumers' needs sometimes manifested itself in a paternalistic concern for the role of advertising in creating, reinforcing, or changing the good or bad habits of ordinary citizens. Such tendencies are not entirely absent in parallel Western sources, to be sure, but the socialist sociopolitical context in Yugoslavia evidently amplified them, especially through the idea, widely honored both in Yugoslav industry sources and in the broader discourse of business and public affairs, that commercial appeals represented just one element of a larger, professionally managed media and public-information system, a network of culture producers self-consciously dedicated to raising standards, shaping tastes, and molding popular consciousness along more or less prescribed lines.

Something Special in the Air: Commercial Promotion, Self-Management, and Yugoslav Exceptionalism

As they pleaded for the acceptance of their work, industry writers responded to this and other argumentative imperatives of Yugoslavia's political culture, and they scrupulously avoided language that might subject them to accusations that they were promoting the shameless manipulation of consumer

---

24. Tkalac, address in *Zbornik predavanja sa seminara vizuelne komunikacije*, 53.
25. See, for example, Miroslav Skalak, "Uloga ekonomske propagande u mijenjanju i njegovanju navika potrošača," *Naš publicitet* 4, no. 1 (1957): 11–12.

desires in the pursuit of profit. Advertising and marketing leaders repeatedly turned to a series of arguments calculated to link the objectives, techniques, and effects of their work with a set of aims and practices already established as desirable and beneficial in the distinctive ideology of Yugoslav self-management socialism. To be sure, they talked frankly about persuasion, about desires, and occasionally even about profit. They could convert profit, a more or less suspect concept, into something positive through the magic of socialist ownership of the means of production. Like other capitalist categories, profit was transformed (superficially at least) through reference to a variety of permissible analogues from the lexicon of contemporary Marxism, with particular attention to how the unusual new Yugoslav variant had updated and translated that lexicon.[26] By 1968 things had progressed so far that one defender of advertising could even argue that "*the only good product* is one that can enter into the competitive battle in the marketplace with the prospect of ensuring its *profitability.* All other factors just amount to a superstructure on this fundamental factor."[27]

The "difference" that made such bold and seemingly un-socialist claims possible was the idea of Yugoslav exceptionalism. If there is a single dominant theme that runs through the literature of the Yugoslav advertising industry, it is the insistence that the relationship between consumers and sellers in this particular and unique country was (and ought to be) something itself particular and unique: a positive, mutually advantageous interaction that aimed to fulfill the rich promise of workers' self-management. This line surfaces repeatedly in the trade sources, where a favored tactic of industry representatives was to depict advertising as an important instrument of self-management socialism:

> The advertising specialist [*reklamer*] must, in the first place, through advertising and promotion [*reklama i propaganda*] *display the directives and the goal of our economy in their entirety.* This is the foundation upon which all our activity is based.... In this way our people will be constantly reminded of the duties that they must fulfill, if we wish to reach the ultimate goal, that is, the struggle for a better living standard.[28]

---

26. For evidence of the very rapid conversion of profit into a potentially positive end, see Deem [Dušan Mrvoš?], "Što znači izlagati komercijalno," *Naš publicitet* 1 (August 1954). There the writer contrasted new, competitive methods of commercial display with the decidedly uncommercial and decorative style of the 1947 Zagreb Trade Fair, where "a peaceful style without rivalry had prevailed." In just a few years following the embrace of market mechanisms, however, things had changed dramatically, and thus the writer observed approvingly that "today...the profitability of every individual operation is in question."

27. Milan R. Jovanović, "Ekonomska propaganda i privredna reforma," in *Ekonomska propaganda i privredna reforma u SFRJ*, ed. Radmilo Dimitrijević (Belgrade, 1968), 43–49, at 49 (emphasis added).

28. Mil. [*sic*], "Proizvodač, trgovac, reklamer, potrošač," *Savremena privredna propaganda* 1 (November 1957): 9–10, at 9 (emphasis added) (the graphic format renders the exact title of the article uncertain).

Or, as another specialist put it almost two decades later, in 1975, "insofar as the problems of *our advertising* are *specifically our own*," the problem for the country's advertising industry, and for its clients, was how to harmonize its functions "with the economic and social goals of the Yugoslav self-management socialist system."[29]

This pronounced imperative to pay tribute to the "special circumstances" of Yugoslav socialism is a species of the more general enthusiasm for Yugoslav exceptionalism that marks the public discourse of the socialist period. The convention is an important one, packed with meaning, and the industry literature is chock full of it. When they attempted to justify a stronger presence for advertising and marketing in Yugoslav society, industry writers continually used language designed to appeal, either expressly or implicitly, not only to socialist values generally but especially to "our specific conditions" as participants in Yugoslavia's hybridized economic system.

These industry experts were, after all, salesmen, and it is quite clear that they realized that they had plenty of work to do to sell their approach in what was still, despite the comparative laxity of Titoist control over ideology and expression, a regulated and restricted marketplace of ideas. Those who wanted to guide the future of the larger enterprise of advertising and marketing in Yugoslavia understood that the success of their craft and the security of their positions among the élites of the emerging Yugoslav business world depended on winning for the industry the respect and confidence of policy makers and business leaders or, failing that, at least reassuring them that the arts of consumer persuasion were either innocuous or, at worst, a mild, manageable, and in any event necessary evil given the country's formal commitment to market mechanisms. One of the keys to their strategy was this constant posture of deference to the "special circumstances" of Yugoslav socialism.

Because self-management made Yugoslavia's economy a special case, Yugoslav advertising was said to be special as well. Typical, for instance, was the observation by Radmilo Dimitrijević that the "role, place, and character of advertising in the new economic conditions have their own specific place in our country, just as the development of our socialist advertising is also specific." In Yugoslavia, Dimitrijević insisted,

> We are *searching for our own specific path in advertising* as well. The automatic acceptance of some Western forms of advertising would be harmful because of existing differences in the social systems. On the other hand, this does not mean that the experience, rich practical knowledge, and various profitable innovations [of the West] cannot be exploited or adapted to our circumstances.[30]

---

29. "Mednarodni simpozij jugoslovanskih propagandistov Portorož, in *MEDIJ: glasilo Društva ekonomskih propagandistov Slovenije* 1, nos. 1/2 (1974): 5–9 (emphasis added).

30. Radmilo Dimitrijević, "Ekonomska propaganda i privredna reforma," in Dimitrijević, ed., *Ekonomska propaganda i privredna reforma u SFRJ*, 9–20, at 9, 13 (emphasis added).

This idea of exceptional advertising for an exceptional Yugoslavia quickly became a central organizing principle of the rhetoric used to defend the trade. It crept into practical handbooks, scholarly treatises, and speeches; it was a stock fixture of both discourse for public consumption and communications to "insiders"—that is, to others in the industry or connected with it.

In one of the first trade journals, for example, we find the suggestion that, as early as 1957, the special nature of Yugoslav advertising had already become self-evident: "Here we won't get into the difference between the methods of advertising in a socialist society like ours and ways of advertising goods in capitalist commerce. Differences exist, and they are fundamental."[31] Speaking to a meeting of Slovenian advertising specialists in 1964, after advertising had already gained something of a foothold in Yugoslav life, the head of the advertising department of the large machine-manufacturing firm Litostroj sounded some of the same themes. "We will have to find," Branko Vrčon insisted, "our own special, domestic expression for these common promotional activities...just as we have already succeeded in giving them our special, socialist content."[32]

Just how that "special, domestic expression" was supposed to appear was far from clear, however, and elsewhere in the address Vrčon implied that much if not all of the technique of the West might be available for Yugoslav use: "We cannot betray the content that belongs to us, but we can make use of all the most modern means of any sort whatsoever....Thus, as a practical matter, in the form and choice of methods of our advertising in the economy there can be no borders. If there are borders, they are only in social ethics, in the ethics of our socialist society, in the content of our advertising."[33]

As examples like these suggest, a primary purpose of invoking the purportedly unique characteristics of Yugoslav society was to assure readers that the country's advertising industry had by no means succumbed to the various insidious vices of Western capitalist practice. In work after work on advertising and marketing, practitioners and academics stressed

---

31. Ž. Ilić, "Reklamer i borba na tržištu," *Savremena privredna propaganda* 1, no. 3 (October 1957): 18–19, at 18.

32. Remarks of Branko Vrčon, *Zapiski s posvetovanja ekonomskih propagandistov Slovenije, od 20. do 22. marca 1964*, 3–12, at 12.

33. Ibid., 9. Nevertheless, in his remarks to the conference Vrčon expressly attempted to distinguish Yugoslav advertising from both that of the Soviet bloc and that seen in the West, which represented, he insisted, "the protection of the interest of the individual, the individual capitalist, the producer of wealth." Ibid., 6. Yugoslav advertising, Vrčon suggested, was seeking its own ways, just as Yugoslav society was traveling along its own "independent path to socialism." Ibid. The notion of Yugoslav exceptionalism became a primary thematic emphasis of various professional gatherings designed to promote advertising. Thus we find, for instance, the Federal Economic Council, as part of its mission to coordinate economic policy in the country, sponsoring a conference in 1971 on "The Role and Place of the Marketing Concept in the Specific Conditions of the Yugoslav Enterprise." Aspects of the conference are discussed in Mihovil Skobe, *Organizacija privredne propagande* (Belgrade, 1973), 5.

that the techniques and theories they were espousing were entirely in accordance with the norms of Yugoslavia's special variant of socialism.[34] This tendency was present in the specialist publications from the very beginning, and it lasted, albeit in somewhat attenuated form, until the very end.

Along these lines, a contemporary biographical sketch of Croatia's trailblazing Dušan Mrvoš assured readers that his professional views and his work "rapidly developed in our specific circumstances" following the end of World War II.[35] The implication was, quite clearly, that Mrvoš was happily able to shed whatever undesirable views and practices he might have acquired in his prior decades of professional experience. In the same spirit, one expert in consumer protection and the legal aspects of advertising, writing toward the end of the socialist period, insisted that "Yugoslav marketing must be harmonized with our social, political, and economic characteristics and interests; it therefore cannot be the sort that we encounter in the economic practice of capitalist states."[36] Arguments of this sort were sprinkled liberally throughout the industry literature, and they found special prominence in works of a pedagogical nature, which likely faced stricter scrutiny.

A quiet neglect of the specifics of the supposed relationship between Yugoslav business and the fundamental values of the society was typical. Though advertising and marketing practitioners often bowed to the concerns of socialist politics and the criticisms of socialist politicians, such gestures ordinarily amounted to little more than ritual obeisance, displays of what would later be called "political correctness." Not infrequently the references to "our particular conditions" constituted, in essence, a rhetorical preemptive strike against an assumed opposition, an obligatory first nod to party jargon. The writers then went on their intended way, largely unconcerned with socialist economics and evidently much more interested in making Yugoslavia's "specific circumstances" a good deal less specific and a good deal more like the circumstances that prevailed in the capitalist West. Even so, the fact that this sort of argumentation turned up so frequently and lasted for so long speaks to the persistence of a serious conflict over the role of advertising and marketing, lingering uncertainty over their future, and pressure on industry specialists to make their work conform, at least superficially, to approved socialist norms.

Yet despite that pressure most of what appeared in the industry's practical programs was incorporated from the theory and practice of the capi-

---

34. See, for example, Josip Sudar, *Ekonomska propaganda: predavanja na postdiplomskom studiju Ekonomskog fakulteta u Zagrebu* (Zagreb, 1975 [1958]).

35. Veljko Klašterka, "Predgovor," in Mrvoš, *Propaganda reklama publicitet*, 4.

36. Franc Pernek, *Potrošnik in njegovo varstvo: marketinški, pravni, in organizacijski vidik* (Maribor, 1986), 34.

talist world with little or no mediation. One therefore finds painstaking attention to the idea that Yugoslav advertising and marketing were supposed to reflect the country's "specific conditions" but almost no discussion of practical means of making advertisements and marketing campaigns actually do so. This was not simply an innocuous carryover of forms and techniques of Western commercial promotion, as the industry's disclaimers insisted. An important ideological transfer was also made to (and through) the Yugoslav cadre. Notwithstanding frequent denials, these masters of persuasion were importing in largely unaltered form an understanding of the centrality and sovereignty of the consumer that had been forged and refined through the experience of capitalist business. The culture of the market was on the move.

The record suggests that the industry, anxious to pursue its agenda without interference, sought to arrange at least a truce with the anti-advertising forces by appealing to and praising the very innovations that, according to the party, set the Yugoslav system apart from all others, whether socialist or capitalist. Bogdan Denitch has observed that the concept of self-management in Yugoslavia became, by the mid-1970s if not earlier, "the unifying social myth of the society, analogous to such broad terms in Western polities as 'democracy.' "[37] Although Denitch is surely correct in seeing self-management as a talisman of social solidarity, the special emphasis accorded the concept in the discourse of Yugoslav advertising and marketing is, in fact, the invocation of an even larger (and perhaps more unifying) social myth: the cherished idea of Yugoslav exceptionalism, of the country as a promising "third way," something appealingly "in between"—not like the West, but also not like the East.[38]

To a great extent, the legitimacy of socialist governance, shaky though it occasionally may have been, was grounded not only on the principle of self-management but also on the idea of Yugoslavia's unique hybrid quality, on its mission to soften the harsh sides of both communism and capitalism, on its geopolitical prominence as the leader of the movement of "non-aligned" states, and on the prestige that these maverick roles brought to the country. When they promised to honor Yugoslavia's "special circumstances," the champions of advertising and marketing were therefore dutifully paying homage to this myth of exceptionalism, acknowledging the special power it exerted over the country's political discourse.

---

37. Denitch, *The Legitimation of a Revolution*, 192.

38. An early example of argument along these lines is found in Mrvoš, "Uloga ekonomskog publiciteta u socijalističkoj privredi," *Naš publicitet* 4, no. 2 (1957): 1–3, at 3. The writer suggested that Yugoslav advertising would differ in its aims and messages from both Western advertising and the kind seen in other socialist countries. As was typical for the trade literature, however, he offered no specifics about which of the "appeals" of capitalist advertising the Yugoslav industry would supposedly reject.

Good & Plenty: The Abundance of Promises and the Promise of Abundance

The rhetoric of advertising and marketing responded to socialist values in other important ways as well. A frequent tactic of the industry's many *plaidoyers*, for example, was the attempt to inoculate commercial promotion against serious criticism by stressing its importance to economic development. "Development" was, of course, a concept with its own notable history in the aggressively modernizing ideologies of state socialism. By the time the Yugoslav trade specialists seized on it as a way to build their legitimacy, Marxist-Leninist thought had already made development the subject of a reverential interest verging on fetishism. Exploiting this natural opening, industry leaders habitually depicted advertising and marketing as sure tickets to development and prosperity—techniques absolutely necessary to the realization of business goals in any market-oriented economy.

The particular paths that capitalist states had taken to achieve their enviable abundance remained suspect, but Yugoslav socialism, like socialisms elsewhere, still treated development itself as a desirable end. If society could harness advertising and marketing to the service of state-sanctioned development, then they might overcome their traditional association with the corrupted practices and values of capitalism. It thus became rhetorically nonthreatening for Yugoslav specialists to cite (almost always with approval) the exemplary successes of developed countries. As with the habitual reference to Yugoslavia's "special circumstances," the task was to cast advertising and marketing as essentially system-neutral and even value-neutral techniques of economic progress, methods that could be made to serve either the harmful ends of capitalism or the positive, healthy aims of socialist society.[39]

As such, the industry's reliance on the rhetoric of economic development reflects an attempt to stake its claims on extraordinarily safe ground. After all, who could argue against prosperity and a brighter future? Especially in connection with this particular theme, the Yugoslav debate was, at times, noteworthy for its tame, oblique quality. Focusing on the presumed economic benefits of advertising and marketing, industry writers seemed to avoid any candid reflections on the potential social and political consequences of the shift toward the acknowledgment of consumer sovereignty that their orientation actually entailed. In lieu of that, they offered mild, uncontroversial, and soothing (not to say vapid) forecasts about the many advantages that an increased reliance on commercial promotion would bring. Consider, for example, how this restrained spirit pervades the following passage from the overview of commercial promotion offered up in Josip Sudar's groundbreaking textbook *Ekonomska propaganda*:

---

39. See, for example, Bogomir Deželak, *Politika in organiziranje marketinga* (Maribor, 1984).

Advertising is an important and beneficial factor in the exchange of material goods in our economy. It has a favorable influence on the raising of living standards; it develops a sense for aesthetics and culture. Through the advertising of, for example, soap powders, standards of hygiene are raised, while the advertising of kitchen appliances helps the housewife to liberate herself from various tasks. With advertising we teach people about the new accomplishments of technology, we educate them, and in this way we spread the common culture. Advertising assists in the development of our economy, and as such, it is justified. It is a part of doing business, and it offers the consumer all the advantages of modern commerce.[40]

This is, as far as it goes, pretty bland stuff, so bland, in fact, that I am almost tempted to apologize for quoting it at such length. But the superficial lack of any potential for controversy in Sudar's flat and unprovocative disquisition on the benefits of advertising is precisely the point. The implicit, more subversive, message was the intimation that advertising itself could and should be treated as something unobjectionable. In the context of Yugoslavia's socialist system, that message was still not beyond dispute, even as late as the 1970s. And so the case had to be made yet again.

The Bible of the new industry in the first decades of socialist Yugoslavia, Sudar's text was noteworthy for the extent to which it avoided what he called "theoretical explanations and general propositions," at least on the subject of the relationship between advertising and socialism.[41] Even more than most of its counterparts, the book confined its message largely to a nuts-and-bolts exposition of advertising techniques, making only a rather weak introductory gesture toward some justification for the expansion of advertising in Yugoslav society—an expansion that Sudar depicted in 1971 as dramatic, if still rather modest in comparison with what was encountered in the contemporary West. That very technocentric orientation, of course, had its own argumentative implications: it moved the work of commercial promotions away from the realm of the sociocultural and onto the reassuring ground of skill, method, and craft. Yet even Sudar, less engaged in the open defense of advertising than many of his fellows, sought to legitimize his calling with reference to the many material benefits of development that would flow from a more complete acceptance of advertising.

---

40. Sudar, *Ekonomska propaganda*, 15.
41. Sudar, *Ekonomska propaganda*, vi (foreword to the 1958 edition); in the 1971 edition, see, esp., 1–30. It is possible, of course, to read Sudar's failure to produce any sustained apologia for advertising as evidence that he thought such justifications had become unnecessary, that is, as a statement of his confidence in the place that the movement had secured in the country by the early 1970s. But in light of the anxieties clearly evident in so many other contemporary sources, I believe it is safer to view Sudar's approach as reflective simply of his own different interests and concerns, or perhaps as evidence of the option for a more understated rhetorical strategy for bolstering the reputation of advertising.

Increasingly, marketing and advertising were characterized as not merely permissible and desirable from the standpoint of economic development, but as essential to economic progress under Yugoslavia's modified market model. As one leading spokesman for the trade, Aleksandar Spasić, explained the situation, Yugoslavia had created "a new type of market and producers," one for which "the function of advertising [was] significant and, we could say, irreplaceable."[42] Industry activists could argue, moreover, that skepticism toward marketing and advertising was tantamount to opposition to self-management, the very centerpiece of Yugoslav socialism. Consequently, resistance to commercial promotion and the marketing approach was at times lumped together with the Soviet-style state-planning models that the Yugoslavs had rejected as rigid and counterproductive.

Although they typically deployed the development theme in a positive, optimistic register, advocates of commercial promotion occasionally relied on a little fear to help make their case. Yugoslavs knew that, although they might be better off than their counterparts in the Soviet bloc, they still lagged fairly far behind Western living standards. The alternative to aggressive economic development was continuing relative deprivation. One handbook thus warned that business enterprises would do well to take full advantage of the benefits of advertising "if they wish to escape the unwanted economic and financial consequences that, in free market conditions, threaten those economic institutions that do not recognize the demands of the marketplace and of consumers."[43] In the view of another commentator, the new business realities of market-oriented socialism absolutely dictated a new openness to advertising: "no one pays heed any more to the old principle of the *čaršija*, the patriarchal merchant elite, that 'the goods sell themselves.' Today the producer has to speak as well, and not just the goods."[44] Though the reference here to the traditional *čaršija* traders harks back to the era before socialism, one wonders if this comment might also have been a veiled criticism of an ingrained passivity acquired in the command economy of the immediate postwar years.

Whether Yugoslav enterprises truly faced any dire penalties if they failed to compete effectively is another matter. Advertising and marketing circles certainly latched on readily to ideas and practices imported from capitalism—and, perhaps even more important, to the *"biznis"* mentality of capitalist commerce as well—but the same cannot be said of the Yugoslav economic structure more generally, which remained lumbering, top-heavy, and unresponsive despite all the enthusiastic new talk about markets and efficiency.

---

42. Aleksandar Spasić, "Naš trenutak sadašnjosti," *Ideja* no. 4 (February 1973): 6–7, at 6.

43. Josip Garvan, "Predgovor," in Čedomir Jelenić, *Ekonomska propaganda u trgovinskom preduzeču* (Belgrade, n.d. [ca. 1971]), 5.

44. "Problem ukusa," *Savremena privredna propaganda* 2, no. 2 (1958): 30. The refutation of the idea that "the goods speak for themselves" is a frequent theme in the industry sources.

Enterprises largely failed to take full advantage of the flexibility and market incentives that the system offered. Only infrequently did they function as profit-seeking, market-oriented "businesses" in the capitalist sense of the term, and few developed the sensitivity to customer needs seen in Western firms.[45]

Nevertheless, the mere fact that Yugoslavia's new way of conceptualizing economic relations allowed the advocates of commercial promotion to threaten recalcitrant enterprises with the specter of insufficient revenues is highly significant, regardless of whether those threats were credible. Although the country's enterprises did not often operate like their Western counterparts, advertising and marketing served as prime conduits of an important, if partially obscured, ideological transfer: the business-speak and business-think of the West gradually invaded Yugoslav economic and political life and seeped into the broader currents of public discourse, even as advertising and marketing leaders continued to describe and defend their work using language imbued with socialist concerns and categories.

It Just Makes Sense: The Rationale for Rationalization and the Perpetuation of Planning

Another striking feature of the industry campaign (and one that, like others, appears calculated to find a warm reception among communist audiences) was the effort to legitimize advertising and marketing with the assertion that they would necessarily promote the rationalization of the Yugoslav economy.[46] Repeatedly the consumer-oriented approach that underlay the modern practice of advertising and marketing was depicted as eminently rational.[47] Like other rationales, this one attempted to connect the mastery of consumer demand with modes of thinking and argumentation that had already been accepted in Marxist ideology as legitimate.[48]

The insistence on the rationality of commercial promotion arose at least partly as a response to enterprise leaders' widespread skepticism about the

---

45. See Lampe, *Yugoslavia as History,* 276; Tyson, *The Yugoslav Economic System and Its Performance in the 1970s,* 23–27.

46. See, for example, Deželak, *Marketing;* Vojislav Zeremski, "Ekonomska propaganda i produktivnost rada" in *Ekonomska propaganda i privredna reforma u SFRJ,* 21–28.

47. On the purported importance of advertising to the proper and efficient functioning of business enterprises, see, for example, "Ekonomska uloga zavoda," *Naš publicitet* 2 (September 1955).

48. The industry's claims to rationality were echoed in other Yugoslav literature on consumption more generally. Thus we read in one analysis of consumption policy from the late 1950s that "the ultimate goal of management [*gospodarjenje*] is the ever increasing satisfaction of human needs and desires and, to achieve this goal, the rational and economic use of the means of production and consumer goods." Aleš Kersnik, *Struktura potrošnje narodnega dohodka in njen vpliv na razvoj našega gospodarstva* (Ljubljana, 1958).

utility of advertising. One of the most prominent themes in the industry literature, especially in the early years, was the effort to refute the notion that advertising expenditures were nothing more than *"bačen novac,"* money thrown away.[49] The embrace of self-management had not managed to squelch more traditionalist Marxists who complained that advertising was an unnecessary, wasteful, and senseless use of resources, a practice that should be discarded in favor of the more rational planning of production and consumption.[50] Facing such doubts and criticisms, promoters of commercial promotion tried to prove that their work was not only effective in reaching and moving its target audiences, but also indispensable to economies that sought to take advantage of the inherent efficiency and rationality of markets, as did self-management socialism.

Here we should note the critical distinction between the thoroughly rationalist message advanced by advertising and marketing leaders when speaking in defense of commercial promotion and the potentially quite different set of messages conveyed to consumers across Yugoslavia through advertising itself. Commercial promotion in Yugoslavia did, to be sure, make considerable use of the themes of rational consumption. Constrained by the political climate and by the country's always modest circumstances, the Yugoslav Dream was a disciplined dream. Yet this emphasis on the measured, moderate, and rational satisfaction of consumer needs was by no means uniform, and, as presented to the public, it was undermined by frequent implicit appeals to status, fantasy, and escape. In contrast, in the advertising specialists' descriptions of their work—as opposed to the work itself—rationality reigned supreme.

Complementing the effort to exploit the allure of rationalization was the industry representatives' tendency to downplay ad hoc elements of their practice and to underscore the highly programmatic nature of advertising and marketing activities. In this way they appealed to the traditional socialist preoccupation with planning, which had survived the transition to self-management surprisingly intact. Even after multiple rounds of market reform, Yugoslavia's economy was administered by a host of planners, and an enduring faith in the value of planning among economic and political elites counterbalanced the new tendency to elevate the significance of consumption. In the reassuring technocratese of the advertising and marketing specialists, managers and officials recognized the attitudes of people whose methods were perhaps not all that different from their own.

---

49. See, for example, Josip Sudar, "Novinsko oglašivanje," *Naš publicitet* 1 (August 1954). As evidence of the effectiveness of advertising, Sudar cited the relatively high level of expenditures on newspaper advertising in the United States.

50. This critique proved quite persistent. See, for example, Dragutin S. Vračar, *Uloga privredne propagande u politici prodaje jugoslovenskih preduzeća: doktorska disertacija* (Ph.D. diss., University of Belgrade, 1972), 214.

In this vein, for example, Dušan Mrvoš explained his favored rendering of the term "advertising" in a way that emphasized "the advantages of goods [or] services in connection with real human interests": *ekonomski publicitet,* Mrvoš maintained, is the form of commercial promotion that results "if we consider the *needs* of the buyer or consumer, or the user of services, for whom we are *organizing planned production* or the *planned provision of services,* attracting attention to them with *planned messages* as well."[51] This systematized understanding of a deliberate, programmed advertising practice accordingly distinguished *ekonomski publicitet* from the *reklama,* which was asserted to be merely the crude offer of goods or services "originating primarily from one's *own* and threatened interest" made when those goods or services are "no longer selling on their own."[52] Carefully framed to maximize their ostensible compatibility with socialist understandings of the distribution of goods and services, planning-centered formulations like this could "sell" more readily in the Yugoslav cultural and political marketplace.

The effort to naturalize the "marketing concept" posed special challenges and offered special opportunities. Marketing arrived in Yugoslavia with an indisputably Western provenance and suspiciously capitalist foundations. Yet these did not prove to be an insuperable barrier. As with their earlier engagement with Western advertising, Yugoslav industry specialists made heavy use of marketing literature from Western Europe and the United States. There were, for example, frequent references to the work of Philip Kotler, "the father of modern marketing," whose influential 1967 text *Marketing Management* was rapidly incorporated into the vocabulary of the Yugoslav industry following its appearance in the West.[53] Again, because Yugoslavia was ideologically porous and its political culture comparatively relaxed, the reliance on Western models tended to provoke only quasi-official grumbling rather than any outright prohibitions.

Even more than advertising, marketing signified the apotheosis of the consumerist orientation. But by the 1970s marketing had gained a firm foothold among those who ran Yugoslavia's economy, and it had done so with impressive speed. Its acceptance, however, was always partial and conditional, subject to ongoing negotiations between those politicians, administrators, and business enterprise leaders who favored less restricted market operations and those who sought to retain a substantial role for economic planning keyed to the priorities of producers and policy makers. The more limited activity of market research per se proved to be a safer endeavor, but the basic conceptual premises of marketing as a comprehensive practice meant

---

51. Mrvoš, *Propaganda reklama publicitet,* 14 (emphasis in original as to needs; emphasis added as to planning).

52. Ibid., 13

53. Philip Kotler, *Marketing Management: Analysis, Planning, and Control* (Englewood Cliffs, N.J., 1967).

that, like advertising, it would never be entirely beyond suspicion during the socialist period. In order to reinforce its legitimacy, it also had to be cloaked in socialist values.

The lexicon of plan and program gave industry specialists an easy way to do just that, and, as the professional literature amply demonstrates, advertising campaigns and marketing initiatives could readily be couched in such terms.[54] There were, of course, basic and enduring tensions between the planning predilections of the administrative elite and the consumer-oriented, Western-flavored style of planning that most marketing specialists envisioned.[55] Industry leaders, however, typically asserted that they could harmonize the two perspectives without undue difficulty:

> The fundamental principles of marketing contemplate a planning approach to decision making on all levels, for without that there is no coordinated development, and so therefore the stable conditions of economic functioning are absent. Assertions that marketing leads to the unchecked [*stihijski*, elemental] operation of the laws of the market are therefore unfounded and are the consequence of a lack of understanding of its fundamental principles.[56]

As numerous such examples suggest, the content of the marketing approach threatened to subvert some of the fundamental values of the Yugoslav system, but its basic style of operation gave it, as a practical matter, a reassuringly socialist "feel."

The marketing concept's ascendancy since the 1960s also had a pronounced effect on advertising practice and on the dominant modes of self-representation among advertising industry leaders. Advertising specialists in socialist Yugoslavia had from the beginning pointed with pride to the highly planned, programmatic quality of good commercial promotion. As marketing came into fashion, that emphasis intensified. The rise of marketing as an independent subdiscipline within business studies led to the growth of a technocratic, market-oriented mirror image of the plan-driven practices that prevailed under the old command economy models.

---

54. For example, Radoslav R. Niketić, *Privredno planiranje: osnovi planiranja privredne propagande* (Belgrade, 1972). Compare the criticisms expressed in "Gde se najviše greši," *Savremena privredna propaganda* 2 (April 1958): 7. There the unidentified author depicts the inability to "construct a solid commercial plan" as a typical failing of the "non-expert advertising worker" [*nestručan reklamer*].

55. See, for example, Stevan Vasiljev, "Uz Nacrt društvenog plana Jugoslavije za period od 1986. do 1990.," *Marketing* 16, no. 4 (1985): 2. A useful overview of the development and reception of marketing in Yugoslavia, published late in the socialist period, is Dragutin Radunović, "Jugoslovenski marketing između teorije i prakse," *Marketing* 17, no. 2 (1986): 80–83.

56. Programski odbor IX. kongresa JUME, "Poruke IX. kongresa JUMA," *Marketing* 15, nos. 3–4 (1984): 2–3, at 2; compare M. Milisavljević, "Marketing i srednjoročni plan 1981–1985," *Marketing* 10, no. 1 (1979): 2.

In the West the marketing approach sought to dislodge the focus on production that, its adherents argued, had unwisely dominated industrial manufacturing. A new, holistic understanding that would place greater stress on market research and on the planning of promotion and sales was to replace the old ways. In the rhetoric of marketing, consumers were sovereign: according to the theory, enterprises were primarily concerned with satisfying the needs and wants of their customers, and were encouraged to orient their production to meet those demands. Advertising was treated as one part, albeit a very important one, of the all-encompassing scheme implied by the marketing concept.

Advertising itself thus became even more an object to be planned and programmed, an implication of the marketing approach that found fertile soil in the "specific conditions" of Yugoslav socialism.[57] In fact, the fascination with comprehensive market planning started to overshadow some of the earlier emphasis on advertising as a primarily declarative, unidirectional, informative practice. The shift that was taking place comes across clearly, for example, in the treatment of this issue found in one rather sophisticated advertising and marketing treatise from the last years of the socialist period:

> Many here think that marketing is, above all, the effort to give the buyer needed information.... That understanding of marketing is not completely accurate.... Marketing is actually the effort to use promotional devices [*propaganda*] and the control of informational processes, on the basis of the great amount of information that circulates within a manufacturing organization... and on the basis of the goals that have been set, in order to provide for the CONTROL and the MANAGEMENT of production and sales processes in their entirety.[58]

Here, once again, those worried about the unsocialist implications of the new world of Yugoslav business could find reassurance in the familiar planned quality of the approach to economic management that was now on offer.

The Miracles of Science: Commercial Promotion as a System of Knowledge

In Yugoslavia as in the West, the professional vocabulary adopted to explain the work of commercial promotion made liberal use of the idea that these activities, if undertaken properly, constituted sciences, or at least highly

---

57. The subordination of advertising to a more comprehensive understanding of marketing functions (one that is emphatically convinced of the value of planning) is evident in, for example, Momčilo Milisavljević, "Planiranje privredne propagande," *Marketing* 1, no. 3 (1970): 20–25.

58. Vladimir Štambuk, "Predgovor," in Mitrović, *O+P+P=: priručnik za upravljanje propagandom*, 7–8, at 7 (emphasis in original).

rational technical practices with a reliability and status closely approaching those of the sciences. Marxist materialism, of course, had long placed a premium on scientific knowledge, and the purportedly scientific nature of modern-day marketing, retailing, and advertising gave Yugoslav advocates a secure rhetorical footing, allowing them to argue more effectively that their work was rational, productive, and legitimate.

Caught up in the new vision of market-communication-as-science, Yugoslav industry specialists, like their Western counterparts, soon became both believers and proselytizers. They seized on the idea that a scientific grasp of human psychology could measure, mold, and manage the appeal and efficacy of advertising, and they accepted marketing's claims of increasingly dependable control of the flow of information between producers and consumers. Hand in hand with the notion that the mastery of the market was an essentially scientific endeavor came a reliance on an associated literature in business-oriented psychology, a field that over the years became increasingly popular and well accepted in the country.[59]

As a result of these trends, the industry's representation of its work quickly became laden with "psychologized," scientific (or pseudo-scientific) characterizations of the power of advertising and marketing. One typical formulation described advertising as "one of the instruments that enables the buyer, or the consumer, to transit the phases of the communicative spectrum (from lack of knowledge through familiarization [*upoznavanje*], comprehension, and persuasion [*ubedjenja*] to action—buying the products and services of the enterprise)."[60] Those familiar with advertising as practiced in the West will recognize echoes here of AIDA (*Attention Interest Desire Action*), one of the catchy encapsulations of theory for which, as shown earlier, the Yugoslav specialists showed such a prodigious appetite. Advocates of such approaches stressed that their essentially scientific techniques produced reliable knowledge and results. Effects could be quantified and measured, variables isolated, and alternative techniques tested and retested, offering businesses the prospect of scientific certainty that their promotional initiatives would pay off.

Representatives of the industry argued creatively that science was on their side. In one revealing example from 1954, an unnamed defender of advertising (quite possibly Dušan Mrvoš, the prime mover of Zagreb's OZEHA bureau) appealed to readers' recognition of the obvious legitimacy of science in order to distinguish the old-fashioned and primitive *reklama* from what

---

59. See, for example, "Psihologija oglasa," *Savremena privredna propaganda* 1 (October 1957): 17; Boris Petz, *Psihologija u ekonomskoj propagandi*, 3rd ed. (Zagreb, 1980).

60. Momčilo Milisavljević, "O značaju Drugog međunarodnog simpozijuma privrednih propagandista '5+1,'" *Zbornik referata sa II međunarodnog simpozijuma privrednih propagandista održanog od 2. do 7. novembra 1969. g. na Bledu* (Belgrade, n.d.), 7–10. See also Milisavljević, "Planiranje privredne propagande," in ibid., 11–16.

the writer characterized as the modern, positive, system-neutral conception of present-day advertising (*publicitet*):

> The *reklama* is the fruit of the elements of capitalist production and distribution. The methods and techniques of this sort of *reklama* have made it very hated around the world. Ultimately, the *reklama* as an economic activity has become a most widely discussed subject at expert conferences and has been defined thus: "The *reklama* works its influence on people using inflated, deceptive, and untruthful information and is carried out using the noisy effects of marketplace barkers, with the aim of effecting a one-time sale of goods." The *reklama*—literally "calling out"—is today counted as part of the inglorious past of our profession....*in our socialist conditions*, the *reklama* has no place, neither as a concept, nor as an activity, nor as a title.[61]

Thus far, the argument advanced here seemed to be headed toward just another affirmation of the familiar, socialist-sounding themes already discussed in detail above. Then, however, the *Naš publicitet* contributor took an interesting rhetorical turn—though ultimately, in the history of Yugoslav advertising, one that would not prove particularly unusual—invoking for the practice of advertising all the authority and certainty of science: "just as 'alchemy'...was transformed into chemistry thanks to investigative work, or as 'astrology' was transformed into astronomy, the activity of influencing people in connection with the sale of goods and services *has been transformed into an exact science,* one for which we do not yet have a corresponding expression or title."[62] Present at the beginning, this sort of adamant insistence on the scientific nature of advertising and marketing would remain a constant in the professional literature throughout the socialist period.

Marxism, of course, had no monopoly on science, and signaling the importance of the appeal to scientific processes here is not meant to suggest that there is anything intrinsically or exclusively socialist about that line of argument.[63] Yet given a field of public discourse restricted in other critical ways, communism's fondness for science-talk did offer Yugoslav specialists an important opportunity to enhance their image in the eyes of those who held political power. They exploited that opportunity repeatedly.

There was the occasional hint of rebellion against all this intellectualization of the trade. Borislav Mitrović, for example, reassured readers that his 1988 handbook would offer a treatment of advertising "without

---

61. M. [Dušan Mrvoš?], "Reklama u socijalističkoj privredi," *Naš publicitet* 1 (August 1954): 4 (emphasis added).
62. Ibid.
63. On American advertisers' embrace of the "science" of marketing, for example, see Susan Strasser, *Satisfaction Guaranteed: The Making of the American Mass Market* (New York, 1989), 146–161.

mathematicism and academicization." With his avowed fondness for simplicity, Mitrović summed up the marketing concept thus: "Selling means 'making people want what you offer them,' but marketing is 'selling people what they want.'" (The reasoning here, it should be noted, shows just how deeply the idea of consumer sovereignty had penetrated into the thinking of the advertising and marketing sectors of the Yugoslav business establishment.) Nevertheless, even this somewhat distanced approach accepted the fundamentally scientific nature of advertising and marketing. Immediately after criticizing the penchant for theory and numbers, Mitrović went on to insist that his "simple" handbook would show "universal laws proven with decades of use and the newest methods that have been applied in developed markets."[64]

The campaign to legitimize marketing and advertising thus evidences a consistent pattern of appeal to categories already accorded substantial legitimacy in the ideology of Yugoslav socialism: rationality, science, technocratic expertise, planning, development, public service, Yugoslav exceptionalism. Even in the industry's early self-representation there were, to be sure, a few occasions when practitioners largely dispensed with any attempt to tailor their exposition of advertising and marketing practice to the values of the prevailing system.[65] But presentations of that type were rare. Much more common were efforts to cleanse advertising and marketing, at least superficially, of the taint of capitalism. With a degree of cosmetic alteration to bring them into apparent conformity with Yugoslavia's "special conditions," the techniques of consumer communication could be, and were, offered up as perfectly acceptable import items.

New and Improved, or Just Window Dressing? The Problem of "Socialist Advertising"

The many recurring references to the special nature of Yugoslav socialism, and to key motifs of socialist ideology more generally, suggest in turn the value of a closer consideration of the idea of "socialist advertising." The Yugoslav case, it turns out, presents an extraordinarily useful point of departure for the study of that problematic concept.

Yugoslavia was not the only socialist society in which the proponents of commercial promotion attempted to articulate an alternative to the theory and practice developed in the West. Steeped as it was in the values and assumptions of unfettered capitalism, the received tradition of marketing and advertising could hardly be imported wholesale into communist lands; some attempt to bring it into line with socialist values was required. Business

---

64. Mitrović, *O+P+P=: priručnik za upravljanje propagandom*, at 11, 17.
65. See, for example, Dinter, *Ekonomsko-propagandna služba u poduzeću*.

leaders and communications specialists in other socialist states also wrestled with the problems inherent in efforts to enhance domestic consumption through the use of commercial promotion.[66] Alongside the specialized literature on the subject there arose in Eastern Europe various professional institutions focused on the practical application of marketing and advertising techniques.[67]

The history of these parallel efforts remains largely unexplored, but my sampling of evidence from a number of potentially comparable cases points toward the conclusion that such activities in most other socialist countries were, both in practical and ideological terms, often quite limited, constrained as they were by the more rigid political and economic structures of the Soviet bloc. Hungary seems to have been something of an exception, as was, at least for a time, the German Democratic Republic. Conservative Czechoslovakia, another relatively prosperous socialist society, did develop its own advertising infrastructure, but compared to what went on in Yugoslavia, the work undertaken there was not just bounded and cautious but downright tame.[68] The large gap between the Yugoslav pattern of practice and the model dominant in more conventional communist states appears to have opened quite rapidly in the mid-1950s, and by the 1960s representatives of the Yugoslav guild were frequently (and proudly) commenting on the extent to which other socialist countries lagged behind. Techniques of commercial promotion were not neglected entirely, but they tended toward the primitive and were pressed into service as a means to sell the plan and not, as marketing's true believers would have it, as ways to plan the sale.

Yugoslavia offered something substantially different. The difference "on the ground" was remarkable, too: the country became a shoppers' paradise for consumers from all over socialist Europe, who came in droves to take advantage of the bounty available to them there and nowhere else. The department stores and boutiques of Zagreb, Ljubljana, and Belgrade were as close to the West as the average shopper from Bratislava or Kraków was likely to get.

---

66. On advertising in East Germany, see Merkel, "Alternative Realities, Strange Dreams, Absurd Utopias: On Socialist Advertising and Market Research," in *Socialist Modern: East German Everyday Culture and Politics,* ed. Katherine Pence and Paul Betts (Ann Arbor, 2008), 323–344; Simone Tippach-Schneider, *Messemännchen und Minol-Pirol: Werbung in der DDR* (Berlin, 1999). On the USSR, see Randi Cox, "All This Can Be Yours! Soviet Commercial Advertising and the Social Construction of Space, 1928–1956," in *The Landscape of Stalinism: The Art and Ideology of Soviet Space,* ed. Evgeny Dobrenko and Eric Naiman (Seattle, 2003), 125–162.

67. See, for example, the work of East Germany's DEWAG organization, as documented in the group's professional journal, *Neue Werbung.*

68. See, for example, the Czechoslovak advertising journal *Propagace* [Advertising]. I am grateful to Bradley Abrams for generously sharing his insights into and sources documenting the Czechoslovak case.

As an unusually robust example of the growth of an advertising-driven, abundance-driven consumer culture under socialism,[69] the country squarely poses the question of the viability of what some Yugoslav specialists and many of their counterparts elsewhere in the communist world called "socialist advertising." The Yugoslav setting—one in which the advertising was genuinely advertising and the socialism genuinely socialist—might therefore seem to offer an ideal case for studying the problems inherent in that notion. Yet the record clearly discloses that, for all the talk about a new and thoroughly socialist conception of advertising, Yugoslav advertisers actually did very little to develop any coherent theory of such a new style of practice, much less to implement it.

They did not fail for want of an auspicious start. The concept of an expressly "socialist advertising" had been advanced quite earnestly in East European circles in the late 1950s, when de-Stalinization sparked considerable interest in the possibilities that advertising might hold for the socialist world.[70] The defining moment of this early phase came in December 1957, when Yugoslav experts, along with their counterparts from the other European communist states, China, Vietnam, North Korea, and Mongolia, traveled to Prague for a major conference of advertising specialists and others interested in promoting socialist commerce. That twelve-day meeting culminated in an elaborately constructed joint resolution of the conference delegates, a document that would become part of the foundation for the study of advertising in Yugoslavia and other socialist societies. The resolution offered a set of sweeping pronouncements on the "fundamental duties" of advertising in a socialist economy:

1. Socialist advertising must lift up and educate the populace with the aim of elevating taste, must develop and stimulate their needs, so as to in this way promote demand for goods produced. The result of this sort of advertising must be reflected in the qualitative improvement of national consumption, as well as in the formation of new needs and new tastes, as a consequence of which the development of new and additional production will be accelerated.

---

69. The People's Republic of China, of course, offers many provocative points for comparison, but one might question how "socialist" that economy has remained. See Charlotte Ikels, *The Return of the God of Wealth: The Transition to a Market Economy in Urban China* (Stanford, 1996); Deborah S. Davis, ed., *The Consumer Revolution in Urban China* (Berkeley, 2000).

70. Worth noting is that the potential for a distinctly and expressly "socialist marketing" seems to have sparked comparatively little interest, perhaps because the marketing concept is undeniably Western in its derivation and so closely tied to capitalist understandings of the nature of business and economic relations. Nevertheless, the industry literature is filled with assertions that marketing, like advertising, could be readily harmonized with the "specific circumstances" of self-management socialism. See, for example, Branislav Đorđević, "Je li koncept marketinga inkompatibilan sa našim društveno-ekonomskim sistemom?" *Marketing* 8, no. 3 (1977): 8–11.

2. The role of advertising includes the assistance that it must offer to the populace in an informative way with respect to rational methods of the consumption of goods. This function of advertising does not reflect merely a new relationship between the retailer and the consumer, but also a concern for the consumer and his needs, and is, moreover, of great significance for the economical and rational use of material goods, which the community creates for the greater satisfaction of the needs of the nation.

3. Advertising must promote the maturity of socialist commerce so that the consumer, thanks to well-organized advertising, will find the goods he needs ever more quickly and make his purchases in the most convenient way, and with the least waste of time. This factor is of great significance and scope, for in this way the fulfillment of production is accelerated, the productivity of the labor of those employed in commerce is enhanced, and at the same time the utilization of existing and available retail space is much more forcefully exploited as well, with the result that the expenses of the commercial distribution of goods are significantly reduced.[71]

As this manifesto suggests, participants in the 1957 Prague conference occupied themselves with many of the themes that had already emerged in the discourse of the young Yugoslav industry, ideas that would maintain their currency among the country's advertising and marketing workers: rationalizing consumption, increasing the efficiency and ease of purchases, stimulating demand for domestic production, increasing income, cutting costs, educating and informing consumers, satisfying needs, and promoting new and higher consumer tastes (this last sometimes paired with a lofty, if ill-defined, notion of improving the common culture).

In Yugoslavia, these ideas became a common refrain in the appeal for the acceptance of advertising, especially in the early decades of the industry's expansion. Although the country was now comfortably outside the Soviet orbit and developments in the Soviet bloc did not heavily influence its advertising practice, the Prague resolution remained a part of the domestic debate for years.[72] Notably, Yugoslav specialists often avoided using the specific designation "socialist advertising" for their own work, perhaps to underscore the distinctiveness of what they were doing, but they did frequently invoke (with apparent approval) the conference itself and the principles of the resolution that it yielded.[73]

---

71. *Rezolucija Internacionalne konferencije ekonomskih propagandista*, Prague, 9–21 December 1957, reprinted in Mrvoš, *Propaganda reklama publicitet*, 502–503, at 502. For a more detailed report on the conference, see the untitled piece by Mrvoš published in *Naš publicitet* 4 (December 1957): 31–40.

72. See, for example, Vračar, *Privredna propaganda*, 136–137.

73. A follow-up conference was held in Poznań, Poland, in 1972. There is some indication that at least the conceptualization of advertising in certain other socialist countries was edging

As its key declarations make clear, the Prague statement on "socialist advertising" proclaimed, in effect, a Marxist-Leninist version of the gospel of efficiency. Although this concern for rationality pales compared to the emphasis placed on these values in the neoclassical economics of the West, it has nevertheless been a strong current of socialist economic ideology (though arguably not a similarly important part of socialist practice). But despite the seeming affinities between some of the ideas expressed in the Prague communiqué and the theoretical and practical justifications of advertising offered up in the capitalist world, the conference delegates insisted that the advertising practices they envisioned had nothing to do with advertising as it had developed in the industrialized West. Socialist advertising [*socijalistički ekonomski publicitet*] would, they said, reflect the realities of socialist life in a way "fundamentally contrary to the substance of capitalist advertising [*reklama*]," which, the resolution stressed, shows no concern for the interests of the masses but instead "serves the interests of individual entrepreneurs with the aim of personal enrichment."[74]

In Yugoslavia, practitioners often described advertising in socialist-sounding terms not unlike those announced at the 1957 gathering in Czechoslovakia. On various occasions, for example, the trade sources reiterated the Prague delegates' conviction that advertising under socialism ought to be justified in both economic *and* social terms.[75] Yugoslav commentators frequently suggested that, in a socialist setting, advertising needed to be a more modest and measured undertaking than the unbridled hucksterism fostered in the West. And they emphasized that commercial promotion had to be limited by the principle "that it must not lead people astray into the purchase of unneeded goods, satisfying the current interests of the producer and not those of the buyer, who does not actually have the suggested need at all."[76] This perspective stressed that "socialist advertising should stimulate in the consumer only desires for goods that he objectively needs and that are, with respect to his capacities, available to him."[77] Or, as another representative Yugoslav source insisted:

> *We are not a consumer society,* and although we accept some phenomena of the market economy, we must adjust them to socialist principles and to our entire socioeconomic system. Keeping this fact in mind, both the marketing concept

---

cautiously toward an acknowledgment of the role of markets in economic efficiency. Whether actual practice elsewhere corresponded to such a trend is a matter for future research.

74. *Rezolucija Internacionalne konferencije ekonomskih propagandista*, in Mrvoš, *Propaganda reklama publicitet*, at 502.

75. See, for example, *Drugo jugoslavensko savjetovanje propagandista [Proceedings of the Second Yugoslav Conference of Advertising Specialists]*, Zagreb, 22–23 February 1963, 8–9 (Zagreb, 1963).

76. Franjo Perič, "Ekonomika propagande," in *Reklama v gospodarski propagandi*, ed. Branko Vrčon (Ljubljana, 1967), 26–45, at 30.

77. Ibid.

itself and the creation of advertising methods within the framework of that concept must include those traits that are characteristic of our vision of socialism. And that means, above all, a humanistic content.[78]

Yugoslav advertising thus remained, at least according to the line typically advanced by its defenders, a distinctly socialist practice, notwithstanding all the flexibility, openness to the West, and ideological innovation of the Yugoslav system.

Yet for all these well-chosen words of caution (or comfort) concerning the ultimate humanity and decency of advertising in the "specific conditions" of Yugoslav socialism, in practice the Western and Yugoslav approaches clearly were thought to be substantially, if not entirely, interchangeable. Again and again, industry leaders defended the introduction of Western techniques, claiming that they would naturally modify them as required for Yugoslav use. Along these lines, the remarks of Branko Vrčon are typical, and typically revealing:

> Here I would caution you especially that in socialism, insofar as the *methods* that we use in connection with advertising are at issue, we would be considering the significance of advertising completely incorrectly if we were to take the position that our socialist economics and our socialist social order warn us against the use of various contemporary, already well-established *methods* from the capitalist world. Abroad, in the markets of the more than seventy countries with which we trade, we encounter all possible forms of capitalist commercial promotion every day. It is fitting, of course, and completely natural that we not only take account of such forms everywhere, but moreover, after transforming them, systematically use them wherever the need for that appears.[79]

This tendency to confess (publicly and insistently) the need to transform capitalist expertise as a prerequisite for domestic application was pervasive in the rhetoric of the Yugoslav trade. Yet little specific attention was given to the thornier question of just *how* to transform the forms of capitalist advertising before putting them to systematic use.

The way the industry talked about its own work left the distinct impression that simply eliminating the private ownership of the means of production and the private profit motive had, in fact, *already* accomplished much of what was thought necessary (at least within advertising and marketing circles) to convert advertising into a force that could serve the interests of ordinary workers and consumers—to render advertising, as it were, sanitized for their protection. One typical analysis explained the distinction:

---

78. Miroslav Fruht, *Kreacija privredne propagande* (Belgrade, 1975), 21.
79. Vrčon, "Reklama kot del propagande v gospodarstvu," in *Reklama v gospodarski propagandi*, 7–25, at 16.

"One must differentiate between and distinguish the methods of advertising from its goals. In addition, one must strictly distinguish between the goals of socialist and capitalist advertising.... It is well known that in capitalism the primary purpose of the economic activity of every entrepreneur is that he attain the highest possible profit. Advertising is subordinated to this purpose as well, whereas in the socialist economy the basic purpose is essentially different, and much higher. The purpose of the socialist economy is social production, from which every member of the society benefits as much as he contributes to the community."[80] Advertising, in this view, was by no means antithetical to socialist economic relations. Rather, it was merely one of the common "instruments" necessary in *any* economic system based on the exchange of goods and money. As such, advertising was not only permissible in the socialist economy but was actually *required*.

It is important to note, however, just how little this approach really asks of advertising. This line of reasoning, and it was a common one, was remarkably undemanding; it implied that most if not all of the methods of capitalist advertising would become acceptable once its "primary purpose"—entrepreneurial enrichment—was removed.

And a neglect of the "hows" of socialist advertising was by no means just the habit of the mature, more secure advertising industry of the later decades of Yugoslav communism. Very much the same tendency was evident from the beginning, as seen, for example, in the seminal 1959 textbook by Dušan Mrvoš. Like the many opinion pieces Mrvoš had published in previous years in OZEHA's organ *Naš publicitet*, this work sought to reassure its audience that advertising posed no real dangers—that it would not, at least in the hands of conscientious experts, prove to be a carrier of ideological contagion. Although Yugoslavia could and would develop advertising practices to achieve some of the same ends served by advertising in the West, Mrvoš said, "we will not imitate the methods of that sort of capitalist advertising that, in the competitive battle, tries not only to press but also to destroy its rival and to drive it out of the marketplace. Likewise, we will not make use of all those criteria of appeal [*apel*] and message [*poruka*] that have been developed in the capitalist economy."[81] Yet in the end this manual, much like its influential counterpart published by Josip Sudar a year earlier, made no substantial effort to conform its specific content to the norms of socialism. It provided very little sense, if any, of what sorts of messages and appeals would have been off-limits.

These samplings from the rhetoric used to defend advertising and marketing in Yugoslavia illustrate the uncertain, vulnerable, even suspect position in which the industry's specialists continually found themselves—a dilemma that led them to favor the unremitting pledge of allegiance, the socialist

---

80. Deželak, *Ekonomska propaganda*, 6.
81. Mrvoš, *Propaganda, reklama, publicitet*, 9.

spin, and the Truth Half Told. Their representation of their work leaves the unmistakable impression that they felt compelled to proclaim the reality of, and their loyalty to, a distinctive new form of commercial promotion, a genuinely socialist species of advertising. Yet in the voluminous record they have left behind, very little suggests that the industry advocates took that charge very seriously in practice. The bulk of what they wrote and what they created leads, in fact, to a completely contrary conclusion. In handbook after handbook, treatise after treatise, we find what seems to be the obligatory introductory apologia: careful justifications for the transfer of all these dubious capitalist methods to the socialist setting, often accompanied by the reassurances that a socialist style of advertising did indeed exist and that it represented something categorically different from its capitalist forebears. Yet beyond the verbiage no sustained attempt to construct an identifiably socialist practice of consumer persuasion can be found in these texts, and the same must be said of the advertisements themselves. The faith in socialist advertising, so frequently invoked in Yugoslavia, appears to have been almost all credo and no praxis.

A few representatives of the industry, it must be noted, were rather more vociferous in their insistence that Yugoslav advertising be something specifically socialist. Such commentators stressed that the lifestyles, living standards, and other fundamental economic features of the West made it difficult and perhaps even unwise to adopt a great deal of Western advertising and marketing practice.[82] Even in the late 1980s, when confidence in socialism had been severely eroded, occasional trade sources expressed pride in the purportedly specific, socialist nature of Yugoslav advertising. Thus the foreword to the advertising textbook published by Borislav Mitrović in 1989 asserted that the author had set forth "the clinical picture, diagnosis, and therapeutic treatment of the advertising specialist in the framework of the self-management market system, in which he invests his hopes," singling out Mitrović for special praise for having done so "without falling into the paleo-capitalistic euphoria of a consumerist economy."[83]

---

82. Along these lines, note the views expressed at a 1975 trade conference by Aleksandar Spasić, a Belgrade political scientist and academic who was a leader in the institutional consolidation of the field and who frequently commented on the development of the domestic advertising industry. "Društveno-ekonomski aspekti ekonomske propagande u mas medijima," in *Mediji komuniciranja s tržištem danas i sutra*, 96–102. Spasić, who in 1973 had been elected the first president of the Yugoslav Advertising Association [*Savez Ekonomskih Propagandista Jugoslavije*], looked askance at the experience of the West and called for a reformulation of the values of advertising along more emphatically socialist lines. But action was not forthcoming.

83. Sergije Lukač, "Predgovor," in Mitrović, *O+P+P=: priručnik za upravljanje propagandom*, 9–10, at 9. Although the handbook in question does indeed devote rather more time than many comparable works to reflections on the social underpinnings of Yugoslav advertising, it, too, is ultimately concerned with how to manage marketing and advertising operations effectively, and in this regard it is heavily influenced by Western practices and experience. For a sense of the continuing tension between the perceived need to criticize the excesses of Western advertising and the high regard in which it was nevertheless held, one need look no further than

Still, even these more ardent affirmations typically amounted to little more than a declaration of good intentions in the introduction to a monograph or an earnest-sounding expression of concern in an address to colleagues at a conference. Here again, there was virtually no effort made to address the specifics of how the practice of advertising, and particularly its content, could be adjusted to the stated norms of what was said to be a distinctive socialist way of doing business.

Historians seeking a truly "socialist advertising" will have to look elsewhere. Yugoslavia did indeed offer advertising *in* socialism, and plenty of it. Commercial promotion in the country was definitively shaped and constrained by the socialist political and ideological context in which it appeared and by the concrete realities of consumption in an economy that was, despite its right-deviationist departures from orthodoxy, still very much a socialist system. Yet the simple fact that we find advertising in a socialist country, and that advertising practice felt the strictures of socialist political culture, does not settle the question (not unless the definitional bar is set far too low, that is). In the end Yugoslav advertising was not "socialist advertising," despite the legitimizing rhetoric that so often accompanied it.

This mismatch between rhetoric and reality does not imply, however, that the ideological context that socialism provided was of only marginal importance. To the contrary, it is apparent that the advertising and marketing community infused the discourse of the trade with formulations designed to appeal precisely to categories already accorded respect and legitimacy within socialist ideology. If socialist values exerted only limited influence on the practice, methods, and content of Yugoslav commercial promotion, they nevertheless had a powerful impact on the structure of the long campaign to secure the place of advertising and marketing in Yugoslav society.

---

to the second of the two forewords to Mitrović's handbook, this one by Vladimir Štambuk. Ibid., 7–8.

4 Fearing It

The Values of Marxism and the Contradictions of Consumerism

The real use value of the product must be the true goal of every system
of production that wishes to label itself "socialist."
                                    —Besim Spahić, *Strategija savremene propagande*

The external form of things must be ever more pleasing and inviting
for buyers, which demands additional expenses, as well as the use of
psychology, an artistic sense for design, and so on, as well as cleverness
in advertising, in order to convince the buyer that the superficial, external
use value of an advertised item is identical with its actual, internal use
value.
                                    —Nada Sfiligoj, "Trg in tržno komuniciranje v našem gospodarstvu"

"The worker is still the humblest of human beings, even when he
drives a Chrysler and has colour television at home."[1] With that comment,
pithy and packed with the sympathy, anger, and skepticism that typified
Yugoslavia's rich Marxist-humanist "deviation" of the 1960s and 1970s,
political philosopher and social critic Mihailo Marković captured the awk-
ward contradictions of the consumer experience in the latest phase of modern industrial production. Ostensibly the observation was targeted at life
under capitalism: although more and more working-class laborers in the
socialist countries were taking in the pleasures of television, we can safely
assume that few or none ever settled into the "soft Corinthian leather" of a
Chrysler Cordoba or enjoyed that special feeling of distinction and privilege
that, the ads insinuated, could be found behind the wheel of a New Yorker,
Newport, or Imperial—all wonderfully cunning names for conjuring up a
sense of class and "class."

Yet with respect to workers and their pleasures, Marković was actually
advancing a much larger argument, and one that came with a special twist.

Sources for the epigraphs: Besim Spahić, *Strategija savremene propagande: prilog demitologizaciji savremene građanske reklame* (Sarajevo: Oslobođenje, 1985), 8–9; Nada Sfiligoj,
"Trg in tržno komuniciranje v našem gospodarstvu," *Bančni vestnik* 35, no. 12 (December
1986): 371–372.

1. Mihailo Marković, *The Contemporary Marx: Essays on Humanist Communism* (Nottingham, UK, 1974), 184.

Much more than simply another leftist criticism of a strictly capitalist species of class narcosis, these few words about "the humblest of human beings" drove to the heart of the dilemma that confronted contemporary Marxism during the anodyne affluence of the postwar years. A "great transformation" of its own sort, this new prosperity, and the subtle rebalancing of class interests and even class definitions that went along with it, forced thinkers in the Marxist tradition to modify their theories and their understanding of history. Marxist-Leninist statecraft, now the order of the day in places far away from the Soviet fountainhead, also had to adjust to current economic conditions that did not neatly correspond to those that had provided the basis for Marx's predictions. Already that model had proven rather shaky when revolution sprang up, contrary to the forecast, in places hardly touched by an urban proletariat. And now recent events rendered the early orthodox theorizing even more problematic, as the material comfort that seemed to go hand in hand with developed capitalism had started to yield a complacency and a realignment of loyalties that could look suspiciously like the *embourgeoisement* of the capitalist working class. Modern industrial production, it seemed, might produce the sort of surplus wealth that could, if spread around liberally enough, undermine working-class consciousness. Which way was history really heading?

If these new dynamics were a genuine worry insofar as they might hinder the emergence of Marxist government in new locales, they provoked even more grave concern when they threatened to thwart the exercise of socialist power already installed. And nowhere was that problem more acute than in Yugoslavia.

By many contemporary domestic accounts, Yugoslavia was hurtling toward the creation of a capitalist-style "consumer society" by the late 1960s. As seen in the foregoing chapters, living standards had risen dramatically, and innovative methods of advertising and retailing had been put into practice all around the country. Along with a fresh set of styles, tastes, and desires, new expectations about what economic policy ought to deliver and a new ideology of consumer sovereignty were spreading throughout Yugoslavia, "imported," to a significant extent, from the West.

But the move toward consumerism—and it was certainly a persistent drift in that direction, if not a headlong rush as some maintained—did not go unchallenged. Instead, consumer culture and the advertising and marketing that propelled it encountered, early on, staunch and ardent resistance. That resistance and its broader implications are the subjects of the next section of the book, which in successive chapters focuses first on the nature and intensity of the Marx-inspired mainstream critiques of market culture, then on the wavering efforts of the party-state apparatus to balance the obvious benefits of consumer satisfaction with the perceived risks of a slide into consumerist values and ethics, and, finally, in chapter 6, on the more uncompromising and bitter opposition to consumerism—and to the communist authorities who allegedly had promoted it—that came from the work of critics like Mihailo Marković and his allies in Yugoslavia's radically egalitarian, antiestablishment, Marxist-humanist movement.

Advertising Age: The Evolution of the Critique of Commercial Promotion

Almost as soon as the elements of a consumer culture appeared in Yugoslavia, a discomfort with it started to surface as well. In its earliest phases, beginning in the 1950s, the reaction against the intrusion of market culture centered mainly on specific styles, techniques, and tropes of advertising. Only later would there emerge a dominant concern about broader issues such as the social consequences of commercial promotion and its role in fashioning popular culture.

Marxism always mattered most in these controversies. It provided the ever present formative context. Yet for the critics, these were by and large not problems considered to be purely internal either to Marxism or to Yugoslavia. Other values and intellectual tendencies mattered, too, and the evolution of attitudes seen in Yugoslavia was also a function of the society's participation in a larger, transnational conversation on market culture and consumption that recognized, drew from, and yet ultimately went beyond Marxist insights. In the 1950s and early 1960s that wider critique was itself still in its infancy, with great changes still ahead. The shifts that occurred within socialist Yugoslavia across four decades consequently reflect the maturation of the international debate from an initial mid-century focus on the propriety of particular appeals and methods to a later emphasis on the relationship of market culture and consumer culture to more expansive and more deeply entrenched structures of economic and political power.

Just how strong a causative force commercial promotion actually exerts over the making of mass culture has long been hotly disputed. During the 1950s and 1960s industrialized capitalist societies saw continued clashes between apologists for the advertising, retailing, and marketing trades and those who viewed such work as fundamentally deceitful and harmful. Against the popular assumption of an ever looming danger of individual and group manipulation, some later observers like the influential media sociologist Michael Schudson cast doubt on the capacity of advertising to bend minds and refashion tastes reliably and efficiently along the lines that advertisers desire. Even the (comparatively) straightforward issue of the effects of advertising is, accordingly, very much in doubt. The messier questions of how market culture is produced and what it means for those who participate in it have shown themselves to be just as difficult, if not more so. Schudson, whose thoughts on the matter reflect a useful mixture of probing empiricist skepticism and a critical sensitivity to the unseen and the subtle, remained unconvinced of the effect of advertisements as "a specific goad to sales" with the power to change buyers' choices as the ad men have claimed and the critics have feared, but he proved more open to the idea of advertising as "a general cultural encouragement toward materialism," believing that with time it may shape social preferences and attitudes.[2]

The dynamics at work in the formation of consumer culture are extraordinarily complex, of course, and advertising is best treated as only a single important piece of the puzzle of causation. These debates over advertising and its consequences are still far from resolved, but whatever the ultimate merits of the broader indictment of advertising as an engine of culture, the matter seemed much more clear-cut to those critics in Yugoslavia who took their cues primarily from Marxist thought. The critique of market culture that began to take shape in the 1950s plainly assumed that the various manifestations of commercial promotion that had become so noticeable so quickly were, in fact, playing a key generative role. Indeed, one of the most revealing features of the debate within Yugoslavia is the critics' insistence that what lay at the heart of the consumerist orientation spreading among the public was the practice, or malpractice, of advertising, retailing, and marketing. They usually traced the problem to these activities rather than, say, to the individualism and exaltation of choice that are arguably implicit in mature diversified markets, to the variety and expressive cultural potential inherent in the products of virtually every developed manufacturing economy, or to some perhaps more deeply rooted set of human urges for pleasure, status, distinction, and self-expression, all of which might prove much less tractable to social and political management, and thus much more unsettling.

As it happened, then, the condemnation fell on commercial promotion as the source of the spreading troubles. But it took some time to arrive at this verdict. Early on, the criticisms that were voiced had a distinctly ad hoc quality. They tended to reflect sporadic upwellings of doubt or irritation rather than any sustained, coherent, or systematic campaign.[3] Recurring complaints that Yugoslav advertising too often slipped into misleading, unfair, crude, or tasteless usages marked the public conversation. There were also indications that some observers had quickly begun to see advertising as a form of visual pollution. One contributor to *Naš publicitet,* the trade journal and promotional organ of Croatia's leading OZEHA agency, thus remarked in 1956 on the misgivings prompted by the growing use of potentially intrusive outdoor display ads like the large painted wall over Zagreb's central square promoting *Vjesnik,* the city's principal daily newspaper. This industry advocate defended the use of such displays but noted "the hostile position of certain citizens in various municipal and urbanistic institutions of some cities, who look down upon the so-called *reklama* [the old colloquial

---

2. Schudson, *Advertising, the Uneasy Persuasion,* 130.
3. See V. Desantolo, "Uz prvi broj časopisa Standard," *Standard* 1, no. 1 (May 1955): 1.

word for advertising, and a term that was, as we have seen, held in disrepute by the professionals] and who fear that something new placed on some square or street might ruin the majestic appearance of their cities."[4]

Others continued to wonder whether advertising was pointless in a society based on socialist distribution,[5] though the developing industry, helped along by the pro-market political climate of the country's distinctive self-management socialism, usually seemed able to put those concerns to rest, at least as a matter of public debate if not always a matter of business practice. Probably the most significant criticisms in these early years, however, were grounded in an abiding skepticism about the fundamental utility and efficacy of advertising. To some, it remained unclear whether advertising really worked or not, and industry specialists still found it difficult to disabuse enterprise managers of their fears that, given the circumstances of the Yugoslav economy, money spent for commercial promotion was as good as thrown away.

The contours of the debate changed with the passage of time, but not entirely. Even as the practice of Yugoslav advertising rapidly matured and industry professionals consolidated their position during the 1960s and 1970s, many of the old sore points lingered on. Despite the dramatic expansion of the trade, some critics and enterprise managers were still to be convinced that advertising was an effective method of boosting sales, much less a cost-effective technique.[6] Even the now undeniable popularity of advertising did not prove wholly persuasive: there remained an unassuaged doubt about whether Yugoslav companies might simply have fallen for a fad, ignoring real economic value and engaging in advertising because it had become "the thing to do," presumably expected of any modern, self-respecting, forward-looking business.

This was the judgment of commentators such as Marjan Rožič, a secretary of the influential Socialist Alliance of the Working People (hereafter, the "Socialist Alliance," also commonly referred to as the SAWP or SAWPY), who suggested in 1973 that advertising and other forms of commercial promotion had simply become de rigueur for some enterprises, with questionable benefits. "Often, funds that have no connection at all with sales results are used for advertising," Rožič claimed. "There is an outpouring of resources, as if this were, for example, advertising for the sake of the advertisement, and not because of the effect on sales."[7] Speaking as a representative of an

---

4. V. Kl. [probably OZEHA's Veljko Klašterka], "Vjesnik na Trgu republike," *Naš publicitet* 3, no. 1 (May 1956); see also the back cover of the same issue, which immediately follows the article, for one of the advertisements in question. For another pleading of the merits of outdoor advertising, see A. J., "Reklama na zidovima," *Standard* 1, no. 1 (May 1955): 15.

5. See Jevrem Brković, "Reklama," *Savremena privredna propaganda* 2, no. 3 (April 1958): 30.

6. See, for example, Otmar Lipovšek, "O ekonomiki propagande," *Bilten DEPS*, nos. 9/10 (n.d. [ca. 1970/1971]): 15–16.

7. Marjan Rožič, quoted in Marjan Serdarušić, "Pod cijenu 'milosti,'" *Ideja*, no. 4 (1973): 5.

extra-party group that served one of the most important institutional "transmission belts" between the public and the communist leadership, this critic found it hard to believe that many of the increasingly common forms of promotion, such as the sponsorship of sports and entertainment events that ran the gamut "from beauty contests to soccer clubs," could have much real economic value to the enterprises involved.[8] Many others expressed a similar concern over the use of contests and games of chance to stimulate sales, and over the advertising of alcohol and tobacco, all of which were also frequent themes in the public debate over advertising and its methods.[9]

Well into the 1970s critical evaluations of Yugoslav practice continued to invoke the need for advertising to be, first and foremost, a means of informing consumers. This was precisely what the defenders of the trade had long held up as the primary mission and purpose of commercial promotion in a socialist country. As seen in the previous chapter, no small part of the critique came from representatives of the industry itself, whose pronouncements on these subjects often attested to a mentality that was sensitive to and tried to recapitulate (not to say parrot) the "correct" Marxist outlook of the party, and who were inclined to preempt those complaints insofar as possible with a widely advertised effort at self-policing. (Such shows of deference and submission, of course, had deep roots in the Marxist-Leninist tradition.) Exercises in industry self-criticism led to continual calls for a higher standard, one more in keeping with familiar formulations of the aims and values of Yugoslav socialism. In this conception, Yugoslav advertising was supposed to be an altogether more straightforward affair, perhaps less artful but in the end more reliable. "The honest commercials (and advertising organizations)," according to Stane Možina, a teacher with close links to the profession, were "those that, instead of sex, vulgarity, *double entendres [dvoumnosti]*, and the like, attempt to establish a connection, that is, solid bonds with consumers, and that respond to the consumers' wishes and observations."[10] But if these were the applicable standards for a socialist society, the critics often found that the work of the domestic industry went wide of the mark.

Small-bore reservations of the sort described above, which persisted until the end of the socialist period, are important in their own right as indicators of a habitual discontent with the specific appeals and products of the industry of commercial promotion. Moreover, all such complaints were

---

8. Ibid.

9. For an example of the criticism directed against alcohol and tobacco, see the comments of Joža Vlahović, originally published in the Zagreb daily *Vjesnik* and excerpted in S. L. M., "Pretjerana revnost jednog komentatora," *Ideja*, no. 7 (1973): 9. Criticism of sales promotions using contests was frequent as well. See, for example, "Slovenski propagandisti protiv nagradnih igara," *Ideja*, no. 9 (1974): 39; cf. M. H., "O dvostrukom moralu," *Ideja*, no. 3 (July 1978): 9–10.

10. Stane Možina, "Vloga potrošniških svetov," *Delo*, 12 January 1974, 19.

noteworthy for the simple fact that they could even be deemed relevant and necessary in a society that, viewed with an eye to the logic of its political system and the potential for state control of business practice, might have been imagined to be virtually immune to such troubling phenomena. But in the main they did not amount to any thoroughgoing indictment of Yugoslav commerce or Yugoslav public culture. Instead, they were suggestions for a bit of helpful corrective tweaking here and there.

Later, however, with burgeoning prosperity and a noticeable (some said rampant) tendency to cater to consumer desires, the terms of the debate shifted, with the changes most rapid and most salient in the late 1960s and early 1970s. Now a wider, more forceful, and expressly *cultural* analysis was beginning to take shape. Rooted as it was in a concern for the changes then sweeping Yugoslav society, this new critique points us toward the deeper meanings of the consumer experience.

The Engineers of Human Souls: Communist Values, Bourgeois Tastes, and the Power of the Advertocracy

As one would expect, many of the most bitter critics were committed Communists, hostile to capitalism as a matter of principle and predisposed to distrust the lifestyles and business practices that they associated with it. Beyond this fundamental ideological antipathy, some recognized in commercial promotion and consumerism a threat to the socialist political and social order in Yugoslavia itself, and these worries grew more intense as time passed and the consumer-oriented economy took hold in the 1960s and 1970s. Practical considerations of preserving the authority of the party may therefore have also motivated their attacks.

Even in the latest stages of the Yugoslav experiment, after all the reforms and all the experimental departures from more orthodox communist methods and doctrines, Marxist understandings clearly continued to claim the dominant position in the critique of commercial practice. The defenders of commercial promotion and the consumer orientation also continued to hold out the promise that the innovations adopted by Yugoslav "business" were, or at least could be, consistent with socialism. But the skeptics remained unconvinced.

Although Marxism, with its concerns about use value, the alienated surplus of labor, and the like, always remained the bedrock of the anti-advertising, anti-consumerist line, the evolving public controversy often revealed that Western critiques and the Western experience had proven all too relevant for Yugoslavia. That was clearly the judgment, for example, of Sarajevo sociologist Besim Spahić, whose contributions to the final episodes of the domestic debate suggested that Yugoslav advertising, even after so many years of promised corrections and conformity, still needed to aim for something radically different from the Western usages it had thus far emulated. By 1983 Spahić had come to a grim assessment of the role of commercial promotion in Yugoslav society, arguing that, both as a matter of theory and practice, the qualities and the function of advertising in Yugoslavia did not differ essentially from those encountered in capitalist systems. A solution, in this view, would have required the near total reconstruction of Yugoslav advertising.[11] Spahić, who had studied at the *École Supérieure de Publicité et Marketing* in Paris and had an intimate acquaintance with the Western practice that formed the primary focus of his disapproval, concluded that capitalist conceptions of advertising showed far too little concern for genuine criteria of value and, as a result, had no place in a society based on Marxist principles. "According to its theoretical foundations," he wrote in 1985, "a socialist system of goods production...must be a manner of production that takes as its point of departure, and is oriented toward, genuine human needs, which are truly satisfied only by *actual use value,* and not by luxurious cosmetics and a perverted meaning of production."[12]

Communist attitudes could at times be extraordinarily punishing, and skeptics of the most implacable sort were not hard to find. In one memorable media flap, for example, Voja Vukičević used the party's official newspaper as a platform to rail against the ascendancy of commercial promotion as "a special force for managing people's desires and dispositions." Writing in early 1973, during a period of heightened scrutiny toward market culture, Vukičević concluded that the practice of advertising in Yugoslavia had become nothing less than an "advertocracy" [*reklamokratija*]—a system of profit-driven psychological manipulation fundamentally antipathetic to self-management socialism. Advertising, he claimed, functioned as a method of psychological "torture" that had been designed to reshape the desire and will of ordinary citizens. Consumers in this view found themselves at the mercy of a "very advanced" psychological technique, one that "skillfully takes advantage of the most refined achievements of intellectual creative work." Contemporary advertising, according to Vukičević, "provokes and excites a person's consciousness, it arouses the emotions and penetrates into the psyche, so that it always appears to be pointing precisely to those human wants and desires that are truly characteristic of the person himself." To make matters worse, whatever benefits were to be had from advertising accrued solely to sellers, who were willing to go to extremes to serve their own interests.[13]

---

11. Besim Spahić, *Aspekti reklame u jugoslovenskom društvu* (Sarajevo: Oslobođenje, 1983), 167–168; see also 158–159.

12. Spahić, *Strategija savremene propagande,* 168–169.

13. References are to Voja Vukičević, "Antisamoupravna moć reklamokratije," *Kreativne komunikacije,* no. 7 (Febuary 1973): 8–9 (originally published in *Komunist,* 15 February 1973).

As a result of this constant subjection to irrational and deceptive advertising messages, Vukičević asserted, Yugoslavs were now frequently becoming "slaves" to the products they consumed: "Under the pressure of everyday life and the desire to stay 'in step with the times,' individual products become items 'you just can't do without.'" And the costs of all this mindless pursuit of fashion would be great: "Under the pressure of the advertocracy," he insisted, "people will strive to use only those goods that are 'up to date,' even at the cost of sacrificing other, elementary material or spiritual needs."[14]

A key element in this line of analysis in Yugoslavia, as elsewhere, was the idea that the creation of consumer culture was inherently linked to a pattern of production relations and to a collection of groups that stood to profit. The problem was therefore not advertising per se, or at least not *merely* advertising, but also the structure of economic and political relations that lay behind it, obscured by its artifice and its tantalizing promises. Ultimately this complex of interests, institutions, and incentives formed a system of domination, the "advertocracy" that seemed to pose such a threat to communism.

In a different time and place, Stalin had hoped that his socialist-realist writers would craft the templates that would permit the reliable mass production of an equally reliable citizenry. Now it seemed that in Yugoslavia it was instead the creators of advertising who had in fact become "the engineers of human souls," and they were manufacturing a class consciousness of a decidedly different sort. Moreover, in the judgment of Vukičević and other like-minded detractors, advertising was doing much more than simply warping individual human psyches, bad as that was. There were broader social consequences as well. Far too much money was being spent on advertising, and practically every enterprise had special funds set aside for it. Like the products it hawked, advertising itself had become something that Yugoslav companies thought they "just couldn't do without," and, as a result, enterprise budgets—and, in turn, workers' incomes—were suffering. A further danger, Vukičević warned, was that the advertocracy was busily generating its own philosophy and ideology, ideas that seemed to intrude into every area of interpersonal relations, and especially into culture. Advertising, from this perspective, now functioned as a species of disinformation, totally at odds with the values of self-management socialism. According to Vukičević, the country's reliance on and subjection to advertising was preventing its workers from becoming "the masters, and not the slaves, of the products of their own work and creative endeavor."[15] The entire socialist enterprise seemed to be at stake.

---

14. References are to Vukičević, "Antisamoupravna moć reklamokratije," 8–9.
15. References are to ibid.

The themes and ideas put forward in this *Komunist* piece were quite representative of the standard Marxist critique circulating in Yugoslavia at the time, as was the unease about the threat to socialism, but the approach was noteworthy for its uncompromising ferocity. In the face of so harsh and frontal an attack, the advertising industry fought back. The reaction was quick, sharp, and dismissive. The trade journal *Kreativne komunikacije*, which had reprinted the Vukičević attack, complained that the so-called "advertocracy" was sheer illusion, something completely "fabricated." The idea that Yugoslavs were becoming "slaves" to advertising came in for special ridicule from *Kreativne komunikacije* columnist Igor Mandič, who bluntly stated that he was "fed up with those self-styled visionaries [*vidovnjaci*] who see a danger for our self-management society in everything we share...*with Western culture.*" Yugoslavia's "apocalyptic prophets" [*apokaliptičari*], Mandič claimed, wanted to erect a "*cordon sanitaire*" around the country, protecting it with a "quarantine against contemporary civilization and all its contradictions, as if we could live as some isolated little society, sheltered away somewhere."[16]

Even though the response in *Kreativne komunikacije* was irate and remarkably bold, it was still quite clearly constrained and subdued by the governing values of the Marxist system in which these debates were taking place. Accordingly, Mandič was careful to point out that the culture of commercial promotion in Yugoslavia remained a safe distance away from the supposedly very different system that prevailed in the West. "We have not yet been flooded," he promised his audience, "with that truly perverted technology of advertising which all around the world is accepted as 'the new global theatre.'"[17] But such reassurances notwithstanding, the battle had been joined. For Marxist social critics, consumerism and market culture now ranked among the most important "internal enemies" of Yugoslav socialism.

Promise Her Anything, But Give Her... The Deceptions and Illusions of Market Culture

Of course, not all the criticism poured out on the country's new culture of consumption was as intemperate as the sort that declared Yugoslavs to be "slaves" subjected to the rule of an "advertocracy." Often enough, the critique proceeded along predictable communist lines, with the equally predictable leaden tones of Yugoslav party ideology, which may have been revisionist in its content but was hardly innovative when it came to rhetorical

---

16. Igor Mandič, "Izmišljene reklamokracije," *Vjesnik*, 24 February 1973; reprinted in *Kreativne komunikacije*, no. 7 (Febuary 1973): 9 (emphasis in original).
17. Ibid.

style. In the most skillful hands, however, the indictment of market culture could ascend to the poetic. That was the case, for example, in a 1974 analysis by Ivan Sedej, a columnist for one of the country's leading daily newspapers, who turned his complaints about a television commercial for ski clothing and equipment into a lyrical reflection on the dangers and deceits of consumer society. (The maker of the advertised products was not mentioned in the piece, but they may well have been manufactured by Slovenia's famous Elan company, one of the firms most successful in taking advantage of the latitude offered by self-management and pursuing an aggressive, brand-oriented marketing strategy that, with time, established the company as an industry leader not only in Yugoslavia but abroad as well.)

The objections in this instance were rooted in a criticism that was, on the face of it, familiar enough: the advertisement was deceptive. And, indeed, complaints about the fraudulent quality of advertising were a frequent feature of the Yugoslav debates. Yet here was evidence that the problem had taken on a new light. It was not that the ad was misleading in the traditional, narrower sense of exaggerated claims, misrepresented features, unfair comparisons, and overstated qualities. Rather, the television commercial under scrutiny in this case stood as an emblem for a larger and more profound illusion, and the trouble was not just with this particular spot but with advertising in general.

The goods being promoted were, in themselves, mundane and seemingly harmless enough, but they held out the promise of something far beyond the everyday, suggesting that "the purchase of expensive, fashionable equipment is the only entry ticket into the society of happy, idle young people who effortlessly amuse themselves in the snow." The implicit message, Sedej said, was that "we can therefore buy a ticket to high society—we can become talented, beautiful, and successful." The commercial, he believed, put forward an "even deeper lesson and suggestion" that free spending was what really made life worthwhile, that "money and the carefree enjoyment of life (in stylish clothes, of course) are the condition for beauty and broad smiles and spirited jokes in the vacation spots of the Alps." And a very good life it promised to be, too:

> The carefree rich guy is always handsome, and the girls who are with him are beautiful—no room here for big-bellied old men and fat old ladies. High society doesn't know them. High society is always beautiful, cordial, and playful. And most important: we apparently can join in it, if, of course, we buy such-and-such fashion product of the famous firm.

Like their counterparts elsewhere in the modern world, Yugoslavs had now found themselves living "in an age of substitutes," one in which companies promoting their own interests promised that "we can, for not much money, buy a substitute for high society and happy youth." Advertising would have people believe that the answer to all their hopes and problems was really quite simple: "Buy yourself satisfaction!"[18]

As this and many other contributions to the ongoing debate attest, opponents of the consumerist mind-set assumed that consumerism could be set in minds in a straightforward and reliable way. They saw the link between the messages disseminated by commercial promotion and the psyches of ordinary Yugoslav citizens as direct, potent, and certain. It was with such fears in mind, for example, that Ratko Božović identified a special danger in the capacity of advertising to mold human desires to its own ends. Božović was a Montenegrin political theorist and sociologist born in Bosnia who, during the course of a long career in Belgrade beginning in the early 1970s, became one of the country's most visible and committed critics of consumerism during the years of its rise to the forefront of public concern.[19] Stressing that the underlying rationale of virtually all advertising was commercial and that it was undertaken in furtherance of the interest of manufacturers and sellers, not buyers, Božović asserted that advertising trafficked in an "excessive recommendation" of consumption opportunities and "prepares people for an uncritical acceptance of everything that is being recommended and imposed."[20]

Worse yet, advertising made the mindless pursuit of the material seem eminently natural to consumers: "It prepares them for the fanatical adoration of things," Božović claimed, and "leads them to a stupefying mode of behavior in which they consider the decision that has been extracted from them to be their own." The larger implications for interpersonal relations—and, the critique suggested, for the future of socialist society—were tremendous. Lulled by the soothing and satisfying message of material plenty, targeted customers were ignoring the fact that business practices were creating an illusory set of needs and interests. They remained blissfully but dangerously unaware that their state of highly manipulated attention and inattention amounted to nothing less than "the beginning of a systematic suppression of their freedom."[21] For a society that had come to take its comparative liberty very seriously indeed, the new market culture seemed to pose potential threats to the freedom and democratization that had proven so essential to the construction of the Yugoslav "difference."

---

18. References are to Ivan Sedej, "Kupite si zadovoljstvo in srečo," *Delo*, 2 February 1974, 20.

19. See Božović's reflections on his career and work in "Izbegli iz normalnog života" (interview with Božović), *Etna: časopis za satiru* 7, no. 65 (1 April 2007), online at http://host.sezampro.yu/aforizmi/etna/etna65/etna8.htm (accessed 19 June 2008).

20. Ratko Božović, "Moral potrošnje," in idem, *Odnos sredstava informisanja prema potrošačkom društvu* (Belgrade, 1981), 29–32, at 30.

21. References are to ibid., 30.

From Stone Hatchets to Vacuum Cleaners to Televisions: Capitalist Tools and the Manufacture of False Needs

The fear that advertising was busily generating a huge number of artificial "needs" among the country's citizens represented another especially noticeable and, indeed, near constant feature of the Yugoslav debate as it matured in the 1960s and thereafter. Time and time again, the opponents of commercial promotion dismissed it as a collection of tactics designed to convince the consumer to pursue something that "in the absence of the methods and influences of advertising, he would not consider to be his interest or need."[22] An underlying difficulty, from the critics' perspective, was the self-interest of producers, many of whom, it appeared, were acting too much like their capitalist counterparts, with a reckless disregard of the damage that market culture could do. In Voja Vukičević's unsparing formulation, for example, those in control of the "advertocracy" plied their trade with the conviction that "it is necessary, whatever the cost, to prove that the product offered on the market represents a primary human need, a pure necessity, and a precondition for any sort of modern and contemporary living."[23]

Although Yugoslav critics thought the stakes were especially high for their own particular society because of the threats that such desires posed to its distinctive socialist principles, the critical rhetoric that took shape in Yugoslavia actually had a great deal in common with the "false needs" line articulated by both Marxists and Western commentators of widely varying ideological persuasions. The comparative intellectual fluidity of Yugoslav public discourse meant that the critics were quite capable of borrowing from Western insights into the capitalist experience in order to hammer home their indictment of consumerism. In that process they made the bad examples of the West even more meaningful—and, for socialism, more relevant. Ištvan Rajčan, the president of the Committee for Information Activities [Savjet za informiranje] of the Socialist Alliance of the Working People, stressed the gravity of the situation by noting that even in the bourgeois world sociologists had the good sense to be talking about "the terror of advertising and the deformation of the consciousness of the consumer."[24] If Westerners could recognize and combat the threat, the critics suggested, it was all the more imperative that Yugoslavs follow suit.

Right up through the final years of socialist Yugoslavia, the "false needs" theme remained prominent (and indeed acquired a new urgency). In the course of one of the most thoroughgoing critiques of consumerism produced

---

22. Svetislav Taboroši, *Odnosi potrošnje u socijalizmu: potrošač u sistemu udruženog rada* (Belgrade, 1986), 135.

23. Vukičević, "Antisamoupravna moć reklamokratije," 8–9.

24. Rajčan, "Idejno-politički aspekti EP," *Ideja*, no. 1 (July 1977): 13–14, at 14 (address to the International Advertising Symposium, Kladovo, 1977).

during the 1980s, for instance, Stanko Ilić argued that in order to find convincing proof of the creation of illusory needs in this socialist society, all that was really necessary was that "we take a good look at the store windows" of towns and cities across Yugoslavia where, he alleged, the evidence was overwhelming. "In them we will see, for example, unusual models of shoes—starting from men's shoes with high heels [*cipele "na sprat,"* or "two-storey shoes"], all the way to shoes with a conspicuous appearance and size that orthopedists would call the best methods for deforming human feet."[25]

Ilić could see no good reason for these odd permutations of modern modishness, but he certainly had no trouble identifying plenty of bad reasons. The problem seemed to lie, first and foremost, in the unholy alliance of style and profit, and here once again we encounter a critic of market culture implying that the pursuit of gain had become far too real a motivation for Yugoslav enterprises: "'It's a question of fashion,' the creators of such consumer goods will immediately say. The single motivation for producing such goods is, actually, the 'creation' of greater profits for the organizations in which they work." From this perspective, the innovations that were marketed as basic "needs" actually ended up imposing real burdens on ordinary Yugoslavs and the economy that was meant to serve them. With just such costs in mind, Ilić complained that "all these additions and changes, all the decorations and beautifications—not only in the case of items of personal apparel but also many technical items (cars, furniture, etc.), and their packaging, too—someone, naturally has to pay for them." Who would foot the bill for desire? For this critic, the answer was obvious, at least to those not already stupefied by their materialistic hunger: "Who else if not—the consumers?"[26]

Occasionally some degree of acceptance of the commonplace "false needs" critique turned up even in industry sources and in training materials for marketing and advertising workers. Along these lines, for example, one commentator for Croatia's *Kreativne komunikacije* acknowledged that "contemporary industrial society forms *a type of manipulated person:* the *consumer,* who in the purchase of certain goods decides more because of the influence of refined marketing methods on his subconscious than because of normal needs."[27] This judgment, appearing in a reflective piece on the role of "marketing in self-management society," comes close to conceding the point advanced by Marxist critics and by their anti-consumerist counterparts in the West. In skeptical analyses of this type, the very category of the "consumer" [*potrošač*] was divorced from the safe, neutral, essentially

---

25. References are to Stanko Ilić, *Put u humano društvo: od socijalizma ka komunizmu* (Belgrade, n.d. [ca. 1984]), 136.

26. References are to ibid.

27. Tomislav Pećarina, "Marketing u samoupravnom društvu," *Kreativne komunikacije,* no. 1 (1972): 10–13 (emphasis added).

functional definition that the proponents of marketing typically had insisted upon. Instead, from this increasingly common critical perspective, the term "consumer" had begun to signify something rather more alarming, acquiring a meaning more along the lines of "practitioner of consumerism."

Not all those associated with the industry were willing to yield their ground so easily, however. In the view of some of the most ardent defenders of advertising, all this anxiety and agitation about false needs was tantamount to an assault on the very idea of progress itself. Thus one contributor to Zagreb's *Ideja* asked, in 1972, "if the creation of new needs is bad, would it have been best for us to have kept on using stone hatchets?"[28] Or as another leader in the field, Boris Petz, put it one year later, "why should we...declare to be 'unethical' or 'immoral' advertising that, among people of contemporary culture, stimulates a need for the aesthetic, the clean, the orderly, the comfortable?"[29] For these insiders, in other words, the critics had gotten it only half-right at best: the consumers' desires did indeed rise to the level of "needs," they were in fact new, and they were, moreover, admittedly the results of commercial promotion. The difference? These desires were good, reasonable, and socially progressive.

Others cast doubt on the whole notion that advertising could really do all the horrible things that the critics claimed. "Today it is positively confirmed," industry stalwart Momčilo Milisavljević objected, "that advertising does not have that capacity to produce needs, but rather can only point to possible ways of satisfying existing needs." While buyers might not be satisfied with every purchase, the advocates of commercial promotion protested, it would be very difficult to sell people something that was not really useful. Against the idea that the wants and needs of shoppers were highly plastic and easily manipulated, Milisavljević ventured a radically contrary proposition: "The consumer," he declared, "is a thinking being." Neither "a king" nor, as some would have it, "a pawn," the consumer was actually "in the best position to decide what he wants and what he doesn't want."[30] This line of defense, of course, is virtually indistinguishable from the rationale habitually advanced by advertising's Western apologists.

This sort of back-and-forth over the issue of "false needs" illustrates perfectly how the distinctive political climate of Yugoslav socialism, by giving ideological and rhetorical ammunition to both sides, made for a controversy that would not only be especially heated but especially enduring as well. As the officially sanctioned point of departure for most analysts and would-be opinion makers in the public sphere, the governing Marxist ethos ensured that consumerism and its cultural markers would frequently come

---

28. "Sudjenje propagande," *Ideja*, no. 3 (1972): 10.
29. Boris Petz, "Bez crno-bijele jednostranosti," *Ideja*, no. 4 (1973): 15–16, at 16.
30. References are to Milisavljević, "Društveno-ekonomska uloga ekonomske propagande," 4.

under attack, accused repeatedly of eroding proper socialist values. But at the same time the remarkable latitude of Yugoslavia's peculiar variant of Marxist-Leninist practice meant that those interested in the expansion of the consumer orientation had considerable power to push back—to test the boundaries of their freedom and, as it were, to resist the resistance.

When You've Got It, Flaunt It: Individuality, Status, and Distinction in a Collectivist, Egalitarian System

The new emphasis on material abundance also opened up disturbing opportunities for what the Yugoslav critics, using the standard jargon of the party, called "social differentiation." It threatened to lead not just to the exaltation of self-interest and selfishness (though there was plenty of grumbling about that), but, worse still, to a new focus on the individual as distinct from and possibly even superior to others. For an egalitarian sociopolitical system that was supposed to be based on collective solidarity, this spelled trouble.

In the view of many of the critics, Yugoslavia during the high times of the 1960s and 1970s was, contrary to expectations, witnessing the persistence (some said the resurgence) of social hierarchy. A large share of the blame for all this status-mongering, they maintained, could be traced to consumption's great power as a social signifier. On these questions of status and distinction, the many who challenged the new consumerist orientation had plenty of ideological ammunition at their disposal. As one would expect, Marx and his intellectual heirs were a staple item and the standard foundation. But, perhaps surprisingly, the protagonists in these fights also relied heavily on classics of non-Marxist social science as well as influential works of contemporary Western scholarship and criticism from Thorstein Veblen to C. Wright Mills to Pierre Bourdieu, illustrating once again just how relevant the experience of the capitalist West, and analyses derived from that experience, seemed to have become.[31]

---

31. The use of consumption as a means of strengthening or even creating a sense of social identity has been the subject of a long and rich tradition of sociological and social-critical inquiry, and many of the Yugoslav critics (and, indeed, some of the defenders of the consumerist course) were well versed in the arguments advanced in and about the West. They drew freely, for example, on economist Thorstein Veblen's classic analysis of conspicuous consumption, with its attendant observation—especially important for a transnational analysis of the Yugoslav experience—that in modern economies the consumption practices of the upper, that is, "leisure" class, and, perhaps just as important, the system of values that accompanies those behaviors, filter down in modified form to others in the society. Domestic commentators were also particularly drawn to the work of sociologist C. Wright Mills, and especially to his provocative 1951 book *White Collar: The American Middle Classes* (New York, 1956). As socialist rule matured, Yugoslav life had seen an increasing bureaucratization, accompanied by the growing significance of the group of mid-rank employees interposed between the élites and the proletarian workers with whom so much Marxist ideology has been concerned. Given these potentially worrisome developments, the Yugoslav critics' choice of Mills was eminently sensible. With the

Communism's leveling imperatives sat uneasily with what the critics saw as the new culture of individual expression. In one testimony to the extent of the perceived problem with "getting ahead," Mladen Zvonarević pointed out how the country's emerging automobile culture had quickly moved beyond considerations of practical utility to become instead a vehicle for the expression of social distinctions. Although the Yugoslav economy in 1973 remained modest enough for *any* car to still count as a status symbol, this critic believed that, nonetheless, inequalities in the distribution of wealth were sufficient to encourage a strong hierarchy of consumer preferences. Ordinary Yugoslav citizens, Zvonarević asserted, were glad to be able to drive their own cars, yet they most assuredly did not remain indifferent to whether the car in question was a Peugeot or merely a "Fića," that is, the tiny, cheap, Fiat-based Zastava 750 that was the first car many of them could afford to buy. These things mattered. Just like the high-status Peugeot and Mercedes imports, such keen attention to the expression of social distinctions through spending was itself brought in from abroad, this observer indicated. The introduction of Western styles, Western tastes, and even Western products was, in this view, inevitably bringing about "a special sort of transfer of feelings" as well. And, as a result, Yugoslavia had seen the arrival of a "statusophrenia, an insanity about status that is, really, the core of what in political jargon we call the consumer mentality and the like."[32]

The contingent, negotiated, multivalent political dynamics of Yugoslav socialism meant that such diagnoses of "statusophrenia," snobbism, and conspicuous consumption would pop up continually in the trade literature on the arts of commercial promotion, appearing alongside subtle and not so subtle defenses of the industry. When Zvonarević warned that commercial promotion had become one of the greatest potential threats to the socialist ideal of a classless society, for example, he did so not in any ideology-laden communist platform but in the pages of the trade review *Ideja*. As was so often the case, the contrast between the opposing views was jarring: here we find one of the country's leading business journals advancing the damning argument that advertising was only "strictly speaking," in narrow and misleading terms, *"the sale of things,"* since it was also "at the same time—whether it wishes to be or not—*the sale of a certain ideology as well."*[33]

Still another commentator for *Ideja,* also writing during the distinct chill in the political climate that took place in the early 1970s, broached some of

---

evolution of the international study and critique of consumption, a number of Yugoslav critics looked to the work of Pierre Bourdieu, whose work offers one of the classic formulations of how preferences in the consumption of "cultural goods" may be the product of, and in turn reinforce, social hierarchy. See Bourdieu, *Distinction: A Social Critique of the Judgment of Taste* (Cambridge, Mass., 1984).

32. References are to Mladen Zvonarević, "Iluzija o 'naivnoj' propagandi," *Ideja*, no. 4 (1973): 17–18, at 18.

33. Ibid., 18 (emphasis added).

the same concerns when he took some of his colleagues to task for designing an advertisement for Ford automobiles that exhorted potential customers to "Establish your worth. Decide on a Ford." The underlying message here, Miodrag Hitrec reasoned, was that people could and should be judged by what they own, and this idea simply could not be reconciled with the values of Yugoslavia's socialist society.[34]

In responses of this sort, we see once again how the debate itself mattered: how Marxist rhetoric and values exerted a powerful disciplining influence over the conduct of the industry and thus shaped the public discourse on advertising, commerce, consumption, and the culture of the market. Yet it is worth pausing here to reflect on what the wide-ranging controversy also indicates about the differences between conditions in Yugoslavia and those seen in other socialist countries. The very fact that a variety of cars made by Ford was being advertised in the country, and advertised in such aggressive terms even at the risk of provoking a backlash, speaks volumes about the nature and extent of the consumerist *folie* taking place there. Although the Ford ad copy in question went on to promise "a *top-of-the-line* car at very favorable prices, with *prompt delivery*," it is telling that this industry critic did not object to such an appeal to luxury, to distinction, and to freedom from the scarcities traditionally associated with socialist production.[35] In this as in so many other instances, the messages were, to put it mildly, mixed. This made for a debate that was, if not reliably transparent, always rich and revealing.

Vigilant Marxists of a more orthodox stripe (though that was always an uncertain category for Yugoslavia) reacted forcefully against the perceived anti-egalitarian trend. Using the party organ *Komunist* to underscore the connections and distinctions between "the heaven of advertising and its earthly foundations," commentator Ivo Paić grumbled about a domestic door manufacturer that, in touting its products with the slogan "Your home is your fortress," had stoked consumers' individualistic desires to withdraw to a detached private house, away from society. This motto was, he charged, "the credo of the person in bourgeois society."[36] Such self-absorption and "bourgeois content," Paić suggested, were all too frequent in Yugoslav television, radio, newspapers, and magazines.

Shadowed by the ever present hobgoblin of snobbism, the relationship between consumer culture and "social differentiation" remained a topic of great concern right up through the last years of communist power. As a result of what had been, by the 1980s, a sustained influx of Western ways and tastes, Yugoslav socialism risked being undone, or so the critics claimed. Slovenian sociologist Jože Goričar saw Yugoslavs as wrapped up in "the

---

34. Miodrag Hitrec, "Nastavljamo li po starom," *Ideja*, no. 5 (1973): 10–11.
35. Ibid., 11 (emphasis added).
36. Ivo Paić, "Reklamno nebo i njegova svjetovna osnova," *Komunist*, 22 February 1976.

imitation of the consumerist lifestyle of the upper levels of contemporary developed capitalism," a bad habit that for too long had been "creating among us some sort of 'socialist-petit bourgeois' [*soc-malomeščanska*] caricature of the Western society of 'abundance'."[37] Some saw the roots of the present crisis in such overspending, status-seeking indulgences. In such times of diminished economic opportunity, the penchant for showy displays of the Good Life could come across as extreme, and these excesses proved especially galling to the critics. Too often, Ratko Božović complained in 1988, Yugoslavs were attempting to impress their neighbors and acquaintances with "castles for houses" and "houses for burial crypts" [*kuće-zamkovi* and *grobnice-kuće*].[38]

The critics' lingering doubts about the legitimacy of consumers' perceived "needs," which, as explained above, was a hot issue in its own right, figured heavily in these debates over status and distinction as well. The problem, Aleksandar Todorović suggested in 1981, was that many Yugoslavs seemed to have lost touch with a sense of their real needs and, as a result, were often spending as a matter of prestige. The consumerist pursuit of acquisitions, Todorović indicated during the early years of the downturn in 1981, was fraught with the potential for *snobizam*:

> When your neighbor, friend, or acquaintance says that he goes every year to Capri, in Italy, then you are supposed to understand that he is "on a higher level" than you, "unfortunate" that you are, traveling around on the Adriatic coast or our hot springs and mountains. How much he really relaxed, what he saw, what he experienced—that is not important. For him what is important is that he spends his summer vacations in an exclusive locale and you in an "ordinary" place.[39]

In this instance, as in so many others, we see how the rhetoric of resistance in Yugoslavia, informed continually by the country's egalitarian socialist public ethos, sought to steer consumption practice back toward what members of the resistance deemed to be an acceptable middle ground of consumer opportunities for Everyman. Typically the critics assumed, as Todorović did, that there was nothing particularly objectionable about the increasingly

---

37. Jože Goričar, "Potrošniška družba—potrošniško obnašanje," *Zbornik znanstvenih razprav* 40 (1980): 89.

38. Ratko R. Božović, *Suočavanja* (Nikšić, 1988), 188–189. Drawing on the insights of economist Thorstein Veblen and his *Theory of the Leisure Class,* Božović concluded that Yugoslavia's consumer culture was modern but not entirely so: it also expressed "influences from the distant past." Veblen's interpretation of conspicuous consumption is noteworthy for his insistence on the archaic origins of modern practices. The leisure class, Veblen maintained, "is found in its best development at the higher stages of the barbarian culture; as, for instance, in feudal Europe or feudal Japan." Veblen, *Theory of the Leisure Class,* 1.

39. Aleksandar Todorović, "Potrošačka psihologija, način života i snobizam," in Božović, *Odnos sredstava informisanja prema potrošačkom društvu,* 52–64, at 63.

popular custom of taking regular vacations at the popular Yugoslav seaside and at domestic resorts.

Indeed, as with many other consumer pleasures, such trips had become, I conclude, precisely the sort of "everyday luxuries" that Yugoslav citizens prized and that the authorities pointed to as evidence of the success of their system. But at the same time it was vital that such expenditures of money and time stay reassuringly "ordinary." Conspicuous consumption "on a higher level" or "in an exclusive locale" remained, in the dominant public ethos if not always in practice, out of bounds.

To Dream the Impossible Dream? Socialism's Limits and the Quixotic Quest for the Best of the West

Compounding the constraints imposed by an official public rhetoric that favored the moderate and the ordinary, another force attenuated the effects of status-building acquisition and display: the simple fact that the option for a socialist economy and political system had made such consumption practices, in a very real way, less possible. In terms both of concrete purchasing power and the range of market offerings (and the diversity of that *asortiman* was itself continually under some degree of pressure from socialist values, albeit usually in subtle ways), Yugoslavs found themselves running up against hard limits on their abilities to spend, enjoy, and express their status and individuality. Even in the best of times, and in the best of socialisms, some things were just not possible.

This mismatch between the hoped-for and the available, between desire and reality, became the source of another primary motif of the domestic anti-consumerist critique. In this respect, the *non*-advertising content of the popular media now appeared increasingly suspect as another major vector of consumerist values. Rejection of the new popular culture as a vehicle for other-worldly escapism was, for example, a prominent theme in the work of Slovenian party leader Franc Šetinc, who embarked on his own high-profile anti-consumerist campaign in the 1970s. Šetinc extended the public argument beyond the familiar indictments of advertising to include the "trash" that was supposedly being produced by Yugoslavia's "boulevard press," arguing that such mass-distribution publications were just as deeply implicated in the merchandising of the unreal. Part of the problem with popular culture, it appeared, was the very fact that communist rule had imposed (properly, in the mainstream view) such significant limits on the possible. Consequently, Šetinc suggested, the need for an array of consumerist diversions arose "because, in our society, there is no way to realize the ideals of the 'self-made man' (the American ideal of the person...who has raised himself, so to speak, from nothing up to unimaginable prestige and wealth)." With such paths foreclosed, the mass media had started to offer all manner of ersatz escapes, with the result that "our trash literature, out of some sort of nostalgia, quite obviously transfers the world of film stars, rich singers, successful managers, and playboys from the Western press to its own pages."[40] As for the welfare of the broad consuming public, Šetinc could only conclude that the popular press often simply "alienates them in a world of empty hopes, for it offers people *a deceptive substitute for what doesn't exist in real life*," essentially abdicating its responsibility to expand their horizons and create a more genuinely fulfilling, and genuinely socialist, mass culture.[41]

In this harsh condemnation of the street press, Šetinc was not alone. The critics seemed ever more convinced that the problem had spread beyond just the fields of commercial promotion to the mass media more generally, which served, as Zagreb sociologist and cultural critic Tena Martinić put it in 1974, as the "faithful carriers of consumer culture."[42] The same sort of concern about the peddling of illusions was, for example, central to Ivan Sedej's excursus on the dangers of the seductive sale of ski fashions and the fashions of the Good Life, which appeared in the same year. Behind these advertising images and others like them, the columnist was convinced, lay a collection of impossible dreams. The commercial depicted a world "that is not ours and that never will be ours."[43]

And why not? Here once again, the critique pointed to what was imagined to be a fundamental contradiction between consumerism and socialism. The discrepancy between images sold and realities lived was not just about economic limits, undeniable as they were. Over and above those more straightforward constraints, Marxist-inspired visions understood socialism to demand—and promise—something different, something that was, in the end, better than the dream worlds of consumer capitalism. Instead of easy escapism, the basic social agreements that were embodied in Yugoslavia's economic and political system required, in this view, an embrace of the truth that the country and its people could only really expect a future of genuine but necessarily modest rewards and, yes, more hard work. Yugoslav advertisers and businesses, the critics maintained, would have had their audiences think otherwise. The promised life of practically limitless consumer opportunity was pure illusion, and yet in the fantasy existence of the commercial, Sedej insisted, "the whispering voice convinces us of precisely the opposite."[44]

So just how many regular Yugoslavs could actually expect to live the kind of life "sold" in commercials of this sort? Who were these miraculous

---

40. France Šetinc, *Smo potrošniška družba* (Ljubljana, 1980), 56; see, generally, 53–62.
41. Ibid., 57 (emphasis added).
42. Tena Martinić, "Potrošačka kultura," *Kultura: časopis za teoriju i sociologiju kulture i kulturnu politiku*, no. 27 (1974): 8–24, at 13.
43. Sedej, "Kupite si zadovoljstvo in srečo."
44. References in the passage are to ibid.

Yugoslavs? Sedej was convinced they were a rare breed. The promised "world of shining whiteness and blue skies" was one that advertising opened up for "successful people, the kind who probably sign their hotel bills without even looking at them," but, at least from this critic's standpoint, there was reason to doubt that the visions produced and reproduced in the standard imaginary of Yugoslav advertising had any basis in the country's economic realities. "The young people who appear in such a commercial are born with money," Sedej cautioned. To actually pursue such a lifestyle, the sacrifices required would have to be quite real and quite painful, since "for the sort of standard of living that advertising offers us, at least ten years' of hard work in an extraordinarily well-paid job would be necessary." The money to chase these dreams would have to come from somewhere, and the consequences would not be pretty: "the well-known factory is convincing young people...that they ought to squeeze the money out of their fathers and mothers." Alongside the "false picture of conditions and false modes of thinking," a pernicious status seeking was once again seen to be at work, too, and as a result the commercials ended up "filling poorer people with feelings of less worth."[45]

In anti-consumerist critique of this type, as in so many instances, the arts of commercial promotion figured as devices of psychological manipulation and, as a result, as powerful forces of cultural change. Sedej argued that advertising "forces us into completely impossible mental and ideological molds; among them the idea about the supreme happiness of carefree extravagance is just the mildest." In so doing, it had conned ordinary Yugoslavs into believing what was, in fact, "an unbelievable duality." It offered up "on the one hand, a clever representation of high society, while on the other, *the persuasion that all this is, strictly speaking, the happy medium, which is quite easy to achieve.*" The sad conclusion, then, was that the way of life shown in such advertisements was absolutely beyond the grasp of ordinary people in a socialist society. Skis and clothes they might be able to afford, but certainly not the wide world of abundant pleasure that was supposed to go with them. Consumers, in this view, were being seduced by the unreal: "Advertising is thus propagating *a life that cannot be our life.*"[46]

A Mind Is a Terrible Thing to Waste: Market Culture and the Making of *Homo consumens*

Whether or not they concluded that Yugoslavia had slipped over the line and become a "consumer society," the adversaries of the new consumerist orientation typically showed some faith that their country, because of its

---

45. References in the passage are to ibid.
46. References in the passage are to ibid. (emphasis added).

socialist foundations, was better equipped to check the spread of consumerism and reform the culture that had sustained it. For some, certainly, the fact that changes in Yugoslav society were still something less than total and irremediable offered only the coldest comfort. Such was the line adopted by Zagreb psychologist and law school lecturer Boris Sorokin, who delivered a caustic review of commercial promotion at one of the early conferences of the Yugoslav Marketing Association. Sorokin argued that although the country had not yet become a consumer society, largely because it was still not wealthy enough, the dangers were nevertheless great. There were ample manifestations of a "consumerist mentality," he suggested, and much of the blame had to lie with advertising. The work of advertising and marketing specialists, according to Sorokin, posed a particular threat to the country's young people: "If we 'educate' a human being as an obedient and highly conformist consumer in his very early years, and especially if we place the value of conformity in the highest position in his system of values, then as producers and sellers (that is, as those who want to make a profit for themselves) we will form that human being so that he will be at our disposal as an obedient consumer for years and years."[47] Such harsh criticism, according to one industry commentator, "shocked the auditorium" of marketing specialists, who took it as either "a dilettante's opinion or a provocation."[48]

Yet Sorokin's remarks were probably more unusual and shocking for their blunt, confrontational tone than for their substance. In fact, such portrayals of market culture as a form of subtle brainwashing came up repeatedly in the broader public debate over consumerism and commercial promotion, and the record of the industry's many professional gatherings makes clear that even these conferences and seminars were frequently the venue for critical assessments of the social impact of the new business styles.[49] Although advertising and marketing leaders might have preferred that "dilettante" outsiders and other like-minded critics had remained silent, many more such "provocations" would be forthcoming throughout the socialist period, and the suspicion that work in these fields amounted to an especially pernicious form of psychological manipulation never fully subsided.

But the problem transcended mere matters of technique. Many of those who put up the staunchest resistance were convinced that the ultimate responsibility for the new consumerist mentality lay with capitalism itself. In reliable Marxist fashion, Ratko Božović thus interpreted the drive toward consumerism as the quintessential product of systems founded

---

47. Boris Sorokin, address to Third Conference of the Yugoslav Marketing Association, Niš, quoted in Gabrijel Sfiligoj, "Podpora ekonomski propagandi na III. kongresu Jugoslovanskega združenja za marketing—JUMA v Nišu," *Bilten DEPS*, nos. 15/16 (n.d. [ca. 1973]): 15–16, at 16.

48. "Zaobilazite ljudske vrednote!," *Ideja*, no. 2 (1972): 21–23, at 21.

49. See, for example, the conference papers collected in Božović, *Odnos sredstava informisanja prema potrošačkom društvu.*

on self-interested capital's exploitation of labor and control of the means of production. The maximization of profit, in this view, depended on the maximization of demand, and this in turn required the "creation of a mass consumerist psychology" and a uniform, conformist "mass person—*Homo consumens.*"[50] The account Božović offered reflected a judgment that market culture bred a mind-set that was not only extraordinarily widespread but extraordinarily petty and intolerant as well, one that led those in its thrall to dismiss any efforts to resist consumerism as foolish, naive, and unnatural. "When the orientation toward *being* [as opposed to *having*] does appear among some rare individuals," Božović claimed, "it is often pronounced to be some form of abnormality by others with a hedonistic consciousness."[51]

It was clear, furthermore, that the syndrome, as Božović and his fellows in the critical mainstream saw it, had now become relevant to socialist societies as well. In some form or another, then, the culture associated with contemporary capitalism, if not its economic foundations, had evidently taken root in Yugoslavia.

The trouble, it appeared, might be lurking almost anywhere. No longer were commercials and consumer goods the only problems. Consumerism had crept into the realm of experience, too. With an eye to the remarkably pervasive quality of the unsettling new ways and the suspicious new values that accompanied them, sociologist Jože Goričar groused about the popularity of Yugoslav "disco clubs" as a "typical example of the 'import' of the consumerist way of life from the West." These dance venues, Goričar complained near the height of the international disco-music wave in 1980, were popping up all across the country, "spreading like mushrooms after a rain," and they had ended up "producing and maintaining an out-and-out disco euphoria among our youth." With more than a little contempt, he reported that one Hollywood disco producer had gone so far as to make the grandiose claim that disco had become not just a music style but a distinctive way of living and seeing the world, a judgment that Goričar acknowledged to be fundamentally correct, with one critical caveat: the dance mogul "just forgot to add that because of that 'way of life' and 'manner of thinking,' the producers of popular records are earning great riches, which are flowing out of the pockets of millions of naive and bored consumers. Ours too!"[52]

Confronted with what seemed to be the construction of a new *Homo consumens* and a massive reshaping of the minds of the young and the restless, the naive and the bored, the critics offered an image of a Yugoslav society drifting away from its moorings, with dismaying results that spoke to the need for even more dedicated resistance. To that end, Stipe Šuvar, an influential leader in the Croatian party who cultivated a high-profile presence as

50. Božović, *Suočavanja*, 177.
51. Ibid., 187.
52. Goričar, "Potrošniška družba—potrošniško obnašanje," 89 n. 25.

a public intellectual, waged a sustained rhetorical campaign against consumerism in the mid-1970s, part of that time from his post as Croatia's minister for cultural affairs, which he assumed in 1974 before rising to further heights in the federal party structure. Cataloguing the typical Yugoslav's wish list, Šuvar again raised the critical issue of the correspondence between hopes and expectations and economic realities: Just how sensible was this new vision of prosperity and well-being? Only a small fraction of Yugoslavs, 10 percent or so, could really expect to fulfill all these "needs" without any substantial difficulties, Šuvar estimated. At the same time, however, he did concede that a reasonably high standard of living was also available to a growing number of others, especially to white-collar employees and better-paid members of the working class: in Zagreb, for instance, 45 percent of all automobiles were owned by workers. But many others found the desired lifestyle harder to attain, Šuvar noted, and so what he characterized as a hunger for the emblems of the Good Life had driven hundreds of thousands of Yugoslavs to seek work abroad—and not just those who were unemployed at home.[53]

Such observations about the increasingly wide reach of consumerist passions deserve special emphasis, for they underscore that although not everyone could expect to build a single-family *vila* or a getaway *vikendica*, or drive off to the fjords in a "top-of-the-line" Ford, the quest for markers of accomplishment and status ended up touching Yugoslav society quite broadly. This was not a malady of the relative few who had already given in to the vices of "enrichment" that, as we will see in the next chapter, so vexed Tito. Instead something quite different, quite sweeping, was taking place. The country's consumer culture, as even some of the critics recognized from time to time, had become all the more troubling—and all the more important—because it apparently could ensnare almost anyone. Values that from a socialist standpoint were woefully misguided had taken hold among rather ordinary Yugoslavs, who seemed to have discovered in the new culture of shopping and owning a tempting opportunity to emulate the lifestyles of the rich and famous.

And so the critics were adamant. For his part, even in the face of aggressive questioning during a post-conference interview by a defender of advertising, Boris Sorokin refused to back down from his "shocking" indictment of the effort to churn out "obedient" and "conformist" Yugoslav consumers. "If we are talking about how advertising could increase the wealth of

---

53. Stipe Šuvar, "Elementi potrošačkog društva i potrošačkog mentaliteta" (1976), in Šuvar, *Samoupravljanje i alternative* (Zagreb, 1980), 163–183, at 173–174. Portions of the piece were drawn from an earlier article by Šuvar, "Potrošačko društvo i potrošački mentalitet," *Treći program* (Radio Beograd) (spring 1973). Consumer society was a leading element of Šuvar's social criticism during these years. Along these lines, see also, in the same volume, the essays "Raspodjela uvjeta proizvodnje i sredstava potrošnje," 148–161 (1975), and "'Srednji slojevi' ili 'srednja klasa' u jugoslavenskom socijalističkom društvu," 245–266 (1971).

this country (and, therefore, of its citizens), that seems all right to me," Sorokin allowed. "But if the price we have to pay for that enrichment amounts to the deformation of people's personalities...then I am fearful of that risk. Doesn't this perhaps resemble the situation that A[ldous] Huxley back in 1932 described [in his] *Brave New World*?"[54] By and large, the mainstream critics were convinced that this sort of "deformation of people's personalities" was real and, moreover, had become widespread enough in Yugoslavia to require an urgent response.

Contemporary observers thus wondered about precisely the sorts of questions that lie at the heart of the historical inquiry that we are engaged in here: Just what was happening, domestically and globally? The critics were aware that Yugoslav society found itself at a particularly important juncture, caught in wider, world-historical processes that were, at best, difficult to understand, much less manage and control. It was with those larger dynamics in mind that Ratko Božović noted how the peculiar Yugoslav variant of consumer culture, notwithstanding "the specific conditions of its social and economic terrain and its traditional cultural inheritance," in the final analysis "had not betrayed its model—the consumer culture of civilized post-industrial society."[55] For skeptics like this, that consumerist "model" was dead wrong, and the implications for the future of socialism very troubling indeed.

The Good Life for All of YU: Consumerism across the Divides of Class and Geography

The very public controversy over consumerism leaves little doubt that ordinary Yugoslavs were not just looking to their more privileged compatriots for models. Instead they were participating in a much broader, genuinely international phenomenon. The critiques demonstrate, moreover, that the external, "imported" dimensions of the new popular culture could prove powerful even if the individual Yugoslavs participating in it were themselves anything but cosmopolitan. Along these lines, for example, Stipe Šuvar observed that consumerism often served an especially significant function in reshaping the values and tastes of the members of a highly noticeable and highly important demographic category in postwar Yugoslavia: the new urban dweller "who has left his peasant life behind, and who would like to indulge in something nearly like that level of life lived by the so-called jet-set of society around the world, which we are otherwise reading about so much in the columns of our so-called entertainment press."[56] Mass internal

---

54. "Zaobilazite ljudske vrednote!" *Ideja*, no. 2 (1972): 23.
55. Božović, *Suočavanja*, 178–179.
56. Šuvar, "Elementi potrošačkog društva i potrošačkog mentaliteta," 176.

migration was rapidly remaking Yugoslav society, and consumerist desire seemed to be rapidly remaking the internal migrants. The chance to join in a broadly shared and highly visible culture of consumption went a long way toward reducing what had been stark differences between the country's urban and rural subcultures.

Ever more salient in Yugoslav society, and thus in the domestic debates, was the linkage between the new styles of consumption and the geographic diffusion of an increasingly uniform, transnational popular culture driven in part by a fascination with internationally famous entertainers and celebrities. The country's mass-media outlets, Šuvar observed tartly, were frequently consumed with such matters as "where some duchess had lunch and what she ate, or where some world-famous film star traveled and how she got there."[57]

Stipe Šuvar wasn't exaggerating. Leaving aside the normative judgments implicit in remarks of this sort, such observations about the content of the Yugoslav popular press were, the evidence suggests, fundamentally correct. The country's "lowbrow" mass media had indeed become astonishingly attentive to European and American movie stars and rock idols, just as they closely followed the latest twists in Western lifestyles and the ups and downs of Western celebrities and their hemlines. The coverage, moreover, was rarely all that politicized or critical. Exposure to the international culture of celebrity, entertainment, and diversionary escape spawned, in turn, a host of Yugoslav variations, elaborations, and imitations, yielding a motley assortment of mass-media offerings that ran the gamut from pop stars to sitcoms to sex symbols.[58]

In a mere two pages of a single representative 1970 issue of Croatia's widely circulated women's magazine *Svijet,* for example, we can see just how far Yugoslav society, and the media that attempted to both shape and reflect it, had moved in this direction. (By this time, a fascination with the international culture of celebrity had figured prominently in the pages of the magazine for several years.)[59] While one photo and caption featuring Soviet actors Nikolai Grinko and Marina Vlady did represent a nod toward mass culture produced outside the West, that piece ran next to a much larger picture of John Wayne (describing the actor's prodigious film career without mention of his well-known anticommunist activism). On the same page, *Svijet* reported with uncritical amazement on the hundreds of millions earned by film stars Barbra Streisand, Lee Marvin, Elizabeth Taylor, Richard Burton, Sean Connery, Sidney Poitier, Sophia Loren, Dean Martin, Rex

---

57. Ibid.

58. See, for example, Magda Weltrusky, "U novim ulogama," *Svijet* no. 26, 30 December 1970, 16–21. In this fashion photo-feature, ten Yugoslav television and stage actresses modeled the styles of the coming year.

59. See, for example, "Koliko ljudi—toliko ćudi," *Svijet* no. 3, 1 February 1966, 36–37.

Harrison, Omar Sharif, and Cary Grant. Yet another photo announced the making of the "Raquel Welch TV Special," which the magazine described as a "huge show" that depicted what life was like for "an unusual girl for whom every dream, even the smallest, comes true." Hollywood had, without a doubt, come to Yugoslavia. Meanwhile from Paris, another glamour capital of the West, the editors treated readers to a bit of fashion photography taken at an exhibition of boats and yachts.[60]

Mixed in with the stars and style and sex were pieces with more direct bearing on the daily lives—or the imagined futures—of ordinary Yugoslav working women. In this manner, news about the rising number of women who had breached a formerly male domain and now earned their living driving trucks, buses, and cabs ("in Paris alone there are approximately seven hundred female taxi drivers") appeared along with a story on the efforts of a British actors' union to look after the interests of auditioners in the face of "the ever increasing number of theater pieces in which the actors have to appear either partially or completely nude." Another report on what was termed (ironically, it seems) "an unusual discovery in France" asserted that the nearly universal presence of television was apparently making women more image-conscious and flirtatious by exposing them continually to images of style, fashion, and taste. In this item, remarkable for the matter-of-fact way in which it presumed the naturalness of such changes in behavior as a consequence of television, *Svijet* printed the comments of one French woman who observed that "when you have a posh and elegant female television host as guest in the house every day, it becomes embarrassing to see yourself in a shabby housecoat, with uncombed hair."[61]

Making an effort, then, was understood to be important, but the magazine suggested that there was always a little room to hope and dream as well, and fortune might smile on anyone. Readers learned that one apparently quite ordinary Jacqueline Bonnard, on an outing to a restaurant in France where she lived, had discovered a pearl in her plate of oysters, but then went on to experience something "that more resembled a film or a fairy tale": in a second shell, yet another pearl. The same page of the magazine, just across from this story, featured a photograph of a glamorous model wearing three baroque natural-pearl rings, a pearl bracelet, and an over-the-top diadem fancifully sprinkled with pendant pearls, the handiwork of the famous

---

60. "Zanimljivi svijet," *Svijet* no. 3, 11 February 1970, 56–57.

61. Ibid. On the role of fashion in the consumer cultures of other communist countries, see Judd Stitziel, *Fashioning Socialism: Clothing, Politics and Consumer Culture in East Germany* (Oxford: Berg, 2005); Katherine Helena Pence, "From Rations to Fashions: The Gendered Politics of East and West German Consumption, 1945–1961" (Ph.D. diss., University of Michigan, 1999); Philipp Heldmann, "Konsumpolitik in der DDR: Jugendmode in den sechziger Jahren," in *Konsumpolitik: Die Regulierung Des Privaten Verbrauchs Im 20. Jahrhundert*, ed. Hartmut Berghoff *(Gottingen*, 1999), 135–158; Katalin Medvedev, "Ripping Up the Uniform Approach: Hungarian Women Piece Together a New Communist Fashion," in *Producing Fashion: Commerce, Culture, and Consumers*, ed. Regina Lee Blaszczyk (Philadelphia, 2008), 250–272.

contemporary London jewelry designer John Donald. All this ran, as it did every two weeks at the time, in each issue, under the rubric "The Interesting World" [*Zanimljivi svijet*].[62]

An interesting world it was indeed. And if the writers and editors comprehended the irony that images and commentary of this sort appeared in the same issue as an interview with Herbert Marcuse, a leading light of the Frankfurt School that had deplored just such emanations of the "culture industry," they did not admit it. Compounding the irony, the interview with Marcuse—of whom *Svijet* reported that the young anarchists of the 1968 generation were proclaiming the slogan "Marx is our prophet, Marcuse is his interpreter, and Mao is his sword"—ran as part of the magazine's regular series titled "Conversations with the Stars," although here at least both the journalist and Marcuse himself acknowledged that the notion that this particular political philosopher had now become a "star" was more than a little discomfiting.[63]

Not all the coverage in this installment of "The Interesting World" was wholly uncritical: the same feature spread also ran a snippet with the title "Competition for Liz?" informing readers that although "until now it has generally been considered that Liz Taylor holds the lead among actresses when it comes to tasteless attire," a new photo of Gina Lollabrigida—shown here garbed in an ostentatious, improbably puffy knee-length fur, heavily made up, and accessorized with matching boots and handbag in a bold, garish snakeskin pattern—demonstrated that the Italian star "had decided to compete with Liz, at least in this field." And while the tone of a companion item on a newly invented electronic cookbook, meal planner, and household budget manager was otherwise excited and glowing ("and best of all, this machine is not out of some futuristic film—it's for sale now"), the report spoiled the fun a bit by adding, "It's better that you don't ask about the price, however."[64] Notwithstanding such little doses of reality, all these excursions through the world of films and fairy tales still struck the critics as a disturbingly easy way to win the hearts and minds of the proletariat and the peasantry—and to win them for something other than the values of socialism.

By the 1960s the cultural shift had been exposed as one that could cut across occupational and regional boundaries and span the country's profound urban-rural divide. The quick pace of urban development and the ongoing transfer of rural populations to the cities had created another conduit for consumerism, and the magnitude and comparative novelty of these demographic and economic trends had, as Tena Martinić observed, made for special difficulties in Yugoslavia. Because the thousands of uninitiated

62. "Zanimljivi svijet," *Svijet* no. 3, 11 February 1970, 56–57.

63. Marko Goluža, "Mislilac široka osmijeha: razgovori sa 'zvijezdama,'" 4; Herbert Marcuse," *Svijet* no. 3, 11 February 1970, 10.

64. "Zanimljivi svijet," *Svijet* no. 3, 11 February 1970, 56–57.

city dwellers were, as Martinić put it, in unfamiliar circumstances and "cut off from their traditional cultural values and completely unprepared for urban living habits," they proved "very susceptible to the content of the consumer culture" that had, by the mid-1970s, taken such a firm hold. The new arrivals were, in this view, all too easily sucked in by the allure of easy entertainment, diversion, and the pleasures of spending. Particularly noteworthy, Martinić thought, were the ways in which the new, more uniform consumer culture of the masses had brought about profound "ruptures with the elements of traditional culture" and eroded what had been Yugoslavia's remarkable and distinctive "multiethnic quality" [*mnogonacionalnost*] and its famously "diverse ethno-national cultural traditions" [*raznolike narodne kulturne tradicije*].[65] Consumerist values and behaviors were, from this perspective, creating an odd and disquieting yet very real *unity* across a society that was, in so many ways, renowned for its disunity and diversity.

If such observations about the transnational and cross-class quality of Yugoslavia's consumerism were substantially correct—and, as explained in more detail in subsequent sections of this book, I conclude that they were—a media-driven popular culture, steeped in the homogenization and standardization typical of the early stages of industrialized mass consumption, was making Yugoslavs *more like each other* at the same time that it was making them *more like their counterparts* in the developed capitalist West. From today's vantage point, of course, after the brutal wars of the 1990s, it might be tempting to view such a tendency toward a pan-Yugoslav mass culture as something welcome and healthy for Yugoslav society, but at the time, especially to cultural critics attuned to the virtues of "high" and "traditional" culture and skeptical of the lowbrow and the middlebrow, any such blurring of ethnic and regional differences could seem like a very real and very dire loss. Worse yet, from the skeptics' standpoint, all this troubling uniformity was arriving in the guise of progress. As Tena Martinić put it, conformity was being cultivated "under the pretext of democratization," with the disturbing result that unwholesome consumerist attitudes and behaviors were now hailed as modernization and "proclaimed to be the extension of cultural values and the elevation of the level of cultural consciousness."[66]

The spread of suspect urban ways beyond the confines of the cities and the connections between modern city life and consumerist thinking proved to be common themes in the ongoing public debate. Like others, Stipe Šuvar's trenchant reading of what was taking place across Yugoslavia acknowledged, correctly, that the new desires and habits did not affect only the urbanized parts of the country. The danger, as had already become apparent by the 1970s, was far more serious. To drive home that lesson, Šuvar offered an account of automobile fever in a village in the hilly Macedonian region of

---

65. References are to Martinić, "Potrošačka kultura," 12.
66. Ibid.

the Šar-Planina, one of the least developed areas of the federation. In this one little settlement, he said, about forty people already owned cars—this even though no road went to their village. Because an automobile was apparently something well worth having anyway, the resourceful villagers kept their vehicles under guard in a parking lot in the small city of Tetovo and used them whenever they went down to town.[67] The peasant insistence on owning cars, in Šuvar's view, verged on the comical: "On rural radio stations people are requesting songs [with an announcement from the disk jockey] in order to inform their neighbors that a person has bought an automobile of this or that brand: Let it be heard! Let it be known!" Once again, such consumerist indulgence, from the standpoint of the critical mainstream, was coming at a very real cost: "People in the villages," Šuvar reported, "are acquiring aspirations for 'automobilization' even in cases when they have not ensured other minimal possessions necessary for a civilized existence."[68]

It seemed, moreover, that status in rural life was increasingly divorced from its traditional ceremonial expressions and reoriented toward modern consumption. Thus Šuvar noted with obvious disapproval that even some small Yugoslav villages had succumbed to "a competition that takes the form of acquiring televisions, installing plumbing, buying kitchen appliances, and getting cars for one's offspring so that they won't run off to the cities. *All this speaks to the borders of the modern consumerist mentality and its infiltration into even the village.*" The hunger for goods and for at least the outward emblems of the Good Life, it appeared, had led some Yugoslav country folk into a way of life that was simply nonsensical. To illustrate the point, Šuvar noted that "in some villages in Serbia people have a television in the house and a water heater installed, even though they don't have electricity yet." Challenged with the apparent absurdity of this sort of spending, the villagers were adamant in the defense of their purchases, he said: "Just let them have these things on hand, and they will be ready for the electricity whenever it comes![69]

Outcomes like this were no doubt extreme, but they call attention to what was, in fact, a genuine and far-reaching restructuring of life beyond the cities, and they effectively dispose of any illusion that the Yugoslav consumer culture was one shared only by urban dwellers or was, as the critics sometimes implied, essentially a vice of the rich (or what passed for rich in Yugoslavia). Quite to the contrary, evidence of a much broader transformation was accumulating rapidly, so much so that by 1980 Jože Goričar could note with some justification that "several categories of our citizens" had fallen victim to the consumerist mentality.[70]

---

67. Šuvar, "Elementi potrošačkog društva i potrošačkog mentaliteta," 174 n. 15.
68. Ibid., 174.
69. Ibid. (emphasis added).
70. Goričar, "Potrošniška družba—potrošniško obnašanje," 84.

O Brave New World That Has Such People In't!
Yugoslavia on the Frontiers of Consumer Society

So Yugoslavia seemed to have slipped over the edge, beyond the orbit of reliable socialist values and into some new condition that looked for all the world like the consumer culture of the capitalist camp, or something awfully close to it. The country was apparently well on the way to becoming, as Ivan Sedej wrote, "a society of consumers," one that had lost its roots in production and in real human values, and one in which "only ne'er-do-wells and fools with some sort of complex cannot and don't know how to make their way to what advertising offers us."[71] The charges here may have been overstated, but evidence of major change was too abundant and too clear to be ignored. Not surprisingly, the prime suspects tried to clear their names. Defending the work of his profession in the years after its rise to prominence, Croat advertising expert Josip Sudar, one of the true luminaries in the field, acknowledged the mounting criticism of the vices associated with commercial promotion, but he insisted that all the problems that the critics so frequently cited were absolutely contrary to the aims and intentions of the much maligned trade. "We don't want to create a consumer society," Sudar protested to his university audiences, "but rather a progressive society."[72]

And so the choice was presented: a consumer society or a progressive society. But what, exactly, was consumer society? Why did it provoke such a tempest? What made it a threat to "progressive" interests? And given the real and potential power of Marxist-Leninist party control, how could it truly jeopardize the socialist experiment?

One interpretative thread that runs throughout the present study is the idea that the Yugoslav case complicates and, indeed, requires a rethinking of the theories and categories typically used to analyze the appearance of market culture and consumerism in their modern, global dimensions, not least with respect to questions of provenance and causation. But, at the outset, Yugoslavia's critics, politicians, and scholars tended to see the matter as rather more clear-cut. The Yugoslav *Lexicon of Marketing,* an influential reference work, thus defined consumer society in 1977 as one in which "the material situation of individuals, prestige through the frequent exchange of consumer goods, and the possession of material goods of lasting use value are the fundamental criteria of the place and role of individuals in the social hierarchy." In this sort of society, it was said, the "sole credo" was the attainment of a high standard of living and the establishment of prestige through possessions. Lest the presumed ideological divide go unnoticed, the *Lexicon* went on to explain that the term "consumer society" was, in fact,

---

71. Sedej, "Kupite si zadovoljstvo in srečo."
72. Sudar, *Ekonomska propaganda: predavanja na postdiplomskom studiju Ekonomskog fakulteta u Zagrebu,* 40.

"a synonym for highly developed capitalist countries that, in their development, emphasize the rapid development of those economic sectors that produce material goods of mass consumption."[73]

Among those critics who voiced the worries of the Marxist mainstream, the generative linkage between capitalism and consumer society was virtually uniform and virtually unquestioned. The sociocultural diagnosis offered up by Tena Martinić, for example, understood the consumerist way of life as one that reinforced the regressive social relations of the capitalistic past and that was, for this reason, fundamentally antithetical to the socialist project. "The mass production of the products of a pseudo-culture or consumer culture," Martinić warned in 1974, "is directed against every critical and historically grounded view of individual and collective values."[74]

But finding clarity about the relationship between consumerism and socialism proved a difficult task, even for those who devoted a great deal of thought and effort to the problem. One of the most sustained assaults on consumerist values came in the work of Franc Šetinc, the secretary of the Central Committee of the Slovenian party organization, who published an influential and frequently cited inquiry into the subject, first in 1979 in a Serbo-Croatian edition and then the next year in his native language. Developed out of a number of essays that Šetinc had contributed to mass-circulation periodicals across the country over the preceding months and years, *Are We a Consumer Society?* (*Jesmo li potrošačko društvo*) was an exercise in the use of the bully pulpit. And the project was, by some measures at least, a success: of the various critiques of consumer culture that appeared during the last two decades of the Yugoslav federation, the continued attacks by Šetinc probably enjoyed the highest public profile. Yet the work is ultimately more noteworthy for the importance of its author, for its prominence in the national debate, and for its representative quality as an exemplar of more or less orthodox communist sentiments than for the novelty, creativity, or power of its arguments. For the most part, it runs through fairly standard complaints about consumerism that were already in circulation and that have been addressed in the foregoing sections.

The central problem presented in *Are We a Consumer Society?* was, at least explicitly, just what the title suggested. In the end Šetinc answered the question in the negative, though he conceded that there were nonetheless

---

73. *Leksikon marketinga* (Belgrade, 1977), 228; quoted in Aleksandar Spasić, "Odnos sredstava informisanja SR Srbije prema potrošačkom društvu," in *Odnos sredstava informisanja prema potrošačkom društvu*, 3–10, at 7 (emphasis added). Although the definition was clearly meant to communicate that Yugoslavia was not a consumer society, it is perhaps unintentionally revealing: the reasoning used here implies some sort of nationwide *option* for the consumerist orientation, a conscious policy choice of consumer production over other possibilities. To this extent, it may in truth be more characteristic of Yugoslavia than of the "highly developed capitalist countries."

74. Martinić, "Potrošačka kultura," at 12–13.

many disturbing manifestations of consumerist "behavior."[75] Confronted with the evidence that Šetinc himself adduced, however, one might well question the writer's reasoning on this point. That the matter was one that elicited a wide assortment of responses was, in any case, beyond dispute. Šetinc's collaborator Boris Majer explained in his introductory essay that the range of opinions on Yugoslavia's relationship with the material world ran "from those who just wave it off in a carefree way, saying 'that doesn't affect us, that's a sickness of capitalist society, we are much too underdeveloped economically to seriously speak about consumerism in our society,' to those who see in the development of our society consumerism and nothing else." This latter group of cynics, Majer suggested gloomily, had concluded that consumerism "has already deformed all of our life with the result that, in this respect, we are increasingly not much different from any contemporary bourgeois consumer society." The book offers further confirmation that the debate over consumer culture had become extraordinarily vital and indeed almost omnipresent. For as Majer emphasized, these were arguments that Yugoslavs could hear "on television, on the radio, in the daily press and in journals, and last but not least on the street in everyday conversations as well."[76]

Ultimately Majer and Šetinc both treated the response to consumer culture in Yugoslavia as tantamount to a referendum on self-management, and the "wrong" conclusion was one they could not countenance. The question was, as Majer framed it, "above all, whether self-management socialism is capable of opening up a different historical alternative to not only contemporary capitalist 'consumer' society but also to contemporary state socialism."[77] In the end, the message of these mainstream Communists was not that the party leadership had done everything right thus far—there was some measure of humility and self-criticism on that score—but rather that no one else, and certainly not the various other opponents of consumerism, had addressed or could address the situation any more successfully. In the final analysis, there was reason to hope: an alternative was indeed possible, resistance was not futile, and the party could be trusted to lead the way.

But from the standpoint of less sanguine observers, those who still denied the existence of a consumer society in Yugoslavia and held out the hope of yet another marvelous Yugoslav "difference" were simply deluding

---

75. See Šetinc, *Jesmo li potrošačko društvo* (Belgrade, 1979). Unfortunately, because the author evidently decided that there had already been too much cataloguing of such behavior, the book lacks the rich and illuminating specificity that makes the works of Šuvar and others so revealing and useful. Curiously, although the Serbo-Croatian text presented the title in an interrogative form, leaving the matter open for debate, the Slovenian version of the book turned the question into a statement, raising the prospect, at least initially, of a troubling affirmation. But whatever the reason for the switch, Šetinc's ultimate judgment remained the same: Yugoslavia was not, in fact, a consumer society.

76. Boris Majer, "Smo potrošniška družba?" in Šetinc, *Smo potrošniška družba*, 7–9, at 7.

77. Ibid.

themselves, proceeding from a false premise and engaging in foolish circular reasoning. In these gloomier readings, social relations in the country had indeed declined to such a sorry state. Ratko Božović, for instance, warned that *having* was displacing *being* as the foundation of Yugoslav life, concluding that the society was now increasingly dominated by a new ethic: "have as much as possible."[78]

And if consumer society had arrived, where had it arrived from? How did things come to this dire pass? The mainstream critical discourse on consumption and market culture left little doubt that consumer society had its origins in the West, produced and reproduced by forces that were not just inimical to self-management socialism but external to it—inimical and external, that is, if self-management was conceived and implemented as the critics thought proper. Yugoslavia had been subjected to what amounted to a forced exportation of ideology and culture from the capitalist world and had not, as yet, been able to resist it successfully. The diagnosis was grave, and the disorder was, some argued, quite advanced. As Božović put it, things had slipped so far that Yugoslavia had seen the creation of "a typical consumerist psychology," one that had been "created as the amalgam of three basic factors: influences from abroad and our new social-historical practice have been grafted onto a traditional tissue."[79] But if consumer society was the apparent product of a sort of cultural "infection," that same fact gave reason for hope that the system might be restored to health if the foreign bodies could be attacked and purged.

Accordingly, the perspectives of the opposition tended to focus on contact with the market culture of the capitalist world as the ultimate source of the new social evils, and the theme of transnational infection remained a frequent and recurring trope in Marxist analyses of Yugoslav consumerism. This was a tricky line of argument, however. Anything that smacked of cultural quarantine might well provoke widespread resentment, since openness to the West had long been a great source of pride, prestige, and satisfaction for the party and for ordinary Yugoslavs. Yugoslavs loved to travel abroad, and they relished their unusual freedom to make personal contact with the even more uninhibited consumerism of the capitalist world, simply by getting in their cars or onto buses and trains and traveling there. This prized mobility, however, was now frequently said to be no small part of

---

78. Božović, *Suočavanja*, 187. Advertising specialists were able to press the "being versus having" distinction into service for their own ends. In one French expert's opinion, reprinted in translation in a trade journal, the new consumer's preference for *being* over having required a new more engaged, more responsible, and more personal type of contact with customers. The headline for the column thus announced: "Marketing Is Over—Long Live Communication!" Jean-Pierre Piotet, "Z marketingom je konec—naj živi komunikacija!," *MM: marketing magazin*, no. 5 (September 1981): 6. Here we see something of the industry's characteristic proclivity for replacing established practice with some allegedly new and improved style.

79. Božović, *Suočavanja*, 178–179; see also 188–189.

the problem. Shopping trips to purchase clothes, shoes, and jewelry in the West, especially in Italy, had become so commonplace and so characteristic of Yugoslav tastes and customs as to represent what Jože Goričar called "a unique sort of typically Yugoslav consumerist myth." Goričar believed these outings had resulted in a serious drain on the Yugoslav economy (which was, it should be noted, always keenly sensitive to hard-currency balances of trade and payments, and all the more so in the crisis years of the 1980s). All these shopping "pilgrims," he noted, were leaving behind over 300 million lira a year in Italy, and that was just in the cities along the border.[80]

Advertising's indisputable links to Western models were also thought to be a major source of the cultural contamination. Goričar, who as late as 1980 could conclude that the country was not—or at least not yet—a consumer society, nonetheless believed that tremendous damage had already been done, and that advertising and marketing continued to be among the primary vectors of a most unwelcome cultural transfer. Yugoslav advertisements, commercials, and other forms of commercial promotion, he observed, were "in most instances directed according to the Western prescriptions of so-called marketing, that is, according to tested and confirmed formulas for the psychological manipulation of buyers with the most widely varying needs and tastes."[81] Commercial promotion in its dominant modes thus seemed to be a dangerous force with the potential to corrupt less-developed societies, one that, as Nada Sfiligoj put it, imposes "new forms of behavior, lifestyle, culture, and so on, and, at the same time, destroys many traditional values and develops new ones, which can be false or alien to the environment into which they are introduced."[82] As shown in the foregoing chapters, it was indisputable that Yugoslavia had been exposed to such outside influences, and exposed to a remarkable extent. The effects of all this contact remained a matter of great controversy, but for the critics, at least, the costs were obvious.

Regardless of their disagreements over whether Yugoslavia was or was not (or was not *yet*) a full-fledged consumer society, the mainstream critics tended to concur in situating Yugoslavia in an especially important and especially vulnerable place. It lay on the frontier of an expanding, transnational popular culture, one that was increasingly homogenized and driven by capitalist interests and a capitalist logic. In this view the developed world, particularly through the agency of huge multinational corporations, was busily imposing its own system on the rest, spawning what Ratko Božović called a "planetary" style of consumption that, in turn, reinforced its own economic and political domination. Consumer culture in "economically backward countries," including Yugoslavia at least for the time being, therefore

---

80. References are to Goričar, "Potrošniška družba—potrošniško obnašanje," 84.
81. Ibid., 89.
82. Sfiligoj, "Trg in tržno komuniciranje v našem gospodarstvu," at 371.

appeared as the product of this global relationship of domination and sub-
jugation.

The ongoing processes of universalization and homogenization were far
from complete, of course, and salient differences remained. Rather than a direct and uniform transfer to the receiving, "dependent" society, the borrow-
ings had resulted, as Božović conceived it, in "a special sort of interweaving
of the new forces of consumer culture, introduced and indigenous, and the
traditional usages of the host country."[83] But as important as those native
holdovers may have been, from the dominant Marxist critical perspective it
was what had made it across the border that mattered so much.

It Takes a Licking and Keeps on Ticking: Hard Times, New Complaints, and the Time Bomb of Consumer Desire

By the early 1980s the potentially destabilizing effects of consumerist habits
and expectations were becoming all the more dangerous, as the Yugoslav
economy now proved unable to sustain the growth and abundance of years
past. In important ways, however, the domestic debate changed. Its intensity
weakened, its tone softened, and the frequency of the attacks diminished,
indicating that Yugoslavs, the critics included, were becoming inured to the
by now very familiar techniques and messages of commercial promotion
and to the life of satisfaction-seeking consumption that the country's business culture encouraged. Habituation is surely an important reason that the
attacks subsided to some extent. Another part of the explanation is that
the normative, critical attention of the politicians, public intellectuals, pun-
dits, and other opinion makers was now turned to the economic crisis at
hand and to the efforts to diagnose and cure that problem. Finally, and
perhaps just as important, the fact that the Good Life now seemed to be
slipping away for ordinary Yugoslavs made the lively, exuberant, and sometimes indulgent consumer culture of the previous decades look rather less
threatening and more appealing.

But the many difficulties and adjustments of this new era of bad feeling
did not mean that either the consumerist orientation or its critics had disappeared. The fundamental conflicts between socialist values and the culture
of consumerism still remained, and some continued to resist that culture bit-
terly. For these people the worsening economy only lent a new urgency to the
critique. As would be expected, most attacks on consumerism during these
last years of socialist, federated Yugoslavia were still rooted in an essentially
Marxist understanding of the relation between production and use. Yet this
final period also evidenced a further evolution of the mainstream critique

---

83. Božović, *Suočavanja*, 177.

and the continued broadening of the intellectual horizons of Yugoslav public discourse. There now appeared a number of analyses more attuned to new and different critical perspectives. This trend was most evident in the contributions of Yugoslav intellectuals, who prided themselves on their freedom to draw upon an expansive corpus of international scholarly literature, including the works of writers such as Roland Barthes and Umberto Eco whose thought took them beyond the familiar bounds of establishment Marxism.[84] As the result of their interests, even more cosmopolitan intellectual tendencies were manifest in the public debate over consumer culture during these last years. Opinion of this sort typically did not challenge Marxist readings of consumption head on—that might still have been outré, if not risky—but instead looked to parallel interpretations and alternative intellectual traditions that could, as needed, be harmonized with Marxism.

As the critique matured, it became evident that even many Marxist critics had, in revealing ways, come to terms with the consumerist orientation. The assessments that appeared thus more often treated the consolidation of a robust consumer culture in the country as a fait accompli, and the flavor of the debate suggested, if not a genuine sense of acceptance or complacency, then at least a resignation to the idea that consumerist values had perhaps become inevitable and were likely to remain an important part of Yugoslav culture. There was less agitation, less provocation, less vitriol, more despair.

As a consequence of the vastly improved living standards of the past two decades, the standards of judgment had evidently evolved as well. Thus the mainstream critique more frequently betrayed a grudging recognition of the popularity of the consumer orientation and the benefits that it had brought to the country. Jože Goričar's 1980 broadside against the looming threat of consumer society, for example, was remarkable for the way it carved out an exemption for expenditures on a whole range of consumer items: vacuum cleaners, washing machines, refrigerators, gas and electric stoves, radios, televisions, and even cars. These "needs of our people," Goričar admitted, "were just yesterday 'on the other side,' but today [are] already 'on this side of material necessity.'" They had become "almost essential for the normal course of work and life."[85] In other words, no matter how skeptically such acquisitions and desires had been viewed in the past, these specific "needs" were no longer "false." Just what counted as "consumerist" extravagance had changed radically.

Such indulgent stances reveal a great deal about both Yugoslav consumer culture and the political and social arena in which it was debated. In particular, they show just how deeply the modern forms of consumption practice had penetrated into the society. Goričar, a critical social scientist working from an explicitly Marxist perspective, proved quite ready to overlook as

---

84. See, for example, Marija Francetić, "Semiologija reklame?" *Sol* 1 (1986): 83–90.
85. Goričar, "Potrošniška družba—potrošniško obnašanje," 84.

"essential" and "normal" a large chunk of the spending that had been encouraged by the Yugoslav advertising and marketing industry. These were, moreover, purchases imbued with considerable cultural, *communicative* significance, including many items that had been the objects of great wariness and derision. It is plain, then, that by the last decade of the socialist experiment, many Yugoslavs, and with them even many opponents of consumerism, had come to find much of what constituted Western-style mass consumption quite natural, quite unthreatening.

For some critics, however, the growing gap between consumerist expectations and financial realities—between the kind of spending that citizens had learned to consider "ordinary" and "necessary" and the kind that the economy could reasonably support—meant only that market culture could now wreak even more havoc in Yugoslav society. Such suspicions had developed to the point that, by 1981, in the early years of the economic crisis, concerned parties had come together at a conference devoted entirely to the thorny topic of "the relationship of the media to consumer society." At this gathering, Aleksandar Todorović underscored what had rapidly become one of the most compelling—and most fateful—dilemmas of Yugoslav consumerism: the country was prosperous enough to encourage a host of consumerist hopes and dreams, but never quite able to satisfy most of them for most of its people. Along these lines, Todorović noted the key role of fashion, a revealing indicator of ordinary consumers' desires. The steady stream of cross-border shopping excursions to Trieste, he suggested, was reflective of an acutely perceived need of many Yugoslavs to stay "in step with fashion."[86] But it also pointed to a failure of the Yugoslav market or, at the very least, a failure of Yugoslav marketing: for many, the height of fashion still meant something brought in from outside. Despite all the efforts made to accommodate shoppers' fancies, it seemed that the country's economy still could not deliver fully on the promises that had accompanied the move to a consumerist orientation.

And the problem was worse than a simple inability to keep up with the latest fashion trends. In light of the dramatic reversals that had taken place in such a short time, the threat now seemed more worrisome, and to some observers, even existential. Not too many years before, as Slobodan Jakšić told the same group of conference-goers in 1981, Yugoslav policy and the buoyant economy had made it relatively easy for families to furnish their homes in a fairly luxurious manner and equip them with modern appliances manufactured either at home or abroad, thanks in part to easy credit. Now, however, with the advent of an energy crisis and a general economic decline, families were caught in a bind. Appetites had been unleashed that now could

---

86. Aleksandar Todorović, "Potrošačka psihologija, način života i snobizam," in *Odnos sredstava informisanja prema potrošačkom društvu*, 52–64, at 57.

not be satisfied, and as a result, Jakšić said, "a special sort of uncertainty about one's own existence has been created."[87]

In objections of this type we encounter the most significant new emphasis of the critique of consumer culture that emerged during the 1980s: the *unsustainable* nature of the consumerist desires that had been so quickly and successfully cultivated in Yugoslavia. The cultural trends and tastes of the past remained largely in place even as new, unpleasant economic realities made for what Ratko Božović in 1988 called "the specificity of the consumer culture" in Yugoslavia: a distinctive (and distinctively troubling) national pattern in which, as a result of outside influences, citizens had become accustomed to a spending habit that "often 'overtakes' and 'eats up' production—more is consumed than is produced."[88] Cultural hybridization, in this view, had yielded a set of "strange contradictions—a consumerist sensation [*divljenje*] without the material and productive means to satisfy it."[89] Two years earlier Nada Sfiligoj had expressed a similar judgment about the worsening mismatch between inculcated tastes and real prospects, and here, too, a market culture imported from capitalist conditions seemed to be at fault. Under the influence of advertising, Sfiligoj indicated, Yugoslav society had taken on a number of the less desirable characteristics of the capitalist, consumerist West. "Our economy still has not reached *that dangerous point at which it would become senseless*," she concluded, "but that danger nevertheless exists, and it is high time that the development of our economy be redirected in such a way that it can fulfill its fundamental tasks," that is, the satisfaction of the people's genuine needs.[90] Weighted down with worries like these, the commentary from the 1980s betrays a strong sense that the desires stoked by the reorientation toward consumer satisfaction had, in the end, rendered the Yugoslav economy frighteningly unmanageable. The country, it seemed, was being consumed by consumption.

The Power of an Idea Multiplied: Lessons from the Yugoslav Resistance

All these efforts of the mainstream critics to check Yugoslavia's consumerism and its vibrant market culture have a significance that transcends their immediate contribution, important as that was, to the battles of the past. First, because the hostility to the consumerist orientation proved so widespread and so intense, and because its opponents so effectively documented the diffusion of market culture as they made their arguments against it, we

---

87. Slobodan Jakšić, "Porodica kao prizma projekcije način života," in *Odnos sredstava informisanja prema potrošačkom društvu*, 65–72, at 70–71.
88. Božović, *Suočavanja*, 178–179; see also 188–189.
89. Ibid., 177.
90. Sfiligoj, "Trg in tržno komuniciranje v našem gospodarstvu," 371–372 (emphasis added).

have ample confirmation that the Yugoslav case does indeed disclose real and important manifestations of consumerism, and that it therefore shows us something that in a number of respects closely resembled the phenomenon seen in the West. The terms of the debate, in effect, help us know what we are dealing with. They give us greater confidence that what Yugoslavia experienced was similar enough to the consumer culture described in the standard studies and critiques to render our comparisons fair, useful, and instructive.

Given the country's political system and its comparatively undeveloped economy, such a finding was not a foregone conclusion from the outset. The manipulated business and media environments characteristic of communist governance, even of the more relaxed Yugoslav sort, raise the possibility that when we now examine the record of retailing and advertising under Yugoslav socialism, what we see is not what people actually got. Undertaken for its own sake, for example, advertising might have functioned as a false front, mimicking the visual forms of "modern" commerce elsewhere without in fact being generative of a widespread and potent consumer culture that amounted to more than looking and wishing. Though such visual and emotional engagement is surely important in its own way, when citizens can rarely hope to do more than hunt and hope, their shared experience—the resultant popular consumer culture, in other words—is one of scarcity, pursuit, and denial, not variety, abundance, and satisfaction.

Indeed, the conclusion I derive from a more limited examination of commercial promotion in the communist countries of the Soviet bloc suggests that they were often prone to offer up an impressive visual presentation of consumer abundance that was disconnected from reality in the stores and from the options genuinely available to citizen-shoppers. Corroborating that judgment, anthropologist Caroline Humphrey reminisces about the retail displays of Soviet-era Moscow and recalls, probably less than half-jokingly, that "in the old days, if you saw something in a shop window it was a guarantee that it could not be bought inside."[91] This coupling of scarcity with the pretense of its absence was a tremendous problem, interesting and important in its own right. Yet the cultural calculus that economies of this sort produced, one typical of places like the USSR, Romania, Poland, and even the German Democratic Republic to some extent, requires an analysis that takes us rapidly toward questions and concerns quite different from those at issue here.[92]

---

91. Caroline Humphrey, "Creating a Culture of Disillusionment: Consumption in Moscow, a Chronicle of Changing Times," in *Worlds Apart: Modernity through the Prism of the Local,* ed. Daniel Miller (London, 1995), 43–68, at 48.

92. See, for example, David Crowley, "Warsaw's Shops, Stalinism, and the Thaw," in idem, *Style and Socialism,* 25–47. For similar problems with commercial promotion in the GDR, see Merkel, "Alternative Realities, Strange Dreams, Absurd Utopias."

In contrast, the very gravity, ubiquity, and earnestness of the arguments against Yugoslav consumerism make it clear that the outward manifestations of consumer society in Yugoslavia were not just a Potemkin village thrown up by managers and the media to make the country's economic system (and its government) look modern, productive, prosperous, dynamic, responsive, successful, and perhaps even a little Western. In Yugoslavia the mass consumer culture of abundance was no illusion, no simple sales job. The Yugoslav Dream was, for a time, the Real Thing.

For this reason the terms of the controversy should also intensify our historiographical interest in the ostensible Western-ness of Yugoslavia's version of consumerism. The debate over consumer society, it turns out, squarely poses the question of whether what Yugoslavia experienced did, in fact, come from the West. As we have seen in the foregoing discussion, many commentators understood the emergence of something very much like the classic symptoms of consumer society as incontrovertible proof that Western influences had intruded into Yugoslav social life, chiefly via advertising, and changed it for the worse. The mainstream critiques thus provide further important evidence in support of the findings set forth in chapters 2 and 3, which explained how Yugoslav advertising and marketing practice first imported and then disseminated a variety of Western notions about what an economic system should offer consumers, how producers and sellers should treat them, and what it means to engage in "business."

Some aspects of the debate, however, raise the provocative alternative possibility that certain key elements of the Yugoslav experience were not primarily the products of cultural and ideological transmission. Rather than invariably a case of "infection" through contact with the West, what we encounter here may instead be evidence that even a highly restrained economy that incorporates limited, buffered market mechanisms may have the capacity to generate its own characteristic culture organized around the selection, purchase, use, and display of consumer goods and experiences, a culture created according to what is, arguably, the market's inherent logic of competition, acquisition, and consumer sovereignty. As chapter 6 will show, a number of other, revisionist critics, while acknowledging the consequences of the importation of Western culture, challenged the mainstream view, tracing the appearance of consumer society back to an origin in the market orientation of Yugoslav socialism itself, a system of production and labor relations that they believed to be, at its core, disturbingly akin to capitalism.

The long domestic controversy over consumerism and commercial promotion cannot, in the end, settle these questions of classification and provenance. But these disputes do heighten the sense that what we discover in the Yugoslav case is an important concrete example of the internationalization of market culture and tendencies toward consumer society through the transfer of capitalist categories of experience into an anti-capitalist economic, political, and social system. "Globalization" would be, of course, an extraordinarily tempting (and extraordinarily fashionable) term for what was taking place in Yugoslavia from the early 1950s on.[93] But if every transaction that crosses the borders between states or culture groups can be deemed an instance of "globalization," the concept ends up with, at the same time, far too much and precious little meaning, and the phenomenon is projected so far into distant history that it loses its power to tell us—as it can and should—truly important things about more recent developments.

As important as it is to trace transnational connections far across the globe and into the deep past, analytical rigor would be better served by reserving the term "globalization" for situations in which structures of governance, management, and ownership have been extended via networks that reach across state borders—for situations, in other words, in which not just contacts but *control* itself has been multinational. This was certainly not the case in socialist Yugoslavia. For this and other cases from the state-socialist domain, even "universalization" is probably too strong a word, and one that may blur critical distinctions between the varieties of consumer experience that actually existed outside the well-studied sites of the capitalist West. Yet it is absolutely clear, as evidenced in the domestic debates and in the larger historical record, that something genuinely "international" (or "transnational") was at work here. Not just business practices but also culture, in the sense of values and attitudes that became widely shared and expressed, ultimately could and did cross the borders of socialism.

The decades-long conflicts over advertising and consumerism in Yugoslavia are of critical importance for another reason as well: they underscore that in this socialist country there was a special potential for *resistance* to the spread of consumer society. Because the opposition to the growth of consumerism was so firmly rooted in the political and social ideology that set Yugoslavia apart from the more classic venues of consumer society, it did help hold the consumerist orientation in check to some extent. It was here that the facts of socialist governance and socialist public ethics mattered most.

By the time some Yugoslavs found themselves with the luxury of finding luxury a cause for concern, criticism of an increasingly international mass consumer culture had become almost a commonplace in many countries. Just as had happened with the styles and ideas of Western consumerism, this new atmosphere of opposition now poured into Yugoslavia from abroad, mixing on arrival with strong indigenous tendencies. From the rebellion against manipulative advertising in the 1950s to the anti-materialist counterculture of the 1960s to the environmental movement of the 1970s, resistance was

---

93. On the emphasis of global forms of consumption in the study of culture, see Daniel Miller, "Introduction: Anthropology, Modernity, and Consumption," in idem, *Worlds Apart,* 1–22.

in the air and on the move. But in the "specific conditions" of Yugoslavia's self-management socialism, resistance mattered more.

We do need to recognize that not every argument made in connection with the mainstream Marxist critiques is properly attributed to socialist values. As we have seen, for example, in the case put forward by Stanko Ilić, a substantial fraction of the Yugoslav critique of consumer culture, with its not infrequent asides about "radicals" and "hippies," betrays some of the crusty social traditionalist's consternation before the vagaries and vacancy of fashion. Ilić's concerns about the harmful effects of consumerism were thoughtful and no doubt genuine, but he was also quite obviously irked by the *à la mode* modes of Yugoslav youth. Consider, for instance, this bit of invective dropped into one of Ilić's footnotes in the course of a larger assault on fictive needs: "In the period of the 'maxi' style," he observed, "footwear was flat and clumsy, and thus women, dressed from head to toe with the intention of appearing stretched, walked in such shoes like men, with long steps and without any real grace."[94] This remark is, in its way, a pointed critique of consumer culture, and a fairly typical rejection of fashion-driven false needs. But all that glitters is not gold, and try as we might, it is impossible to interpret such comments as expressing a particularly *socialist* point of view, even (or especially) when it comes from a writer whose work was otherwise deeply committed to a progressive socialist agenda. Nor does kvetching like this have very much to do with any of the weightier arguments against consumer culture raised by other critics across the political spectrum.

Here we would do well to remember just how important and variable a role subjective moralities have played in the analysis of consumption practice, including moralities that have little direct derivation from political theory per se. As Svetislav Taboroši acknowledged in the course of his otherwise very critical efforts to make sense of his country's love affair with the world of goods, there is always the danger that when determining the fictive character of needs, the "false" ones will turn out to be those that the person making the judgment does not have or does not approve of.[95] That observation was meant to underscore ordinary consumers' capacity for self-deception, but it might easily apply to the blind spots and biases of the critics, too. At any rate, in the particular circumstances in which the Yugoslav debate went forward, traditionalist reactions like Stanko Ilić's reluctance to walk a mile in someone else's "two-storey shoes" were clearly a part of the ideological mix, often blended inextricably with genuinely progressive socialist politics. Therefore, as we analyze the sources of antipathy to consumer culture, conservative hostility of this sort needs to be acknowledged as well: if not filtered out, then at least factored in. Resistance mattered more

94. Ilić, *Put u humano društvo: od socijalizma ka komunizmu*, 136 n. 38.
95. Taboroši, *Odnosi potrošnje u socijalizmu*, 83.

in Yugoslavia because Yugoslavia was a Marxist society, but not all the resistance offered by Marxists was, in fact, Marxist resistance.

Of course, some of the limits imposed on the growth of consumer society in Yugoslavia stemmed from the weakness, relative and absolute, of the country's economy. The Yugoslav version of the Good Life did not, to be sure, rise to the level of Western wealth. This undoubtedly placed real restraints on the development of consumer culture. When advertisers offer up a carefully crafted look at life and people, at better homes and gardens, good housekeeping, and the essence of a cosmopolitan woman's day—in other words, at *us*—they are not fabricating outright fantasies. Much of the allure of these images depends on a fundamental (though certainly not exact) correspondence to economic and social *reality*. As Marija Francetić observed in the course of her 1986 analysis of the semiotics of commercial promotion, "advertising *must* rely on that which is already accepted and recognized, in order for it not to run the risk that the advertising itself would not be accepted."[96]

This point is especially important, and it is an insight consistent with my finding that the country's consumer culture was, to a notable extent, built on the continuing delivery of successful results "on the ground." Yugoslav advertising, in its effort to enlist the public in the country's particular version of the consumerist dream, could not afford to peddle images of luxury and leisure that were too far removed from the daily experiences—and reasonable expectations—of ordinary Yugoslavs. Divorced from authenticity, the dream loses its appeal: consumer society's vision of abundance must be at least plausibly attainable, if not right now, then at least someday soon.

Hard and cold economic facts thus inevitably intrude, serving as an important brake on the development of consumer culture wherever it appears. And it must be acknowledged that the basic realities of Yugoslav life, even in the happiest days of the 1960s and 1970s, remained at a considerable remove from the more accommodating circumstances enjoyed by ordinary Westerners. But lingering economic "backwardness" can only explain part of the story. As discussed in chapter 1, Yugoslavia's economy was, for much of the postwar period, extraordinarily dynamic. It produced huge relative gains, and even considerable absolute wealth. And coupled with the Titoist indulgence of tastes and habits that to many did not seem reliably socialist, it could indeed support an approximation of Western lifestyles that was, if not always entirely convincing, still noteworthy for its surprising distance from the bleaker prospects of most of the Soviet bloc.

Economic limitations clearly mattered in Yugoslavia, just as they no doubt have curbed the growth of consumerism in many other less developed countries. But as the debates covered here strongly suggest, something else

---

96. Francetić, "Semiologija reklame?" 89 (emphasis in original).

was also working to check the spread and "excesses" of Yugoslav consumer culture: the public climate of serious skepticism, even outright hostility, that greeted the ascendancy of advertising, marketing, and the new consumerist orientation, and the potential linkage of that antagonism with real political power (a topic explored in more detail in the following chapter on the action and inaction of the party and state).

Other societies have, to be sure, seen determined opposition to the growth of consumer culture. In Yugoslavia, however, there was a critical difference: because a socialist political system was in place, and because the values that undergirded that system had some considerable degree of popular support, opponents of consumerism wielded unusual power to create, as it were, a counterculture, to set meaningful if often informal social and cultural boundaries, and to thereby limit its expansion.

The debates also offer us valuable evidence that speaks to another critical question raised throughout this book, namely, the degree to which the popular culture of consumption touched the various social and economic strata of Yugoslav society. Was this, as the focus of some critiques of consumption suggested, a phenomenon confined mostly to the wealthy or driven primarily by the special tastes and habits of the nouveaux riches? Or was Yugoslavia witnessing something more broadly based? Who, in the end, were the *subjects* of the new consumer culture?

As the critics noted, the extent of the consumerist enthusiasm in the 1960s and 1970s was nothing short of extraordinary, spilling as it did from the prosperous north and west to the underdeveloped south and east, and from the sophisticated big cities to the tiny, "backward" hilltop villages. That range indicates that in the new consumerist Yugoslavia, the relationship between consumption and privileged status had changed dramatically since the mid-1950s, when Milovan Djilas had complained of a New Class marked by its special access to the material tokens of power. In the formulation that Djilas presented, only a small group of bureaucrats, politicians, and administrators commanded sufficient resources to spend freely and conspicuously: power begat consumption. If the critics' diagnosis was accurate, however, the new combination of more widespread prosperity with an ad-driven veneration of things as repositories of status and identity had now reversed that old equation: consumption begat power. Increasingly it was the symbolic potency of consumption that established a person's importance in Yugoslav society.

The contemporary opponents of consumer culture in Yugoslavia often saw it as symptomatic of the destruction of the more radical egalitarianism of the immediate postwar years, the token of a distressing new social hierarchy. From that perspective, the trickle-down theories of Thorstein Veblen and the distinction-reinforcing interpretations of Pierre Bourdieu and his followers came to the fore, joining the Marxist line in emphasizing the cultural dominance of élite models that were continually attractive yet persistent in their exclusivity.

Much of the evidence of Yugoslav consumer culture as it was propagated and lived out in everyday experience "on the ground," however, leads toward a rather different interpretation. A closer look at what was happening on a day-to-day basis in the shops and store windows and streets suggests that the critics erred in their judgment that élite practices counted for so much. For most Yugoslavs, consumer desires and tastes were not patterned directly upon the spending habits of those at the highest levels of society. Indeed, they could not have been. Yugoslavia was prosperous, but not *that* prosperous.

Instead, a simpler model prevailed: the modern but modest, rewarding but reasonable, Yugoslav Dream. Contrary to what the critics often alleged, village dwellers and urban workers were not pining away for the "must-have" Mercedes and the chance to fritter away a million dinars on a jet-setter's vacation to Fiji, as one antagonistic party figure implied.[97] They were, instead, putting in extra hours, holding down second jobs, and leaving home for months to work as *Gastarbeiter* in order to scrape together enough money to buy a television set, some modern household appliances, and perhaps a fairly pedestrian little Zastava sedan for family vacations and weekend outings. This was mass consumption, not massive consumption.

To be sure, Yugoslav society was not without social distinctions, and the country certainly did witness a number of the phenomena described by Veblen, Mills, Bourdieu, and the Yugoslav critics who invoked them and other like-minded analysts. But, in important ways, consumer culture in Yugoslavia and the content of the commercial promotion used there were restrained by socialist ideology and the prevailing sense of public morality. As a result, the Yugoslav variant of consumerism did not promote social differentiation through consumption nearly as much, or as explicitly, as the more free-wheeling practice of the West. True luxury goods or items prized because of their scarcity, such as certain Western products that even the expansive Yugoslav economy could not manage to offer or replicate, needed little if any advertising to maintain their power as emblems and generators of élite status, of course. Consequently the creation and projection of distinction remained, but it went forward on different terms.

That difference is critically important. Viewed from up close, and only within the internal framework of Yugoslav ideology and experience, the "social differentiation" that consumerist abundance made possible could be quite salient and quite troubling. Viewed from without, however, with reference to the comparative, the world-historical, and the *longue durée*, the experience of everyday life in this socialist country was more noteworthy for the *compression* of differentiation that Marxist values and socialist practice

---

97. See "Napredka ni mogoče podariti" (interview with Stane Kavčič), *Delo*, 13 November 1971, 13–14, at 14. The complaints of Communist Party leader Kavčič about Fiji junkets are discussed in more detail in chapter 5.

brought about. The distinctions become less meaningful, the commonalities more noticeable.

The mainstream critiques, infused with the spirit of Marx, had difficulty recognizing such dynamics. The socialist tendency to focus on the habits of the enemy class—on the wealthy, on the evils of social differentiation, and on the most conspicuous consumption by the most unusual people—tended to blind them to the more subtle but just as important effects of consumption on a much broader swath of society. Their Marxist inclinations steered them away from some of the deeper and perhaps more unpleasant truths about the social origins and consequences of consumerism. Class identities were certainly not disappearing or becoming unimportant, but contemporary consumer culture was changing the very nature and content of those identities. Class was becoming more fluid—and more cultural.

Yet Yugoslav socialism seemed reluctant to acknowledge the new alignments. Schooled in the traditions of class struggle and trained by Marx and later critics to see consumption practices as, above all, the projection and defense of class privilege and status, Yugoslav opponents of the consumerist orientation were largely insensitive to the capacity of a consumer culture, in the right circumstances, to build broader, cross-group solidarity and to diminish social distinctions.

The reasons for this blind spot no doubt included what we have seen to be a common insistence that consumerism was and would remain a creature of capitalism, and a concomitant unwillingness to analyze capitalism in terms that might be seen as giving the capitalist model credit for positive developments. Such tendencies were prominent in the critical mainstream, and their implications come across quite clearly, for example, in the analysis of post–World War II capitalist society offered by sociologist Jože Goričar. Drawing heavily on the critique of consumerism offered by Herbert Marcuse in his 1968 classic *L'Homme unidimensionnel*, Goričar echoed Marcuse, and the Frankfurt School analysis more generally, with his argument that the West was busily exporting consumerist values along with its capital, computers, and "know-how." But the undeniable postwar prosperity of the West required socialist critics to engage in some tricky distancing. Thus, while Goričar targeted consumerism as one of the essential characteristics of contemporary capitalist experience, he stressed that the West deserved no real praise for its innovations in the world of goods. "We do not wish," Goričar insisted, "to create any illusions about 'people's capitalism' or 'equal opportunity societies,' or embrace the theory about the *embourgeoisement* of the working class, about the end of ideologies, and the like."[98]

If theorizing about the expansion and fluidity of capitalism's middle classes proved so unpalatable as to require an outright rejection as "illusions," the

---

98. Goričar, "Potrošniška družba—potrošniško obnašanje," 84.

thought that consumption practices and consumer culture might actually be working to erode social distinctions and diminish class divisions within *socialist* society—just as some observers have concluded was happening in the West—remained even further from the Yugoslav critics' minds. My determination, however, is that something very much like that was indeed taking place. Yugoslavia's distinctive consumer culture and the commercial promotion that sustained it often did work to replace the old-style communist leveling with a different sort of egalitarianism based on participation in a new Yugoslav Dream, one rooted in consumption. There was, to be sure, real and significant social differentiation in Yugoslavia, just as the critics maintained. But ultimately the country's advertising did not urge its citizens toward some lofty heights of opulence that they could never really hope to attain. It pointed instead toward a more realistic middle ground of consumer spending for Everyman: modern, comfortable, gratifying, and even a bit indulgent, but also rather modest and, in the end, noteworthy precisely for that reason.

5 Taming It

The Party-State Establishment and the Perils of Pleasure

> Comrade Tito, on the Adriatic coast there are tens of thousands of *vikendice*, weekend houses. There are, of course, little *vikendice*, there are people who have taken out credit or who have set aside part of their paychecks to build some little family house. But there are also many enormous villas, there are people who own a house in Zagreb and in Belgrade and still another at the seaside...and who along with that have two or three cars, motor boats and so forth. Is it possible to acquire all that by working?
>
> —Dara Janeković, interview with Tito at his villa on the island of Vanga, October 1972

Socialist critics found, as we have seen, plenty to say about the new Yugoslav culture of commercialism and the promotional activities that were driving it. But the record also reveals that even as late as the 1980s the Yugoslav political-administrative establishment had produced, in fact, surprisingly little in the way of official or even quasi-official rules or guidelines regarding these phenomena. To the extent that we may fairly speak of a "party line" on advertising or the rise of consumer society, any such code was at least as noticeable for the practical latitude it granted to the development of consumer culture and market culture as it was for its restrictive and disapproving tone.

Given how sharp and sustained the attacks on consumerism proved to be, and given communism's reputation for fusing state administration with rigid ideological control, this relative absence of directives and regulatory decrees from on high is especially noteworthy. As demonstrated both in the archival record and in the treatment accorded these questions of political and regulatory context in industry literature, high-level party and state interventions on these issues turned out to be infrequent, inconsistent, and inconclusive. Party members may have been deeply troubled by the directions

---

Source for the epigraph: Dara Janeković, interview with Josip Broz Tito, *Vjesnik*, 8 October 1972, 1–4. Although this question was posed without a trace of irony, the interview took place at the Adriatic retreat—one of many such getaways for Tito—where the Marshal himself very publicly pursued the Good Life.

that Yugoslav consumerism was taking. But there is little if any indication that they were willing to back up their vocal misgivings with purposeful state action designed to rein it in. This absence of concrete governmental measures to restrict the culture of the market and check the perceived excesses of consumer attitudes, values, and behaviors is, in the final analysis, one of the most noticeable and distinctive features of the political history of consumption in Yugoslavia.

On this point, it makes sense to pause to ask whether we can trust the record produced by the authorities themselves. Just as the legitimacy of socialist governments in Eastern Europe was always open to at least some doubt, the evidentiary quality of sources generated by socialist officials frequently comes into question, and with that, because of worries over censorship and self-censorship, sometimes even the fundamental credibility of sources that simply have originated *within* socialist societies. These problems are by no means eliminated in the context of Yugoslavia's unusually loose style of socialism, but they are alleviated to a significant extent. The comparatively unthreatening quality of most of the questions at hand here helps as well. As regards less sensitive issues like those that surrounded the rise of consumerism, the official documents that emerge from Yugoslav files tend to reflect a reasonably wide range of opinions and intensity, and for our purposes such sources are, I conclude, usually not much more duplicitous or self-serving, if at all, than are typical archival finds from the collections of public administrative bodies in noncommunist countries. Similarly, when it comes to published sources, it is likely that, in comparison with what appeared in the Soviet bloc, readers can somewhat more easily trust what they find in Yugoslav publications to be representative of real sentiments among the population. That reliance should not be blind: the Yugoslav press was not entirely free, and self-censorship and "soft" implicit censorship were serious matters. But the Yugoslav debates were free enough to leave us with a historical record that is fairly indicative of the true contours of public decision making.

It seems, in many instances, that when decisions were made, the decision was to leave well enough alone. Explicitly, at least, advertising and marketing activities were not heavily regulated. Practice was influenced from above but not dictated. Rather, both the critical appraisal of consumerism and the practical demarcation of advertising's proper place in the society usually devolved to lower levels, where they were a matter of ongoing negotiation, a constant give-and-take between competing interests that never left matters clearly resolved. Again, this way of doing business typified the larger pattern of Yugoslav administrative practice, which had become decentralized quite early on and grew even more so with the passage of time, especially with the implementation of the Constitution of 1974.

These processes of negotiation and contestation were by no means static. At times the consumerist orientation was given more latitude, whereas at others, especially during the party's reaction against the market-loving excesses of "liberalism" in the early 1970s, the pendulum swung in the opposite direction, setting advertising and marketing workers on the defensive and leaving them uncertain about the future of their craft.

But this big chill during the 1970s proved to be, in fact, the central episode in the party-state effort to tame consumerism. For those who had embraced the consumerist orientation and for the makers of market culture who were accused of feeding it, this was as bad as things ever got, at least once they had secured a firm position in the country's commercial establishment. (The situation was obviously much bleaker in the command-economy years and their immediate aftermath.) Yet even this time of comparative stricture and disapproval did not, in fact, yield any dramatic rollback of Yugoslavia's consumer culture. All the harsh talk may have created a climate of caution and self-censorship, but for the most part all the harsh talk was just that: all talk. It did not amount to the kind of determined and thoroughgoing state assault on the culture of consumption that might have made for a lasting difference.

Just Do It: The Absence of Effective Legal Restrictions on Market Culture

The positions expressed at the highest party levels clearly did set a tone and determined the general direction of administrative policy. This, in turn, had implications for the use of advertising and other aspects of commercial promotion. But in most cases the official stances appear not to have specified definite outcomes with regard to advertising, marketing, and retailing practice. There was hardly any rulebook when it came to commercial promotion, and the express rules that did exist do not come across as particularly socialist. Only a few legal provisions directly governed the deployment of advertising messages, and these were reminiscent of familiar provisions against dishonest or unfair practices seen elsewhere, including countries outside the socialist camp. In such circumstances, market culture could and did evolve without much hindrance. A review of the enormous body of sources produced by industry specialists leaves the strong impression that the few explicit legal restrictions that were in place, moreover, rarely became the subjects of any great concern in their business affairs.

This was the case, for example, with the appearance of a new consumer-protection movement that gained strength in the 1970s and 1980s. A substantial literature on the rights of Yugoslav consumers accompanied that movement's institutional efforts at the local and republic levels, addressing problems like defective products, false advertising, pricing irregularities, and procedures for dealing with customer dissatisfaction. In many ways, to be sure, this particular response to the new role of advertising, shopping, and retailing in Yugoslav society merits more scholarly attention.[1] We might question, for example, the extent to which domestic advocates of consumer-protection laws drew explicitly upon Western models and the problems they may have encountered in attempting such a transfer of legal reasoning to the socialist setting. Some Yugoslavs were, for instance, keenly interested in Ralph Nader's early crusades. Frequently commentators thought the solution to the perceived threat to consumers' rights (as with so many problems in the complex arrangements of Yugoslav socialist governance) could be found in the organization, on a "self-managing basis," of the various interest groups involved.[2] There were numerous discussions about how consumers might best be integrated into the elaborate structures of self-management. In this way, the consumer-protection movement appears to offer yet another example of the Yugoslav system's propensity to bureaucratize, and thereby control, social tendencies with genuine, grass-roots popular support. Consumers' rights could, it seemed, be made to "fit" in the self-management scheme.[3]

In the end, however, this type of organizing was concerned primarily with the enactment of narrowly tailored protective measures, the establishment of consumers' rights organizations, and other similar, fairly restricted issues. Our analysis here, in contrast, aims at a different target: the deeper

---

1. Along these lines, compare the fairly vigorous consumer-protection movement that developed in Poland. See Malgorzata Mazurek and Matthew Hilton, "Consumerism, Solidarity and Communism: Consumer Protection and the Consumer Movement in Poland," *Journal of Contemporary History* 42, no. 2 (2007): 315–343.

2. See, for example, Taboroši, *Odnosi potrošnje u socijalizmu*, 136–158. In 1977 party theoretician Edvard Kardelj suggested that organization for consumer protection was best undertaken at the local level, given the danger that a high-level organization might, as he said was often the case, "transform itself into some sort of unqualified adviser which gives reprimands for the management of the economy [*koji daje lekcije privredi*] but which does not itself assume any sort of responsibility for it." Kardelj, "O ulozi poslovnih zajednica za proizvodnju i promet i samoupravnih interesnih zajednica za snabdevanje u ostvarivanju celovitog koncepta gradova," address to the Stalna konferencija gradova Jugoslavije, 12 May 1977; quoted in Taboroši, *Odnosi potrošnje u socijalizmu*, 157. Compare Sfiligoj, "Trg in tržno komuniciranje v našem gospodarstvu," 372.

3. One contributor to the party organ of the League of Communists of Yugoslavia argued against the idea that any fundamental opposition existed between consumers and producers. "It is not necessary even for a moment," Slobodanka Zekić said, "to consider the consumer as some separate category which is in confrontation with the working class." Instead, she insisted, consumers ought to be treated "as working people and citizens." Zekić further observed that "the Law on Associated Labor and other laws insist that organized consumers have an influence on production (quality and variety), on the prices of products and services, and the determination of opening hours, [and] on supplies." She concluded, however, that Yugoslavia was far from realizing this goal. Zekić, "Ne emotivno o interesima," *Komunist*, 19 January 1979, 9. On this point, compare the observations of Svetozar Stojanović: "The quality of socialist society depends to a large degree upon the manner in which the consumer is educated. In our country, quite a bit has been said about the association of producers, but all too little about the association of consumers." Stojanović, *Between Ideals and Reality: A Critique of Socialism and Its Future*, trans. Gerson S. Sher (New York, 1973), 133. Originally published as *Izmedju ideala i stvarnosti* (Belgrade, 1969).

connections between, on the one hand, Yugoslavia's culture and politics and, on the other, the consumerist values and behaviors that by most accounts had taken root so rapidly. For the consumer-protection movement, no broader social commentary on the role and influence of consumerist values in Yugoslavia was part of the portfolio.[4] As such, representatives of this tendency are best understood as not offering what I have highlighted throughout this book as *resistance* to the new consumerist orientation. They sought to prohibit those techniques of sales and marketing that they deemed abusive, but such initiatives did little to challenge the place that consumerism had assumed in the country's social life. In the West, Naderite restraints on advertising may indeed have had the collateral effect of slowing down the expansion of market culture to some extent, but in Yugoslavia the more central problems were raised by those who thought consumer society was unsafe at any speed.

For their part, advertising specialists actually seemed to embrace a certain degree of regulation of their craft, probably because they believed this would have bolstered the industry's claims to honesty, decency, and professionalism—thereby giving advertising some cover against critics—and because such measures were seen to be fundamentally akin to the professional standards that governed their counterparts in the West, whose practice they so admired. If anything, Yugoslav advertising and marketing leaders seemed to want *more* rules, or at least more rules of their own devising. A main theme of the industry literature was, in fact, the quest for a *Kodeks* that would establish a professional code of conduct (and that would, at the same time, shield advertising work against criticisms based on practices not included in the regulations and, perhaps even more important, establish the craft itself as a more reliably "professional" undertaking). Although the discussion went on for years, the code itself was not adopted until 1976.[5]

One domestic expert could thus observe three years earlier that "Yugoslavia is one of very few countries without any special legal regulation for advertising," noting that beyond basic laws against unfair competition, there was "nearly not a single limit for the use of advertising media."[6] In this unusual legal and administrative context, advertising practice and advertising content were not burdened by any explicit body of political, or even highly politicized, prescriptions and proscriptions. Instead, the process of regulation, such as it was, proved much more vague, open, and indeterminate.

---

4. See, for example, Stojan Cigoj, *Varstvo potrošnikov in naloge javne uprave*, 1. zvezek (Ljubljana, 1982); Pernek, *Potrošnik in njegovo varstvo*. Compare Stane Možina, "Zaščita potrošnikov in proizvajalcev," *Delo*, 9 March 1974, 16.

5. On the (in)significance of the *Kodeks*, see, for example, Mitrović, *O+P+P=: priručnik za upravljanje propagandom*, 30; Spahić, *Aspekti reklame u jugoslovenskom društvu*, 150–151, 158.

6. Julije Drasinover, "Juridical and Institutional Marketing Framework," in European Society for Opinion and Marketing Research/World Association for Public Opinion Research, *Marketing East/West: A Comparative View: Report on the Work of the ESOMAR East/West Marketing Group* (Amsterdam, n.d. [ca. 1973]), 1–6, at 4.

The nature of that regulation is therefore harder to characterize with certainty, and issues of causation become rather more slippery. Advertising and marketing work was, as the output of the industry itself confirms, often restrained compared to Western practices. Establishing precisely who and what held the Yugoslav industry in check, and to what extent, is a task that will likely prove impossible, however, given the limited nature of the extant documentation. In the end, decisions about such matters as what might be included in an advertising campaign evidently rested within the discretion of the media enterprises that would ultimately be responsible for broadcasting or publishing the advertisements. A sensitivity to political consequences, of course, shaped the use of that editorial discretion. And, quite naturally, it molded the intellectual work and business decisions of advertising's creators as well: they doubtless carried out their jobs with caution and a substantial degree of self-censorship. Industry specialists were keenly aware of the political climate, and the record suggests that they most often conformed their own practice to the implicit boundaries established by the political environment.

And though there was, undeniably, something of a restless spirit among Yugoslavia's advertising and marketing leaders, we have to remember that these were not open rebels. Although their practice and their creations did carry, as I argue repeatedly here, an ideology that could prove subversive of socialist authority, this subtle and, perhaps, often even unconscious antiestablishment activity was the work of people who were, in the end, "establishment types": increasingly successful businesspeople who wanted to further increase their success, who relished their work and their newfound importance to the economy, and who, by all indications, sought to secure their positions *within* the system. As such, compromises could be made.

Further complicating this picture is that industry leaders may often have found themselves with divided loyalties. As successful members of the business élite, they were not infrequently also party members. Moreover, influential party members sometimes served in important positions in the various professional associations. The president of the Croatian Marketing Society [*Društvo za Marketing SR Hrvatske*] in 1976, Ivan Mecanović, also served as a member of the Executive Committee of the Presidency of the Central Committee of the League of Communists of Croatia, for example.[7] Even in the absence of a strict party line on market culture and consumerism, it is not hard to recognize how such persons could serve as transmission belts, channeling the then prevailing communist sentiments from the higher levels of the party organization downward and outward to the guild. (Of course, the transmission sometimes may have worked in the opposite direction, thus helping to secure the legitimacy of advertising and marketing.) Well-placed

---

7. For a sample of Mecanović's views, see the interview with him published as "Trgovina— sastavni dio procesa reprodukcije," *Ideja,* no. 7 (June 1976): 4–5.

party and government functionaries also were, it should be noted, frequent speakers at the discipline's many professional conferences and seminars, and this, too, communicated a sense of how the political climate was shifting at any given time.

The Old Man and the Sea: Josip Broz Tito on Consumption and Consumerism

In the absence of many hard and fast rules, we need to consider more closely how the transmission belts worked, that is, how members of the party-state apparatus sought to deploy the less definite, unofficial or quasi-official constraints that remained at their disposal. Tito himself only rarely voiced any special criticism of consumer culture. Given his centrality to Yugoslav political life both before and in many ways even after his death in 1980, he is remarkably absent from the pages of Yugoslavia's advertising, marketing, and retailing literature and, perhaps even more surprising, from the citations of those who attacked what they saw as excesses in Yugoslav business and the social pathologies which, they were convinced, market culture helped to create. Most of the references to Tito that do turn up are, in fact, rather oblique. Typically the statements attributed to the party leader in the public debates over consumerism and consumer culture did not, in fact, speak directly to those issues but represented instead some broader, more general position that could then, as a matter of rhetorical tactics, be harmonized with the position that the writers or speakers involved had already adopted. Tito's views could thus serve as indirect support for either an attack on or a defense of the consumerist orientation.[8]

Tito's most straightforward attacks on consumerism and the culture that nourished it appeared as part of the stepped-up campaign against "liberalism" that the party launched in 1972. In October of that year, he joined the federal communist leadership in an important open letter to all party organizations that declared, among other things, "we need a more decisive opposition on all fronts to the pressure of consumerist psychology, to the manifestations of an unscrupulous relationship toward labor and social resources, to carelessness, and to all forms of wastefulness and parasitism."[9]

---

8. For an example of this technique in one of the most significant contributions to the debate, see Šetinc, *Smo potrošniška družba*, 62–75. Šetinc used tangentially related party proclamations and statements from Tito and Edvard Kardelj to bolster his anti-consumerist position.

9. Josip Broz Tito, "Pismo Predsednika SKJ i Izvršnog biroa Predsedništva SKJ," quoted in Aleksandar Spasić, "Odnos sredstava informisanja SR Srbije prema potrošačkom društvu," 4. The document is reprinted, along with the 1972 *Vjesnik* interview cited in the next note, in Savez komunista Jugoslavije, *Nova inicijativa u SKJ (Pismo predsednika SKJ i Izvršnog biroa Predsedništva SKJ; Intervju Predsednika SKJ Josipa Broza Tita Vjesniku)* (Belgrade, 1972.) The quoted passage appears at page 10.

At almost exactly the same time, the issue of consumer society also surfaced in an interview that Tito gave to an editor of the main Zagreb daily *Vjesnik*. During her questioning, the newspaper's Dara Janeković expressed sharp criticism of the new culture of commercial promotion, urging Tito to consider the powerful unhealthy influences corrupting Yugoslav young people, "especially in that portion of youth which is opting for the fashionable and easy life." Much of the blame, she suggested, lay with the new culture of material comfort and consumerism. "It's enough if we consider, for example, our advertising, on the streets, in the stores, in the cinemas, in newspapers, on radio and television," Janeković asserted. "What kind of profile of young men and women is being propagated here, Comrade Tito?! The most negative kind, the kind that accompanies consumer society, and let's not even mention other things."[10]

Notably, although Tito had otherwise used this interview to complain again and again, in harsh terms, that some Yugoslavs were amassing unseemly and impermissible personal wealth, the party leader offered no direct response to this question about consumer society. Still, the editor of the Belgrade trade journal *Privredna propaganda* saw trouble here: "only the politically naive," Žozef Lončar reasoned, could believe that the question was posed "coincidentally."[11] (Janeković was herself a well-placed Communist with a long history reaching back to the Partisan resistance.) In any case Lončar, like a number of his colleagues, took the interview as an occasion for those who worked in the field to engage in some critical reflection on their failings. Advertising and marketing leaders, it appears, were concerned that "the Old Man" had developed serious misgivings about their work.[12]

The anti-consumerist remarks in the party leadership's open letter of 1972 were forceful and pointed to be sure, but both they and the campaign in which they arose were ultimately limited. Moreover, apart from these, Tito had little to say publicly about consumerism and consumer society or about

---

10. Dara Janeković, interview with Josip Broz Tito, *Vjesnik*, 8 October 1972, 1–4, at 4.

11. Žozef Lončar, "Pismo glavnog urednika," *Privredna propaganda* 3, nos. 17–18 (September 1972): 3. He did note, however, perhaps with some relief, that "reportedly, Comrade Tito did not directly answer a question that must seriously worry" the entire Yugoslav advertising industry. Ibid.

12. Aleksandar Spasić, the first president of the Yugoslav Advertising Association, quotes Tito as making much more direct comments in the Janeković interview. According to Spasić, Tito declared that the party "must fight more energetically against the petit-bourgeois psychology of consumer society which alienates, dehumanizes, and degrades [*obezvreduje*] people, and which is also causing great harm to the League of Communists and to the development of our self-management society, but this has been spreading, especially in the cities." This quotation, however, is not to be found in the text of the October 1972 interview as printed (and reprinted); Spasić appears to have made an error in attribution. Given the stir that the open letter and the *Vjesnik* interview caused in advertising circles, it is still significant that, years after the fact, this otherwise authoritative industry source was presenting the quotation as one directly from Tito's famous interview. See Spasić, "Odnos sredstava informisanja SR Srbije prema potrošačkom društvu," 4.

the negative influences of advertising and marketing. The comparative silence here is telling, perhaps. Tito was, as Mirko Tepavac has noted, very much "a reluctant reformer" and one who, in the end, "preferred socialism to prosperity, if and when the two seemed to conflict."[13] My reading of Tito's engagement with these questions, both in the clampdown of the early 1970s and at other times, suggests that he ultimately found no major threat to continued communist control in the expansion of consumer culture. This, at least, is the most plausible interpretation of Tito's (in)action on this front.[14]

Much the same disapproving tone that had emerged in connection with the events of 1972 was still strongly in evidence two years later at the Tenth Party Congress, which turned out be a showcase for the new ideological turn against the alleged excesses of the market.[15] The resolution produced at that gathering spoke, for example, about the need to "oppose the intrusion of commercial interests" and, similarly, to "oppose the penetration of bourgeois and petit-bourgeois concepts and the norms, lifestyles, trash, and kitsch that are characteristic of them." These were, the party leadership concluded, "an expression of the approval of primitive taste and sensationalism." In this vein, the resolution complained that individual publications were placing too much emphasis "on the acquisition of revenue at any cost."[16]

Still, even at this time, a particularly harsh one for advertising and marketing work, potent countervailing tendencies were at play. As for the Old Man himself, for all his insistence on the perpetuation of communist authority, Tito proved to be anything but an opponent of the general prosperity, material wealth, and contentment that Yugoslavs enjoyed during the 1960s and much of the 1970s. Quite to the contrary, in his pronouncements on economic and social policy we find evidence of an indulgent attitude toward the accumulation of material comforts, or at least toward those that a great

---

13. Tepavac, "Tito: 1945–1980," 71.

14. See also, for example, Josip Broz Tito, "Borba za dalji razvoj socijalističkog samouprav-ljanja u našoj zemlji i uloga Saveza komunista Jugoslavije," address to the Tenth Congress of the League of Communists of Yugoslavia, May 1974; cited in Sudar, *Ekonomska propaganda: predavanja na postdiplomskom studiju,* 32. In these lectures, as elsewhere in his work, Sudar comes across as not especially burdened by Tito's attitudes toward commercial promotion. Although he was otherwise quite attentive to leading socialist conceptions of the role of advertising, he cites the party leader only for fairly general complaints of the sort described here. Later in the lectures he quotes Tito's insistence that market forces be subordinated to social considerations and to the familiar modes of communist governance. Accordingly, in Tito's view, the development of the market was not simply to be left to "elemental forces" [*stihija*] but instead was to be "guided" using "planning on the basis of self-management." Ibid., 58.

15. Fred Singleton, writing shortly after the 1974 conference, captured the spirit of the times with his characteristic skill, sensitivity, and economy. See Singleton, *Twentieth Century Yugoslavia,* 284.

16. References are to the Resolution of the Tenth Congress of the League of Communists of Yugoslavia, *Komunist,* 3 June 1974, 25–26; quoted in Sudar, *Predavanja na postdiplomskom studiju,* 33.

number of Yugoslav citizens already enjoyed or to which they could reasonably aspire.

Thus, when Tito in a 1971 speech called attention to "the question of personal enrichment" [*bogaćenje*], he made certain to qualify his remarks so as to cast no shadow of blame on the many fairly ordinary people whose thrift and hard work had left enticing vacation spots like the Adriatic seacoast dotted with *vikendice,* handsome little (and not so little) second homes. On every holiday and summertime *vikend,* Yugoslavs bundled off to these houses in droves. When they could not make the trip to the sea, the dwellings could be rented—for hard currency, naturally—to the tourists who had become the mainstay of one of the country's most important industries. There was even talk in some communist circles of expropriating these weekend homes, a suggestion that apparently found little support in the broader party. The idea was roundly rejected, for instance, in one internal report prepared for the members of the Croatian Party's Executive Committee.[17]

Yugoslavs were certainly getting comfortable, and many of them may even have been getting comparatively wealthy, but these more common and accessible markers of the Good Life were not offensive to Tito: "In this regard," he said about the problem of Yugoslavs' "getting rich," "I am not thinking, for example, about weekend houses but rather about the manifestations of real personal enrichment, by means of which a new capitalist grouping is being created within our socialist system."[18] The focus, it appeared, was to be on how Yugoslavs came by their money, not on how they spent it.

Part of the problem that the regime faced was the simple fact that there was nothing else for Yugoslavs to do with their cash but spend it. Investment in the traditional sense was not an option. For a time, before the experimentation of *liberalizam* was effectively squelched, there was considerable interest in reforming the economy to allow some form of individual shareholding in business enterprises. This move, advocates thought, might also tamp down some of the most excessive spending. Before his ouster, for example, Slovenian party leader Stane Kavčič had shown some openness to the idea. In an interview with the main Ljubljana daily, he made the case for shareholding with a blunt and memorable challenge to the wisdom of existing policy: "Look, instead of someone going to Fiji and spending a million dinars, he could give that money to some enterprise that would invest it and give him back interest and possibly something extra as well, depending on

---

17. Neki elementi za ocjenu stana na području socijalnih nejednakosti i za političku akciju Saveza komunista Hrvatske: Radni materijal za sjednicu Izvršnog komiteta CK SKH, March 1972. Hrvatski Državni Arhiv, collection Centralni komitet, Savez komunista Hrvatske, HDA-1220-5928.

18. Josip Broz Tito, address to a delegation of the Savez udruženja rezervnih vojnih starješina Jugoslavije, Karlovac, 5 October 1971; quoted in Šuvar, "'Srednji slojevi' ili srednja klasa," 256.

the profitability of the investment. What do you think? In which case would socialism have more?"[19] In response to such proposals, Janko Liska countered that ordinary consumers were not at issue here: "Where did the people who are forced to go to the Fiji Islands get their money from?" he asked. "Was it really in accordance with the will of the people? Or was it a question of fraud or the misuse of public office...? If the money they now spend on private swimming pools, Mercedes cars, profitable weekend houses, and pleasure trips to Fiji is diverted to investment in enterprises, will they acquire self-management rights?"[20] As Liska's heated response suggests, a suspicion that these displays must have been fueled by ill-gotten gain ran throughout the debate over conspicuous consumption. Corruption, illegal economic activity, and misappropriation were among the chief targets of the party's concerns at the time, and because of the luxurious lifestyle associated with such pelf, the attack on this front was conflated with the anxieties over consumer society. (Even when it came to outright corruption, there was concern that formal legal regulation—or as one frustrated high-ranking member put it in a closed session of the Croatian Party's Executive Committee, "merely law after law"—would not work.)[21] But it was, in fact, this concern over improper earning that most clearly marked Tito's assault on "enrichment" during his October 1972 *Vjesnik* interview with Dara Janeković.

With regard to spending, however, there was evidently much more leeway. Tito was himself a celebrated *bon vivant* and was, moreover, genuinely sensitive to the importance of high living standards for Yugoslavia's citizens. He was, for example, famously emphatic about the need for government policy to offer a comfortable life to the Yugoslav working class, and to do so almost immediately. As he put it, "The generation that is alive right now and that is building a new society with its efforts must enjoy the fruits of its labor, not just some distant, future generations."[22] Given this fundamental commitment, it is understandable that the party leader would look upon weekend houses as fine fare for the common man and would take care to explain that when he criticized undesirable wealth he had in mind something more egregious than these more "ordinary" luxuries.

19. "Napredka ni mogoče podariti" (interview with Stane Kavčič), *Delo*, 13 November 1971, 13–14, at 14.

20. Janko Liska, quoted in Singleton, *Twentieth Century Yugoslavia*, 296 (original source not attributed); for more on Liska's response, see Šetinc, *Smo potrošniška družba*, 66. Mihailo Marković was equally skeptical: "Money made in speculation in land and 'week-end houses,' from stealing and corruption and in hundreds of other illegal ways waits to be transformed into shares and to begin bringing in profits. There is constant pressure to introduce the necessary legislation." Marković, *The Contemporary Marx*, 136.

21. Dragutin Plašć, transcribed statement in Magnetofonski zapisnik sa proširene sjednice Izvršnog komiteta Centralnog komiteta Saveza komunista Hrvatske, održane 14.III.1972. godine. Hrvatski Državni Arhiv, collection Centralni komitet, Savez komunista Hrvatske, HDA-1220-5928, VIII/1–VIII/2.

22. Josip Broz Tito, quoted in Šetinc, *Smo potrošniška družba*, 64.

In this regard, it should be noted that the creators of Yugoslavia's market culture were themselves sensitive to the need not to pitch their campaigns to a standard of living that would appear unattainable or even unseemly. As one industry writer explained it in 1971, "advertising is intended for the majority, and the majority represents the average. The advertising specialist operates with averages and knows that the average person is proud to be average. Therefore, to the extent our consumer is able to achieve the average, we may assert that we have contributed to a better life for him, and we accomplish the same thing even if we just convince him that he has achieved the average."[23] This observation speaks to what I conclude is a compelling need for advertising to sell a vision of life that comes across to the target audience as something real and attainable. Actual conformity to economic and social realities is not necessarily at issue. As Robert Goldman has noted, "advertisements can tell us nothing directly about how social relations are actually lived....Although no claim can be made that ads depict real life 'one can probably make a significant statement about them, namely, that *as pictures* they are not perceived as peculiar and unnatural'."[24] Ultimately it is the semblance of reality that proves critical, and this held true for the Yugoslav case as well. Neither Tito nor the ad men strayed too far from what had by that time emerged as an agreed-upon semblance of reality.

Trickle-Down Authority: The Transmission of the Party's Anti-Consumerist Concerns

As with Tito's own personal involvement, many of the most significant initiatives against consumerism that other party and state leaders undertook grew out of the broader effort to trim back the influence of the market that began around 1972. Communist officials during this period often did press a critical line—sometimes oblique, at other times joltingly direct—with a substantial bearing on questions of consumer culture. As seen in the preceding chapter, this was most notably the case with the careers of Croatian Party heavyweight Stipe Šuvar, who engaged in a long and very public crusade against what he saw as a runaway consumer frenzy, and Slovenian Party leader Franc Šetinc, who mounted a heated anti-consumerist campaign of his own. With time, other well-placed officials joined the fray, strongly affecting the tenor of the public debate.

Yet for all the excitement and worry they unleashed, direct interventions from the higher levels of the party and state administration need to be placed in the proper perspective. Much of the serious and sustained engagement

---

23. Marjan Pintarič, "Komu služi EP?" *Bilten DEPS*, no. 11 (1971): 25–26, at 26.
24. Goldman, *Reading Ads Socially* (London, 1992), 35; quoting Erving Goffman, *Gender Advertisements* (New York, 1976), 25.

with consumer culture took place elsewhere, and the debates over advertising, marketing, and consumer society are, in fact, noteworthy for how rarely the *grands hommes* make their appearance. Yugoslav communist ideology, and Marxist thought in general, indisputably exerted a very real restraining influence on the philosophy, even the practice, of marketing, advertising, and retailing throughout the socialist period. Yet there is surprisingly little to suggest that many of those in the upper ranks were committed to an intransigent opposition to the way that market culture was reshaping the country or even that they were attempting to thwart the new business practices in some more silent fashion, as *éminences rouges* behind the scenes.

To be sure, there was a fair amount of talk about the troublesome topics of consumerism and market culture. The archival records of various official entities charged with such questions show that worries about an out-of-control consumer culture did surface from time to time in internal discussions. In a meeting of the Croatian Party's Executive Committee in 1972, for example, one member pointed with a mixture of pride, disbelief, and concern to the fact that a foreign newspaper (most likely the *Times* of London), had just printed a story titled "Yugoslavia: A True Paradise for the Consumer," using this image of (ostensible) success as part of his larger argument about the need to remedy social inequalities and spread the Good Life more equitably.[25] Even in this time of strong suspicion toward the culture of the market, communist officials proved less concerned with consumer mentalities and the abuses of advertising and the media than with the familiar demons of unjust enrichment and social differentiation, which by the early 1970s had already been topics of hot concern for years.[26] Along these lines, another expressed worries to his colleagues that Yugoslavia had moved toward "the establishment of a structure in our [socioeconomic] relations that corresponds to capitalist society and that we now want to bring closer to some socialist relationship by means of social-democratic palliatives in our tax and other policies."[27]

Though consumerism and market culture per se evidently took a back seat to these concerns about income distribution and unearned wealth, these topics did figure from time to time in the internal discussions of the party

---

25. Dušan Dragosavac, transcribed statement in Magnetofonski zapisnik sa proširene sjednice Izvršnog komiteta Centralnog komiteta Saveza komunista Hrvatske, održane 14.III.1972. godine, II/1. Hrvatski Državni Arhiv, collection Centralni komitet, Savez komunista Hrvatske, HDA-1220-5928. No citation to the article was given, aside from a reference to the "*Times.*"

26. On the problem of "enrichment," for example, see Stenografski zapisnik—13.VI.1968 sa prvog sastanka održanog u CK SKH na temu: visoke zarade i bogačenje, 13 June 1968. Hrvatski Državni Arhiv, collection Centralni komitet, Savez komunista Hrvatske, HDA-1220-3751.

27. Milutin Baltić, transcribed statement in Magnetofonski zapisnik sa proširene sjednice Izvršnog komiteta Centralnog komiteta Saveza komunista Hrvatske, održane 14.III.1972. godine, XIII/6. Hrvatski Državni Arhiv, collection Centralni komitet, Savez komunista Hrvatske, HDA-1220-5928.

leaders. In one presentation to a party gathering in 1972 on "ideological-political activity," for example, Božidar Gagro warned of the power of the mass media, including television's "narcotic" function, and insisted that the Yugoslav media were guilty of spreading a "neocapitalist" ideology "that is being offered in the most open fashion in that part of the media content that is not political in the narrow sense." A holistic approach, he maintained, was necessary, one that would recognize politics where it seemed to be missing and scrutinize content more broadly and thoroughly.

In the absence of that kind of control, Gagro argued, the media enterprises and publishing houses had ended up spreading "a system of values that systematically renders worthless every effort toward the creation of a revolutionary and humane individual consciousness." Along with other unwelcome antisocialist phenomena, the party was obliged to criticize and take action against what Gagro called the *"terror of the consumerist ideology."*[28] Some speakers at the meeting at which this report and other media assessments were discussed echoed these views, although in a milder fashion, and with little or no affirmation of the idea of consumerism as a form of "terror." One member, concerned that the League of Communists had become too "ideologically heterogeneous," complained about the inroads that a "consumerist psychology" had made not just in the broader society but in the party ranks as well, bringing with it a "bourgeois consciousness and bourgeois ideology."[29] Another offered up what he described as "a rather horrible reflection in the domain of everyday life": the country was experiencing, Milan Prelog said, "a change in the system of values that today exists, really, in Yugoslav life in its entirety" [*u čitavom našem životu*]. "Far be it from me to negate the value of improvement in the material standard in a state such as ours," Prelog insisted, but the critical "social standard" of living had been supplanted to a large extent by the narrow "individual standard," with the result that "today we evaluate people's success or lack of success" on that basis of personal wealth and lifestyles. The challenge that socialism had set for itself, he countered, was to raise up working people *"with* their class," but Yugoslavs now seemed preoccupied with lifting themselves *"out of* their class."[30] Still another commentator in these party discussions reminded his colleagues about the lessons to be learned from sociologist C. Wright Mills's conclusions on the media's traditional role as instruments of the

---

28. References are to Božidar Gagro, SK i sredstva javnog i masovnog komuniciranje (text of presentation to conference), 5–7, incorporated into the document Magnetofonski zapisnik sa savjetovanja o aktualnoj idejno-političkoj situaciji i zadacima komunista u idejno-političkom djelovanju, održanog 6.VII.1972. godine i 7.VII.1972. Hrvatski Državni Arhiv, collection Centralni komitet, Savez komunista Hrvatske, HDA-1220-6145 (emphasis added.)

29. Jovan Mirić, transcribed statement in Magnetofonski zapisnik sa savjetovanja o aktualnoj idejno-političkoj situaciji i zadacima komunista u idejno-političkom djelovanju, održanog 6.VII.1972. godine i 7.VII.1972, 25/2–26/2. Hrvatski Državni Arhiv, collection Centralni komitet, Savez komunista Hrvatske, HDA-1220-6145.

30. Milan Prelog, transcribed statement in ibid., 24/1–24/3.

wealthy, suggesting that these concerns had become applicable to the Yugoslav media scene as well.[31]

But even in this time of rising antipathy within the party-state apparatus toward consumerist popular culture and the business-media complex that was alleged to drive it, the authorities opted for pressure instead of rules. As the president of the Croatian Party's Central Committee, Savka Dabčević-Kučar, said in 1969 to a meeting of key leaders in media and journalism from around the republic, "I don't intend to give directives, because the party congress has already given them, and the Central Committee of the League of Communists of Croatia will give them as well."[32] In a fine example of the sort of trickle-down authority that typified the process of official control in matters like these, she then proceeded to apply the party pressure so characteristic of Yugoslav governance, taking care to hear out the views of the media representatives while at the same time ensuring that the Communists' growing displeasure was communicated.

Then and later, however, the "directives" given by the party and the state that it dominated would remain less than explicit, and less than lock-tight. As usual there was wiggle room, though less of it than before. The considerable latitude left to the industry was manifest in the extraordinary vagueness of most of the party's statements and guidance on these questions. Yugoslav ideology differed from the state socialisms of the Soviet bloc in important ways, but its rhetoric, like party-speak elsewhere, could at times be impenetrably murky, and sometimes in the criticisms of consumer culture it was hard to understand just what was desired. Equivocations and inherent contradictions abounded.

Along these lines, for example, consider the assessments offered in 1975 by Dušan Popović, a member of the Executive Committee of the federal party leadership and the president of the party's Commission for Informational and Propaganda Activities [Komisija za informativno-propagandnu delatnost SKJ]. Popović's stance evidenced the characteristic ambiguity and ambivalence of party pronouncements on advertising and marketing. Like many Yugoslav officials, he treated "the importance of economic information in the development of socialist market relations"—that is, the asserted basic purpose of advertising—as beyond dispute, and he acknowledged "the results that individual informational publications have achieved in the construction of contemporary methods of marketing."[33] But that recognition

31. Antun Žvan, transcribed statement in ibid., 17/2.

32. Savka Dabčević-Kučar, transcribed statement in Iz stenografskog zapisnika razgovora Predsjednika CK SKH drugarice Savke Dabčević-Kučar novinarima zagrebačkih redakcija štampe, radija i televizije, 27 May 1969 (meeting with journalists and media representatives), III/7. Hrvatski Državni Arhiv, collection Centralni komitet, Savez komunista Hrvatske, HDA-1220–3678.

33. Dušan Popović, *Informisanje u društveno-ekonomskom i političkom sistemu* (Belgrade, 1975), 20; quoted in Sudar, *Predavanja na postdiplomskom studiju,* 31.

and approval came with reservations: "It must be emphasized," Popović continued, "that we have not arrived at a worthy social consideration of a great number of questions, especially ideological ones, that emerge from the complex of commercial promotion [*ekonomska propaganda*] and advertising [*oglašavanje*] in general."[34] The tone taken thus mixed reassurance with a measure of menace. In the remainder of his statement, Popović took more direct aim at the industry. Advertising, he concluded, was suspect both for its content and manner of presentation. Especially troubling in this view was that advertising frequently served to legitimize ideas and practices that, if they appeared elsewhere in the same publication or in others produced by the same media enterprise, would provoke the most serious political controversies. These unhealthy values ranged, he said, "from the petit-bourgeois race for social prestige to tastelessness and idleness."[35]

The authorities' tendency toward grand generalizations, imprecise complaints, and loose invocations of socialist values is evident in the comments offered in 1973 by Mate Oreč, the head of the Information Service of the Federal Conference of the Socialist Alliance of Working People of Yugoslavia. Part of the problem, Oreč suggested, was that Yugoslav advertising and commercial promotion had not yet become something definitively Yugoslav: "We do not have our own system of social values with regard to a series of questions, nor in advertising as well, but instead we very often imitate trendiness [*pomodarstvo*] as well as, ultimately, trash [*šund*]."[36]

This criticism was perhaps clear enough, but the accompanying prescription for the cure was virtually undecipherable. The way out of the current dilemma, Oreč indicated, was for all who were involved with advertising in Yugoslavia to ensure that everyone in the society "recognizes the true phenomenon and the true character of this social activity." Moreover, he wrote, "this social activity needs to be understood more deeply in order to comprehend its significance for our rapid social and economic development, and for our market economy both in the domestic and international marketplace."[37] Faced with disapproval of this sort, advertising and marketing leaders could easily have concluded that they had displeased the authorities, but it would have been difficult to formulate any specific, satisfying response. This dilemma

---

34. Ibid.

35. Popović, *Informisanje u društveno-ekonomskom i političkom sistemu*; quoted in ibid., 32.

36. Mate Oreč, "Kako da se premoste nesporazumi," *Ideja*, no. 4 (1973): 19. In addition to his work with the Socialist Alliance, Oreč was also a lecturer [*docent*] at the Political Science Faculty of the University of Belgrade, a position that demanded and conferred substantial political influence. Although the piece opens more questions that it answers, the writer clearly argues that, in its proper sense, commercial promotion [*ekonomska propaganda*] did not include bribes, corruption, and squandering money on the sponsorship of sports teams, as some critics apparently believed.

37. Ibid.

may help explain the sweeping generalities about socialist values that appear throughout the industry's own literature, as shown in chapter 3.

Much the same sort of agitated vagueness was still evident a few years later when, in March 1977, two federal-level political committees charged with oversight and policy recommendations regarding the media and information services met in Belgrade and produced a "Summary and Position Paper on the Role of Advertising in a Self-Management Society" in which they outlined their conclusions as to the proper use of commercial promotion. The document, lengthy and full of leaden, bureaucratic, sometimes repetitious prose, need not be set forth here at length, but a few of its essential provisions do warrant careful examination, as they offer a solid sense of the direction that official policy was taking in the aftermath of the assault on what was deemed pro-market zealotry. The twelve-member joint session noted the existence of "several phenomena that are unacceptable in terms of their social and economic content and in terms of their ideological and political implications: unfair competition, deception of customers, a flood of games of chance (*sličice*, lotteries), ideologically alien influences on children and youth, the intrusion of luxury products, snobbism, and the like. Throughout all this, petit-bourgeois styles often dominate, and the idea of acquiring goods the easy way, without work, is imposed."[38]

Often, the committee members maintained, advertising messages were essentially contradictory to the editorial and political policies of the media enterprises in whose publications and broadcasts they appeared. Part of the problem, they concluded, was the lack of direct legal or political oversight. They suggested that advertising activities were still largely "alienated from associated labor" and were undertaken with too much autonomy within various media enterprises and advertising agencies. Characteristically the remedy was seen in the structures and practices of self-management: workers' councils, according to the committee members, ought to exercise the ultimate authority over the form and content of commercial promotion, and advertising ought to be conducted in accordance with the interests of producers and buyers, something these representatives said was "still not the practice."

The panel found that, contrary to the desired result, advertising practice was becoming an arena for "privatized relations, wastefulness, and private commissions." Troubling sums were being spent outside the control

---

38. "Rezime i stavovi o ulozi ekonomske propagande u samoupravnom društvu," reprinted in *Ideja*, no. 2 (February 1978): 4–6, at 4. The text was prepared by the Commission for Propaganda and Informational Activities of the Executive Committee of the Presidency of the Central Committee of the League of Communists of Yugoslavia [Komisija Izvršnog komiteta Predsjedništva CK SKJ za propagandnu i informativnu djelatnost] and the Council for Information Services of the Federal Conference of the Socialist Alliance of Working People of Yugoslavia [Savjet Savezne konferencije SSSRNJ za informiranje]. Later in the year the position paper was delivered to the Advertising Federation of Yugoslavia (Savez ekonomskih propagandista Jugoslavije).

of workers' councils, resulting in private profit not commensurate to the work invested in the activity. Advertising expenditures, it was noted, had swelled to approximately three billion dinars annually for the entire country, with about one billion of that spent in Slovenia alone (this even though that republic represented less than one-tenth of the country's total population).[39]

Reacting to the tendency of Yugoslav advertising to go its own way, the Central Committee and Socialist Alliance committees treated commercial promotion as something that definitely had to be subordinated to established government policy: "Advertising [*ekonomska propaganda*] is obligated to contribute fully to the efforts of the entire society toward establishing the dominance of associated labor in the society, to affirm the interests of social ownership, to develop socialist commercial ethics [*poslovni moral*], to be constantly involved in current social efforts with the aim of stabilizing our economy, to increase social engagement regarding savings and increasing the productivity of labor, to increase the orientation toward domestic raw materials, to increase the integration of science and productive labor, and so forth. [Point 1]" This was, of course, precisely what the ad creators said they *were* doing. It all sounds very much like the quasi-apologetic introductory remarks that, as we have seen, were offered by many advertising and marketing specialists to establish the trustworthiness of their textbooks, articles, conference papers, and other presentations. But whereas the other content of industry publications often suggested that such assurances may have been only perfunctory obeisance to party ideals, here we encounter here the other side of the coin: the official exposition of party values that, depending on how the individuals charged with implementing those values exercised the fairly broad discretion that the system granted them, may not have required much in the way of real, practical changes.

Like most party pronouncements in Yugoslavia, the joint committees' findings represented more than a simple exhortation and less than a simple decree. How things would be worked out "on the ground" could thus vary significantly, and though such interventions do appear to have exerted an influence on actual practice, the results were typically mixed, changing, and marked by strong regional and even local variation.

Nowhere in the committees' statement do we learn much about *how* advertising and marketing practice was supposed to achieve the social goals indicated, some of which might more properly be considered the province of production rather than sales promotion. The document was rather more explicit, however, about the need to reinforce mechanisms of social control. Advertisers and the creators of advertising, the statement suggested, should have decidedly less freedom about how to structure their appeals than had

---

39. "Rezime i stavovi o ulozi ekonomske propagande u samoupravnom društvu," 4–5.

been the case in recent years. One solution was thought to lie in the power of media editors, who were clearly believed to be more reliable guardians of ideological propriety:

> It is indispensable that advertising, on the basis of common social goals, be clearly determined by editorial understandings of proper use of the means of public communication in order to overcome the practice whereby economic information, advertising reportage, announcements, and other messages of a commercial-promotional nature are prepared and published independently of editorial policy and the programmatic orientations of the media themselves. The [administrative] councils of the public media [*javna glasila*], editorial bodies, and other forms of social influence also must analyze and introduce the positions of the society concerning the advertising messages that appear in the public media. [Point 3]

What we see here is a suggestion that the soft, informal censorship that characterized Yugoslav media practice needed to be tightened considerably. There was also a call for more self-censorship: "All those who participate in the preparation and the dissemination of advertising messages and information must commit themselves fully, so that advertisements [*reklame*], announcements [*oglasi*], and other messages that are ideologically unacceptable from the standpoint of our social relations and socialist values will not appear. [Point 7]" As these passages suggest, by 1977 the party authorities had come to see advertising and its messages as forces that were dangerous, unruly, and potentially destructive of the country's social cohesion and efforts to eliminate class distinctions. Despite Yugoslavia's comparative openness to foreign influences, the position paper also leaves little doubt that the advertising industry's steady westward gaze was viewed with great concern. A wariness about ideological contamination, the committee members concluded, was especially warranted when foreign products were advertised or when foreign advertising itself was used. [Point 7] In the end, notwithstanding the occasional obscurity of its rhetoric, the document speaks volumes about the kinds of pressure applied to advertising and marketing work in the socialist era, forces that had become more intense in the early to mid-1970s following the crackdown on "liberalism."

A short time earlier, in 1976, the party organization in Slovenia—which was then becoming a notable hotbed of innovative commercial promotion—had issued its own position paper on advertising.[40] This document, rather more elaborate than the one produced by the federal-level committees, is noteworthy for, among other things, its insistence on the role of Slovenian

---

40. "Stališča komisije CK ZK Slovenije za agitacijo in propagando o vlogi in problemih ekonomske propagande v naši družbi," 22 December 1976. The document is published in Serbo-Croatian as "Savez komunista o ulozi i problemima EP," *Ideja*, no. 1 (July 1977): 6–12.

advertising in "affirming" a unified Yugoslav market. Implicit here was the idea that advertising work ought to counter the spread of particularistic and parochial economic activity that might give rise to nationalism. Like the members of the federal committees, the Slovenian party also emphasized the requirement that advertising respect socialist ideology, and they stressed, in particular, that appeals could not be permitted to invoke a standard of living inaccessible to ordinary people doing common work. "Luxury goods," the Slovenian Central Committee warned, "are to be shown only as products that our market already offers and that may be purchased, but they may not be represented as a necessity without which life is less valuable or unpleasant."[41]

Franc Šetinc, the party leader who chaired the committee group that produced the paper, later used the essays compiled in his book *Are We a Consumer Society?* to underscore the party's concerns over what he liked to call unwelcome "manifestations" of "consumerist behavior." (Šetinc was intent on distinguishing examples of bad "behavior" from a more sweeping consumerist "mentality," which he said was typical, and could be typical, only of the West.) Advertising, Šetinc said in his gloss on the official document, had veered away from its primary duty of providing reliable information to consumers. Foreign goods, foreign ideas, and even the foreign names of advertised products were undermining Yugoslav production with their insinuation that quality was to be found elsewhere. Corrupted by forms and characteristics imported from capitalist practice, advertising was encouraging consumerist attitudes, and too many citizens were thinking "my neighbor has it and so I have to have it, too!"[42] At the time, Šetinc was in the process of making himself a key figure in the nationwide debate over consumer culture, and this committee report represents in some ways the high-water mark of his efforts to translate anti-consumerist critique into more effective anti-commercial control.

But such campaigns largely failed. Though high-level political interventions did have an effect as they filtered down to party organizations on lower rungs of the system, that is, within institutions and business enterprises, they did not result in harshly restrictive regulation. This was evidently the result of an option to avoid such legal strictures in favor of informal pressure, that is, an option for business as usual. Even comparative hard-liners on questions of consumer culture did not muster much enthusiasm for a true state crackdown. Stipe Šuvar, for example, who was as ardent as any Communist on these matters, told his Croatian Party colleagues in internal discussions that outright censorship was not in order, backing away from legal solutions even as he launched a special commission of the Central Committee charged with combating media excesses, under his chairmanship. "We don't need

---

41. Ibid., 11.
42. Šetinc, *Smo potrošniška družba*, 50–52.

restrictions and bans," Šuvar insisted, "but rather critique and convincing disputation."[43]

There were, to be sure, some real results. The trickle-down transmission of authority that did occur seems to have been most important when media enterprises incorporated into their operating policies some recognition of the party's insistence that socialist norms guide the use of advertising. In October 1975, for example, the party council within the principal Slovenian broadcasting company, Radio-Television Ljubljana, issued its own pronouncement about the need to bring advertising practice into line. Recently, the council observed, advertising had become the subject of intensified social scrutiny, and Communists themselves were obligated to devote "special attention" to its development, "because it is untenable that along with the regular bases of programming, which are built on the ideological and political standpoints of the League of Communists and on constitutional provisions, we are, precisely in the case of advertising, permitting opposing forces in this respect."[44] Coming from one of the republic's main venues for advertising, this sort of antagonistic stance was bound to have a further cooling effect on the energetic promotional activity that had been the hallmark of the first several years after the 1965 reforms.

Yet while communist attitudes clearly worked most often to restrain the influence of advertising and marketing, party leaders could sometimes lend important support, too. In the last years of federal Yugoslavia, for example, the country's advertising and marketing industries found a kindred spirit in Ante Marković, the president of the Federal Executive Council, whose pro-market policies were just the sort of prescription that many leaders in the field believed was in order.[45] Marković's benevolence toward advertising came, of course, at a time when a number of communist politicians in Yugoslavia were themselves actively advocating, or at least seriously considering, a much more thorough introduction of market mechanisms.

But even during the industry's darker days, some well-placed officials offered encouragement. Consider, for example, the opinions expressed in 1973 by Marjan Rožič, then secretary of the Council of the Association of Labor Unions of Yugoslavia [Vijeć Saveza sindikata Jugoslavije]. Asked during a television interview whether the government's policy of economic stabilization might not be leading to a dramatic reduction of advertising activity, a change that had become noticeable recently in the newspapers and on television and radio, Rožič responded with a rather strong affirmation of

---

43. Šuvar, transcribed statement in Magnetofonski zapisnik sa sjednice Komisije CK SKH za idejno-političko djelovanje i kulturu, održane 25 travnja 1972. godine, 24 April 1972, 5. Hrvatski Državni Arhiv, collection Centralni komitet, Savez komunista Hrvatske, HDA-1220-5995.

44. "Komunisti RTV Centra Ljubljana o ekonomskoj propagandi," *Ideja*, no. 3 (December 1975): 2.

45. See Ivica Vidović, "Duh (ne)vremena," *Ideja*, no. 2 (summer 1989): 5.

the positive role of advertising. Commercial promotion, he insisted, was essential: "For me, the normal dimensions of advertising are a constituent part of the process of production [*reprodukcija*]. I think there cannot be any dilemmas over whether we need advertising or not, for the answer is: yes." Although advertising should not be allowed to turn into a wasteful exchange of resources between producers and their advertising services—Rožič suggested this was too often the case—it was similarly important that the stabilization efforts not mutate into a "campaign to hound out useful advertising."[46]

The Big Chill: How Official Resistance Trimmed Back Market Culture

What we encounter in these interventions from the early and mid-1970s is the power of the anti-consumerist resistance at its strongest, especially in terms of the connection between party ideology and the actual practice of Yugoslav business. In the wake of the 1972 open letter from the party and state leadership, and coinciding with the general suppression of what the Communists called "liberalism," a climate more hostile to market culture prevailed for several years.

Advertising was, no doubt, under the gun. Even when the authorities' complaints were aimed at an unhealthy cultural slippage that was cast in broader terms, and not directed at market culture and advertising, marketing, or retailing per se, industry leaders and advocates obviously saw in such moves a potential threat to their work and their status. Indeed, the disapproval caused some in the field to strike a very conciliatory pose.[47] In one representative instance from 1973, in the midst of the unpleasantness, industry proponent Aleksandar Spasić acknowledged that, as he put it, the newest initiatives of Tito, the party, and "the entire society" dictated that advertising and marketing specialists were "obligated to contribute to the affirmation of socialist ethics [*moral*] in their entirety—especially in our field—and also to uphold new values that will affirm even more forcefully the Yugoslav self-management system." Spasić was certainly trying to be accommodating during what was a very hard time for the profession. He

---

46. Marjan Rožič, interview on Zagreb television broadcast "Novinarski klub," 14 February 1973; quoted in "M. Rožič: protiv hajke na propagandu," *Kreativne komunikacije*, no. 7 (February 1973): 6.

47. For some time after the publication of the 1972 open letter and the interview with Dara Janeković, industry publications frequently engaged in a careful, measured defense of advertising and marketing against the charges made. See, for example, "Propagandisti o provođenju pisma," *Kreativne komunikacije*, no. 5 (December 1972): 16–17. Along much the same lines, see "Ahilova peta naše propagande," *Kreativne komunikacije*, no. 8 (March 1973): 16–18 (results of a survey of leading Yugoslav specialists); "Društvo ekonomskih propagandista SR Hrvatske predlaže Program rada SEPJ za razdoblje 1976–1978. godine," *Ideja*, no. 5 (February 1976): 4–6 (Croatian specialists' proposed agenda for the Yugoslav Advertising Association).

went so far as to admit that "uncritical, frequent, and uncultured uses of foreign methods" had resulted in "a very evident affirmation of petit-bourgeois taste" and "the subsidization of the lowest sort of trash through advertisements." Still, the line that industry figures such as Spasić adopted was by no means a simple capitulation, and they insisted that advertising work had brought great benefits to the country as well.[48]

A similar sort of defensive reaction to the official pressure is seen in the formal response of the delegates to the fifth pan-Yugoslav advertising conference, held around the same time. They recognized "various deviant forms" of advertising practice in the country and the need to reorient advertising to its proper informative role. "We feel an obligation," the delegates confessed, "to actively eliminate all negative phenomena in our field, to exclude from our ranks those who encourage them, and to identify those who are not involved in advertising as a function of business policy but rather as a form of pure commercialization independent of the essence of advertising." Perhaps more impressive still, these industry representatives signaled their recognition of the value of new levels of internal surveillance and control over their work and signaled their willingness to accept such interference. "The presence and permanent influence of numerous members of the League of Communists in our ranks," they suggested (in a shining example of diplomatic understatement), "will make possible a more rapid resolution of these current problems of the profession." But at the same time they stood up for the work of commercial promotion as an "indispensable and important economic instrument."[49] Clearly, in the wake of recent events, the makers of market culture were cowed, yet not completely submissive. These responses provide as good an example as any of the defensive mode, at once apologetic and defiant, into which Yugoslav industry leaders continually retreated when faced with sharp or weighty political criticism.

The years surrounding the purge of "liberalism" also produced some of the most vivid and notable critiques of advertising, further attesting to the growing official hostility to the consumerist orientation. One event indicative of the inhospitable climate and the increasingly public profile of these disputes was a mock trial broadcast on Croatian television in October 1972, with advertising itself placed in the dock as the defendant. In the end, after arguments pro and con were presented, the jury found for the defense, exonerating advertising by a seven-to-three margin. In any event, the trial seems to have been a rather more sedate spectacle than the programmers might

---

48. References are to Aleksandar Spasić, "Naš trenutak sadašnjosti," *Ideja*, no. 4 (1973): 6–7, at 7.

49. "Društvene vesti: Izredni bilten udeležencev Petega mednarodnega zbora ekonomskih propagandistov '5+1,'" *Bilten DEPS*, nos. 15/16 (n.d. [ca. 1973]): 3–4. A Serbo-Croatian version of the document is found in "U kostac s negativnostima," *Ideja*, no. 3 (1972): 14–15. Compare Fedor Rocco, "Što je, zapravo, u pitanju?" *Ideja*, no. 4 (1973): 14; Boris Petz, "Bez crno-bijele jednostranosti," *Ideja*, no. 4 (1973): 15–16

have hoped. The "prosecution" was led by Goroslav Keller, a design expert with strong connections to the industry, and anything but a real adversary of advertising—in other words, a sheep in wolf's clothing. Attention went to specific minor misdeeds of the practice rather than to any more grand idea of advertising as a form or source of social pathology. The commentary in the trade review *Ideja* claimed that the fundamental concord evident in the broadcast was all very much in order, proof that "today in this country there is no attempt at a blanket, general negation of the social and economic role of advertising and commercial promotion." The journal's reviewer was particularly relieved that the debate was "free of vulgar, unfounded and conservative disqualifications of advertising per se" and that the prosecutor did not let his star turn on television lead him off "down the path of a priori, blanket rejections of advertising, that is, into conservative, anti-market, unscientific and even quixotic [*donkihotske*] positions."[50]

One of the industry's overarching messages, as we have seen, was that advertising and marketing were not only useful to the Yugoslav economy but were essential and inevitable as well. Not surprisingly then, given this orientation, *Ideja* was quite pleased to see the appointed inquisitor refuse to tilt at windmills. But the line of argument advanced here really seems little more than a swipe at a straw man, and a rather lightly stuffed one at that: by the time of this televised mock trial, criticism of advertising, consumerism, and consumer culture had gone a good bit beyond the sort of reflexive, all-encompassing nay-saying that the review's commentator was so glad to see avoided. Rather more to the point, it would seem, were the observations of another viewer, cited in the same piece. The mock trial, it turns out, had not fared especially well with the popular "Citizen X," an anonymous columnist for the widely circulated entertainment magazine *Studio* who in each issue passed judgment on the previous week's television offerings. Citizen X was disappointed: the show, "although it debated an interesting subject, advertising, missed its goal because the prosecution and the defense were really arguing the same point."[51] As that comment suggests, the show's various audiences may have expected a more hard-hitting interrogation of the social consequences of advertising. Although the "trial" may not have produced the desired fireworks, the very fact that it aired is strongly suggestive of the intense pressure and high level of public scrutiny directed at advertising at this time. Such episodes help explain the markedly defensive tone of the industry's self-presentation, and they illustrate the atmosphere of suspicion and resentment that surrounded advertising and marketing work at the time.

The unfavorable ideological environment that resulted from the party's initiatives had real consequences for the practice of advertising as well: for some time afterward, the decrease in the amount of advertising in the public

50. "Sudjenje propagande," *Ideja*, no. 3 (1972): 10.
51. Ibid.

media was so noticeable that the editor of *Kreativne komunikacije* complained about the "freeze" in his industry's activities, and wondered, "Is this the requiem for our advertising?"[52] In particular, business enterprises faced real pressure to limit expenditures for advertising. This was the proposal, for example, of Stane Dolanc, an anti-reformist leader of the Slovenian party organization.[53] The demands grew so intense that one writer complained of a "campaign" against advertising expenditures.[54] As it happened, reports of the demise of advertising were greatly exaggerated, but the concrete effects at the time were no illusion, and my sampling of advertising in mass-circulation publications confirms the downturn.

Even after the "campaign" against advertising abated, specialists in the trade were never completely liberated from ideological interference in their work. They were not strictly regulated, but they were not strictly free. One prominent industry expert from Slovenia, for example, recounted how a proposed television commercial for a deodorant was nixed for inappropriate content by those in the television enterprise charged with the review and approval of advertisements. In the commercial the deodorant user, presumably after applying the product, would rise into the air, a transformation that in the minds of the ad's creators was supposed to suggest airiness and freshness, that wonderful lighter-than-air feeling that consumers would enjoy. To some, however, the spot seemed to have dangerous religious, and hence anticommunist, overtones: the skyward rise was thought to be too reminiscent of the Ascension of Jesus following his resurrection or of the Assumption, in which, according to Roman Catholic doctrine, a sinless Mary "after the completion of her earthly life" was taken up "body and soul into the glory of heaven."[55] The incident probably testifies more to the power of communist defensiveness and the lingering censorial impulse at work in Yugoslavia's relatively free media institutions than to any real danger of reawakening the religiosity of what was already a rapidly secularizing Yugoslav populace. The idea that audience members would make the same connection that the good Marxist reviewers had seems a real flight of fancy—an assumption, as it were, of the most dubious sort.

In another representative instance of the effects of communist ideology on real-world practice, three texts proposed for use in radio commercials promoting the nonalcoholic beverage Stil were rejected by editors at Radio

---

52. Ante Batarelo, "Pismo glavnog urednika," *Kreativne komunikacije*, no. 7 (February 1973): 5.

53. See Aleksandar Spasić, "Naš trenutak sadašnjosti," *Ideja*, no. 4 (1973): 6–7, at 6. See also, for example, the various journalistic attacks discussed in the Slovenian society's professional journal: Branko Musar, "Ocvirki na račun ekonomske propagande," *Bilten DEPS*, nos. 15/16 (n.d. [ca. 1973]): 11–13.

54. Musar, "Ocvirki na račun ekonomske propagande," at 13.

55. Personal communication with Zlatko Jančič, 4 December 1997. The quotation of the doctrine is from Pope Pius XII's 1950 pronouncement *Munificentissimus Deus*.

Ljubljana because of their unwelcome social or political implications. To overcome the limitations of radio, the writers of the proposed texts had quite clearly tried to use a playful approach to language to engage listeners. Their approach proved, it would seem, rather too playful. One version, prepared in the notoriously inelegant street parlance of *ljubljanščina*, the local dialect of Ljubljana, was squelched—not surprisingly, really—for its outright vulgarity. Another text, designed to communicate in the language of *bonton*, that is, elegance and good manners, was evidently suppressed for no other reason than its use of the word *dama*, "lady," which apparently was thought to invoke a suspect, pre-communist notion of class and style.

Finally, and most significant, a third proposal was rejected for its unwanted parody of "socialist realist" [*socrealistično*] modes of thought and speech. This particular ad copy is extraordinarily revealing and thus warrants a reproduction in full. For our purposes, it serves both as an example of the kind of work that might be reined in for political reasons and as a curiously ironic commentary on the Titoist notion of consumption-as-worker's-reward and the democratization of spending opportunities. The script for the commercial toyed with the familiar tropes of party rhetoric:

> With his own hands, calluses, and struggle, our working person has fought for and won the right to be the lord of his own land and master of his own deeds. Restaurants, which were once reserved for fat capitalists and their spoiled sweethearts, are today in the hands of the producer-worker who, after he has spent eight hours slaving away at his machine and created new and useful things for the great community of workers and farmers, can step up to the bar and order, freely and with self-confidence, "two deciliters of Stil."[56]

One of the great virtues of popular culture in socialist Yugoslavia was a delight in self-mockery and a willingness to treat practically any subject with a healthy dose of light-hearted satire. There were some limits, however, and this particular effort evidently took as its targets certain features of public life that were, in 1983, still no laughing matter. This kind of joking was apparently too Yugoslav even for Yugoslavia.

Refrigerator Socialism with the Door Ajar: Defrosting (and Spoilage?) after the Big Chill

In the final analysis, then, we see that the culture of the market in Yugoslavia did prove amenable to some control. It could be tamed—a little. Advertising

---

56. Jernej Repovš, "V velikem stilu—Stil," *MM: marketing magazin*, no. 26 (June 1983): 10. The texts in question were developed by the Studio Marketing agency, which was at the time associated with Ljubljana's *Delo* publishing house.

was, of course, a distinct business practice with definable content, and one undertaken by easily identifiable business and media institutions that were, by the very nature of their presence as economic actors in the socialist system, directly amenable to state supervision, as were the similarly identifiable individual practitioners who might be made to pay a price for transgressions. Advertising, in other words, gave a communist government real and discrete *targets*. In practice, however, advertising was not tightly monitored in the "hard" sense of straightforward state action designed to prevent antisocial (and antisocialist) "abuses." The party and state authorities could set the tone, and from time to time they did use a heavier hand to do just that. Yet the effects of such actions were limited at best. As applied, the control was not reliable, uniform, or direct, and it proved to be more a matter of informal suasion at the local and enterprise level than of administrative intervention with the force of law. This was, in other words, more a matter of control by the party (control by party colleagues and coworkers, really) than control by the state.

Moreover, even the party's ambitions to discipline market culture were inconstant. The chill that began in the early 1970s was followed by a thaw and an easing of tensions, and then by a period of benign neglect as the authorities, confronted with an economic collapse that made the heady days of consumerist excess look downright appealing, moved on to "the crisis" and to other problems.

We also need to set the Yugoslav effort at party-state control in a comparative context. The results of the Communists' resolution to get tough(er) on the culture of the market in this country in no way resembled the aftermath of the East German authorities' decision in 1975–1976 to ban almost all consumer-related advertising. Instead, the Yugoslav power structure took, even in the midst of the struggle against excessive advertising, a comparatively light touch. Perhaps even more significant, it then drifted back toward a pattern that looked more like the comfortable times of the 1960s: a modus vivendi that was, at worst, an uneasy truce. Although there were periodic retrenchments and further grumbling from the adversaries of consumerism and commercial promotion, and advertising practice still faced continuing scrutiny at the local, enterprise level (as indeed it had before the big chill), there was no major move to compare with the crackdown—if, indeed, it can be called that—of the early 1970s, nothing that felt like a "campaign to hound out useful advertising."

Looking at the long arc of Yugoslav history after the 1950s, we are therefore left with a picture that shows how market culture—that is, the market practices shaped by the specific cultural products of advertisers, producers, sellers, and the media—could manage, despite some interference and interruption, to proliferate and take root largely unimpeded by state regulation. That being true of market culture, it is the case, a fortiori, that the key features of the broader popular *consumer culture* could in the same way continue to function beyond the reach of effective state control. Whereas the culture of the market is to a greater extent the product of business actors and actions, consumer culture, in contrast, is more the result of genuinely public processes of culture-making: the product of ordinary citizens' everyday responses to the consumption opportunities that they encounter. Consumer culture is not just what gets "sold" but also what gets "bought"—and how. As such, it remains far more intractable to state management.

And therein lies the rub: for opponents of the new consumerist orientation in Yugoslavia, the problem was at least as much one of consumer culture as of market culture. Yet the proposed responses tended to seek out the easier, more immediate targets—namely, Yugoslav business. Moreover, effective control proved lacking on both counts. The Yugoslav party-state apparatus, for all its power and competence as a Marxist-Leninist formation, would have been hard-pressed to prescribe the way that ordinary citizens came to share and express their values, attitudes, and interests with regard to consumption. These matters resist control even in aspirationally "totalitarian" societies, and Yugoslavia had long since ceased to be even aspirationally totalitarian. At the same time, as we have seen in the analysis just presented, that same Marxist-Leninist state found only limited, temporary success in disciplining the influential business actors who had become so deeply invested in building a vital and alluring market culture.

The absence of effective state action on these fronts was fateful. By the 1960s Yugoslav society was well along the path to what the critics of parallel phenomena in Hungary derided as "refrigerator socialism." The Yugoslav party-state authorities were comfortable enough with this policy option, but the leadership wanted to have it both ways: they would have liked to throttle consumerism while at the same time supporting ever expanding consumption. The evidence suggests, however, that they never found the proper means to accomplish that. Ultimately, at least in this case, even the more powerful toolbox of Marxist-Leninist governance did not yield dramatic results. As we will now see, however, some critics outside the party mainstream would remain convinced that the failure was not one of means but of will.

6 Fighting It

New Left Attacks on the Consumerist Establishment

and the Yugoslav Dream

Praktična žena [Practical woman] promoted practices totally different
from those that were analyzed by *Praxis*.

—*Leksikon YU mitologije,* 2005

Although most of those who expressed misgivings about Yugoslavia's consumerist orientation drew on a decidedly left-wing and cosmopolitan tradition, Marxism did not occupy the entire critical field. Even frank conservative reactions against market culture and consumer society also marked the public discussion of the issue on occasion. Along these lines, for example, Roman Catholic theologian Franc Rode turned to his institution's long history of anti-materialist teaching in mounting a traditionalist critique of both the global phenomenon of consumerism and the socialist practice that, he claimed, had willingly embraced it. Rode, a highly influential cleric with strong Vatican connections who after the Yugoslav breakup was installed as the archbishop of Ljubljana, implied that the inculcation of consumerist values was, in fact, completely in accordance with the Communists' desires. No one should have been surprised, he suggested in the midst of the domestic controversy, that Yugoslav policy had generated a socialist version of consumer society, for socialism, at its heart a materialist political philosophy, could ultimately promise nothing more. "We talk a lot about the construction of socialism, about a humanistic society, about progress," Rode observed. "But if we leave these abstractions behind and step onto the ground of reality and ask ourselves what this really means, we may perhaps recognize that in the end, and in the best case, this is all a matter of a higher form of consumer society." Ultimately such efforts could only prove empty, Rode contended, as they were grounded not in spiritual values but in the fleeting satisfactions of material experience:

If we pull back that illusory veil in which we constantly wrap socialist society, we will see that this ultimately boils down to the fact that [when we live in such

---

Source for the epigraph: Iris Adrić, Vladimir Arsenijević, and Djordje Matić, eds., *Leksikon YU mitologije,* 2d ed. (Belgrade, 2005), 320.

a society] we will all eat well and drink well, we will live in beautiful surroundings, we will live in brotherhood and friendship with everyone, we will freely
create our cultural and aesthetic values. That is all fine, but is this enough for
people and civilizations that are slated for death? What is the sense of all this,
if death has the last word?[1]

Such formulations obviously share a great deal not just with the familiar
anti-Marxist line of the Roman Catholic Church but also with the broader
Catholic critique of consumerism, an anti-materialist perspective that has
had considerable impact elsewhere in the world. Catholicism in the late
twentieth century had found itself struggling against materialism of two
stripes, marketist and Marxist, and in the Yugoslav case it seemed that,
perhaps worse still, the two could coexist.

The events of 1989–1991 would largely settle one side of the matter
among the Yugoslavs and their neighbors in Eastern Europe, but the world-
historical debate remains unresolved. After the collapse of communism in
Europe, Catholic opinion would continue to struggle with the relationship
between socialism and consumerist values, as evidenced, for example, in
Pope John Paul II's warnings during his 1998 visit to Cuba in which he
suggested that Cuba's experience of material deprivation could make the
prospect of consumer society dangerously seductive.[2] Marxist materialism,
in this view, may through its failures serve to make the marketist version all
the more attractive.

Even in the comparatively mild ideological climate of Yugoslavia in the
1960s and 1970s, tough anti-materialist approaches such as these had few
prospects for success. They asked for too much, and asked it of too many.
Rode's theologically inspired attack clearly went too far for Yugoslav officialdom: while the Communists typically used a rather light touch when
it came to censorship, the publication of this particular text was forbidden,
though several excerpts were apparently published abroad in the emigrant
journal *Naša luč* [Our light].[3] Although communist party leader and consumption critic Franc Šetinc obviously felt compelled to address these claims
as part of his defense of state policy—and, perhaps perversely, republish
them for a far broader Yugoslav audience—Rode's perspective and others
like it appear to have had little influence outside narrow Catholic circles,
and such explicitly spiritual arguments did not figure prominently in the
mainstream debate over market culture. Whether it was a matter of eagerly
exploiting the latest shopping opportunities or trying to resist the consumerist tide in the name of socialism, much of the rest of Yugoslav society, it

---

1. References are to Franc Rode, "Resnično krščanstvo pri nas danes in jutri," quoted in
Šetinc, *Smo potrošniška družba*, 39; see also ibid., 25.
2. See "The Pope in Cuba," *New York Times*, 23 January 1998.
3. See Šetinc, *Smo potrošniška družba*, 39; see also 25.

must be remembered, was in one way or another already committed to some version of materialism.

Nevertheless, despite their secondary status, conservative viewpoints did remain a detectable strain of critique throughout the socialist period. Thus one writer for *Nova revija*, the most important outlet for nationalist intellectuals in Slovenia during the last decade of the federation, argued in 1990 (after the collapse of state socialism elsewhere but before the ouster of the Yugoslav party) that a communist-*sponsored* consumerism posed a direct threat to both democratization and the Slovene national cause. The authorities, Jože Snoj claimed, had deliberately encouraged "profit-seeking consumerism" [*pridobitniško potrošništvo*] in order to direct attention away from the many failings of the regime. Consumption practices in Yugoslavia, from this perspective, thus functioned as a form of "self-administered narcotic for the populace" [*ljudska samoomama*]. Moreover, the consumerist impulse was harming women by luring them away from their traditional roles as mothers. In combination with the elimination of subsidies for children, Snoj maintained, this cultivated addiction to wealth and acquisition had driven women away from their families into largely unremunerative jobs. In the process, it was alleged, communist policy had driven down the birth rate, thus endangering the very existence of the Slovene nation.[4] Critically, Snoj's traditionalist perspective implied that the socialist critique of consumer society amounted to not much more than an exercise in hypocrisy or, at best, self-deception. In this view, the creation of a consumer society was exactly what the Communists *wanted*, notwithstanding all the Marxist insistence to the contrary.

At the opposite end of the political spectrum, other commentators identified a very different kind of feminine oppression in the impact of commercial promotion and consumer culture. Along these lines, for example, feminist scholar Maca Jogan attacked advertising as an instrument of women's oppression. Endorsing most of the familiar communist objections to consumerism and the excesses of advertising—the propagation of false needs, the alienation of the worker, the narcotizing use of consumption for class pacification, the underlying conception of "the person as thing or robot"—Jogan focused on the ways in which advertising perpetuated dramatic inequalities between men and women. "In the advertising messages of consumerist capitalist society," Jogan observed, "there prevails a model of woman stripped of most human qualities, that is, a beautiful puppet, a being of sexual passions, something enchanting and something that can be dominated, and interesting to society as a stimulator of consumerism and as a direct participant in consumption."[5] Although she thought the classic consumerist vision of feminine nature had an unmistakable Western derivation,

4. Jože Snoj, "Tisoč let samote," *Nova revija* 9, no. 95 (March 1990): 250–259, at 252.
5. Maca Jogan, "Potrošniška usmerjenost in vprašanje emancipacije," *Teorija in praksa* 18, no. 10 (1981): 1218–1223.

Jogan believed that Yugoslav advertising had also latched on quite readily to this aspect of the imported ideology of consumerism. And once again, she suggested, Westernization was being equated falsely and simplistically with progress: "According to some," Jogan wrote, "the acceptance of that sort of model of the woman from the 'developed countries' in our social conditions of 'backwardness' is supposed to signify a revolutionizing effect, enlightenment, and the possibility for a transition to a more modern state of interpersonal relations." Jogan remained skeptical. She interpreted the sexist conventions of Yugoslav advertising as just more foolish and harmful imitation of the West. "It seems," she said, "that this example, like others, warns us about the error of the idea that everything modern (in the West) is also progressive, and that our obligation is simply to model and adapt ourselves to the more developed countries and, at the same time, to dismiss everything that does not carry the label 'made in the good Free World.' "[6] A society in which commercial relations were theoretically grounded upon social ownership of the means of production, Jogan argued, ought to be able to express a much higher level of respect for women.

In critiques of this nature, which highlight a vision of the consuming female as "a beautiful puppet" who proves valuable both because of her vulnerability to consumerist impulses and her allure for creating them, there are obvious echoes of a line of analysis then being elaborated with increasing sophistication and force among feminist scholars and cultural critics in the West. This attitude toward the gender dynamics perceived to be at work in the culture of the market—one that focused on women's endeavors as an arena for deception, manipulation, and domination—would with time become a familiar fixture of anti-consumerist rhetoric. But in Yugoslavia the encounter with feminine consumption was hardly univocal or, for that matter, unequivocal. Alongside such feminist-inspired reproaches there also appeared interpretations that defended and even celebrated women's activities in the marketplace, treating women as active, engaged, informed, and skillful agents who not only responded to consumption policy but could, through the expression of their needs and desires, drive it as well. Amplifying an image that would be sustained in the country's market culture and the popular media from the 1960s on, the cultural commentary of women's magazines often proceeded in this register, offering up a vision of the modern *Jugoslovenka* as a talented shopper who recognized (and demanded) quality and, in the process, maximized value for herself and her family. Across the country, in widely circulated periodicals such as *Svijet, Naša zena,* and *Jana,* this sort of representation was standard fare.

Similar views were seen elsewhere in the communist world as well. In the USSR of the Khrushchev Thaw, for example, Susan Reid has found that

---

6. Ibid., 1221–1222.

the new consumption regime propagated in the discourse and action of the party and state conferred on women, "in their capacity as consumers and retailers, a particular kind of power and expertise as the state's agents in reforming the material culture of everyday life"—a posture that in a variety of ways continued the Stalin-era approach to women as "consumption experts."[7] Along somewhat different lines, Mary Neuburger observes that Communists in Bulgaria also took special note of women's distinctive capacities as consumers, suggesting a link between the state's modernizing initiatives in fashion and "the general assumption that women were inherently more materialistic than men." As such, Neuburger concludes, "the regime presumably could be most effective by pandering to their sensibilities as 'material girls.' "[8] But the similarities of socialist societies with regard to the gender dimensions of consumption, important as they are, only go so far. Yugoslavia's unusually close embrace of consumerist values and marketing messages, coupled with its equally unusual capacity to indulge in problems of abundance rather than problems of scarcity, meant that this particular socialist society's engagement with consumption would, when it came to women's roles, end up having much in common with the gendered readings typical of, and developed for, the "affluent societies" of the West.

As much as the alternative analyses rooted in feminism, nationalism, and religion reveal about the complexity of Yugoslav society and the range of reactions that its variant of consumer culture provoked, such commentary must, in the end, be recognized as outside the mainstream debate. Yugoslavia was decentralized and even comparatively pluralistic, but it preserved a Marxist-Leninist political order, and in that system Marxist analyses of consumerism still mattered most.

Far more central, then—and far more threatening—was another distinct strand of antiestablishment opinion that emerged alongside those more conventional analyses discussed in the preceding chapters. This was the urgent, unorthodox socialist critique of consumer culture developed by a group of revisionist Marxists skeptical of, and even openly antagonistic toward, the market-oriented premises (and promises) of self-management socialism. Most important in this uncompromising confrontation was the disapproval that issued continually from a circle of critics aligned with the celebrated journal *Praxis*. From 1964 until its publication was suppressed in 1974–1975—in other words, precisely during the most dramatic expansion of consumption opportunities in Yugoslavia—this sociologically oriented

---

7. Reid, "Cold War in the Kitchen," 220–221. Such power notwithstanding, the new Soviet discourse placed women in "an ideologically inferior role," marking out advances in "self-government" and "socialist democracy" as distinctively male. Ibid.

8. Neuburger, "Veils, *Shalvari*, and Matters of Dress," 182. The Bulgarian government also used its leading women's magazine, *Lada*, to elaborate "a socialist rationalization for shopping and vanity." Ibid.

review of politics and culture functioned as a vital outlet for left-wing Marxist-humanist thought, attacking not only contemporary capitalism and the inhuman face of Soviet-style state socialism but official Yugoslav policy as well.

Both at home and abroad, the journal proved extraordinarily influential. It energized Yugoslav communism and annoyed the party leadership, while among left-wing intellectuals in the West it raised hopes for the future of democratic socialism in Eastern Europe and beyond. As part of their broader interest in criticizing capitalism and restraining the influence of the market in Yugoslav society, members of the *Praxis* group devoted sustained attention—and, as we will see, plenty of unforgiving criticism—to the social problems that stem from modern modes of acquiring and using goods and services, while at the same time they struggled to define the proper role of consumption in a socialist economy.

Amid all the stir that surrounded the journal at home and abroad, the centrality of market culture and consumer culture to the worldview of these Marxist-humanists has frequently been ignored, a neglect evident both in the contemporary reception of *Praxis* and its work and in the historical analysis of its legacy. If not overlooked entirely, the uncompromising indictment of consumerism in the humanist line has at least been largely forgotten—overwhelmed, it seems, by a greater attention to the Praxists' critique of authoritarianism.

The competing authoritarianisms of the Left and Right represented a concern that could, of course, easily find traction with Cold War–era sensibilities. The issue was elevated to even greater prominence by Yugoslav officialdom's uncharacteristic heavy-handedness in shutting down the journal, a response that made *Praxis* a cause célèbre and underscored the uncomfortable fact that, even in this most tolerant of communist societies, forbearance had its limits. Accordingly, as remembered thus far, the *Praxis* story has usually shaded into the easy rhetorics of insider authority and outsider opposition that have so often marked our historical accounting of the communist era, influenced mightily by the long-prevailing paradigms of "totalitarianism" and "dissidence."

It is true that even the milder communism of the Titoist party provoked its share of dissidents, and it may even be fair to count at least some of the *Praxis* circle in that number. But seen in the context of the larger historical arc of socialism, members of the country's Marxist-humanist movement were, ideologically at least, "insiders" themselves. It does not diminish their serious anti-authoritarian objections, nor the very real costs that they and others like them paid for their intransigence, to suggest that we need to look beyond the highly salient *oppositional* qualities of their positions to search for the deeper lessons that these intra-Yugoslav, intra-Marxist debates may offer us about the challenges then facing socialism not just in Yugoslavia but in the broader communist world as well.

Manufacturing Consumption: Hedonism, False Needs, and the *Praxis* Critique of Capitalism

The Praxist critics took a decidedly comparative, social-scientific, and global approach to their work as analysts and commentators, and much of what they had to say about consumer culture was prompted by its more overblown manifestations abroad, in the wealthiest of the capitalist countries. They were well aware of how consumerism was rapidly reshaping life in the West, and they were none too pleased with what they saw. The fundamental objections emerged fairly early on, as seen, for example, in the distressing diagnosis of contemporary culture offered by *Praxis* collaborator Miladin Životić in 1967. Identifying bureaucracy and the "affluent society" as the two dominant features of modern life, Životić elaborated a binary typology that interpreted ordinary citizens and workers in the developed capitalist world as the captives of what he called the "hedonistic-utilitarian culture." This culture served, as he viewed it, as the logical concomitant of the other dominant modern type, the state-heavy, profoundly bureaucratized "authoritarian culture" (although, as we will see, the hedonistic alternative was not without purportedly authoritarian features of its own).[9]

It was in connection with the hedonistic-utilitarian culture, naturally, that the issue of consumer society arose. According to Životić, the essential qualities of the hedonistic paradigm included "the separation of the need to consume from other needs, the reduction of human needs to the need for commodity-monetary values, and the emergence of a nonproductive relationship toward these values."[10] Where this culture prevailed, an emphasis on spending and displays of wealth was said to dominate social life; even the fundamental values of society ended up "directed toward consumption." Beneath all this seeming luxury, however, the Praxist interpretation detected an appalling poverty of the spirit. "A society of material abundance," Životić thus argued, "creates a man for whom, in Marx's words, the totality of manifestations of human existence is not necessary. In place of a wealth of human needs we notice in such a society *the reduction of needs to the need for consumption and the amassing of goods.*"[11] What these theoretical observations translated to in practice was a distinctly unpleasant way of life, despite its superficial richness, comfort, and freedom: "This modern hedonist is not a happy man: he lives only through the senses and not by means of the spirit.... Modern sociological research shows that

---

9. Miladin Životić, "Between Two Types of Modern Culture," in *Praxis: Yugoslav Essays in the Philosophy and Methodology of the Social Sciences,* ed. Mihailo Marković and Gajo Petrović (Dordrecht, 1979), 187–197; originally published in the Yugoslav edition of the journal as "Izmedju dvaju tipova savremene kulture," *Praxis,* nos. 5–6 (1967): 802–812.

10. Životić, "Between Two Types of Modern Culture," 190.

11. Ibid. (emphasis added).

the spread of hedonist life styles is accompanied by the spread of neurotic syndromes, despair, insecurity, and the absence of a sense of reality."[12] In the far-reaching and comprehensive interpretation of the *Praxis* school, the consumerist orientation could thus be seen to be at the root of a whole host of seemingly unrelated social ills.

But the Praxist analysis was ultimately anchored to a broader, more expressly political agenda. Deploying the trope of modern-man-as-consuming-man that was then so current in international cultural-critical circles, Životić brought the fight against consumerism back to his movement's larger concerns with human freedom and the battle against oppressive political and economic structures, seeking in the process to quash any unduly sanguine inferences about the presumed advantages of the play-passions of the West. "Contemporary *homo consumens*," he thus concluded, "is not a self-directed individual but an object of manipulation by authoritarian social forces."[13] While consumerism may have been associated with the ostensibly more "free" of the two prevailing cultural variants, from the *Praxis* perspective it robbed people of their liberty just as surely as the bureaucratic-authoritarian culture did. It simply worked by stealth.

Not surprisingly, these left-revisionist critics saw Western advertising as one of the main instruments of what they sought to expose as a quiet capitalist version of authoritarianism that bent consumers to its own ends. Here they picked up the familiar denunciation of advertising as a generator of false needs created only to serve selfish commercial interests. The result, Životić believed, was a disturbing emphasis on the need to consume over all other needs and the concomitant elevation of the hedonic over all other aspects of human existence: "While they comprise a part of the total make-up of man, sensory pleasures have a limit: when they are isolated from other human needs they become limitless. Man develops an uncontrolled desire for possessions, an aspect of his nonproductive relationship toward consumption values."[14] The consequence, it appeared, was a shocking sterility of mind and culture: "Artificial needs cause man to lose all sensitivity to authentic spiritual values. In this vacuum the need for empty amusement becomes the only need."[15]

All this emphasis on hedonism might seem to betoken a theory that treated psychological considerations as taking precedence over all others, but this was not the case. To be sure, questions of culture, spirit, psyche, and intellect were distinctive emphases of the *Praxis* approach more generally, and they proved central in this instance as well. Such matters were not, as traditional Marxist formulations urged, relegated to the sidelines

---

12. Ibid.
13. Ibid.
14. Ibid.
15. Ibid.

as mere "superstructure." Yet in the end the Praxist analysis remained a Marxist analysis, and economic relationships still mattered more. Accordingly, the humanists' interpretation pointed to the conclusion that what we encounter in modern consumer society is the pleasure principle harnessed to the service of capitalist production relations. "Contemporary hedonism," Životić argued, "creates the political and intellectual apathy of modern man. It preserves the 'incompetence of the masses'…upon which rests the authoritarian-bureaucratic, 'competent' management of society."[16] In such understandings, the cultivation of consumerist values emerged as the latest capitalist device for stripping ordinary citizens of their freedom and power. Consumption, it would seem, had supplanted the Marxian original as the new "opiate of the masses" or, perhaps more apt, as an exhilarating but ultimately debilitating new hallucinogen.

The offensive against consumerism was anything but a one-off sortie or passing affair. Quite to the contrary, throughout the high times of the 1960s and early to mid-1970s, the *Praxis* group made attention to consumption, in both its global and local Yugoslav dimensions, a profound and recurring emphasis of their work. Mihailo Marković, for instance, probably the most prominent member of the circle, clearly shared the worry of his collaborator Životić about the dominance of false needs in modern affluent society. This anxiety was, moreover, an abiding concern. Writing in 1981, some time after the heyday of the movement and its journal, Marković described human needs as phenomena that, though not invariably artificial, were still clearly historically contingent and socially constructed: "The fact is that 'need' is a historical concept," he asserted. "In some countries or in some past times one 'needed' a bicycle. Some people nowadays 'need' a second, or even a third, car."[17]

As Marković noted, the prioritization and ranking of needs underwent rapid changes in once poor countries with expanding economies (a shift with special significance for societies that, like Yugoslavia, found themselves on unusually steep development curves). "At first," he observed, "most money goes on food, later, at a higher level, on clothing, then interest concentrates on furniture, next is better accommodation, later a car, still later one's own house, travel abroad, expensive hobbies, another car, a weekend house, etc."[18] As we have seen in the foregoing chapters, this was just what critics at the time were saying had happened in, and to, Yugoslavia—and not without reason.

The psychological and cultural implications of all this change were, from the Marxist-humanist perspective, profound: "It follows then that all human needs can never be satisfied. Even in the most abundant society that one can

---

16. Ibid.
17. Mihailo Marković, *Democratic Socialism: Theory and Practice* (New York, 1982), 93.
18. Ibid.

imagine there will still be a scarcity in some kinds of goods and services."[19] The single-minded use of consumption for the pursuit of satisfaction was, in this view, a ticket to frustration. Something else, a genuine humanist alternative to materialist hunger, was required.

The problem was particularly acute, Marković believed, for the world of contemporary capitalism. There the economic logic of the system itself demanded a constant drive to acquire newer, better, and more goods. Such hunger, of course, could not be fully sated, but this mix of satisfaction and lingering emptiness was exactly what the profit imperative of capitalism required. Bourgeois society, in this analysis, had become utterly dependent upon constant, massive expansion in material production and consumption. "Without such growth," Marković claimed, *without making out of accumulation and consumption the basic criterion of good life,* capitalism would be unthinkable."[20] He noted with approval that the explosion of consumerism in the West and its spread to new lands had prompted significant opposition, leading in some places to "a radically changed anti-consumerist consciousness."[21] This observation, however, came with the warning that some who rejected consumer culture, especially the young, had simply replaced the pursuit of things material with the "excessive consumption of *cultural* and *pseudo-cultural* goods."[22] The Praxists seemed none too comfortable with the countercultural bent of a portion of the New Left, and it may be this unease that led some of them to chide Western critics of consumerism for their excessively radical stances. Consequently, for the short term, Marković could only offer a less than rosy prognosis, notwithstanding some encouraging signs of resistance. In much of the developed world, he concluded gloomily, "exponentially growing industry continues to increase its output, to create artificial needs, and to encourage a wasteful consumption" of resources that were beginning to seem all too limited.[23]

For Our Freedom—and Yours: Contemporary Capitalist Consumption and the Challenge to Socialism

Yet for all their disapproval of latter-day capitalism, the Praxists plainly understood the affluence of the West as a new and especially difficult obstacle to socialist aspirations. Modern life in the developed West presented them with a dilemma, much of it wrapped up in consumerism. In many ways, the

19. Ibid.
20. Ibid., xiii (emphasis added).
21. Ibid., 152.
22. Ibid. (emphasis in original).
23. Ibid., 51.

postwar "Rise of the West" clearly *looked* better than life under actually-existing socialism: more affluent, more comfortable, more free. The *Praxis* critique betrays some discomfort before these difficult facts, but members of the circle were able to argue deftly that what the West seemed to promise was hollow: the comfort transitory, the freedom illusory, the wealth ultimately quite costly.

In the end, however, the Praxist analysis did not deny that for those who wanted to bring about a socialist revolution, or in the Yugoslav case preserve one, the advent of modern consumerism had changed the rules of the game. Svetozar Stojanović, another central figure in the group, summed up the new situation beautifully: "One need not accept the exaggeration of the theories of the 'affluent society' and the 'consumer society' in order to see that the proletariat in the West is *no longer a class which has nothing to lose but its chains.*"[24] As Stojanović noted, much of the Western working class, and in some countries even a majority of workers, had become "aristocratized," undermining traditional Marxist theories about the role of poverty in the genesis of revolution.[25] He did not comment directly on whether the Yugoslav working class was itself becoming aristocratized. In light of the country's growing prosperity and the spread of consumerism, however, it seems sensible to wonder if something very much like that was, in fact, taking place.

Given these fundamental changes, the lessons of the West were understood to be clearly relevant (as indeed they were for more orthodox Marxist critics, as demonstrated in the foregoing chapters).[26] The globally oriented, social-scientific mind-set of the Praxists led them to conclude that socialism was unlikely to be spared the problems classically associated with Western affluence, even though life under socialism was, in most places, a good bit more spare. Socialist societies, it appeared, were caught between their desire to raise living standards and their responsibility to promote a truly humanistic orientation toward culture and interpersonal relationships. The dilemma had not yet become real for many socialist states by the 1970s, but Stojanović conceded that the problems bred by wealth might nonetheless prove endemic to the socialist world, too. "Obsessions with production and consumption," he observed, "threaten the prosperity of socialism in any country which seeks to emerge rapidly from a state of backwardness."[27] In

---

24. Stojanović, *Between Ideals and Reality*, 70 (emphasis added); see also 205.
25. Ibid., 71.
26. Despite certain obvious efforts to distance their analyses from those of Western critics of consumer society, the thinking of Stojanović and a number of members of his circle was, in fact, substantially indebted to such critiques. There are clear similarities, for example, in the approaches of the *Praxis* group and those laid out by John Kenneth Galbraith in his pathbreaking 1958 book *The Affluent Society*, an extraordinarily influential work that was at the peak of its popularity around the time when these Yugoslav scholars rose to prominence.
27. Stojanović, *Between Ideals and Reality*, 129.

the *Praxis* view, of course, the "prosperity of socialism" meant something well beyond the purely economic. Instead, a prosperity of the spirit, of genuine socialist values, was at stake. "A poor socialist society must concentrate upon the creation of material abundance," Stojanović acknowledged. "But we should keep in mind that material wealth, which ought to be a means, can take the place of the basic goal, i.e., human wealth. *Homo economicus*—man mastered by the pursuit of material goods rather than of human existence—jeopardizes the development of *homo humanus* and his community."[28] Perversely, affluence now appeared as much a menace as a boon.

Stojanović's colleague Mihailo Marković expressed a similar opinion regarding the threat of consumerism to socialist aims. The successful pursuit of higher living standards, in this view, spawned not only consumerism but an especially galling sort of political hypocrisy as well. "Individual needs in an insufficiently developed society," Marković cautioned, "will tend to be primarily needs for material objects rather than intellectual and cultural aspirations."[29] This propensity to secure material requirements first may have been natural enough, but from the Marxist-humanist perspective it threatened to produce a massive disjunction between actual behavior and publicly proclaimed ideals. Along with this came a potential perversion of the aims of socialist politics, with the resulting need for pretense and duplicity about what was really going on. "While developing its productive forces," Marković asserted, "society tends to reproduce a type of *homo consumens*, well-known from highly developed capitalist society, but at the same time it still preaches modesty and, at least verbally, sticks to Marx's humanist ideal of man who wants to *be* and not just to *have*."[30]

Like much of the Praxist critique, the observations here were phrased in general terms, speaking to a common dilemma of socialist statecraft. And indeed it was. Even in those countries where leaders were least able to claim that they were successfully satisfying consumer demands, the tension between socialism's material and psychic aims was at work, and that fact was apparent to a number of the most thoughtful and reflective champions of communism. As Ernesto "Che" Guevara suggested, the natural Marxist emphasis on the material could divert attention from the deeper humanistic dimension of the ongoing revolution. "It is not a matter," Guevara insisted, "of how many kilograms of meat one has to eat, nor of how many times a year one goes to the beach, nor how many pretty things from abroad you might be able to buy with present-day wages. It is a matter of making the individual feel more complete, with much more internal richness and much

---

28. Ibid.
29. Marković, *Democratic Socialism*, 162.
30. Ibid.

more responsibility."[31] Clearly, then, the Praxists' worries had at least potential relevance for the entire Marxist project, wherever it had taken root. Yet the immediate practical implications of their diagnosis were indisputable: a look around the socialist world at the time left no doubt that this particular problem touched contemporary Yugoslavia most acutely of all.

Notwithstanding their partisan commitments, the Marxist-humanist commentators appeared to recognize that the surprising performance of Western economies following World War II had definitively altered the terrain on which future socialist political struggles would go forward. New rules seemed to be in effect. Marković therefore took pains to stress that his critique did not depend on a rejection of affluence itself. It would be foolish, he reasoned, to deny that "only in a society of abundance will people *definitely* cease to be obsessed by the bare motive of possession and emancipate themselves for the development of the whole spectrum of deeper and more refined human needs."[32] Wealth, in this view, was a worthy and necessary goal, and indeed even the market, that most troubling of capitalist devices, was deemed necessary as "one of the essential objective indicators of economic efficiency and rationality."[33] But the market brought its own set of threats to other vitally important socialist ideals. From the standpoint of the *Praxis* critics, a major concern was the importation into socialist economics of a Western liberal understanding of the market and, critically, the underlying *ideology* associated with that concept. As Marković expressed it, "real socialism" had borrowed certain of the "worst features" of industrialized capitalist society and non-European civilizations. Socialist governments had embraced both "Oriental despotism and the Western ideal of an unlimited, wasteful material prosperity."[34] That, for the Praxists, spelled trouble, and trouble that hit too close to home.

Market Socialism and Market Culture: The Compounding Contradictions of the Yugoslav Experiment

With the expansion and reinforcement of market mechanisms in Yugoslavia, the problem could no longer be shrugged off as someone else's: the fetishism

---

31. Ernesto "Che" Guevara, "Man and Socialism," in *The Cuba Reader: History, Culture, Politics*, ed. Aviva Chomsky, Barry Carr, and Pamela Maria Smorkaloff (Durham, N.C., 2003), 370–374, at 373.

32. Marković, *From Affluence to Praxis: Philosophy and Social Criticism* (Ann Arbor, 1974), 141.

33. Ibid., 141–142; see also Marković, *The Contemporary Marx*, 180–181, 184. Despite his willingness to accommodate market mechanisms in the short term, Marković envisioned a mature socialist order that ultimately would transcend market relations. A useful guide to the work of the key *Praxis* members on this point is David A. Crocker, *Praxis and Democratic Socialism: The Critical Social Theory of Marković and Stojanović* (Atlantic Highlands, N.J., 1983); see, esp., 258–267.

34. Marković, *Democratic Socialism*, 178.

of commodities had now started, as Marković put it, to "infect" Yugoslav socialism as well.[35] As we have seen in the preceding chapters, that ideological infection was real. There were abundant reasons to conclude that Yugoslavia had indeed seen the transfer of commercial and cultural practices from "outside," accompanied by new ideologies of consumption and the nature of business, and borne by key vectors in the fields of advertising, marketing, retailing, and the mass media. For their part, the *Praxis* critics were convinced that such forces were at work, and they treated them as part of a comprehensive analysis in which commercialism joined the ruthless logic of the market as the clear villains. According to Miladin Životić, for example, Yugoslav policy had yielded a "unique interweaving" of the hedonistic-utilitarian and the bureaucratic-authoritarian types of culture. The creation of a genuine humanistic culture, he alleged, had been postponed, subordinated to the immediate rush to affluence. With the introduction of market mechanisms, the country's culture was being driven to ever more deplorable levels through a vicious cycle in which "mass, depersonalized tastes" became the criteria for commercial success. The state-sponsored emphasis on competition and material wealth was steering the country away from a properly humanist understanding of culture and toward a falsely palliative consumer society.[36]

The Praxists recognized, of course, that the rush from scarcity to abundance had been—and indeed almost certainly had to be—the condition of virtually every European socialist society after World War II. Still, the phenomenon had proven particularly severe in Yugoslavia, where, as Stojanović put it, the society had undergone a two-stage process: an initial period of consolidation, "permeated by a sort of production-oriented socialism with exaggerated emphasis on investment and production to the neglect of consumption," followed by nothing less than "a sort of 'consumer socialism.' "[37]

As a consequence of this shift, members of the *Praxis* group were extraordinarily displeased, on many counts, with the direction of Yugoslav society. Among its many failings, consumerism especially offended the deep and radical egalitarian tendency that the Praxists shared. With so much of the idea of progress wrapped up in consumption, they took pains not to have their resistance appear as an antidevelopment stance per se. The thoroughgoing concern for equality was therefore not to be equated, Stojanović suggested, with any sort of "collectivistic and ascetic egalitarianism" expressed in the "the morality of undeveloped, immature communism," an attitude which, he said, embraces self-denial and "resists material interest, efforts to satisfy

35. Marković, *From Affluence to Praxis*, 142.
36. Životić, "Between Two Types of Modern Culture," 191, 196.
37. Stojanović, *Between Ideals and Reality*, 129.

personal rights and personal interests, the desire for a more comfortable life, and differences in income."[38]

Nevertheless, as we have also seen to be the case among their more conventional compatriots, it is not hard to detect in the Praxists' critique some nostalgia for the purportedly purer socialist values and methods of years past. Mihailo Marković lamented, for example, the nobler, communitarian spirit that had prevailed in the first two decades of socialist Yugoslavia, when times were tougher but social bonds stronger. All this caring, *caritas,* and camaraderie, he said, had been largely dissipated by the mid-1980s, "drowned in the icy water of bourgeois egoism" as the result of the competitive, income-oriented system introduced beginning in 1965.[39]

Particularly repellent to the Praxists was the use of consumption to reinforce social distinctions, and though they were certainly no friends of the truly rich, they were also harshly critical of the struggles of the middle class to defend its position in the capitalist cultural hierarchy, at the expense, naturally, of the next rung down: workers. Along these lines, for example, consider the insights of another *Praxis* collaborator, Ivan Kuvačić, into the implications of contemporary consumption for class identity. Kuvačić depicted a pecking order that, with its clinging to the narcissism of small differences, bordered on the pathetic:

> The middle class wants to differ at all costs from those at the bottom, which is the most prominent feature of its way of life. As many employees have rather small incomes, they are all their life torn between their actual economic position and the ideology they have accepted. Their only alternative is to differ from the lower strata fictively. They accomplish this by "correct dress" and a "genteel" education of their children, imitating the manners, fashions, etc. of the upper classes.[40]

In some respects, of course, this sounds quite like other, familiar indictments of the tastes and habits of the Western bourgeoisie, including some from the pens of *members* of the Western bourgeoisie. And indeed, on one level, it is exactly that. Yet these comments also tell us something more. What is really so startling about this and other Praxist critiques of the middle-class consumerism fed by the West is that their authors deemed the analyses so eminently relevant to Yugoslavia's *socialist* society.

The point warrants special emphasis. Looking at Yugoslav consumer culture, outsiders would do well to stop from time to time to appreciate just

---

38. Ibid., 201.

39. Marković, "Self-governing Political System and De-alienation in Yugoslavia (1950–1965)," *Praxis International* 6, no. 2 (July 1986): 159–174, at 170.

40. Ivan Kuvačić, "Middle Class Ideology," in Marković and Petrović, *Praxis: Yugoslav Essays,* 346; originally published in the Yugoslav edition of *Praxis* 9 (1972): 351–375. Compare Kuvačić, "Potrošačko društvo," in Kuvačić, *Znanost i društvo* (Zagreb, 1977), 167–173.

how peculiar concerns like these were in the broader context of contemporary Marxist-Leninist governance. The more one becomes accustomed to the specifics of Yugoslav daily life in the 1960s and 1970s—the more all these weekend houses and washing machines and cars and European fashions begin to seem natural, commonplace, and unexceptional—the more difficult it may become to appreciate the greater importance of the Yugoslav case. Deadened, perhaps, to some of the significance of consumer culture by a lifetime of advertising messages and relative affluence, a Western observer risks becoming inured to its novel dimensions. The problem may afflict even those who specialize in consumption studies. Indeed, throughout this investigation, I have had to struggle against my own insensitivities along these very lines: at first, the idea that consumer culture would also have developed in Yugoslavia appeared to be quite consistent with the "natural" order of things. In the West this was, after all, the way of all flesh. Even much of the social-critical commentary on consumer society communicates this very sense of inevitability. Later, once I had immersed myself in the subject and its particular manifestations in Yugoslav life, consumer culture once again came to seem natural simply because of its sheer omnipresence. The more familiar consumerism is, the more it may seem normal and normative, unavoidable and unproblematic.

For members of the Praxist circle, however, familiarity did not breed contentment. They were distressed and dismayed, fearful and furious, in the face of the changes taking hold across Yugoslavia. Thus Kuvačić warned that the country was coming dangerously close to embracing "the formula which best camouflages the inner social and human essence of modern market economy," that is, the ideology of the middle class. That ideology, according to Kuvačić, would have had Yugoslavs, and all of us, believe that "every man by acquiring, producing and enjoying, produces and acquires for the enjoyment of others."[41] The Yugoslav experience, he concluded, offered further confirmation of the observation by the contemporary American sociologist C. Wright Mills that the middle class is a rear guard that "in the shorter run, will follow the panicky ways of prestige, [and] in the longer run, will follow the ways of power, for, in the end, prestige is determined by power."[42] Like Kuvačić, many members of the *Praxis* group were deeply concerned about what they believed to be the persistence of the Yugoslav middle class (or, perhaps more accurately, about its apparent ascendancy, given that bourgeois influence in the pre-communist period had been very slight). As Kuvačić warned, consumer society's mass culture was now "permeating all spheres of life." Driven by the mass media and by advertising, the new Yugoslav popular culture was encouraging ordinary Yugoslavs to live well beyond their means. As a result, he argued, the Yugoslav middle

---

41. Kuvačić, "Middle Class Ideology," 354.
42. Ibid., 355, quoting Mills, *White Collar*, 354.

class was becoming increasingly influential in the country's political and economic affairs.[43]

The perceived class implications of the consumerist impulse were also central to the analysis of another contributor to the journal, Rudi Supek, who complained that Yugoslav society had preserved, even encouraged, substantial class inequalities. Even in the recent times of expanding prosperity, Supek wrote in 1971, the Yugoslav working class continued to be exposed to great hardships, "while at the same time our streets are choked by automobiles, expensive imported goods (a pair of shoes for 30,000 dinars which represents one half of some workers [*sic*] salaries), a deluge of weekend houses, etc."[44] In his view, the new emphasis on wealth and consumption had led the country astray, with results that were obvious to even the most casual and uninformed observers: "People who visit Yugoslavia," Supek noted, "often get the impression that it is not a country of workers and workers [*sic*] self-management, but of nouveau riche. A great segment of our press, perhaps the part that is most read, has greatly contributed to the creation of a 'consumer's culture' with all of its petit-bourgeois stupidity and snobbism."[45]

Like many of the more orthodox antagonists of Yugoslav consumer culture, Supek believed that much of the blame lay with the country's media culture. His accusations were unambiguous:

> The media of mass communication helped to form the petty-bourgeois mentality. They quickly oriented themselves toward the logic of market "money/goods relations," and they considered themselves progressive if they began to develop their readers' taste for West European "consumer society." They believed that the same laws are applicable to culture and "sausage sales."[46]

As a result, along with some of the more theoretically inclined party insiders, the Praxists concluded that Yugoslavia had seen the rise of something akin to the "culture industry" described by critics of the Frankfurt School. Supek, for example, recounted what had happened when the ideology of consumption and the notion of the market's inherent virtue had taken hold in the country's mass media: "Consequently everything reminiscent of Marxism

---

43. Ibid., 350. Kuvačić distinguished between the "new" middle class, comprised largely of white-collar employees and technocrats in businesses and state offices, and the "old" middle class of tradesmen, innkeepers, and restaurateurs, and certain freelance professions. The latter, he argued, was fading into insignificance in Yugoslavia, despite attempts to revive it. Ibid., 350, 354.

44. Rudi Supek, "Some Contradictions and Insufficiencies of Yugoslav Self-Managing Socialism," in Marković and Petrović, *Praxis: Yugoslav Essays*, 259; originally published in the Yugoslav edition of *Praxis*, vol. 8 (1971): 347–373. Compare Supek, "Stabilno društvo kao revolucionarna suprotnost potrošačkom društvu," in Supek, *Ova jedina zemlja: idemo li u katastrofu ili u treću revoluciju?* (Zagreb, 1973), 219–229.

45. Supek, "Some Contradictions," 259.

46. Ibid., 261.

soon disappeared from their pages.... 'New values' appeared—sensationalism, pathological forms of social behavior, eroticism, pop music, fashion snobbery, nude models on new models of automobiles—everything that would appeal to the petty-bourgeois parvenu."[47] As such contributions suggest, the Praxists took a decidedly grim view of contemporary Yugoslav culture. Its Marxist character, they believed, was quickly being stripped away. Small wonder, then, if some of these activists whom communist leader and consumption critic Franc Šetinc had tagged as "ultra-leftists" might indeed have returned the animosity, considering him a "superficial optimist" and a self-interested champion of the party élite's status quo.

Like a number of analyses offered by many other writers assembled around *Praxis*, Supek's diatribe against Yugoslavia's own "culture industry" reveals an unusual, sometimes puzzling, combination of intellectual and political influences. Such perspectives mixed a scrupulous sensitivity to the freshest and most dynamic trends in contemporary social-critical theory with a yearning for the good old days of Partisan simplicity and earnest struggle. As a result, the critique of Yugoslav consumerism wavered between a sharp, sophisticated sociological reading of the cross-cultural effects of advertising and a curious sort of grumbling about the vices of modern living.

That fusion surfaced repeatedly in the work of the Praxist writers, as it does, for example, in this delightful jibe from Supek, who had clearly had his fill of immodest excess in the Yugoslav popular press:

> Just try putting a photograph of a working girl in a red kerchief or crowd scenes in the Mao-Tse-Tung manner on one of our newsstands amid the display of bare female breasts and bodies, you will immediately notice that you are confronted with two different cultures that exclude each other, and which are easily defined. These are extremes, but just let anybody try to define what values exist between these extremes in our country.[48]

This is, to be sure, an awfully doleful assessment of Yugoslav culture, and we might fairly wonder whether things were really as bad as Supek made them out to be. He was correct, however, that the Yugoslav "boulevard press" was increasingly filled with sex and celebrity, with an especially noticeable soft-core porn aesthetic in papers and magazines targeted at men. For his part, Supek acknowledged that what he called "the style that has taken over in our country" remained "below the level" of Western consumer society, but he was convinced that it nevertheless signaled dire consequences for Yugoslavia and its people. Such processes, he insisted, had reinforced the group consciousness and solidarity of the country's middle class and had even "brought about a dissolution of class consciousness in the workers,"

---

47. Ibid.
48. Ibid., 261–262.

with the results that "our society possesses less and less of a 'socialist consciousness,' and that it, in fact, *even refuses to have it.*"[49]

With all its seductive power, consumerism had thus become, in this view, a major barrier to the realization of the socialist program, if not indeed *the* key obstacle. Surprisingly, however, the specific *instruments* of consumer culture in Yugoslavia did not run up against especially frequent or bitter criticism in the work of the Praxis group. Indeed, Supek's essay is unusual within the Yugoslav Marxist-humanist oeuvre for the extent to which it concentrates on the culpability of the media in creating and sustaining the consumerist orientation. The critique for the most part reached toward a more global reading of the problems linked to consumption, and perhaps for this reason it took little notice of the specific excesses and deformations of Yugoslav advertising and marketing work.

Yet there should be no doubt that representatives of the Praxist tendency believed that advertising and marketing shouldered a great deal of the blame for the recent course of events. The interpretation that Mihailo Marković offered regarding advertising's key role as a capitalist tool, for example, suggests that an awareness of the cultural power of commercial promotion figured importantly in the *Praxis* analysis of consumption. "Contemporary consumer society," Marković argued, "can only maintain its high rate of profit if the enormous psychological pressure exercised by the advertising industry (which spends some 16 billion dollars p[er] a[nnum] in the U.S.A.) succeeds in finding further artificial needs, and if it can realise these needs when the worker has the necessary spending power. Thus his wages will be increased, and in return the last modicum of strength will be wrung from him."[50] Even here, however, the analysis turned quickly from the specifics of ad-industry practice to, once again, the underlying ideologies of market relations and, in particular, the cruel marriage between capitalism's profit logic and the generation of fictive needs and desires. "It is inessential," Marković thus asserted, "that the majority of commodities will not in fact satisfy his real needs; what is essential is that this process guarantees high rates of profit, avoids economic crises and, by excluding the worker from the political sphere, succeeds in integrating him into the *status quo.*"[51]

It Gets the Red Out: The Glorification of the Market, *Homo consumens*, and the *Praxis* Critique of Yugoslav Self-Management

The critics gathered around *Praxis* were, as the above comments suggest, undeniably sensitive to the cultural, political, and economic significance of commercial promotion, even going so far as to blame advertising for the

---

49. Ibid., 262 (emphasis added).
50. Marković, *The Contemporary Marx*, 184–185.
51. Ibid.

democratic dysfunction and paralysis—"excluding the worker from the political sphere"—that they believed was symptomatic not just of the West but of Yugoslavia as well. Yet the primary concerns of their critique lay elsewhere, and well beyond the day-to-day transgressions of the culture makers of the media enterprises and the advertising, marketing, and retailing specialists. Among the main features of their work was an unflagging effort to demythologize the market and thereby reduce its influence. This was a more universal aim of the internationalist *Praxis* program, but it was at the same time one understood to be particularly urgent in the case of Yugoslavia. Along these lines, for example, Svetozar Stojanović took issue with "Yugoslav anarcho-liberals who *glorify* the market in socialism," arguing that, as part of a larger Yugoslav tendency to "fetishize and universalize the market," they were "provincially repeating the mistakes of pre-Keynesian bourgeois economics."[52] The implication here, to be sure, was that such "anarcho-liberals" had grown far too influential in Yugoslav government circles, if they were not indeed already setting policy. In this view the market mechanism itself may have been inevitable, but it was nonetheless inherently and perhaps even fatally flawed. "It is generally recognized," Stojanović continued, "that the market reacts mainly to the existing level of demand and that it also creates artificial and even harmful demands."[53] In the aftermath of the country's option for more autonomous markets, its culture and values had, not surprisingly, followed suit. And as a result, Stojanović argued, "even the very concept of the standard of living is increasingly reduced to a material standard, rather than being seen as a human standard."[54]

Yugoslav economics, in the *Praxis* view, had moved far too close to the models and practices of the West, settling for imitation where resistance was needed. Mihailo Marković thus described the pro-market tendency in Yugoslav politics as "fundamentally a rationalization for blind economic forces." From this perspective, the glorification of the market and the exaltation of the consumer were part and parcel of a decidedly un-Marxist approach to economic relations:

> It is characteristic of this view, which may be called *economism*, that man is essentially an economic being (*homo oeconomicus*), and a consumer (*homo consumens*), that the essential motive of production in capitalist society is the attempt to maximize income and that, therefore, the most important thing for socialism at this moment is *complete liberation* of economic laws and the *undisturbed development* of commodity-money relations.[55]

---

52. Stojanović, *Between Ideals and Reality*, 132–133, 217 (emphasis in original).

53. Ibid., 132–133.

54. Ibid.

55. Marković, *From Affluence to Praxis*, 110–111 (emphasis in original). Arguing that this stance could in no way be reconciled with Marx's views, Marković acknowledged that "economism" did not actually correspond to the official doctrine of the Yugoslav government following

From this perspective, the country's much vaunted markets were tantamount to an exercise in capitalist production and distribution. "Yugoslav experience," Stojanović maintained, "only confirms what we already know from capitalism—that individual groups (self-governing, now) can use the market to encourage the most uncultured of needs and make quite a bit of money in the process. It is indisputable that *capitalist civilization still dictates our structure of needs and consumption to some degree.*"[56] Worse yet, the problem could not be solved with minor tweaks to existing policy. It was structural, pervasive, and inherent. "So long as it exists," Stojanović claimed, "the market will try to impose itself over society as the supreme regulator and criterion of human relations so that it may thereby restore the economic basis of bourgeois society."[57] In the end, then, while culture truly mattered, and market culture was truly bad, the Yugoslav consumerist syndrome, even if not a simple instance of epiphenomenal "superstructure," could still not be taken as purely or even primarily a matter of culture. The irreducible problem was the market itself.

The bottom line, the *Praxis* critique implied, was that Yugoslav policy was now increasingly driven by the bottom line. While Titoism had quite rightly rejected the authoritarian excesses of Stalinism, or at least the worst of them, reform in Yugoslavia ultimately had produced not "self-managing socialism" but rather what Rudi Supek called "petty-bourgeois capitalism," with a hunger for quick profits and "take it while you can get it!" mentality.[58] Supek acknowledged that Yugoslavia's version of "capitalism," marked as it was by "a petty-bourgeois sense of usury and momentary profit," was rather different from that of the West, but this seemed to be more a distinction of degree than of essence. The country's indulgence in capitalist practices, he said, "remains far below the level of contemporary corporation capital in capitalist countries, because of its entire lack of any sense for modern organization and developmental policies."[59]

The allegation here, though blunted somewhat, is stunning in its implications. The Praxists were suggesting that, in effect, the Yugoslav Communists had opted for capitalism. For them, the elevation of market mechanisms in the name of self-management amounted to nothing less.

The rigid rejectionist anti-market stance of the *Praxis* proved to be, in some ways, a phenomenon of the moment, fueled by the profound changes of the mid- to late 1960s and the early 1970s, and lifted by the flourishing internationalist New Left movement of the same period. By 1975, however, the journal itself had been suppressed, with many of its protagonists ousted from their positions and otherwise silenced or marginalized. With time,

---

the reforms initiated in 1965, notwithstanding some strategic efforts to portray it as such. Ibid., 118; see, generally, 120–145.

56. Stojanović, *Between Ideals and Reality*, 132–133 (emphasis added).

57. Ibid.

58. Supek, "Some Contradictions," 261.

59. Ibid.

moreover, the intellectual market for such stark dismissals of the world of comfort, pleasure, and desire appeared to shrink. Even many of the critics would cast their lots with the broader Yugoslav public and thus come to at least a grudging acceptance, if not a genuine embrace, of the consumption-oriented Yugoslav Dream.

Still, even long after those shifts, resentment and resistance lingered. Especially in more academically oriented circles, the Marxist-humanist sensibility that the *Praxis* project cultivated would outlive the journal itself, remaining an influential current in the public debate right up until the disintegration of communist rule and the breakup of the federation. Even as late as the end of the 1980s, for example, another sometime contributor to *Praxis*, Croatian economist Branko Horvat, saw reason to repeat the judgment that the market and its companion ideology had gotten out of control in Yugoslavia. Rather more favorably disposed toward market mechanisms than his Praxist colleagues, he argued that the market, though necessary, could not be left unrestrained. "We want to preserve the fundamental autonomy of the consumer," Horvat conceded, "for socialism is founded upon the preferences of individuals who make up the society." His position, however, took several steps back from the idea of consumer sovereignty that, as seen in the earlier sections of this book, had been expressed—often quite candidly—in the literature of Yugoslav advertising and, particularly, marketing.

In Horvat's vision, consumers may have been autonomous, but they were definitely not sovereign. He suggested, in fact, that the idea of unbridled consumer freedom was downright dangerous. "Consumer choices," he reminded readers as part of a larger refutation of the appeal for a more laissez-faire Yugoslav market, "are not justified. They are often irrational, formed according to habits and custom, and without sufficient information." It was for this reason, Horvat believed, that while almost no one bought books or visited the theater, plenty of purchasers "chose" alcohol, junk food, and forms of "boastful" consumption. And in a socialist society, such consumer preferences had to be moderated by overarching considerations of social welfare. "If our choice is socially determined," Horvat continued, "then we need to better consider how to control the forces that are responsible for that determination and stop flattering ourselves that we enjoy great personal independence." Ultimately, for this economist as for the *Praxis* movement more generally, the market remained "an instrument of planning"—a subordinate, not sovereign, force, and one always to be held in check by political decisions designed to foster socialist values and culture.[60]

---

60. References are to Branko Horvat, *ABC jugoslavenskog socijalizma* (Zagreb, 1989), 62–65. Earlier Horvat had written of the need to suppress consumerism in favor of a more humanistic Marxist field of values: "We must begin to replace coercion [*poticaj*] with self-determination, competition with cooperation, bargaining [*razmjena*] with solidarity, the accumulation of things with personal development, having with being....A free person very likely will not squander his life in accumulating unneeded things, in desperation over a few extra

Can't Get No Satisfaction: Blaming Titoism for the Consumerist Tide

By now it should be evident that, with regard to the nature and consequences of consumerism, the language and terms of analysis used by the Praxists and by more orthodox Communists were, in some respects, reasonably consistent. Although the rhetoric may often have been harsher, the analysis more penetrating, the judgments more unforgiving, and the campaign more relentless, the *Praxis* critique was manifestly Marxist and, moreover, not meant as any fundamental challenge to communist governance per se. And yet the Marxist-humanist interpretation ultimately proved intolerable to the party mainstream. Why?

What seems to have earned the Praxists the great enmity of the establishment types was their willingness to diagnose consumer society as *a necessary outcome of the basic market orientation of the distinctive Yugoslav system* and, in so doing, to equate self-management with capitalism.

These were dangerous waters. Because the idea of self-management was what Bogdan Denitch has identified as the "unifying social myth" (some might say the sacred cow) of Yugoslav socialist governance, it was off-limits for severe political criticism. The Praxists violated this taboo, and they violated it unflinchingly. Their dispute was not with the basic idea of workers' self-governance, which they held in high esteem as a vehicle of democratization. Marković, for example, believed that the initial 1950 reforms had launched "a process of true transcendence ('withering away') of the State."[61] Rather, as we have seen, they could not be reconciled with the market orientation that had been progressively incorporated into the system's conventional conception and practice. The 1965–1967 market reforms, Marković claimed, had gone so far as to return the country "to a nineteenth-century model of a laissez-faire economy" while at the same time "preserving a far more elitist and authoritarian political system than a developed system of participatory democracy could tolerate."[62] The Praxists' emphatic (and, to many, convincing) assertion that they were advancing a more pure Ur-Marxism left the communist authorities in a bind, without particularly persuasive rhetorical tools, and groping for an effective, credible

---

dinars, or in begging for the favor of his superiors." *Politička ekonomija socijalizma* (Zagreb, 1984), 424; cited in Božović, *Suočavanja*, 195.

61. Marković, "Self-governing Political System and De-alienation in Yugoslavia," 162.

62. Marković, *The Contemporary Marx*, xi–xii. As Marković noted, the most ardent advocates of the reforms would themselves later be ostracized as perpetrators of "liberalism" and "nationalism," and those who resisted them from a Marxist perspective were excoriated as "abstract humanists," "utopians," "revisionists," "anarcho-liberals" (a term that at least one of the Praxists used for his pro-market opponents!), "neo-leftists," and "extreme leftists." Ibid., xii. It was the latter formulation that the party insider Franc Šetinc seemed to favor in *Are We a Consumer Society?* and his other works.

response. Along these lines, at the height of the confrontation between the two camps, one Radio Free Europe analyst suggested that "the Yugoslav information media's current attempt to depict the Praxis professors as 'capitalist stooges' does not appear to be altogether accurate. If they 'sinned' at all—concerning the problem of 'market socialism'—it was in their claim that the market, coupled with political privileges, has been the main source of increasing social differences in Yugoslavia."[63]

Tied in this way to other critical issues, the Marxist-humanist indictment of consumer culture, though undoubtedly sincere and important in its own right, also became a proxy battle over the fundamental direction of Yugoslav society and the legitimacy of those in power. Like their more immediate skirmishes with the Yugoslav authorities over the right to publish their iconoclastic interpretations, this fight, in the end, was one that the *Praxis* critics could not win. In the short term, at least, they lost, and lost big.

In addition to the practical sanctions imposed on the *Praxis* scholars in their writing and teaching careers, their accusations provoked a bitter rhetorical response from the party-state mainstream. One leading exemplar of the position of Yugoslav officialdom, Franc Šetinc, betrayed the establishment's keen sensitivity to the fact that the domestic controversy over consumer society had increasingly come to be understood as, at base, a critique of Yugoslav self-management socialism itself. In his role as the defender of the mainstream party approaches, Šetinc seemed much more interested in hammering the unorthodox opponents of consumerism back into line than in developing any subtle or profound analysis of affluence, markets, choice, and the place of consumerism in a socialist society. His major ideological contribution, *Are We a Consumer Society?*, was most remarkable for its extraordinarily defensive tone and for what it revealed about the importance of consumer culture in the broader arc of Yugoslav politics.

It shows, moreover, how much the *Praxis* critique had stung the Yugoslav leadership. In the introduction to the collection of essays, for example, Šetinc's party colleague Boris Majer sought to distinguish this particular study of consumer society in Yugoslavia from that of other, unnamed critics on the right and the left (and wherever it was on the political spectrum that the "advocates of bureaucratic-statist socialism" might properly be placed). All these, Majer asserted, contented themselves with nothing more than a superficial, ineffectual analysis of consumerist values. There was altogether too much impotent fretting, defeatism, and useless handwringing, he suggested. Other would-be critics had surrendered to the idea that nothing could be done to stop the erosion of the healthier values of self-management socialism. In particular, Majer insisted, the "ultra-leftist pseudo-revolutionary critique of everything that exists," no matter how

---

63. Slobodan Stanković, "Campaign against Belgrade and Zagreb Professors," RAD Background Report/6 (Yugoslavia), Radio Free Europe Research series, 17 January 1975, 3.

noisy and appealing, was not going to get the job done. What was needed instead was "the organized theoretical and practical revolutionary action of the deliberate socialist forces of our society."[64] Here and elsewhere, Majer and Šetinc locked horns with anonymous "ultra-leftists," including one unidentified "Belgrade critic." Given the time and context, it is a virtual certainty that the most important targets here were the members of the *Praxis* circle.[65] Clearly the Praxists had made themselves heard—and unwelcome.

What, then, was the ultimate significance of the Praxist critique? How accurate were the assessments of these "ultra-left" activists? The Marxist-humanist diagnosis of what was taking place in Yugoslavia ultimately offers extraordinarily useful material for the construction of an interpretative and conceptual framework that, when set against the empirical evidence of the Yugoslav record, permits us to test and gauge this particular (and particularly significant) case with an eye to better comprehending just what it was, in fact, that brought about the changes that the critics so disliked. Through its radicalism, the critique posits new explanatory possibilities that have to be taken seriously if we are to truly understand how the society changed and what changed it.

Chagrined by what they believed were the inevitable consequences of self-management's fondness for the market, the Praxists would have us understand that when we encounter phenomena in Yugoslavia that look surprisingly like capitalist consumer culture, what we are really seeing is precisely that: capitalist consumer culture. As explained in more detail elsewhere in this book, however, I believe the evidence compels a conclusion that the country's economic system, despite its market modifications, was certainly socialist enough to vitiate this particular Praxist claim, and the great weight of scholarly authority on the Yugoslav economy, which consistently recognizes its socialist character, corroborates that view. Explanations that look not to creeping capitalism but rather to transnational contacts and processes of cultural transfer and mimesis provide a far better answer, at least in the Yugoslav instance.

Moreover, although the domestic participants in the debate did not anticipate it, there is yet another alternative explanation for the drift toward consumer society in Yugoslavia, one that points us back toward foundational anthropological and sociological insights into the world of goods and the conceptualization of consumption practice. It may be the case that the country's consumerist values and behaviors were neither primarily the

---

64. Majer, "Smo potrošniška družba?" 8.

65. There were clearly other "ultra-leftists" as well. Šetinc also relates, for example, his polemic with the editors of the Slovenian student review *Tribuna*, a dispute dating back to 1971. The students were advocates, as they put it, "for original communism, for an uncompromising moral, egalitarian order." Quoted in Šetinc, *Smo potrošniška družba,* 35; see, generally, 35–38.

product of an imported capitalist culture, as so many argued, nor the predictable outcome of a crypto-capitalist economic system, as the *Praxis* group tended to believe. Instead, the indicia of consumer society might be a more general result of *any* system of modern industrial production, regardless of its underlying political and economic framework, that manages to produce substantial consumer abundance, variety, quality, and choice. Neither the many domestic controversies over consumer culture nor the Yugoslav case itself can, standing alone, provide us with sufficient evidence to resolve these questions. Still the import of the Yugoslav experience is tremendous. Its significance lies precisely in that it frames and clarifies the debate so productively, posing, so starkly, these questions of provenance, causation, agency, and effect, and underscoring their importance to the historical study of consumption.

Even assuming that the Praxists were right, another important question would remain: Just how much "capitalism" is enough to do the trick? (Or, as they would have it, just how much is too much?) If it was indeed capitalist economics that produced such a rich market culture in Yugoslavia and spawned, in turn, a socialist variety of consumer society, were any other parts of the socialist world "capitalist" enough to experience the same thing? For insights into that issue, we need to look to events in Hungary, which in the aftermath of the failed 1956 revolution attempted to satisfy consumer desires and experimented with market mechanisms in a far less thoroughgoing way. Conversely, evidence from the German Democratic Republic and Czechoslovakia, which were substantially industrialized and comparatively wealthy by communist standards but effectively untainted by the market, may offer a useful way of testing whether socialism *itself* may be generative of consumer culture in the forms so familiar from the modern Western experience. At least in the case of the GDR, however, we cannot rule out the possible effects of cultural "infection" from the West. Although the country after 1961 was largely cordoned off from most direct contacts, a familiarity with and understanding of the economic successes of West Germany clearly goaded policy planning, with obvious potential implications for consumption and consumer culture.[66]

If, on the other hand, the cultural "infection" paradigm really holds the key to why consumer society has appeared outside the developed West, we need to ask just how much exposure is enough. Yugoslavia itself was, as we have seen, very exposed indeed; the "dose" of Western-ness that the country and its people received, one administered through the use of advertising and in many other ways as well, was heavy, sustained, and repeated. Something less, however, may well have sufficed. With respect to all these questions,

---

66. See Zatlin, "Consuming Ideology: Socialist Consumerism and the Intershops, 1970–1989," in *Arbeiter in der SBZ-DDR*, ed. Peter Hübner and Klaus Tenfelde (Essen, 1999), 555–572.

the record of latter-day China, Vietnam, and other "not quite communist" countries may hold important lessons as well, as may the experiences of various corporatist and other similar "not quite capitalist" nations. The Yugoslav case therefore suggests the most promising subjects for future research and, critically, helps set the parameters for an ongoing inquiry into the historical processes by which consumer society has achieved its global diffusion.

7 Loving It

Ordinary People, Everyday Life, and the Power of Consumption

Science is falling behind, the economy is falling behind, the statistics are falling behind—no one is able any longer to match the pace of the Yugoslavs and predict how they will continue to rise and flourish in the future.

Children can hardly wait to be born. We have come just that far. There are already several hundred candidates to become the twenty-millionth Yugoslav. There is nothing more beautiful or more full of promise than to be a Yugoslav today.
— Matija Bećković, "O Jugoslovenima" [On the Yugoslavs], 1969

The life of the modern housewife, especially one who is employed, has become downright unimaginable without a refrigerator and a vacuum cleaner, just to mention the biggest items, all the way down to the smallest, such as a coffee grinder or a toaster. Along with all these, electric grills, washing machines, and dishwashers are becoming ever more pervasive.
— "Kućanski strojevi," *Svijet,* 1970

In contrast to the harsh judgments that the critics poured out, the sentiments expressed by many other Yugoslavs often communicated a strikingly lenient attitude toward both the consumerist orientation and the business and press institutions that drove it. Ample evidence suggests that, unlike those Marxists and others who saw advertising and the media's indulgence of consumer desire as dangerous agents of unsuitable capitalist values and as an engine of false needs, many if not most ordinary Yugoslavs saw the needs in question as real enough. They were neither especially vexed by market culture nor much concerned about its potentially harmful effects. For the Yugoslav "man on the street," and, just as important, his female counterpart, the polemics launched against consumerism never seem to have had the profound chastening effect that those critics desired. If it had now become possible to identify a separate subspecies of contemporary spenders,

---

Sources for the epigraphs: Matija Bećković, "O Jugoslovenima," in idem, *Dr Janez Paćuka o međuvremenu* (Novi Sad, 1969), 83; "Kućanski strojevi," *Svijet* no. 9, 6 May 1970, 45.

Homo consumens yugoslavicus, few members of the wider public seemed to think that this was a particularly distressing discovery.

In light of the way recent Yugoslav history had unfolded, this reaction probably should have been expected. Even in the 1970s, when the consumerist upswing had been under way for some time, the country was not far removed from the memory of scarcity and rationing, and even more serious deprivations during wartime. Many people had experienced quite enough enforced asceticism; they were in no rush to adopt any voluntary version just because their new needs were deemed "false" and their motives suspect. Moreover, in justifying such reactions, they were not without some recourse to the political culture of Yugoslav socialism itself. Throughout the period after the introduction of self-management, official or quasi-official discourse was sending mixed messages about consumption: consumerism was alleged to be the origin of a whole host of social evils, and yet at the same time the pronounced emphasis on increased living standards was also often treated as a desirable and natural aim of state policy, a just reward for the working class. Many people clearly preferred the latter interpretation.

This is not to suggest that ordinary Yugoslavs were blind to their acquisitiveness. Quite to the contrary, a recognition of their own indulgent natures became almost a commonplace, a critical (and in some ways self-critical) part of their understanding of who they—as part of an expansively conceived Yugoslav "we"—had recently become. Alenka Puhar, a commentator for the leading Ljubljana daily newspaper *Delo* who inserted herself into what had developed into a limited but vocal anti–anti-consumerist backlash in the popular press, suggested in 1979 that this sort of self-aware reflectiveness about consumerism "had become, so to speak, a part of the most general culture."[1] Clearly the long barrage of critique was having some effect on the public mentality: real if not quite profound, tempering if not quite chastening. Yet people mainly seem to have accepted their label as conspicuous spenders as a badge of honor: a confirmation that they indeed *could* spend conspicuously.

It was quite possible, furthermore, to treat the new opportunity to spend as emblematic of a larger and arguably more important kind of independence. With an emphasis on the individuality, choice, and self-expressive power thought to be inherent in consumer behavior, some of those Yugoslavs who praised the new freedom to spend underscored what they viewed as the genuine autonomy and agency of ordinary consumers. In certain ways, readings of this sort approached the understandings of those against-the-tide Western interpreters who, with their defenses of consumer culture, have stressed and commended its liberative qualities. Reflecting on the remarkable events of the recent past during the late 1960s, Montenegrin-Serb essayist Matija Bećković pointed to just this sort of break with authority in the attitudes and actions

---

1. Alenka Puhar, "Krivda in nekrivda potrošništva," *Delo*, 14 April 1979, 21.

of his free-spending compatriots. "The Yugoslavs," Bećković asserted, "have obviously separated themselves from the state and from its problems and difficulties, and they have stopped being the victims of its subjective and objective weaknesses." In stark juxtaposition to a governmental apparatus that was "always lacking something or other," this reading called attention to the fact that so many savvy and enterprising ordinary Yugoslavs had found a way clear to work extra hours at extra jobs, to develop profitable little side businesses, and to even bend (or break) the rules when necessary, with the result that they were managing to do rather nicely for themselves. In this manner, then, the dreams of Yugoslav socialism had indeed come true, albeit along a most unlikely route: "Accordingly, the state will wither away, not according to scientific and political prognoses but rather through the elemental force of a vital mentality," Bećković declared. "But the Yugoslavs will remain healthy and alive, beautiful and happy. Bravo for them! This was, after all, the very goal of all our efforts and aspirations up to now."[2]

There was, as observations like these suggest, a profoundly popular, public dimension to the consumer culture that Yugoslav society created. This was something not just enjoyed by everyday people but built and sustained by them as well. In many ways, the transformation had taken place outside the sphere of state action—indeed, beyond the state's effective control. The rush to consumption could therefore seem like a restorative, sensible, even laudable pursuit, something that gave the populace vigor and élan, that made them "beautiful and happy."

If there were occasional forays into this interpretive genre of consumption-as-liberation, it must nevertheless be said that the very open debate over consumer culture in Yugoslavia was otherwise marked by a near total absence of defenses of consumerism on the grounds that it may encourage a beneficial, stimulative sort of dreaming about the future and a healthy form or release (not to say escape) from the burdens of the Everyday. Such interpretations have appeared from time to time in the capitalist West, most often in industry apologetics, more rarely in consumption scholarship. But while Yugoslav commentators on consumer culture often followed the international literature on these subjects closely and were quite familiar with the range of arguments made both pro and con, analyses along these lines still seemed to be disfavored. If, in fact, they were not off-limits—for not much in Yugoslavia was, especially toward the end—they nevertheless held little obvious appeal for those who wrote and spoke in defense of consumer culture.

Matija Bećković's evident purpose in taking up the subject of the remarkable material transformation of Yugoslav society was not so much to lionize his acquisitive (not to say greedy) fellow citizens as it was to capture and wonder at the power of their resilient (not to say insatiable) consuming passions. His essay "On the Yugoslavs" at once celebrated and satirized their tastes, their habits,

2. References are to Bećković, "O Jugoslovenima," 82.

and their exertions. But with the references to the struggles of the people, the withering away of the state, and various "scientific and political prognoses," this sharp-eyed commentator was obviously also poking fun at the programs and promises of the Marxist state. And it is clear where his sympathies lay: with the regular folks who, with admirable if sometimes risible abandon, were enjoying this wild new time when, as Bećković put it, "there is nothing more beautiful or more full of promise than to be a Yugoslav today."[3]

As wry commentary of this sort suggests, Yugoslavs' consumption habits, and what was now understood to be a *characteristically Yugoslav* habit of consumption, had with time become the butt of good-natured humor, a development that, at bottom, is best read not as a condemnation but instead as solidarity with the public's ratification of the new consumer culture. Evidence of this type of joking recognition of "our" seemingly unquenchable thirst for the Good Life was to be found in abundance in the Yugoslav public culture of the 1960s and 1970s. Often it seemed that, indeed, an indispensable part of living the Good Life was to engage in a bit of not-too-guilty self-mockery about doing just that. Columnist Alenka Puhar noted, for example, that the widespread hunger for automobiles had reworked the familiar appeal from the Lord's Prayer, *fiat voluntas tua* ("Thy will be done"), into a new formulation: "*Fiat 600 voluntas tua*"—roughly, "Let it be Thy will for me to get a Fiat 600."[4] As her joke here indicates, the public's eager engagement with the world of goods had managed to produce a broadly held, scaled-down, reasonable (and as a result, suitably Yugoslav) version of the sentiment that had been immortalized in American popular culture as "Oh Lord, won't you buy me a Mercedes-Benz?"

In observations of this more forbearing sort we see both playful teasing among friends and, no less important, a recognition that such attitudes, if transgressions at all, were at least ones in which the sinners had plenty of company. The widely shared, genuinely popular consumer culture that buyers and shoppers and wishers had built for themselves could be, in other words, funny and fun, not just self-indulgent but self-aware and self-deprecating—something the anti-consumerist critique barely noticed. When all was said and done, many ordinary Yugoslavs seemed quite aware of their consumerist tendencies, and to some extent even willing to see them as foibles, but they were not especially displeased or inclined to change.

If Loving YU Is Wrong, I Don't Want to Be Right: The Backlash against the Backlash against Yugoslav Consumerism

With time, furthermore, the unforgiving critique of consumerism provoked a serious and uncompromising backlash, one that took the critics to task for

---

3. Ibid., 83.
4. Puhar, "Krivda in nekrivda potrošništva," 21.

going too far. With its ardent insistence on defending the desires of everyday people, this counter-reaction reveals a lot about what was going on in the minds and living rooms of ordinary Yugoslavs. From the perspective of those who decided it was time to fight back, the anti-consumerist line was unduly harsh, out of touch, and quite possibly elitist as well. One telling example of this sort of judgment, with the suggestion that the enemies of consumerism were themselves untrustworthy, came in the form of a mordant little essay in defense of advertising penned by the Bosnian Serb writer Momo Kapor, one of the country's most popular literary figures. The piece appeared in 1982 in the trade journal published by Ljubljana's Studio Marketing agency, which at the time was rapidly becoming the country's most aggressive industry representative of a pro-market, consumerist orientation toward business. The essay is short but crammed with insights into how the mounting critique of consumer culture and advertising was perceived. Coming as it did from one of the preeminent observers of the Yugoslav Everyday, and from a writer whose popularity rested on his talent in capturing, reflecting, and channeling the experiences and sentiments of "regular" Yugoslavs, it warrants a detailed examination.

Kapor launched his broadside by relating one fond memory of growing up in the midst of advertising. He told of his boyhood fascination with the image of a smiling, beckoning Arab, dark-skinned and wearing a fez, that was widely known in interwar Yugoslavia as the trademark for coffee sold under the Mocca brand. (Taking a swipe at the country's new culture of shortages in the 1980s, Kapor pointed out that in the new Yugoslavia of the economic crisis neither the smiling Arab nor coffee itself could be found anywhere, but this, he allowed, was the subject of a different story.) Continuing, the writer warned his readers that he had never really appreciated advertisements until he was deprived of them as a consequence of the strict, distributionist policies of the immediate postwar years:

> I want to tell you that at the end of the war, kids like me found ourselves in a world without advertising. Food was distributed on a point system. Only the strange names high up on the walls of old buildings, remnants of some different civilization, testified that advertisements once actually did exist. We sounded out their names letter by letter and tried to divine their unknown meanings—Cimean, Alga, Bali, Borselino—and we read educational Soviet books about how today's progressive man had once and for all done away with religion and advertising.[5]

In the harsh light of shortages and ideological repression, even the very modest economy of interwar Yugoslavia could seem to people who were, like Kapor, without economic privilege and, indeed, on the edge of poverty, like

5. Momo Kapor, "Reklamokracija," *MM: marketing magazin*, no. 12 (April 1982): 6.

a vaguely remembered and irretrievable Eden. In contrast, the heady consumerist economy of the 1960s and 1970s appeared to be, notwithstanding all its potential excesses, a paradise regained.

As a result of his acquaintance with want, this keen chronicler of the old and the new Yugoslavias had absolutely no use for people who hated advertising. Their complaints were based on a kernel of truth, he admitted, but their zealotry blinded them to an even greater and much more important reality:

> I often encounter fanatical opponents of advertising. These sorts of people write hurried protest letters to the editorial boards of newspapers and television stations. "Why are you violating us with those advertisements? Advertisements are stupid! They are the remnants of capitalist attitudes toward the market!" I'm not saying that this is not true. But the world is not divided into capitalism and socialism. The world, in fact, is not divided! The world is being multiplied. And many things that make our lives easier and nicer are multiplying as well. And we have to find out about those things; someone has to inform us that they exist, whether we live in capitalism, socialism, or feudalism.[6]

Advertising, Kapor maintained, was a necessary and useful part of a way of life that was, on balance, highly desirable. To resist it verged on a foolish and totalitarian denial of choice and pluralism. The impulse to suppress advertising was, in this view, fundamentally akin to the desire to limit free thought and free expression.

Momo Kapor did not use the word, but he clearly seemed to be suggesting that hostility to advertising amounted to old-style Stalinism, which Yugoslavia itself had experienced for some time. And the critics' rejection of the new style of market culture harked back to an unwanted past in more ways than one: in those warmly remembered good old days of deprivation for (almost) everyone, he said, only a few "human-demigods" could find the nice things that everyone really wanted. They did so in the so-called diplomatic shops, and because of their privileged position they were naturally able to make their way to an abundant life without the assistance of advertising. In other words, the critics of the new New Class seemed disturbingly nostalgic for the heyday of the old New Class.

The antipathy to advertising, according to Kapor, also concealed a great distaste for competition, individual decision making, and even personal autonomy. Yugoslav opponents of commercial promotion, he insinuated, did not trust ordinary people to judge for themselves what was good and useful. They apparently would have preferred that everything be approved in advance "by some sort of council, or some body or administrative organ."[7]

---

6. Ibid.
7. Ibid.

In the end, the stance Kapor adopted toward advertising was, to be sure, distanced and somewhat ironic—he was, after all, a humorist—but the bottom line was nothing if not indulgent. "Don't get me wrong," he protested. "In fact, advertisements really bore me. I put up with them, because *they are a guarantee of freedom.* And one other thing: beautiful, undressed girls continue to appear in them—and I have to say that I much prefer to watch pretty girls than broadcasts from symposiums and conferences."[8] With this last appeal to the indulgent, pleasurable, even titillating aspects of advertising—and the parting dig at the country's bureaucratized official culture—Kapor was clearly suggesting that, as was typical of his work, his own attitude had much more in common with that of the "man on the street" than the harsher views espoused by the critics of consumer culture. And on that count he was almost certainly correct.

Challenging the attitudes that reigned in public discourse, others went beyond these more limited defenses of advertising and dared to ask whether the consumerist impulse itself was really quite as bad as the critics allowed. Along these lines, *Delo* columnist Alenka Puhar pointed out that explicit efforts to defend the consumerist orientation as such had been extraordinarily rare up through the late 1970s, at least as far as public discourse in official or quasi-official channels was concerned. Typically, she suggested, the discussion of consumer culture had been more a one-sided polemic than a debate. (Here Puhar was not far off the mark: as we have seen, even the advertising and marketing industry carefully attempted to distinguish its vision of consumer sovereignty from the much despised embrace of consumerism.) Practically every problem of contemporary society, or so it seemed to Puhar, could if so desired be blamed on the consumerist mentality and the struggle for prestige; the ideological environment made consumer culture a natural and easy target. More than a little irked by all this, she questioned whether the country's many manifestations of consumer society could really be held responsible for all the social ills they had allegedly caused.

In this contrarian view, the urge toward critical self-reflection had gotten out of hand, and it was now time for reflection not just on the consumerist bent but also on the attitude "that makes the consumerist mentality into a scapegoat for everything." The critics were busy unearthing the evils of consumerism everywhere: "Low natality and high suicide rates, the dying off of folk music and the enthusiasm for rock, high mortality by heart attacks and automobile accidents, the divorce rate, the shattering of bonds between parents and children, juvenile delinquency and the yearning for private [that is, single-family] houses—we have learned to connect all this to the craving for possessing things." Even feelings of low-self esteem vis-à-vis the West could be chalked up to the lust for the Good Life. If the critics were to be believed,

---

8. Ibid. (emphasis added).

Puhar said, the new values were now culpable even for "our 'tendency to kiss foreigners' asses' [*ritolizništvo do tujcev*], which in the past grew out of an inferiority complex, often out of fear, but now sprouts from a vampirized consumerist spirit.'"[9] Consumerism was a real issue for Yugoslav society, Puhar conceded, but she insisted that it was by no means as villainous as its many detractors made it out to be.

In support of that position, Puhar pointed to the observations of another Slovenian writer, Primož Kozak, who had also suggested that much of the critique of consumerism was unwarranted and probably even harmful. Specifically, Kozak claimed that the anti-consumerist attitude amounted to something quite like xenophobia: "I don't believe in any sort of reservations," he said, "not cultural, and not historical." The retreat from modern consumerism, he insisted, was a quixotic and foolish effort to wall off the society into a cultural preserve of sorts, where it would be secure against the frightening influences of modern life:

> It is possible to imagine a utopia, thinking that if we didn't have this ugly consumerism, then we would be more cultured and, to a greater extent, we would be Slovenes. If there wasn't this hunt for money, cars, and weekend houses, there would be more for schools and culture. If there wasn't this anarchical liberalism, we might be better able to guarantee the status of Slovene culture and identity [*slovenstvo*] and keep it pointed in a safer direction.[10]

By defending the Communists' bugbear of "anarchical liberalism," Kozak was taking aim at the familiar party line, but these observations pointed to a more particularist and decidedly unorthodox basis for resistance to consumerism as well. Consumerism, as this response illustrates, was also perceived by some as a threat to specifically *national*—that is, ethno-national—interests. These were elements of the anti-consumerist critique that were not much in evidence in the more conventional Yugoslav literature on consumer culture, although they may well have been more common in public opinion and in circles of thought too conservative to find outlets in the mainstream press.[11] From Kozak's perspective, this sort of clinging to an imagined national past and future, pure in principle but now threatened by consumerist individualism's neglect of the community, was just so much idealist twaddle.

---

9. References are to Puhar, "Krivda in nekrivda potrošništva," 21 (internal quotation unattributed in original).

10. Primož Kozak, *Peter Klepec v Ameriki* (Maribor, 1971), quoted in ibid.

11. Along these lines, recall *Nova revija* writer Jože Snoj's traditionalist complaints about the consumerist erosion of women's familiar roles and the menace to Slovene natality, discussed in the preceding chapter. For another indication of the nationalist tendency to resist the cosmopolitan implications of the modern consumerist "melting pot," see Ivan Gams, "Skozi Srednjo Evropo v Evropo?" *Nova revija* 9, nos. 101–102 (September–October 1990): 1338–1340, at 1340.

Leaving aside the wisdom or error of Kozak's judgments on the harm done or not done by consumerism, there was, I conclude, some reason for ethno-nationalists to worry: in the Yugoslav setting, consumer culture appeared to the public with both a pan-Yugoslav and a cosmopolitan, cross-border face. Even though the internationalized image of modern affluence frequently was, as I argue throughout this book, scaled down to produce a fittingly modest and distinctively Yugoslav vision of the Good Life that might accord well with the country's expanding but still limited economic horizons, potent cosmopolitan elements were undeniably present. But no matter whether the representations of market culture encountered by ordinary citizens were cosmopolitan and international or more specifically Yugoslav, they did not, in any case, have a strong ethno-national flavor.

Quite obviously, consumerism in Yugoslavia (as elsewhere) often worked to substitute a new, modernist, transnational culture for more traditional means of cultural expression. Here, once again, ideology ran up against the loves and likes of ordinary people. Youth, for instance, wanted jeans. They had little interest in traditional styles and could barely be induced to put on national garb even for special celebrations. As a result, for those who cared strongly about the preservation of the older ways with their more specific national content, consumer culture seemed to pose a serious danger. In the end, however, this particular nationalist brand of resistance to consumerism proved quite limited, at least during the life of the socialist federation. Yugoslavs loved their international style, and they loved the fact that their largely unhampered ability to participate in that international style, something unique among the people of communist societies, was one of the things that made them special—one of the things that made them Yugoslavs.

For his part, Kozak sided unequivocally with the cosmopolitans on this issue. Setting up a traditionalist utopian "reservation" to keep out consumer society could indeed be accomplished, he suggested, but it was a terrible idea:

> All this could be possible and, elsewhere, is possible—for a price: backwardness, isolation [*odrezanost*], and provincialization. And with an ironic, mischievous twist of history: wherever the pulse of contemporary consumption is not permitted to function or cannot function as a real structure for life, it arrives as a religion, as a cult, as a myth, as the thing that is most desired and most precious. And we can almost say that in such a case it causes greater destruction among people and in people than it does where it functions in all its concreteness.[12]

Resistance to consumerism, in this view, was synonymous with resistance to progress and, perhaps even more important, to the sense of connection

---

12. Kozak, *Peter Klepec v Ameriki*; quoted in Puhar, "Krivda in nekrivda potrošništva," 21.

to the rest of the world that so many Yugoslavs prized so highly (and that was seen to be so sorely lacking in the "elsewhere" of Soviet-style state socialism). Kozak's observation is revealing on one final count as well: it suggests that Yugoslav society, despite its seemingly great distance from the Soviet-bloc experience of consumer scarcity and limited choice, was actually not so far removed from that competing model (or from the deprivations of the postwar period) as to make fears of slipping backward seem utterly baseless.

Snap, Crackle, Pop! Yugoslavia's Very Public Enjoyment of Consumer Wealth

The pleasurable and appealing aspects of contemporary consumption—and, with them, certain of those self-expressive dimensions that some cultural critics have seen as potentially liberating—were not lost on many ordinary citizens. Yugoslavs rather liked their consumer culture, and they clearly enjoyed participating in it.

For further proof, we need only examine the output of the Yugoslav popular media at the time. When the makers of the country's media images set out to capture the incidents and emotions of the Yugoslav Everyday, it was, with a remarkable consistency and directness, to the consumer experience and the eager pursuit of the Good Life that they turned. Over and over again, from the 1960s on, the pages of the country's popular press sought to illustrate and document just what the Yugoslav people were finding so attractive about their new freedom to consume—and, when the Yugoslav system sometimes fell short, what they were *not* finding in the shops, stores, and supermarkets.

As such, the coverage offered up in the mass media fulfills a number of evidentiary functions for historical inquiry. In the foregoing chapters we have seen in detail how images and ideas of the importance of abundance were transmitted to Yugoslav citizens through the various instrumentalities of market culture. To be sure, these processes were at work in the non-advertising, non-promotional content of the mass media as well. There, too, the abiding fascination with consumption in the popular press attests directly to the ways in which one set of culture makers, the media elites, "sold" Yugoslavia's distinctive consumer culture to the broader public. This particular relationship of cultural production and transfer—top-down, certainly, though in a way rather different from what is usually assumed of most state-socialist societies—cannot be ignored.

But more was going on. The popular media, whether in straightforward news reportage or in looser, more artistic representations of the Yugoslav experience, also served an important documentary function: when the makers of media representations set out to show their Yugoslav readers and viewers "our" everyday life and the way it increasingly revolved around consumption, they were at the same time serving to record, albeit in a mediated manner, the various ways in which a very different set of culture makers—ordinary Yugoslav consumers—were creating a world of shared values, styles, attitudes, and behaviors for themselves, and doing so "on the ground," in a decidedly non-elite, bottom-up, "mass" fashion.

Media representations of the popular engagement with consumption, in other words, now serve to tell us not just what was being "sold" but also what was (in more senses than one) being "bought" by the public, and what members of the public were making of the various things and experiences that they bought, sought, and shared. As a result, we can now mine such sources to find solid evidence of the texture and content of popular opinion, that is, indications of the views and behaviors of the "little people" (*kleine Leute*) that, as Alf Lüdtke has underscored, are the chief concerns of the academic investigation of everyday life.[13] In taking this approach to the media, I am, of course, keenly sensitive to the problem of public reception that attends any such use of the press. The knowledge of the past that comes to us in this way is indirect, but given the frustrating popular silences that socialist governance so often produced (and, beyond this characteristic dilemma of communist historiography, the general difficulty of securing contemporaneous documentary evidence produced by the "little people" in *any* political system), these sources have to rank among the best evidence available.

Even more to the point, and beyond these issues of relative quality, there is actually very good reason to treat them as very good evidence in absolute terms. What can be unearthed from the popular press often may be, in fact, reliable and representative, at least for historical questions like the ones that concern us here. Especially given the comparatively light touch applied to the Yugoslav press, outright government censorship on coverage of matters such as the living standard, shopping, spending, and the like was not a serious issue. Nor should there be, for the study of topics like these, any paralyzing concern about the effects of self-censorship. The socialist press does pose problems, but the Yugoslav press was not a typical socialist press. And consumption coverage was even less typical. Skepticism is always prudent, but there is good cause to conclude that we may often trust the Yugoslav media to tell us what the public found satisfying.

The same goes for dissatisfaction as well. For frequently it was the practice of the Yugoslav mass media to highlight the views of ordinary citizens and allow them, within fairly broad bounds, to voice their many complaints about current conditions. Reactions to the country's culture of consumption fell within this wide latitude given to the expression of candid and free

---

13. Alf Lüdtke, "Introduction: What Is the History of Everyday Life and Who Are Its Practitioners?" in *The History of Everyday Life: Reconstructing Historical Experiences and Ways of Life,* ed. Alf Lüdtke, trans. William Templer (Princeton, N.J., 1995), 3.

judgments about where government policy was headed and how well the Communists were doing. (Indeed, by the downturn of the 1980s, popular media coverage was chock-full of grumbling and irritation about the decline in living standards.)

The output of the Yugoslav mass media throughout the history of the socialist federation was, of course, immense, and any effort to interpret its connections with consumer culture requires some project of sensible representative sampling. To gauge the reactions of ordinary Yugoslav consumers of the sort that the popular media were courting and whose experience they attempted to capture, I examined in detail the coverage of a wide range of issues related to consumption as those subjects appeared in the pages of *Svijet,* the leading Croatian women's magazine, and *Jana,* its popular Slovenian counterpart, along with a more limited sampling of other key mass-market publications.

Like their analogues elsewhere in the country, these important women's magazines blossomed during the years of the Yugoslav boom. Zagreb-based *Svijet* was a well-established fixture of the Yugoslav media scene. Published by the large media combine centered around *Vjesnik,* Croatia's leading daily paper, it first hit the newsstands in 1953, initially as a monthly and later more frequently. Early on, the magazine confined itself to fashion. Beginning with the May 1962 issue, however, the scope of *Svijet*'s coverage expanded dramatically to include a full spectrum of women's issues or, as the editors put it, "all those questions and problems that may interest the contemporary woman, not just the mother and homemaker, but also the woman who participates in public life." The review promised—and ultimately delivered—a rich survey of contemporary women's concerns, and it did not shy away from questions of politics, sex and relationships, the difficult lives of working women, gender equality, economic conditions, "and, naturally," the editors reassured readers at the time of the switch, "fashion and cosmetics."[14] With the shift in coverage in 1962 came a heightened emphasis on consumption issues, with attention to topics that went far beyond fashion, and *Svijet* now featured new consumer goods in a photo-and-text section titled "For You in the Display Windows of Our Country's Stores" [*Za vas u našim izlozima*]. Essentially a mixture of informational and promotional activities, this regular full-page spread not only publicized the products but directed consumers to retail outlets as well.[15] Another variant of this type of feature that later appeared in the magazine's pages was titled "The Display Window

14. "Obavijest našim čitaljicama," *Svijet* no. 5, May 1962.

15. On the importance of retailing as an engine of consumer culture in the Western capitalist context, see, for example, Leach, *Land of Desire;* Strasser, *Satisfaction Guaranteed;* Michael B. Miller, *The Bon Marché: Bourgeois Culture and the Department Store, 1869–1920* (Princeton, N.J., 1981); Kim Humphery, *Shelf Life: Supermarkets and the Changing Cultures of Consumption* (Cambridge, 1998); Sharon Zukin, *Point of Purchase: How Shopping Changed American Culture* (New York, 2005).

of Desires" [*Izlog želja*].[16] The world of *Svijet* was, by the mid-1960s, a world thoroughly and, for the most part, unselfconsciously rooted in the expansion of the Yugoslav Dream.

A comparative newcomer with a similarly broad scope of coverage, Slovenia's *Jana* first appeared in 1972, when the Yugoslav economy was still generally quite strong, and after the reorientation toward consumerism was well under way. Not surprisingly, then, *Jana's* coverage was, from the start, keenly attentive to questions of consumption, lifestyles, and living standards. Published regularly throughout the remaining years of the socialist federation, these periodicals offer a valuable window into the daily concerns of Yugoslavs in the country's most prosperous regions. Through their ongoing attention to issues of everyday life, we can see how much the system did manage to deliver to ordinary citizens: much of the coverage of consumer issues during the 1960s and 1970s communicates a strong sense of popular satisfaction with living standards. This would change, not surprisingly, as the economy worsened after 1978 and living standards began to fall. With these jolts, the magazines were forced into a new role as chronicles of harder times, tighter budgets, shortages, and popular dissatisfaction. But while the good times lasted, *Jana* and *Svijet* showed just how good the good times were.

Regarding the dynamics of consumer culture, *Jana* and *Svijet* warrant special emphasis as key indicators of the public's reception of changing consumption opportunities and engagement with the various social, cultural, and political issues that the new consumer practices implicated. First, as publications targeted at women, they offer abundant evidence of the attitudes of, and messages directed to, one of the most significant market segments for most advertisers. In Yugoslavia, as in many other countries, women controlled a substantial portion of personal consumption, especially with respect to items bought and used frequently. They were heavily involved in decision making about big-ticket items like cars and major appliances, and they were directly responsible for the purchase of many of the "ordinary luxuries" like gourmet and specialty foods, fashion, and cosmetics that, I conclude, so strongly characterized the Yugoslav consumer's experience of abundance.[17] Moreover, the magazines' broad circulation and obvious efforts to communicate the perspectives of the regular citizen, the "woman-on-the-street," suggest that they not only mirrored (as accurately as any such publication could) but also molded public opinion.

---

16. See, for example, "Izlog želja," *Svijet* no. 24, 15 December 1966, 42.

17. For a discussion of the importance of such "ordinary luxuries," and parallels to and divergences from the Soviet experience, see Jukka Gronow, *Caviar with Champagne: Common Luxury and the Ideals of the Good Life in Stalin's Russia* (Oxford, 2003); Gronow, "Caviar with Champagne: Good Life and Common Luxury in Stalin's Soviet Union," *Suomen Antropologi/Finnish Journal of Anthropology* 23, no. 4 (1998): 29–40.

Figure 20. The *Modna kuća* (Fashion house) apparel store in Praška ulica, Zagreb, designed by architect Ninoslav Kučan, ca. 1960s. Photograph from the collection of Ninoslav Kučan. Courtesy of Mara Kučan-Smešny and the estate of Ninoslav Kučan.

Finally, as periodicals from Slovenia and Croatia, *Jana* and *Svijet* give us an insight into Yugoslav consumer culture at its most expansive: these were easily the wealthiest of the Yugoslav republics, and the ones with the easiest connections to the West, most notably to the shopping centers of Trieste, Tarvisio, Klagenfurt, Villach, and Graz. Slovenes and Croats thus had seen the best Yugoslavia had to offer, and a great number of them had been able to compare it with the abundance of capitalism. Many, in fact, could hop over the border to go shopping without much time or trouble (in not much more than an hour's time from many parts of Slovenia).

Wherever they were able to do it, Yugoslavs loved their shopping. Accordingly, *Svijet* and *Jana* reported regularly on consumer opportunities, offering a mixture of appreciative comments and, for good measure, plenty of criticism of perceived shortcomings. Nor were Slovenian and Croatian media alone in this approach: the Serbian press, too, was quite attentive to these issues, as seen both in well-established sources like Serbia's women's magazine *Praktična žena* as well as upstarts like *Beogradska nedelja*, which

Figure 21. A bustling department store in the regional center of Osijek. From the report on conditions in the stores: "'Our shops are stuffed with merchandise. But in spite of that, when we want to get something truly nice and modern, whether it's for the home or something to wear, we have to travel to Zagreb or Belgrade or Ljubljana, because here where we are they don't have it.' That's how people in the cities in the provinces have been complaining for years. Is that how it really is? Hasn't the situation changed in recent years? Or are we, perhaps, talking about complaining and moaning as a matter of habit?" *Source*: M. G., "Najprije što, a onda koliko," *Svijet* no. 18, 28 August 1968, 4–5, at 4.

briefed readers from time to time on what was going on in the capital's shops and department stores.[18] Consumption had become, by the late 1960s and early 1970s, a near constant feature of mass circulation periodicals of this sort. *Jana*, for instance, featured a regular column that briefed readers on conditions in the stores, keeping shoppers informed about new products, availability, and prices. Quality and value were major concerns as well; at times, the weekly sent its own force of shopping inspectors into the stores to check such factors as variety, quality, and service.

---

18. I am grateful to Brigitte Le Normand for alerting me to the revealing reportage in *Beogradska nedelja* and for sharing with me a number of sources with respect to the coverage of shopping. On Yugoslav women's magazines, see Zrinka Pavlić, *Svijet i praktična žena* (Zagreb, 2006).

Fashion, not surprisingly, was a frequent and much discussed subject in both the magazines, and their reporters visited fashion shows and trade fairs, reporting on trends at home and abroad. Photo spreads on fashion, including coverage of international fashion shows and such revealing items as *Svijet*'s reportage on High Street shopping in England and *Jana*'s updates and snapshots of what people on the street were wearing in Trieste, were common.[19] But the reviews also made it quite clear that fashion was alive and well on Yugoslav streets and in Yugoslav stores.

The writers and editors of these magazines treated fashion as a generalized European and, indeed, global phenomenon. Modernity was most assuredly "in," and fashion ranked as a prime index of modernity. *Svijet,* for instance, found the wildly varying skirt-length norms of the late 1960s and early 1970s a virtually irresistible subject. As one article summed things up for readers, "an essential question of the present day is, of course, the dilemma: mini, midi, or maxi?"[20] For a time all of this was, it must be remembered, a burning issue. Judging from the reportage in the popular press, many Yugoslav consumers took the hemline controversies very seriously indeed. As one woman interviewed for yet another report on the problem observed, the conflicting styles became the focus of personal loyalties and genuine concern:

I was, simply put, in love with the mini-skirt. Both on myself (although, of course, I never overdid it) and on other women. That was an extraordinarily fresh, youthful style, in a word—amazing. When the longer skirts first appeared on our streets, I didn't pay attention to that at all. I thought there was no way that they would win out over the mini-skirt. I see that my predictions didn't come true. And you see, I capitulated![21]

Another interviewee, this one from Macedonia, noted that even this comparatively underdeveloped part of the country was by no means isolated from fashion trends. "For more than a year already," the woman reported in late 1970, "I've been wearing a skirt that goes down to the ground. Almost all Skopje women have taken up the maxi style."[22] At least while it lasted, the maxi-skirt was held in high esteem among Yugoslav women.

Four years earlier *Svijet* had focused on the rise of the mini-skirt with much the same sense of fascination and marvel, calling it "one of those short-lived caprices of fashion of which there are so many," and noting that

---

19. For a critical take on the British infatuation with fashion, see, for example, A. H., "Vašar modnih ludosti," *Svijet* no. 13, 1 July 1970, 60–61.

20. "'Argusovo' 1001. zanimanje: modni urednik (ali samo ovih dviju stranica)," *Svijet* no. 26, 30 December 1970, 14–15, at 14.

21. Majda Sepe, quoted in Dževad Budimlić et al., "Mini ili midi ili Maxi ili?" *Svijet* no. 24, 2 December 1970, 6–7, 36–37, 60, at 60.

22. Snežana Lipkovska, quoted in ibid., 7.

the style was one that seemed to hold the promise of transforming grown women into "the image of a schoolgirl." Yugoslavs were eagerly following a trend that "many, not to say all, creators of fashion are responding to."[23]

Svijet's initial reactions may have betrayed a bit of skepticism, but it proceeded to hype the mini-skirt in the intervening years all the same, as it did with practically every other *nouvelle vogue* to hit the Yugoslav streets. As such episodes suggest, the coverage of fashion in these mass-circulation journals was generally enthusiastic, and often downright promotional, in its tone. From what appeared in print, it seems that the writers and editors of women's magazines (like their counterparts in the publishing world of home improvement and design) took it as a given that styles could and would and indeed *should* change. But fashion coverage was by no means an unadulterated exercise in boosterism. *Svijet*'s notices of new footwear styles for 1970–1971, for example, let loose with a volley of complaints about shoes that did not have "feminine charm" and were "too heavy, thick, and large." With their new collections, the magazine said, the fashion designers had "made use of the styles of the 1930s, the shoes of our grandmothers and great-grandmothers, of boy scouts, gauchos, and who knows what else."[24]

No matter what quibbles they had with the occasional odd trend, *Jana* and *Svijet* were by no means resisting fashion per se. The pages of these magazines, like others in Yugoslavia, treated the nexus between feminine allure and the ability to consume as strong, positive, and largely self-evident. In response to the question "Why have Yugoslav women become more beautiful?" *Svijet* reported in 1966 that there was, in fact, "a definite answer"—and one directly related to the country's radically new consumption horizons. "Changes in lifestyle, housing, dress, and eating habits have hastened the improvement of their outward appearance," *Svijet* concluded. Interestingly, for this inquiry into the hows and whys of the beauty transformation, the magazine's male writer let other men do the talking. Those more scientifically minded interviewees attributed much of the change to developments in health and nutrition, but others among them identified very different aspects of the shift in consumer habits. One artist interviewed for the piece asserted his conviction that "women are more beautiful simply because they are reading the fashion magazines more and because the stronger economic conditions make it possible for them to use more in the way of high-quality cosmetics, and to take advantage of modern hair styling more often." A second respondent, a television director, observed that "our fathers' ideal was a good, smart, and obedient woman, but our ideal is an emancipated, defiant, elusive, and provocatively beautiful companion." The increase in feminine beauty, he said, was simply "a demand of our times." Yet another man interviewed for the piece, a popular singer, admitted that the all this progressive

23. See, for example, "Mini—zašto?" *Svijet* no. 20, 15 October 1966, 8–9, at 8.
24. "Cipela: moderno i (ne) lijepo," *Svijet* no. 21, 21 October 1970, 3.

beautification was the product of the "numerous helpful devices" that had recently become available to women in the stores and salons, but he was satisfied with what he called "the final product." "Yugoslav women are increasingly beautiful," he insisted. "The difference between women today and the women of ten years ago is beyond comparison."[25] Men, it seemed, loved what the culture of abundance with its "numerous helpful devices" was doing for *Jugoslavenke,* the women of the country.

Furniture, household items, and foods also figured prominently in the world of the women's journals, and in this respect, too, their coverage offers a strong sense of the considerable attention Yugoslavs were devoting to their shopping and buying, even for comparatively minor purchases of inexpensive, everyday items. One typical article from *Svijet,* for example, reported on the steps taken by the country's food-products manufacturers to adjust their offerings to the shifts in demand necessitated by Yugoslavia's switchover to the new, "European" work schedule. That modification, which moved the normal workday back by as much as two hours to an 8:30 or 9:00 a.m. starting time, proved to be a major cultural shift in Yugoslav everyday life, and it made for real changes in the schedules and responsibilities of working women. With supper now likely to be the main meal of the day (instead of the traditional mid-afternoon lunch), *Svijet* believed that grocery sales needed to adjust to "the contemporary rhythm of living" that "does not recognize the luxury of time" but instead "conserves it." Here, too, the magazine's writer insisted, consumer industries had their part to play. "A good packaged food," she observed, "is a way of saving time." The results had been, thus far, only mixed, the report concluded, but there were encouraging signs of change in that many companies were "adapting to the modern manufacture of products that simplify life and reduce the complicated preparation of food to more or less a rapid process."[26]

To make sure readers paid even more attention to what was on offer, *Svijet* and *Jana* naturally featured a substantial amount of advertising. The promotional content of *Svijet,* for example, though comparatively limited in the early 1960s, underwent striking growth over the course of that decade and into the 1970s, by which time the magazine was laden with ads. *Jana,* too, included numerous advertising messages.

Through all this promotion and commotion, the centrality of the new consumption regime proved unmistakable. It was, accordingly, to precisely these features of everyday life that one frequent *Svijet* contributor looked when he sought to capture the experience of "the average Yugoslav

---

25. Pero Zlatar, "Zašto su se Jugoslavenke proljepšale?" *Svijet* no. 22, 15 November 1966, 4–5. The term "companion" [*drugarica*] in the quotation here is ambiguous; the word was also the standard usage in Yugoslav communist parlance for "comrade."

26. Magda Weltrusky, "Sajamski jelovnik po novom random receptu," *Svijet* no. 9, 24 April 1968, 4–5, at 5.

woman" in the new Yugoslav "Babylon," that is, her situation "in today's world, surrounded by paradoxes" such as conflicting work and personal responsibilities, bracing modernization alongside persistent traditionalism, and lingering economic limitations mixed in with a host of new hopes, dreams, and expectations. The average *Jugoslavenka,* Pero Zlatar suggested, was firmly rooted in a world of consumption and the prospects for improving it: "What is her main preoccupation? The living standard, above all." The availability of the Good Life, he indicated, lay at the heart of what had turned Yugoslavia into a place of exciting and pleasurable, but sometimes chaotic and bewildering, pursuits. "The contemporary household, in contrast to the one of three or four decades ago, wishes to fill up the house as quickly as possible with a refrigerator, with a washing machine and a dishwasher, an oil-burning furnace, a television, a tape player, and all the other technical splendors." But the ability to achieve this was not without its difficulties, Zlatar acknowledged. The typical Yugoslav woman found herself needing to skillfully manage her family's finances and economize carefully in order to make ends meet each month, he said, "because of this desire to, somehow or other, keep pace with the living standard that a Central European family has."[27]

In their quest for an ever more satisfying version of what Yugoslavs referred to simply as "the standard," the readers of *Svijet* and *Jana* were well informed about what was to be had in the marketplaces of their Babylon, and what, on the other hand, might require them to take to the trade routes. The magazines reported periodically on shopping opportunities abroad, usually in Austria and Italy, but sometimes, for comparison's sake, in other socialist countries as well. Throughout this ongoing coverage of what the public was already at the time calling "consumer tourism" [*potrošački turizam*], it was obvious that Yugoslav shoppers were continually wondering, as one story put it, "where does it pay to go for what?" [*gdje se što isplati*].[28] Stories on the consumer bounty that returnees reported at customs checkpoints (or failed to report—smuggling was an open secret) made it quite clear what the Yugoslav economy was not yet delivering successfully to its consumers.

But even when they devoted this kind of attention to the appeal of foreign shopping, popular magazines documented the basic success of Yugoslavia's consumer orientation. Their coverage made it clear that cross-border trips were largely targeted at limited and specific items, often those thought to be at the cutting edge of fashion. In most ways, and for most needs and wants, Yugoslavs were satisfied with what was to be found at home. They were, above all, savvy shoppers, and through the workings of a profoundly interpersonal, truly popular consumer culture built on frequent word-of-mouth

27. Pero Zlatar, "Jugoslavenka u Babilonu," *Svijet* no. 3, 11 February 1970, 4–5, at 4.
28. A. Horvat, "Živjela mala razlika! ili: 'potrošački turizam' i njegovo naličje," *Svijet,* no. 21, 21 October 1970, 6–7.

exchanges, they knew what could be found at home, or found more cheaply, and what might require a cross-border hop.

In the mass media, however, there was some indication that the public did not quite know everything and that domestic buying opportunities had been overlooked as this avid subculture of transnational treasure-hunting took root. A *Svijet* report from 1968 pointed out that the shopping finds to be had in Ljubljana, just two hours away, might spare Yugoslavs the trouble and expense of bundling off to Italy. The "Trieste Myth," writer Melita Singer suggested, was coming under pressure from competition closer to home. Ljubljana would not satisfy every desire (and neither would Trieste, readers were cautioned), but a shopper headed there "will find much that she won't find here." All this showed, the story concluded, "much more serious efforts in the battle for the market and for consumers" on the part of Ljubljana's business circles—in other words, "a greater sense for modern and sophisticated retailing (and as a result of that, adequate accomplishments)."[29]

Somewhat like the many élite critics of consumer culture, the women (and sometimes men) who expressed their opinions in the pages of *Svijet* and *Jana* did at times communicate a certain skepticism about the Yugoslav fascination with shopping, buying, and owning. There were, for example, occasional rumblings of disapproval about various episodes of consumerist "fevers." Some ordinary citizens seemed well aware that they were being sold an image of modernity, style, and European-ness that typically linked the urbane with the urban. In this spirit, one letter writer griped to the editors of *Jana* that the imagery of the modern woman they tended to present was unnaturally skewed toward the young, fashionable city dweller: "I think it wouldn't be unaesthetic at all," this reader complained, "if, here and there, you were to choose for your cover pages a woman who works in a factory, or perhaps a mother from a farming family who is not adorned with false eyelashes, a wig, and all sorts of makeup."[30]

Conversely, many readers suggested that the urbanization of tastes and habits associated with consumer culture was not taking place quickly enough. It was undeniable, of course, that a major shift in rural life was under way, and the mass media were generally enthusiastic about its benefits and impressed by the rate of change. One whirlwind history of cosmetics in *Svijet*, for example, sought to counter the idea that Yugoslavia's consumer culture was only for urban elites. Starting from the premise that makeup had once been more or less the exclusive province of rich women in ancient Egypt, Greece, and Rome, the columnist in this report-*cum*-product-promotion article noted effusively that in the post–World War II era the art of cosmetics was no longer the domain of "the higher strata of the society of those

---

29. Melita Singer, "Umjesto 'Idem u Trst'—'Idem u Ljubljanu'?" *Svijet* no. 2, 17 January 1968, 8–9.

30. Anica Čeh, letter to the editor, *Jana* 1, no. 8, 17 February 1972, 3.

times" but had, "alongside the substantial growth of the living standard of the population, cleared new paths to the wider masses of the feminine world." Those developments, she said, now had become a part of Yugoslav everyday life as well: "In great measure, this is precisely the value of Margaret Astor—a new cosmetics firm for our times. The orientation of Margaret Astor is, specifically, the highest quality in a broad selection and with a very large series of products," and, happily, these new offerings had now come to Yugoslavia through a production agreement with Maribor's Zlatorog enterprise. "All this," the *Svijet* piece emphasized, "makes for a considerable reduction of production costs and makes renowned cosmetics accessible for virtually all girls and women, both in the cities and the countryside."[31]

Both with respect to socioeconomic strata and to geographic segmentation, then, the mass consumption of small, easily accessible everyday luxuries such as these often was seen as having a profound democratizing effect on Yugoslav life. Although the transfer of city tastes and commodities to provincial areas remained only partial and imperfect, the extent of the societal transformation wrought by consumer abundance, even in rural areas, was clear enough.

In the view of a number of ordinary Yugoslavs, however, the country's economic system had not done a good job in ensuring that the benefits of consumer abundance were distributed broadly outside the major urban centers. In this vein, a *Svijet* report on the state of fashion in Tuzla in 1966 (part of the magazine's continuing series on "fashion on the streets of our cities") conceded that "from time to time" fashion shows did make it to the provincial Bosnian city but noted that "this 'from time to time' was, on the last occasion, four years ago!" But the small-town style deficit was actually even greater, it seemed: "Worse than that is the fact that, afterward, it was never possible to see a single model that had been on display at the fashion show anywhere in the Tuzla shops."[32] Along the same lines, another letter to the editor published in *Jana* complained that those who lived at some distance from all that was offered in the bigger cities ended up experiencing "a form of differentiation that we can't really call 'social.'" In other words, Yugoslav society was, to some extent, experiencing the "social differentiation" that Marxist ideologists and politicians so deplored, but something other than the familiar class-based diagnoses of Marxism was at issue.

The complaints that arose from the urban-rural split were not baseless: at least with regard to the images shown to the public as representations of the Yugoslav Dream, those who crafted the most prominent visual features of the country's market culture did tend to ignore Yugoslavia's rural population, which, although steadily declining in numerical strength, remained

---

31. References are to Mana Molin, "Vrhunska dekorativna kozmetike za najšire krugove," *Svijet* no. 3, 11 February 1970, 2.
32. "Moda na ulicama naših gradova," *Svijet* no. 6, 15 March 1966, 15.

quite substantial. This bias was manifest in the pages of high-circulation periodicals across the country. And clearly there were real problems in channeling the dominant urban-centered styles out to the countryside. With that in mind, the *Jana* reader quoted just above (a man) continued:

> In our stores here in the countryside the same items are always available, and it seems to us that they are the kind that people are carting off from the city warehouses on purpose, thinking "the people out there in the country really aren't that picky, it'll be good enough for them." When we were in one of the department stores in Ljubljana a few days ago (I won't mention the name, so it won't sound like an advertisement for it), we saw things which people have never dreamed might fill our markets.[33]

These difficulties, the evidence suggests, afflicted much of the country. A *Svijet* story from 1968 took up the same subject and uncovered similar complaints. "I still have to visit all the shops in order to find everything that I need for my bathroom," said one disgruntled Osijek woman in the piece. "I don't deny that the stores have a better selection and more courteous service than before, but you still waste too much time in the store trying to find something specific, to the extent you can find it at all." Another interviewee conceded that "the selection of women's ready-made clothing and knitwear is bigger. Nevertheless," this customer fumed, "it is not clear to me why I have to buy goods from the Angora or Rašica brands in Zagreb or Belgrade. It's true that they sometimes show up in our stores, too, but they run out right away. Obviously the buyers are demanding them, so the stores need to purchase them more often, and in greater quantities." Still another shopper despaired that "it's pointless to look for nicely designed items made of wrought iron, but without them, it's hard to be able to put together the atmosphere of a modern apartment. And we have all of that here in Yugoslavia [*kod nas*]. It just seems that the Osijek commercial establishment hasn't 'discovered' it. Or maybe they think that there wouldn't be buyers for that?"[34] Clearly, even in fairly remote places like Osijek (situated in far eastern Slavonia some 280 kilometers from Zagreb and only slightly closer to Belgrade), Yugoslav shoppers were arriving in the stores with exacting requirements, refined tastes, and expectations of variety, quality, ease, and satisfaction. They had been offered a lot in recent years, and they had come to expect even more.

Complaints from the public printed in the Yugoslav media could be quite harsh at times. "I think when it comes to the choice of models," seventeen-year-old student Ružica Milosavljević complained in 1970, "our clothing

---

33. Tone Mlinarič, letter to the editor, *Jana* 1, no. 8, 17 February 1972, 3.

34. The shoppers are quoted in M. G., "Najprije što, a onda koliko," *Svijet* no. 18, 28 August 1968, 4–5.

stores very often remind you of antiques shops."[35] Even in thoroughly "establishment" media outlets, there was plenty of precedent for the expression of real dissatisfaction about consumer offerings. Along these lines, for example, one review of the recently concluded exposition season in 1960, published in Belgrade's leading daily newspaper *Politika,* bemoaned the fact that so many of the promising "new successes" of Yugoslav industry and commerce unveiled at these trade fairs seemed indefinitely unavailable: "At the exhibition booths for the manufacturers of radios and televisions, furniture, textiles, and other goods of mass consumption," *Politika's* reviewer concluded, "it was a rare occurrence when they were able to offer us more complete information about prices and about the delivery date for these products in the stores of our cities."[36]

So there was complaining, and plenty of it. But it must be noted that carping of this sort did not mirror the worries of the anti-consumerist critics. Quite to the contrary, it represented a recognition of the profound appeal of the purchasing power that Yugoslavia had thus far managed to deliver, coupled with a demand for more of those goods, services, and experiences. In the main, these mass-market magazines, as vital shapers and monitors of the experience of Yugoslav women, leave little doubt that a consumer culture rooted in expectations of the regular delivery of abundance had become a thoroughly integrated—and thoroughly welcome—part of everyday life.

In the end, to examine what ordinary citizens were reading in their magazines and newspapers is to understand that instead of "Are We a Consumer Society?" as Franc Šetinc and like-minded critics would have had it, the burning question in Yugoslav everyday life during the good years of the 1960s and 1970s was often something more like the one that, in the midst of it all, *Svijet* posed to its readers: "A Toaster—Yes or No?" (The answer: though perhaps not "indispensable," the new appliance offered remarkable benefits and convenience, compelling a conclusion that "in any case, we can establish that a toaster is not a luxury." Nor was, for that matter, a dishwasher, as a companion piece confirmed.)[37] The complaints of ordinary Yugoslavs were real and regular, and they are indeed highly revealing. But some perspective is required. When shoppers have the luxury of lamenting that they cannot find the stylish wrought-iron pieces needed to put just the right finishing touches on "the atmosphere of a modern apartment," it is clear that most, if not all, of the basic existential problems of individual consumption have been solved. Historically speaking, this is an enviable position for any society to find itself in.

---

35. Quoted in L. Garić, "Moda pod unakrsnom vatrom," *Svijet* no. 18, 9 September 1970, 6–7.

36. Živojin Todorović, "Izložba najmodernih dostignuća ali i najostalijih navika," *Politika,* 31 October 1960, 5.

37. "Pržač kruha—da ili ne?" *Svijet* no. 9, 6 May 1970, 45; "Je li stroj za pranje posuda luksuz?" *Svijet* no. 9, 6 May 1970, 47.

The Love Parade: Living Large on the Small Screen

Elsewhere in the Yugoslav mass media of the times we find evidence that points to the same conclusion. Another particularly revealing source for insights into the public mood toward questions of consumption is Yugoslav television. Television was, by the late 1960s, well on its way toward becoming a near necessity for many households in the country. Even if families had not managed to acquire one yet, it was often an object of keen desire nevertheless, and they sometimes managed to find ways to watch broadcasts. The medium's connection to the profound restructuring of leisure practices and social relations comes across clearly, for example, in one revealing interchange from a 1966 *Svijet* interview with a farm wife and her family from a little village outside Zagreb, when the magazine's questioner turned the subject to this most modern of conveniences. "'I see,'" the reporter asked the man of the house, "that in the village there are lots of television sets. There are many antennas on the roofs. You don't have a television?" At that point, the teenage son of this fairly modest household interrupted, "dejectedly" we are told, that "in Lekenik almost every house has a television," before being effectively silenced by his still skeptical elders. Later on, readers learned that the parental opposition here was not to television per se but rather was a matter of consumer priorities (and control of the purse strings): the mother in this peasant family, who believed it best to put off buying a television until it would no longer interfere with her son's studies—and until she had gotten herself the electric stove and refrigerator that she desired—nevertheless made it a practice to watch TV at her neighbors' homes, and she did so, by her own account, both "often" and eagerly. "On Saturdays it's a must," she told the interviewer.[38]

So what were Yugoslavs watching, and how did television connect with the country's evolving consumer culture? During the years of the most rapid change, a number of the most popular broadcasts focused precisely on issues of everyday life. Along these lines, two now legendary series, *Vruć vetar* (A hot wind) and *Grlom u jagode* (Headfirst into strawberries), stand out as especially relevant and revealing. Producers of these shows held up a mirror to the Yugoslav society that was, as they captured it, caught up in the pursuit of the Good Life. The rhythms and rituals of the everyday—and with them an unending series of consumption experiences, big and small—take center stage in these programs.

Most of the protagonists of *Vruć vetar* are, by design, profoundly ordinary folk. This ten-episode series, which aired originally in 1980 and is still being rebroadcast today, follows its bumbling, torpid, Švejkian anti-hero Borivoje "Šurda" Šurdilović, as he moves (slowly, it should be said) from

---

38. Košutić, "Želje počinja sa fridžiderom," 8.

his quiet and modest life as a barber from the provinces through a succession of adventures and misadventures in prosperous, bustling, sometimes money-mad Belgrade.

The opening shots of the series give us Šurda ambling through the streets of the city, peering into the windows of furniture shops and shoe stores at all that the new consumer culture has to offer. For the moment, however, the hapless protagonist is still very much "on the outside," caught in the rain without even an umbrella, and forced to make do by trying to shield himself with *Politika* [Politics], the leading Belgrade daily—the newspaper's big, bold, and distinctive Cyrillic masthead, instantly recognizable to viewers across Yugoslavia, features prominently in the scene (Episode 1; Figure 22).[39] It soon becomes clear, however, that Šurda may need to rely on more than *Politika*—or *politika*—to keep him dry, comfortable, and happy. For most of the series, he moves none too successfully from job to job, including some time as an undercover security guard working to thwart shoplifters in a large supermarket. Even in this bright, modern slice of consumer heaven, not everything is perfect, it seems: as Šurda is told by his boss, "They steal everything" (Episode 4; Figure 29). Along the rather bumpy way, the audience sees Šurda deal with such milestones as marriage, the arrival of a son, and the effort to buy an apartment and a new Zastava 101 automobile using that financial innovation of the period so loved by the Yugoslav public, consumer credit.

A counterpoint to Šurda's diffidence comes from Vesna, his confident, acquisitive, ambitious, go-getter wife. Like Yugoslav society itself at the time, the characters of *Vruć vetar* form a circle of family and friends that can manage to make room, warmly and comfortably, for both those who, like Vesna, aimed for "success" and those who, like Šurda, were indifferent to material wealth (or at least not willing to work zealously to get it). In Šurda Šurdilović viewers saw a man uncertain, even paralyzed, in the face of the new Yugoslav culture's celebration of economic opportunity, and daunted by the concomitant expectation that opportunity must be pursued when it presented itself. Over time, with a bit of good luck and a lot of hard work (mostly from Vesna, as she takes pains to point out), the family prospers and moves through a series of increasingly comfortable and well-furnished apartments.

But although the images presented in *Vruć vetar* capture an increasingly available Good Life, with few exceptions the characters are not among the Yugoslav "rich." Viewers do see occasional representations of the upper crust: an elegantly dressed *dama* in central Belgrade who is outraged when Šurda refuses to take her equally well-coiffed poodle as a passenger in his taxi; a successful businessman taking advantage of the duty-free service to

---

39. All visual and textual references are to *Vruć vetar*, DVD, directed by Aleksandar Đorđević (1980; Belgrade, 2005). The series first aired on Televizija Beograd. It is published on DVD as part of the PGP/RTS Zlatne Serije series, item number 1140204.

In pursuit of the Good Life—the hit television series Vruć vetar (A hot wind), 1980.

22. So much to buy, but for now not even an umbrella—Šurda Šurdilović the Yugoslav Everyman hero of the series—Episode 1.

23. Lifestyles of the rich—Vesna Šurdilović at work on a JAT Yugoslav Airlines DC-10—Episode 7.

24. Not enough space and privacy—Vesna and Uncle Firga suffer the inconveniences of the old ways—Episode 5.

25. "How many years have to pass until we pull ourselves out of this hole?"—an old-fashioned washday—Episode 6.

26. A deluxe apartment in the sky—moving into a newly built *blok*—Episode 6.

27. All the mod cons—the modern living room and kitchen of Šurda's new flat—Episode 8.

Source: Vruć vetar, DVD, directed by Aleksandar Đorđević (1980; Belgrade: PGP/RTS [Radio-Televizija Srbije], 2005). Actor credits: Ljubiša Samardžić as Šurda, Miodrag Petrović Ckalja as Firga, Vesna Ćipčić as Vesna, Radmila Savićević as Šurda's grandmother.

Getting a piece of the Yugoslav Dream—Vruć vetar, 1980.

28. New furniture for the living room and dining room—Episode 7.

29. "They steal everything"—Šurda works as a security guard for a modern supermarket—Episode 4.

30. The ordinary, everyday luxuries that socialism made affordable—Šurda finally makes it big in his own hair salon—Episode 10.

31. Money doesn't always buy happiness—complaining about the wife's latest department store purchases—Episode 9.

32. Šurda and Vesna living the Yugoslav Dream—Episode 9.

33. Will "a bathroom lined with tiles" guarantee a "happy end"?—Episode 10.

Source: Vruć vetar, DVD, directed by Aleksandar Đorđević (1980; Belgrade: PGP/RTS [Radio-Televizija Srbije], 2005). Actor credits: Ljubiša Samardžić as Šurda, Miodrag Petrović Čkalja as Firga, Vesna Ćipčić as Vesna, Radmila Savićević as Šurda's grandmother.

**Reminiscing about the things it took to "become a real person" in the 1960s—
the hit television series Grlom u jagode (Headfirst into strawberries), 1976.**

34. Bringing home the first family television—
Episode 1.

35. A Yugoslav Home Companion—gathered
around the TV—Episode 3.

36. The Živković family at home—Episode 10.

37. Leisure and style on the Croatian coast—
Episode 7.

38. Disco comes to Belgrade, wearing "two-storey
shoes"—Episode 4.

39. Brand new—showing off the Levi's label on a
recently acquired pair of jeans—Episode 6

Source: Grlom u jagode, DVD, directed by Srđan Karanović (1975; Belgrade: PGP/RTS [Radio-Televizija Srbije], 2004). Actor credits: Branko Cvejić as Branislav "Bane Bumbar" Živković, Danilo Stojković as Sreten Živković, Olivera Marković as Olivera Živković, Đurđija Cvejić as Seka Štajn, Rahela Ferari as Bane's grandmother, Predrag Miki Manojlović as Miki Rubiroza, Gordana Marić as Goca, Bogdan Diklić as Božidar Boca Simić, and Aleksandar Berček as Slobodan Đorđević.

40. Crowds at the Belgrade used-car market—Episode 10.

41. Friends, fashions, and a *Fića*—Episode 8.

42. Success and "social differentiation"—Episode 10.

43. Movin' on up—a new high-rise flat—Episode 10.

44. A modest, modern Yugoslav home—Episode 9.

45. Super-shopping the modern way—Episode 1.

Source: Grlom u jagode, DVD, directed by Srđan Karanović (1975; Belgrade: PGP/RTS [Radio-Televizija Srbije], 2004). Actor credits: Branko Cvejić as Branislav "Bane Bumbar" Živković, Danilo Stojković as Sreten Živković, Olivera Marković as Olivera Živković, Đurđija Cvejić as Seka Štajn, Rahela Ferari as Bane's grandmother, Predrag Miki Manojlović as Miki Rubiroza, Gordana Marić as Goca, Bogdan Diklić as Božidar Boca Simić, and Aleksandar Berček as Slobodan Đorđević.

buy a carton of Kent cigarettes (L&M and Marlboro are also on display, as are bottles of Johnny Walker Scotch whisky) while traveling first class on a new wide-body DC-10 flown by JAT, the national carrier (Episode 7; Figure 23). These wealthy characters with their emblems of *snobizam* are only peripheral to the protagonists' journey, however, and the central concerns of the series are with the lives of ordinary people with whom audiences could readily identify and empathize.

In *Vruć vetar*, those who cannot quite keep up with the rapid pace of change are the subjects of good-natured humor, as happens when the cosmopolitan, image-conscious, young Vesna sends Šurda's aging uncle Firga off to the store to procure an English-branded beauty product, spoken of on the show as "Skin Life Emulsion for Oil Skin." (Skin Life was a line of cosmetics developed by America's Helena Rubenstein firm, manufactured under license in Yugoslavia, and promoted with heavy and sophisticated advertising in mass-market magazines such as *Svijet, Jana,* and *Naš dom.* As such, it would have been familiar to viewers as a prestige brand, one of the "ordinary luxuries" that had recently transformed the Yugoslav marketplace.) The hapless Firga, who is anything but cosmopolitan, suffers terribly trying to memorize and pronounce the English name of the product, butchering it over and over again to Vesna's great consternation and, no doubt, the audience's great delight (Episode 9). More difficulties ensue when Firga and Vesna square off over space in their old home's none-too-modern bathroom, in a scene that speaks to the troubles that Yugoslavs faced with having to "live on top of one another" in the persistent postwar housing crunch (Episode 5; Figure 24). But even if they are unsophisticated, the crusty old Firga and those like him in *Vruć vetar* are, in the end, highly sympathetic characters, and in their struggles to adapt, Yugoslavs no doubt saw their own lives (or the lives of their funny old uncles and grandmothers, which in all likelihood would only have reinforced the point of Yugoslavia's generational shift toward consumer modernity).

In the show's system of values, being a "typical" Yugoslav is, clearly, good enough. Though her conduct sometimes suggests otherwise, even the success-oriented Vesna is willing to reassure her insecure mate, when he becomes jealous of one of her wealthy, polished, and successful male colleagues, that she is satisfied with the regular sort of fellow that she already has. When the anxious Šurda inquires suspiciously about what she really wants out of life, she tells him that simple and normal is plenty:

VESNA: I want a man!
ŠURDA: Some kind of special man?
VESNA: An ordinary one. The most ordinary kind. (Episode 8)

At the outset of the series, it appears that success, at least in the material terms in which the public increasingly defined it, will continue to elude this particular ordinary Yugoslav man. Yet, over time, Šurda and his family do advance to a higher standard of living. Their first home is a leaky old bungalow that he and Vesna share with his grandmother and uncle, a place bereft of up-to-date household appliances, and one that nothing more than the work of a rainy wash day can turn into a farcical little hell of washtubs, hand-wrung linens, and dripping, sagging sheets strung up on clotheslines that transform the kitchen into a wet, steamy maze (Episode 6; Figure 25). These cramped and decidedly old-fashioned conditions prompt Vesna to ask, "How many years have to pass until we pull ourselves out of this hole?" (Episode 6). With time, however, they do manage to move up and out, following the Yugoslav Dream into a high-rise apartment with all the modern conveniences, more space and privacy, television, radio, and plenty of new furniture (Episodes 6, 7, and 8; Figures 26, 27, and 28).

There is some hint, however, that all the consumer spending has gotten out of control. Viewers see this skepticism, for example, when Šurda, electric toaster in hand, confronts his wife over what he thinks are her excessive purchases (Episode 9; Figure 31). He is hard-pressed to believe that Vesna has acted rationally in bringing home not just this appliance but also a blender and hand mixer from one of her recent outings to the department store. To Šurda, these needs seem to be, to use the rhetoric of the critics of consumerism, false: "So this means that a lady can no longer beat eggs without a machine?" (Episode 9). (The play on the words *razbijati jaje,* "to beat eggs," in the original Serbo-Croatian gets lost in translation here. Another implication of the question might be, "So now a lady has to have a machine to break a guy's balls?") But a few complaints like these notwithstanding, the little (and not-so-little) consumer indulgences proliferate over the run of the series. In the Yugoslavia of *Vruć vetar,* the arc of the economic universe is short, and it bends toward affluence.

When all is said and done, Šurda actually does end up realizing the Yugoslav Dream, living comfortably after "making it" as the owner of a popular urban hair salon, where he finally achieves success as a purveyor of the type of "everyday" luxuries—with cosmetics, fashion items, and personal services like hair styling not least among them—that Yugoslav socialism managed to put within the reach of ordinary consumers (Episode 10; Figure 30). By the end of the series, Šurda and Vesna are living in a sophisticated apartment, smartly appointed with modern furniture and plenty of the bright orange plastic lampshades that were de rigeur for the times (Episode 9; Figure 32). The family is no doubt comfortable—they do get, literally and figuratively, the gleaming modern "bathroom lined with tiles" that Matija Bećković had rhapsodized about in his piece "On the Yugoslavs"—but it remains a bit unclear what, exactly, will assure a "happy end" (Episode 10; Figure 33).

Šurda makes good less through hard work and drive than through a combination of luck, talent, and a knack for exploiting the system and the opportunities for quick advancement through connections that it occasionally presented. (If anyone in the series is shown as "grabbing, just grabbing," it is Vesna, a fact that might well be read as a contemporary commentary on the perceived gender dimensions of the country's consumption dynamics.) Here, too, *Vruć vetar* offered a message for viewers. By the time the series was broadcast in 1980, Yugoslavs had certainly developed a popular stereotype of themselves as savvy seekers of the Good Life. They had not, it is fair to say, developed a corresponding stereotype of themselves as driven, diligent workaholics who were intent on laboring incessantly to finance all that material abundance. (There were, to be sure, some regional variations in this respect, especially regarding the Slovenes' stereotype of themselves, and there was an ample basis on which Yugoslavs from any part of the country could have supported a self-image as hard-working, thrifty, and goal-oriented. One need only look at the sacrifices made by the hundreds of thousands of *Gastarbeiter* to recognize that. But the images sustained in popular culture went in the opposite direction.) *Vruć vetar* suggested that being just an ordinary Yugoslav—more bon vivant than Stakhanovite—might be, in fact, enough. And that was, in the end, a message about the ultimate accessibility of the Good Life and the Yugoslav Dream.

Many of the same dynamics of material striving and material achievement were at work in another popular Yugoslav series of the time, *Grlom u jagode,* directed by Srđan Karanović, shot in 1975 and aired initially on Belgrade's TV 2 in 1976, with distribution and repeat broadcasts around the country later. The title of the show—literally, "with one's throat into strawberries"—is an idiom that connotes an action done with no preparation, impulsively, without planning or restraint, perhaps in pursuit of something attractive. Virtually impossible to translate neatly, it might be adequately rendered as "Headfirst into Strawberries," which captures something of the idea of a rash rush toward a tempting target, or perhaps as "Up to His Neck in Strawberries," which would connote a sense of being overwhelmed and incapacitated by circumstances that would otherwise be, if not for their excess, pleasing and rewarding. A fixture of the Yugoslav television landscape in the years since it premiered, *Grlom u jagode* showed viewers, time and time again, just how captivated ordinary Yugoslavs were by the consumer culture that surrounded them, and just how much there was to love.

The central thematic device of the show, as voiced by the characters on a number of occasions, was the problem of "how to become a real person" [*kako postati čovek*]. That phrase in Serbo-Croatian also has the connotation of "becoming a man" or "growing up," and over the course of the ten episodes, viewers saw the characters of the show, like socialist Yugoslavia itself, grow older, richer, and (perhaps) wiser, or at least more worldly. Shot as a combination of flashbacks coupled with present-day mockumentary interviews with the now adult members of the cast, the series followed its hero Branislav Živković, known by his nickname Bane Bumbar, and an ensemble of his friends and love interests from their school days into young adulthood and employment. Each episode is anchored to one year of the decade from 1960 to 1969, with more flashbacks used to illustrate the protagonists' childhoods in the simpler times of the 1950s (these shown in black and white, unlike the rest of the series). As it catalogued the lives of this generation born at the end of World War II, *Grlom u jagode* moved, fittingly enough, from the comparative austerity of the postwar decades through the achievements, abundance, and adaptations of the 1960s. And it left no doubt that by the mid-1970s, when the series was produced, Yugoslavs were already coming to see the preceding decade as one of tremendous change and maturation: the time when Yugoslavia grew up.

Along with the year-by-year arc through the 1960s, each episode was tied thematically to important aspects of everyday life: courtship, leisure time, sports and play, popular music and movies, travel and tourism, sex, fashion and style, illness, transportation, money, work, and much more. When viewers looked back in a given episode at "How Bane Dressed, 1946–1965," "How Bane Got Around, 1945–1967," or "How Bane Lived at Home, 1945–1969," they were surely recalling more than just this single character's experiences. Bane Bumbar's story was, by proxy, Yugoslavia's story.

And in episode after episode, audiences saw just how much Yugoslavia's story across those three decades was one of rising standards and rising expectations—and the joys and anxieties that came with all that new abundance. Simply put, the culture of consumption was everywhere. The very first action shot of the entire series, in fact, shows Bane doing the shopping in a large, bright, modern, and bustling urban supermarket, just one of hundreds of images of a radiant present (and a just as radiant recent past) that appear in the course of *Grlom u jagode*[40] (Episode 1; Figure 45). The quest for the Yugoslav Dream turns up again and again throughout the series, as does, revealingly, the realization of that dream: this was a show, in many ways, about the Good Life *lived*.

There were, to be sure, some twists and turns along the way. Struggles and setbacks and misunderstandings abounded, and it is clear that the members of Bane's privileged postwar generation were, in some ways, very different creatures from their parents and grandparents. Audiences saw this mismatch, for example, in one delightful interchange that illustrated how an understanding of modern fashion did not always cross the generational

---

40. All text and visual references are to *Grlom u jagode*, DVD, directed by Srđan Karanović (1975; Belgrade, 2004). The series was produced in 1975 and first aired on Belgrade's TV 2 in 1976. It is published on DVD by PGP/RTS as part of the Zlatne Serije series, item number DV-1130204. In 1985 Karanović brought the ensemble back together for a feature film titled *Jagode u grlu* [Strawberries in the throat]. Made from the vantage point of the economic decline of the 1980s, the movie is something akin to a Yugoslav version of *The Big Chill*, a darker nostalgia trip that tracks the further twists and turns of the characters' lives, with a good deal of emphasis on what had been lost and compromised in the intervening years.

divide. In this encounter Bane's father asks him, with a mixture of earnestness and exasperation, "Why are Partizan brand jeans worse than Lee's 2E or, what are they called, Johann Strauss?" "*Levi* Strauss!" comes the equally exasperated reply (Episode 6). Obviously not all of Yugoslavia was changing at the same pace, or headed in the same direction. But Bane, like so many others of his generation, gets his Levi's in the end, and shows them off proudly (Episode 6; Figure 39).

The series was gently nostalgic, but it did acknowledge that the Good Life was not necessarily the Easy Life for most Yugoslavs. By and large, the characters in *Grlom u jagode* do end up "making it." Yet there are plenty of struggles. In that spirit, one of Bane's friends reflects on the difficulties of getting an apartment of one's own:

> For me and me generation, and for many residents of Belgrade and Yugoslavia, an apartment was, and remained, the biggest problem. We spent hours, days, months, years in conversations, daydreams, and schemes about how we could work it out to get an apartment. As the years passed, this kept happening more and more often. We had the impression that having the right to an apartment was, really, having the right to live. We complained, we panicked, we got desperate. Really, it was hard. (Episode 10)

The show also gave voice to some misgivings about the culture of consumption or, at the very least, about whether the new engagement with abundance really could deliver all it had once appeared to promise these young Yugoslavs. Having "arrived" in the mid-1970s, many of the now grown-up characters in the ensemble seem to realize that real satisfaction in life will not come purely from material attainments. As one of Bane's companions muses in another of the self-reflective present-day monologues that are a recurring motif of the series, the children of the postwar years were utterly consumed with consumption, but in that frenzy to acquire they had misunderstood something about what it took to "become a grown-up":

> The biggest problem for me and for my generation was that we knew more about what we had to have than what we were actually able to have.
> We had to study, but that cost money. We had to have an apartment. That cost money as well. A car cost money. Not to mention those little things like going to the movies, to the theatre, to cafes, outings with a girlfriend. All that cost money....
> We thought that first we had to have all those things, and then we would become real people.
> Life, however, wanted us to become people first, and then slowly, step by step, we would get all those things we desired so much.
> And now we have them—for the most part, we have them—but we no longer have that youthful desire to enjoy them. (Episode 9)

Here and elsewhere in the show, there was no small dose of ambivalence about the perceived imperatives to consume, even for those who had "made it" and could afford a big, single-family *vila* and a Mercedes (Episode 10; Figure 42). Clearly *Grlom u jagode* meant to give its viewers more than just a shallow paean to the pursuit of wealth.

Nevertheless, the series was, in its fond gaze back to the 1950s and 1960s, more than a little indulgent toward the material markers of the Yugoslav Dream. Judging from what Yugoslav audiences could see in *Grlom u jagode,* the Good Life looked, in a word, good. And it was clear that for more or less ordinary Yugoslavs like Branislav "Bane Bumbar" Živković, that way of living offered a lot to love. The struggles had paid off. The obstacles had been overcome. Impatience and grasping gave way to some relaxation and enjoyment. The "conversations, daydreams, and schemes" turned out well enough.

To complete that picture, viewers were presented scene after iconic scene of Yugoslav everyday life: the purchase of the Živković family's first television (Episode 1; Figure 34) and evenings spent gathered around the set (Episode 3; Figure 35), plentiful meals in a comfortable and well-furnished home (Episode 10; Figure 36), pleasurable vacations spent by this Serb family on "our" Adriatic coast in Croatia (Episode 7; Figure 37), the full-on pursuit of high style and brand-name fashion, and the hip high life of the young "in" crowd spent in bars, nightclubs, and discos (Episode 4; Figure 38). They saw the struggle—successful enough, in the end—to find, fit out, and afford an apartment for an independent, grown-up life, one that would be suitably modern, stylish, and comfortable (Episodes 9 and 10; Figures 43 and 44). And they watched a generation's progression from bicycles and public transportation on to Vespas and motorcycles, and then on again to auto fever (Episodes 8 and 10; Figures 41 and 42), all capped with a poignant and telling scene of a once treasured little Fića, the object of so much pride and care and celebration when it was purchased, now abandoned and rusting by the side of the road: the youthful love no longer good enough for those who had learned that they could love bigger, better, and more.

Feeling the Love: The Culture of Abundance in Public Opinion

While the changing experience of modern consumer abundance reshaped the daily lives of ordinary Yugoslavs, it also had profound effects on the fortunes of the Yugoslav government and the League of Communists. As explained in chapter 1, the Communists, as leaders of a broad-based resistance movement during World War II, began their administration with substantially more legitimacy than their counterparts in most other socialist states. Their authoritarianism and cruel treatment of enemies, real and imagined, quickly dissipated a considerable amount of that initial goodwill, however, leaving the party continually on the lookout for ways to repair its image and restore the popular support it had lost. In the 1960s and 1970s, the country's dramatic economic growth and the vast new opportunities for consumerist satisfaction gave the government and the party a means of repairing some of the damage. For all their complaints about the socially corrosive effects of consumer culture, the Yugoslav authorities plainly enjoyed a much more secure position because of it—at least, that is, while the good times lasted.

The connections between the government's consumption policy and its support among the Yugoslav public were fairly intuitive matters for many, and contemporary commentators both sympathetic to and hostile toward Yugoslavia's socialist experiment frequently noted those links. Yugoslav-American journalist Duško Doder, for example, saw the government's promotion of high living standards as one of its most spectacular achievements. Like a number of the critics of Yugoslav consumerism, he tended to read the country's experience as an exercise in "bourgeois socialism," although, for Doder, this was clearly meant as a compliment, not the slur that the phrase was originally intended to be.

Analysts who, like Doder, interpreted the consumerist expansion as a prime source of popular support for the government were certainly correct, as was the observation that consumer culture might, in the long run, yield even greater stabilizing and unifying effects. "The trend toward middle-class existence," as Doder recognized in 1978, just at the end of Yugoslavia's long run of good fortune, "carries with it both a promise and a threat." For Yugoslav socialism itself, consumerism and its satisfaction seemed to hold out the prospect of both salvation and undoing: "*The promise is that a large body of citizenry will develop a vested interest in the system,*" one that might ultimately even help accomplish the much-desired goal of multiethnic unity, helping to "weld together the Yugoslav nations into a socialist commonwealth and gradually blunt the edge of nationalist animosities." But there were dangers for the security of the one-party monopoly as well. "The threat" was that the further evolution of the population along "middle-class" lines would also bring with it "the long-term prospect of pluralistic evolution," which would have been unpalatable, and indeed untenable, to the communist leadership.[41]

In linking prosperity and the growth of consumer society with the "threat" of uncontrollable pluralistic change, Doder's argument here recapitulates the once fashionable Western belief that the market and democracy necessarily go hand in hand. Market reforms were at one time the standard prescription for the political ills of the socialist world. That theory was, in the end, overtaken by the events of 1989, while the evolution of China since the 1980s stands as the most glaring contradiction of the thesis.

---

41. Dusko Doder, *The Yugoslavs* (New York, 1978), 60 (emphasis added).

As it happened, Yugoslavia never had a genuine occasion to put this principle to the test. Doder's observations appeared just as the Yugoslav economy was about to slide toward a near total collapse. At that point the government had reaped the benefits of a consumerist policy for years, but given the sad course of history, it would never be given the opportunity to enjoy the deeper transformation of the sort that Doder envisioned, whereby consumers who were happy enough for the moment would be converted into committed supporters with a genuine stake in the preservation of the system.

Instead, the benefits of consumerism for the Yugoslav regime were shallow and impermanent, a predicament probed in more detail in the final chapter. Nevertheless, the payoff was quite substantial while it lasted. For a long time Yugoslavs were inclined not only to buy, but to "buy in" as well. We must remember that when times were good, in the 1960s and 1970s, many ordinary citizens were quite pleased with what they had, and proud of their country for achieving that.

At least before the massive downturn of Yugoslavia's last decade, public opinion polling generally showed widespread approval of the economic accomplishments of the system thus far, and similarly high expectations about what the future would hold.[42] When asked, for example, just after the economic reforms of 1965, "Do you believe that the living standard will generally improve in the coming year?" fully 54 percent of all Yugoslavs surveyed answered affirmatively, 28 percent foresaw no increase in standards, and 18 percent responded that they did not know or provided no answer.[43]

In addition, the country's economic success was, by the mid-1960s, becoming both a characteristic and a characteristically well-liked feature in the minds of the public. Along these lines, in response to the question, "What do you like the most about Yugoslav society?" Yugoslav respondents in 1964 placed a strong emphasis on economic development and the improvement

---

42. See, for example, Svetozar Ćulibrk, *Želje i strahovanja naroda Jugoslavije* and Zlata Grebo, *Želje i strahovanja jugoslovenske žene* (jointly published in one volume) (Belgrade, 1965); Ljiljana Baćević et al., *Jugoslovensko javno mnenje o aktuelnim političkim i društvenim pitanjima*, volume 3, 1964, in Jugoslovensko javno mnenje, Series A: Izveštaji o rezultatima anketnih istraživanja (Belgrade, 1964), 63–82, 146–166; idem, *Jugoslovensko javno mnenje o aktuelnim političkim i društvenim pitanjima 1965*, volume 6, 1965, in ibid. (Belgrade, 1965), 77–96; Mijat Damjanović et al., *Jugoslovensko javno mnenje o privrednoj reformi 1965*, volume 7, in ibid. (Belgrade, 1965), 57–61, 77–82, 83–89, 90–98, 99–102, 103–108, 109–114, 145–151; idem, *Jugoslovensko javno mnenje 1966*, volume 8, 1966, in ibid. (Belgrade, 1967), 9–18, 19–52, 74–95.

43. Damjanović et al., *Jugoslovensko javno mnenje o privrednoj reformi 1965*, 66. The data document some drop-off in expectations from responses offered to the same question a few months earlier in May 1965, just before the introduction of the reforms, when the figures were 61%, Yes; 20%, No; and 19%, Don't Know/No Answer. Ibid. Price hikes associated with the reform caused consumers to reduce their spending in certain areas, especially those for which demand was most elastic (e.g., entertainment, eating out, tobacco, and beverages). Ibid., 145–151.

of the living standard, with 25.8 percent of all respondents identifying one of these features as the most appealing. Although more Yugoslavs pointed to freedom, democracy, and equality as the society's best features, and fully 9.9 percent answered "everything," when asked what they liked most about Yugoslavia, these results do show how important the improved function of the economy had become by this time.[44] Just as important, the results of this survey offer us a rich sense of just how the economic changes and improvements in consumption opportunities were experienced by ordinary Yugoslavs. That comes across clearly, for example, in these selections from the respondents' statements about what they liked most:

The possibility to purchase everything that a person desires [male, about 38 years old, illiterate, private farmer, from Bosnia-Herzegovina]

That we have electricity and that nice buildings have been built [female, 60 years old, illiterate, housewife, from Serbia]

That our government treats all national groups [narodi] *equally, and that it is trying to raise the backward national groups* [zaostali narodi] *out of their centuries-long backwardness, in which the other national groups are assisting unselfishly* [female, about 41 years old, semi-skilled worker, member of the Partisan resistance, member of the League of Communists of Yugoslavia, from Slovenia]

The cinemas and theaters [female, 20 years old, literate, unskilled worker, from Serbia]

That everyone is able to find employment and to live well, and that everyone goes to school [female, 26 years old, worker, eighth-grade education, from Serbia]

That we have roads, factories, hospitals, schools, transportation, construction. We have everything we need, and if we work, we are also able to buy what

---

44. Individual free responses were coded to one of eight categories. The figures for the entire federation were as follows: Freedom and democracy, 25.2%; equality, 21.7%; economic development, 13.3%; the improved standard of living, 12.6%; self-management, 6.8%; social and health insurance, 3.2%; other, 7.3%; "everything," 9.9%. There were interesting regional differences: respondents in the developed republics of Croatia, Slovenia, and Serbia proper (without Kosovo or Vojvodina) were substantially more likely to identify either the improved standard of living or economic development as the elements of Yugoslav society that appealed to them most; those from Bosnia-Herzegovina, Kosovo, and Montenegro were much more likely to emphasize freedom, democracy, and equality. Baćević et al., *Jugoslovensko javno mnenje o aktuelnim političkim i društvenim pitanjima*, 3:63–82. Compare the results of a companion survey from 1965, when, in response to the question, "What do you like *least* about Yugoslav society?" 14.6% of all respondents offered an answer that was coded by the survey administrators in the category "the low standard and the overly wide range of personal incomes." The figure for respondents for Slovenia was, for this category, a remarkable 25.1%, far higher than that for the territory with the next highest rate, less-developed Macedonia, at 18.3%. Ibid., 6:79. The coding here is problematic, however, as it prevents us from distinguishing dissatisfaction attributable to living standards from complaints about income inequality.

we need [male, about 39 years old, member of an agricultural collective, from Bosnia-Herzegovina]

Everything is nice, and especially our little village, which has been developed and gotten electricity [female, about 60 years old, housewife, illiterate, member of the Partisan resistance in World War II, from Macedonia]

With each passing day, life is getting better [female, about 49 years old, semiskilled worker, elementary-school education, from Croatia][45]

As sentiments like these suggest, through the emphasis on raising living standards, the Yugoslav government had found ways to bolster its legitimacy in the eyes of ordinary citizens. By creating "the possibility to purchase everything that a person desires," the system helped ensure that many would, in effect, buy in. Policy had become personal.

Strong endorsements of the path that Yugoslav society had taken continued to hold through the mid-1970s. One survey of four thousand Yugoslavs published in 1976, for example, reported overwhelming levels of popular satisfaction with living standards. Asked whether they were pleased with their home, for example, only 15 percent answered that they were dissatisfied; 39 percent reported that they were mostly satisfied, and fully 46 percent said they were totally satisfied. Satisfaction with other chief elements of consumption was higher still: with regard to their clothing, 36 percent expressed total satisfaction, and 56 percent said they were mostly satisfied; only 8 percent reported that they were dissatisfied. For the quality of Yugoslavs' diets, the corresponding figures were 53 percent, 43 percent, and 4 percent, respectively.[46]

Ordinary Yugoslavs became, moreover, deeply attached to their ability to pursue the Yugoslav Dream. Consistently, there was massive resistance to the idea that living standards might have to decrease in order to improve the overall functioning of the Yugoslav economy, and such objections proved even stronger after the economic collapse hit in the late 1970s. In one series of public opinion surveys conducted in Slovenia, the fraction of respondents who judged "less money for increasing personal incomes and the living standard" to be an unacceptable economic remedy remained remarkably high from 1971 through 1988, dipping below a majority only in 1972, during the party's most intense campaigning against "liberalism" and "enrichment," and once more in 1980. In the hard times of the mid- to late 1980s, almost three-quarters of those surveyed deemed any such effort to reduce incomes and living standards unacceptable.[47]

---

45. Ibid., 3:78–82.
46. "Stavovi jugoslavenskih potrošača prema EP," *Ideja*, no. 8 (July 1976): 8.
47. Niko Toš et al., *Slovenski utrip: rezultati raziskav javnega mnenja, 1988–1989* (Ljubljana, n.d. [ca. 1989]), 135.

To a remarkable extent, regular citizens even seemed to like and enjoy their exposure to advertising and the other trappings of market culture. For example, according to one poll conducted in the 1970s concerning the effectiveness and desirability of television commercials, approximately 75 percent of the surveyed group judged such advertisements to be very useful or somewhat useful, whereas only 4 percent found them to be mostly not useful or not useful at all.[48] Being "useful," of course, is not quite the same thing as being well-liked, but on that count Yugoslav advertising seems to have done fairly well, too. In another survey, published in 1976, 53 percent of respondents indicated that they liked the ads they encountered on television, on the radio, in the press, and elsewhere ["*svidaju mi se*"—"I like them," "they appeal to me"]; 34 percent reported that they did not pay attention to advertising; and only 13 percent reported that advertising annoyed them ["*smetaju me*"].[49] This high level of general approval of advertising proved quite durable, persisting even after the sharp economic downturn replaced the optimism of the 1960s and 1970s with tighter budgets, disappointed expectations, even shortages. According to one 1983 survey, for example, approximately 74 percent of the Yugoslav population believed advertising and commercial promotion [*reklame* and *ekonomska propaganda*] to be generally useful and beneficial.[50]

As encountered earlier in the discussion of the rise of the industry of commercial promotion, viewership of television commercials remained quite high. Compared to Western audiences, fewer Yugoslavs seemed inclined to simply tune out the advertisements. In a survey conducted among residents of Vojvodina in 1990, for example, only approximately 22 percent of respondents indicated that they rarely or never listened to or watched advertisements on radio and television; almost as many, 18 percent, said they regularly paid attention to such programming, and 25 percent reported that they often did so.[51]

There were, to be sure, occasional complaints from the public about excesses, along with suggestions that Yugoslavia's rush to adopt modern fashions and the most intense styles of commercial promotion was perhaps somewhat overblown. But the evidence from Yugoslav sources repeatedly reflects a largely positive popular reception of market culture. In the main, the record leaves the unmistakable impression that advertising practice benefited by being so tightly associated with the country's new culture of

---

48. Tkalac, address in *Zbornik predavanja sa seminara vizuelnog komunikacij*, 55.
49. "Stavovi jugoslavenskih potrošača prema EP," 8.
50. The study further revealed that women and young people from eighteen to twenty-four years of age were more likely to have favorable opinions; men generally paid less attention to advertising. Negative attitudes were expressed most frequently by the uneducated. See *MM: marketing magazin* 3, no. 3 (March 1983): 12.
51. Branimir Brkljač, *Efekti ekonomsko-propagandnog programa koji se emituje na radiju i televiziji* (Novi Sad, 1990), 9.

consumption, something that many ordinary Yugoslavs cherished even if they understood that some of their compatriots thought they should feel otherwise.

Buying In and Selling Out: Consumers Who Love Too Much and the Leaders Who Love Them

Others benefited from those links to the new culture of abundance as well. Critically, it helped to cement the widespread popular image of Yugoslav exceptionalism, which the regime valued and cultivated. During the fat years of consumerist expansion, it was easy for Yugoslavs to believe that their country represented something special—perhaps uniquely successful. Hard as it may be to imagine this from today's vantage point, many Yugoslavs saw themselves as having found a place among the winners in the larger global game of politics and economics. As they experienced the pleasure of seeing their living standards approach those of at least some parts of Western Europe, their attitudes about themselves and their neighbors began to change as well. A past sense of inferiority began to disappear, with unexpected and, for some, unsettling results. If they had once gone shopping in Italy out of a sense of real deprivation, now things were different: "Yugoslav visitors in Trieste," Richard West observed, "were smug, even triumphalist." West relates how one Yugoslav shopper in the Italian port-city-turned-international-shopping-center explained to him how the meaning of those legendary cross-border buying binges had shifted with the changing fortunes of Yugoslavia's socialist system: "We used to come here to buy better quality, now we come because it's cheaper."[52]

Italy, like much of Western Europe during the 1970s, was then suffering through significant economic difficulties of its own. The effects of that downturn would spill over soon enough into Yugoslavia, burdening its economy as well, but at the time the reversal of fortunes, albeit still just relative, apparently proved a source of great annoyance to some Triestini. The perceived strength of the Yugoslav system is evident in these comments West recorded during visits to Trieste in the 1970s.

> We depend on the Yugoslavs now…Fifteen years ago I had a car and the Yugoslavs had nothing to eat. Now they have a car and I don't have two. The fact is they are advancing and we are going backwards…They don't have our wages but they don't have our worries about paying for health and their children's education. The money they make they can spend and have a good time here in Trieste…It's terrible here, strikes, inflation, and an old lady like me

---

52. Richard West, *Tito and the Rise and Fall of Yugoslavia* (New York, 1994), 278.

doesn't dare go for a walk at night. But over in Yugoslavia it's fine. If we could vote again, I'd vote for Trieste to go to the Yugoslavs.[53]

These sentiments are extreme in a few respects, but they communicate a fundamental truth about the international image of the Yugoslav system during the 1960s and 1970s and, accordingly, about the relative security of the Yugoslav government at that time. Italo-Yugoslav relations following World War II had gotten off to a dreadfully rocky start—ironically, precisely over Trieste, the city that was serving so conspicuously to soak up the demand for fashion and modernity that the Yugoslav economy still could not quite satisfy. The two sides had very nearly gone to war. Now, however, as the result of its many apparent successes, the Yugoslav system had begun to look not only acceptable but downright admirable as well. And the country's soaring reputation in international circles was not, of course, lost on regular Yugoslavs, many of whom were well aware that their system was increasingly mentioned as a model for the rest of the developing world.

If many ordinary Yugoslavs were, as the evidence suggests, eagerly "buying in" to the system, we must wonder whether they were, at the same time, "selling out." Some observers of the country's embrace of consumerism have interpreted the events of the 1960s and 1970s as plain evidence of the party-state's instrumentalist grasping for legitimacy, that is, for public support of continued communist control. Mihailo Marković and his fellow Praxists, for example, took precisely this view, incorporating it into their broader critique of the country's drift toward consumer society. From this perspective, Yugoslavia's surrender to consumerism had achieved precisely the result the governing Communists had desired: the authorities' standing in the eyes of the public was buoyed, at least for a time, by constantly rising living standards. In this respect, Marković saw the Yugoslav strategy as one common to all socialist regimes, many of which were, in fact, able to dramatically increase living standards in the immediate postwar decades and thereby ensure that their citizens would be less restive, if not exactly contented. But although the Praxist critique in this case, as elsewhere, was couched in general terms, the Yugoslav government was clearly being singled out for the most intense criticism. For, obviously, no country fit the description Marković offered as well as Yugoslavia: "Once the followers of Marx established themselves safely in power," he wrote, "the means became an end in itself. A cult of material production gradually lost its earlier function of overcoming poverty, and of generating a basis for self-development of all individuals. *The good life was reduced to a comfortable life, a wealth of needs to a need for material wealth—like any bourgeois society.*"[54]

---

53. Ibid.
54. Marković, *Democratic Socialism*, 178–179 (emphasis added).

In the interpretation that Marković put forth, consumer society was, in fact, practically the *only* real source for communist legitimacy in Yugoslavia. Having betrayed its original commitments to worker control and a radical devolution of power to ordinary people, Marković suggested, the Yugoslav government was now in most respects just a self-serving, power-loving, "real socialist" regime like any other. An instrumentalist approach to consumption was therefore, if not the only strategy available, certainly the least threatening. "This new Statist society," he argued, "was not able to legitimate itself by meeting either the socialist demand for more social equality, nor even the customary bourgeois demand for more political liberty. *Its main virtue was its ability to produce goods and increase consumption.*"[55] Ultimately, he concluded, consumerism only served to paper over the deeper failings of the Yugoslav system, which "stayed half way between Statism and self-government, oligarchy and democracy, political centralism and decentralization, the plan and the market."[56]

As uncomplimentary as this assessment is, critics could sometimes voice their disagreements with the government's approaches, and their suspicions of its motivations, in even harsher terms. Duško Doder recounts being told by a "left-wing sociologist" from Yugoslavia (quite possibly another Praxist) that Yugoslavia's profound consumerist orientation had been undertaken deliberately in the interest of social pacification and, perhaps not so obviously, for social discipline as well. The government, in this view, had encouraged the wholehearted adoption of a consumerist mind-set, and then, in the most Machiavellian manner, had used consumption policy as both carrot and stick to keep the populace in line and on course:

> What is so diabolical about this regime...is that they have figured out how to use consumerism for their own ends. You have the entire country wrapped up in a pseudo-bourgeois culture with everybody trying to move up. You give the majority of people what they want and their attention is diverted from politics and other such things. But every now and then the regime wants to remind us that whatever we have is ours only because we have been allowed it. It is like a privilege we were granted by the regime, a privilege that can be taken away. They don't want to do that, they just want to remind us of these facts."[57]

It was possible, then, to interpret the reorientation of Yugoslav society toward consumerism as a deliberate, "top-down" phenomenon. From this perspective, consumer society appears to have been imposed on the country much like self-management was; there was little that was democratic

---

55. Ibid., 179 (emphasis added). The author went on to observe that, after 1977, the growth rate declined rapidly, and so this most critical source of legitimacy quickly evaporated.
56. Ibid., 186.
57. Doder, *The Yugoslavs*, 55.

about it. And if consumer culture was not, in fact, intentionally created as a tool of social control, it was, in this view, at least consciously managed to that end.

The problem, in other words, was that the Yugoslav system had indeed delivered abundance and opportunity, and that too many Yugoslavs were, in a word, loving it. But is it fair to conclude that the Yugoslav government relied on consumerism to lull its citizens into a happy stupor that distracted them from the country's pressing problems and their own lack of any substantial control of the political system? Had Yugoslav Communists swindled the people into blithely trading away freedom for Fiats, worker control for washing machines, democracy for dish soap? Had the authorities deliberately used consumerism, as domestic critics of various stripes suggested, as a new opiate of the masses?

As explained in the preceding examination of the rise of the industry of commercial promotion and the genuinely hostile response to consumerism that came from party circles, the record points to a contrary conclusion. This is not to suggest, of course, that the Titoist approach was blind to the prospect that widespread consumer satisfaction would bolster the popular support and acceptance of the regime. It was not. Clearly, the government was sensitive to the many benefits of consumer abundance. But as shown earlier in this volume, the complaints that issued from government and party leaders were frequent enough, and earnest enough, to void any claim that Yugoslav society had been remade along consumerist, crypto-capitalist lines as part of some conscious, diabolical scheme.

If the popular culture of consumption was the creature of anyone's *conscious* plans, it was constructed not by the authorities but largely through the work of a dedicated cohort of advertising and marketing specialists. In this respect, it cannot be characterized as purely a "bottom-up" phenomenon, for these industry workers were themselves part of an economic and political élite, positioned at neither the highest nor the lowest levels but rather somewhere in between. Some of the heightened attention to consumption was no doubt generated naturally through the give-and-take of competitive relationships between Yugoslav firms (which were themselves led by members of another important economic and political élite). But as explained earlier, we must remember that the Yugoslav business environment, at least in terms of decision making at the enterprise level, was really not all that competitive. A number of firms adopted a genuinely competitive orientation toward the marketplace; many did not. Thus I conclude that consumer culture was built and sustained more by the *creators* of advertising—who did have, as we have seen, a strong and genuine conviction in the value of competition and the market—than by the wishes of the advertisers themselves. On this count, it bears noting once again that for a long time the advertising and marketing industry struggled to convince many enterprise leaders that commercial promotion was truly necessary and effective in the Yugoslav context. Yugoslav business surely had a considerable stake in the rise of a consumerist orientation, but the most interested, most motivated parties were the advertising and marketing specialists and ordinary consumers themselves.

It would, of course, be a mistake to overlook the effects of the government's actions in creating and nurturing consumer culture in Yugoslavia. The country's communist leadership did indeed permit, and even sponsor, the new orientation toward the satisfaction of consumer desire. Ultimately, however, it would be even more misleading to ignore the genuine *popular* roots of the new culture of consumption. Consumerism was not simply imposed from the top down as a matter of state policy; in many important ways, as we have seen, it also developed from the ground up. If Yugoslavia managed to arrive at something that looked rather like Western consumer society in some respects, it did so primarily as the result of the wishes, wants, needs, and hopes of ordinary consumers, that is, through the everyday actions of millions of citizens who opted for this new way of living over and over again as they shopped and made their purchases and then enjoyed (and enjoyed displaying) their wealth. Some or even many of these yearnings for the Good Life quite possibly were, as the critics suggested, "false"—that is, called forth and scripted through the black(ened) arts of consumer persuasion. False as they may have been, they were nonetheless *felt* to be genuine by many Yugoslav consumers, and, in that sense, they had a very real quality that cannot be ignored. Through that reality, these new desires made and changed Yugoslav history.

To see such needs and wants as exclusively or even predominantly the device of either a cynical and calculating communist cabal or an equally manipulative business establishment runs the risk of stripping out of the Yugoslav story the popular will of ordinary citizen-actors, thereby compounding a problem that is already severe enough in the historiography of communism. Even assuming for the sake of argument that the party and state leaders actually were happy to see consumerism turn citizens into docile sheep, as the harshest opponents of the new orientation suggested, such a strategy could only work successfully if the indulgence in consumerist desires was, in fact, something highly valued and deeply held by a large share of the population. As such, the popular engagement with shopping and spending and wishing had to amount to a repudiation of, or at the very least a disregard for, the attitudes of the critics. The flourishing culture of consumption could only inure to the credit of the socialist system as long as millions of ordinary Yugoslavs were, in other words, loving it.

For many years they were, with very real and very serious consequences for the cohesion and stability of Yugoslav society. If we can, as I believe we should, see our way clear to interpret their history as not one of near total manipulation but instead one of intentionality, choice, and expression, we end up with a new and different understanding of what made Yugoslavia—and, with it, socialism—work, at least for some time. Yugoslavia was not a democratic country, but in the end the popular culture that mattered most for its political life—Yugoslav consumer culture—was much more a product of the *demos* than its critics were able to recognize or admit.

8 Needing It

The Eclipse of the Dream, the Collapse of Socialism,
and the Death of Yugoslavia

With each passing day, life is getting better.
> —Croatian public opinion survey respondent, 1964

—Daddy...what does "happy end" mean in English?
—Happy end?
—Yeah.
—That's something that doesn't exist in real life, son.
—What do you mean, it doesn't exist?
—That sort of nice, happy ending doesn't exist!
—And "biznis," what does that mean?
—Drop it! I have to get ready—you see that I'm in a hurry!
> —from the final episode of the Yugoslav television
> series *Vruć vetar,* 1980

In socialist Yugoslavia, consumerism created a new New Class. Contrary to Marxian models and the stated goals of Yugoslav socialist policy, which imputed class identities based on a person's role in a system of production, membership in this New Class was predicated, in essence, upon participation in a modern style of mass consumption, a complex of behaviors, tastes, and attitudes that in many respects resembled those seen in the classic Western sites of contemporary consumer society. As the case presented throughout this volume demonstrates, its emergence was triggered by the government's acknowledgment of a perceived need to satisfy consumer desires as a central goal of economic policy, then further encouraged by the self-management system's nod toward the values of the market. Once the idea of consumer sovereignty had gained some rhetorical foothold in the country's dominant ideology, the nascent industries of commercial promotion steadily advanced that concept as a legitimate and necessary premise

---

Sources for the epigraphs: Ljiljana Baćević et al., *Jugoslovensko javno mnenje o aktuelnim političkim i društvenim pitanjima,* volume 3, in Jugoslovensko javno mnenje, Series A: Izveštaji o rezultatima anketnih istraživanja (Belgrade: Institut društvenih nauka, Centar za Istraživanje Javnog Mnenja, 1964), 81; *Vruć vetar,* episode 10.

for the conduct of virtually all Yugoslav business. A remarkable expansion of advertising, marketing, and retailing followed, working in tandem with deep-seated popular yearnings and government policy (or at least sufficient governmental inaction) to produce decades of consumption and consumerism so ardent and unreserved that Yugoslavia became, in the end, quite unlike any other communist country.

Paired with the market culture cultivated by the new business elites, a vital popular consumer culture also became a defining feature of Yugoslav daily life. In the wake of these transformations, however, the sharp slump in the country's economic fortunes that began in the late 1970s left businesses with a pool of potential customers eager to buy and more open than ever to promises of consumer abundance, but without the financial wherewithal to satisfy their desires. In the 1960s and 1970s Yugoslavs learned to dream big. Later, they could not hope to make their dreams come true.

The nature of the consumerist New Class and its implications for this final stage of downturn and disillusionment are the subjects of the analysis in this concluding chapter. The ordinary Yugoslavs who made up the new New Class had not only habituated to the abundance that had become the familiar surroundings of everyday life; they had developed a profound reliance on it as well. They had, in other words, come to need it. Just as much, they needed realistic prospects that it would continue. Failing that, one of the most important foundations of social solidarity, and system legitimacy, was stripped away.

Yugoslavia flourished because of its embrace of consumption, and, in the end, consumption helped destroy it. Yet for all that significance, the Yugoslav experience reveals more than just the meaning of consumer culture and market culture in this single specific locale. In questioning the particulars of what happened in Yugoslavia, we should be sensitive to how it may also extend our understanding of the deeper significance of consumption in socialist societies as a wider category. Here we encounter a critical testing ground for what contemporary consumption scholarship has customarily analyzed as the global spread of cultural forms produced by specifically capitalist economic relations. Yugoslavia's experience gives us a much richer picture of the causes, conditions, and consequences of those processes of diffusion—as well as their possible limits. It helps us see what in these new cultural patterns and cross-border transfers was (and was not) "capitalist," and it sheds new light on the power of business practices to structure social relations, politics, and culture.

Beyond that, and on a still more expansive conceptual plane, the case also raises serious questions about the broader relationship of consumer abundance, and popular cultures built on that abundance, to the efficacy, stability, legitimacy, and public approval of economic and political systems more generally. The Yugoslavs, it must be remembered, were not alone in needing it.

It's How You Use It: The Consumer Experience and the Making of a New Class

In some respects, what Yugoslavia experienced might be interpreted as only a much stronger, more clear-cut, and more pronounced example of a phenomenon seen more generally across socialist Europe. As Bogdan Denitch observed just before his native country fell to pieces, "one has only to spend a brief time in Eastern Europe, the Soviet Union, and, of course, Yugoslavia, to see genuine, avid hunger among all strata of the population for manufactured needs and products, both for commodities and cultural styles, and even for ideas from the capitalist West."[1] Comments like these suggest that there were indeed certain clear continuities between the Yugoslav example and the experiences of other socialist countries. Some, like the thirst for things Western, are fairly obvious and by now have become familiar fixtures of the standard interpretation of Europe's experiments with Marxist-Leninist government.

But some of the seeming continuities may be deceptive. In the final analysis, Yugoslavia's acquaintance with consumerism may have been so thorough, and the paths it took so unusual, that it makes more sense to judge the Yugoslav record as reflective of a fundamental departure from the pattern established in most, if not all, of the other European socialist polities. The "Yugoslav difference" was so pronounced, in fact, that it was apparent not just to specialists in the affairs of communist Europe but to casual visitors and vacationers, too. Perhaps most telling, it was obvious to the ordinary citizens of other socialist countries who, when they could afford it, "voted with their feet," traveling long distances just to shop in Yugoslavia. For these people, Yugoslavia certainly was something different—as close as most of them were likely to get to the contraband pleasures of the West.

While Denitch saw clear parallels to other socialist systems, he was also alert to the fact that consumerism had reshaped Yugoslav society in a unique fashion. His perspective is that of a democratic-socialist émigré scholar in America, yet like a number of critics in the country, he interpreted the effects of consumer culture as, first and foremost, strengthening the position of the middle class. Commenting on the potent combination of policy and popular desires, he thus observed in 1990 that "the great hunger for Western consumer goods and the relative openness of Yugoslavia, economically and in terms of what the domestic market supplies, has created a fairly large consumerist middle class."[2] As explained in chapter 1, by this Denitch clearly did not mean the "traditional" middle class of small-scale private business

---

1. Bogdan Denitch, *Limits and Possibilities: The Crisis of Yugoslav Socialism and State Socialist Systems* (Minneapolis, 1990), 48.
2. Ibid.

owners, which he viewed as largely inconsequential, and in that respect he is
certainly correct. But while it is hard to find a more sensitive, sensible, and
humane critic of twentieth-century Yugoslavia than Bogdan Denitch, I believe his formulation just misses capturing what actually took place from the
mid-1950s on. Plainly, I agree that Yugoslav attitudes toward consumption
did, as Denitch says, encourage the development of a distinct social grouping within Yugoslav society. That group was, furthermore, important, ascendant, and patently consumerist. It was even, as I shall explain, a stratum very
much positioned "in the middle." But, critically, the new New Class that
consumerism built in socialist Yugoslavia was not, in the prevailing senses
of the term, synonymous with the Yugoslav "middle class."

Rather, this New Class was defined predominantly by an embrace of, and
participation in, a lifestyle created and expressed through myriad acts of
shopping, browsing, buying, and using, behaviors that were less important
for their concrete economic significance (real as that was) than for their
power to communicate symbolically, to oneself and to others, a sense of belonging in a modern, forward-looking, cosmopolitan society—a sense that,
as Yugoslav citizens, they had indeed "arrived" and become part of the "developed world"; that is, this New Class of consumers was defined in primarily *cultural* terms, and only to a lesser extent by socioeconomic factors. By
advancing a culturally derived understanding of class in this instance, I am
not suggesting, of course, that we discard more traditional understandings
of class based on factors such as a person's level of wealth and income or,
in the classic Marxian formulation, an individual's position in the division
of labor within the prevailing system of production. These were and remain
indisputably valid and useful definitional criteria, and neither in Yugoslavia
nor elsewhere did the advance of consumer society cause them to disappear.
Rather I propose that, for socialist Yugoslavia, an important part of what
was most distinctive about this very distinctive society can best be understood by taking a step or two back from the familiar social and economic
analytics and looking instead to an expressly cultural understanding of class
identity.

What the Yugoslav record demonstrates is that a potent new, culturally
grounded identity emerged alongside the more familiar notions of group
belonging. The old understandings did not go away. Indeed, as we have seen,
they were the touchstone of the Marxist interpretations offered up continually by party leaders and critics of consumer culture. But the new cultural
option of belonging to a much more expansive community of Yugoslav consumers gradually worked to undermine their importance and to erode the
sharp edges of more traditional class categorizations.

Many of the domestic critics of Yugoslav consumer society, of course,
believed it to be primarily a vehicle for social and economic differentiation
along rigid and more or less familiar class lines. But whether that judgment
was right or wrong (and it does miss the mark in important ways), the fact

remains that a momentous shift had occurred: as seen time and again in the discussion of the furor that developed over consumerism, even those who interpreted class differentiation as characteristic of Yugoslav consumer culture nonetheless indicated that the cleavage planes were made manifest not in traditional terms but rather through the symbolic power of shopping for, purchasing, and displaying consumer wealth. Or, more simply put, to recall Stipe Šuvar's diagnosis of Yugoslavia in the 1970s, the society had become one in which "it's not the one who works who has been important, but rather, the one who spends."[3]

As the domestic debate over consumer culture thus suggests, Yugoslavs' identities were now no longer a predictable function of their roles in the system of production but were instead increasingly grounded in, and expressed through, their participation in a system of consumption. "Identity" is, of course, a much disputed term,[4] but the time has not yet come to jettison it entirely. Rather, more subtle and flexible problem-specific approaches are warranted, with an understanding of identity that looks not to explicit self-identification as a member of a particular group but rather to a more personal sense of values, of what is really important about life. Those values may be divined through a careful and sensitive reading of the attitudes and behaviors of ordinary Yugoslavs. I do not mean for a moment to suggest that Yugoslav citizens would ever have responded to an inquiry about their identities with the response "I am a consumer" in the way that they might well have said "I am a Croat," "I am a Yugoslav," "I am a worker," "I am a peasant," and so on. But that said, the evidence makes it quite clear that, from the 1960s on, many Yugoslavs increasingly viewed consumption and the attainment of the Good Life as among their most important goals. In this sense, the opponents of consumer society were right: ordinary citizens' sense of self-worth did indeed appear to be, as the critics suggested, tied closely to their ability to acquire, spend, and display personal wealth.

Obviously the culture that lay at the heart of this sort of classification was intimately connected with economic factors. Some of these, to be sure, were cold, hard, and unforgiving. At the extremes, economic considerations alone almost certainly could trump the power of culture to create a new class-consciousness. Given the structure of Yugoslav society, such exclusions from the New Class obviously happened much more often at the lower extreme. The variant of consumer culture that Yugoslavia created was decidedly more modest than that encountered in less restricted Western European settings, and the differences from the no-holds-barred American style were clearer still. Yet for citizens at the poorest margins of society, it was no doubt difficult to participate in even this scaled-back version. Cash-strapped agriculturalists in

---

3. Šuvar, "Elementi potrošačkog društva i potrošačkog mentaliteta," 177.

4. See, for example, Rogers Brubaker, *Ethnicity Without Groups* (Cambridge, Mass., 2004).

remote regions of Bosnia-Herzegovina or Macedonia and poorly paid miners and factory workers in Kosovo or Montenegro undoubtedly had fewer opportunities to enjoy the Yugoslav Dream (though even many of these learned that they could leave for the West and then return to buy their share of that dream using German marks or Swiss francs). Clearly economic forces could work to prevent full participation in the consumerist New Class.

What other factors might have brought about the same result? Yugoslavia was home to millions of committed consumerists, but the country also had a genuine, widespread, and honored revolutionary tradition with its own radically egalitarian and sometimes even ascetic cultural styles. Those who opted out of modern consumerism on this basis were, no doubt, quite rare, but the demonstrative symbolic importance of their example was surely disproportionate to their numbers. Communist ideology and Partisan hagiography had their own effects on culture, and these always worked to hold consumerist styles in check to some extent. As we have seen earlier, however, the messages sent by the party were by no means uniform and straightforward. The ideal of revolutionary simplicity lingered on in more or less peaceful coexistence with Tito's yachts and his string of palaces and retreats across the country, and the habits associated with the old New Class that Djilas lamented never quite disappeared. As Svetozar Stojanović has pointed out, the varying cultural styles adopted among party activists had something of a remedial quality: "Communists who have grown up in an impoverished and envious environment, like Tito," he observed, "are most often inclined to enjoy material privileges and a high lifestyle. Communists from well-to-do families usually endeavor to 'redeem' themselves by despising material comforts and benefits."[5] The cultural importance of expressly ascetic communist styles no doubt had some effect in reining in consumer society, but it is hard to escape the conclusion that, in the end, any such exemplars were simply swamped by a torrent of contrary messages communicated through advertising, the mass media, and the thoughts and deeds of friends, family, neighbors, and coworkers. Moreover, many rank-and-file party members were themselves often enthusiastically consumerist.

Probably much more important as a limiting factor on the growth of the new New Class were those social groups whose culture had little in common with, or was even openly hostile toward, the aggressive modernity of contemporary consumer culture. Chief among these were rural populations, elderly people, and social traditionalists. (Obviously these groupings could overlap considerably and, when they did, the distance from modern modes and meanings of consumption was almost certainly multiplied.) People in many parts of the country were, especially in the 1960s and 1970s, still deeply committed to traditional, sometimes frankly patriarchal, ways of life. In these circles,

---

5. Svetozar Stojanović, *The Fall of Yugoslavia: Why Communism Failed* (Amherst, N.Y., 1997), 51.

some of the new style promoted by Yugoslavia's urbanized and urbanizing consumer culture may have been received as more a curse than a blessing.

But peasants and rural folk were hardly immune to materialism, and to the extent that their finances permitted it, many happily took up the quest for the Yugoslav version of the Good Life. In the end money, not traditional mores, may have been a more significant limiting factor on the spread of consumerist values to rural Yugoslavia, and when their pocketbooks made it possible, many peasants spent and displayed wealth as avidly as their urban comrades. Moreover, a tendency toward the generational distribution of labor in the rural economy made modern consumption more available to peasant families. While the older generations often remained engaged primarily in agricultural work, their children encountered a new economy with dramatically different aims and potentials. They frequently took jobs in nearby factories, joining a modernizing industrial working class that quickly acquired equally modern consumerist tastes. In turn, members of the third generation often sought to leave the working class for a more tempting life as "white collar" types not unlike those described by C. Wright Mills in his study of American society. The new lifestyle of the younger generations, and the extra discretionary income that their jobs brought, helped fold even the rural population into the new culture of consumerism.[6]

If this New Class was indeed so expansive and so widely distributed, how was it created? In the simplest, most immediate sense, the rise of a new consumerist orientation was a consequence of the Yugoslav state's reorientation of economic policy away from heavy industry and toward the satisfaction of consumer needs. But while this may have been a necessary condition, it was surely not sufficient. Other socialist governments, to varying degrees, also attempted to accommodate consumer demand, and my ongoing investigations into comparable cases suggest that those regimes appear to have done so without spawning the kind of thoroughgoing social transformation of attitudes and behaviors that left Yugoslav social critics worrying about the vice and venality of consumer society. Other aspects of government policy also clearly had a role in the change. As we have seen, the introduction of self-management as the governing practical and ideological premise of Yugoslav society also catalyzed the reorientation toward consumerism. The new system's flexibility permitted (but did not compel) a shift toward the market, which in turn allowed interested firms to cater to customers' tastes and wishes, gave advertising and marketing specialists the latitude to argue that their approaches were fully consonant with the values of Yugoslav socialism, and, more generally, helped provide an important ideological justification for theories and practices that treated consumption as equal in importance to production, if not, in fact, of even greater weight.

---

6. I am grateful to John Fine for his insights into this particular social dynamic.

Just as important as the government's commitments, however, were the concrete economic results of those choices. Yugoslavia's communist leadership sought—and obtained—dramatic increases in living standards, and in the period of just over a decade and a half, from 1956 to 1972, the country's living standard jumped by a factor of 3.5.[7] (The case thus raises the important question of whether other countries that managed to achieve relatively high living standards, and that did so at a similarly rapid pace, also experienced such changes in culture.) This new wealth created in turn the demand for still more wealth, opening the door to profound changes in attitudes and expectations about what the country's economy could and should deliver to ordinary citizens.

It is critical to recognize, however, that the raw statistics on economic improvement conceal an inherently fraudulent element of the transformation: as we have seen, the government's policies on credit and incomes helped push incomes and spending to unrealistic and unsustainable levels. Much of Yugoslav consumerism, then, was undertaken with the indulgence of a government that operated on the basis of what might best be described as a charge-card mentality. And by the end of the 1970s the country had, both literally and figuratively, exceeded its credit limit.

Another indisputable factor in the creation of consumer culture was Yugoslavia's comparatively easy communication with the consumerist market economies of the West. As described in chapter 2, direct contact with the creators of Western advertising and marketing, and fluency in the ideas that they disseminated, indelibly stamped the theory and practice of Yugoslav commercial promotion. For Yugoslavs not connected with the industry, a familiarity with the ways and wares of the West was just as important. The ideas and expectations that they brought back from their travels were one of the great engines of the new Yugoslav consumerism. Here again, the domestic debate helps substantiate the point. Along these lines, consider the insights of Svetislav Taboroši, a fierce critic of the Yugoslav approach to consumption, who concluded that the economic and cultural impacts of the foreign workers were immense. Largely because of the enormous financial contributions of the guest workers, he asserted, aggregate demand continually remained above the level of domestic production. Moreover, and perhaps more important, the experiences of the *Gastarbeiter* had wrought a fundamental change in the quality of Yugoslav consumption as well. Observing the long-term development of the tastes and spending of the foreign workers, Taboroši saw them as a group particularly subject to co-optation into the new consumerist model. "Because of the cultural unpreparedness of [migrant] workers for their new living conditions," he claimed, "they prove to be especially unable to resist the constant production of new needs. Guest

---

7. Bilandžić, *Historija Socijalističke Federativne Republike Jugoslavije*, 389, citing Eva Berković, "Porast životnog standarda," in *Trideset godina socialističke Jugoslavije* (Belgrade, 1975), 71.

workers tend to eliminate their increased psychic instability using the only sort of identification that is possible for them: the defense of their own personal dignity in the realm of consumption, where formally, they have equal rights." This was, apparently, the only solution: "at a disproportionately high rate, they purchase various technical innovations and engage in those forms of consumption-for-prestige that are available to them (large automobiles, for example)." As a result of the constant contact with Western commercial promotion and consumerist attitudes, Taboroši concluded, "the lowest segments of the consumer culture of the West" were being "transplanted"—first to the *Gastarbeiter* and then to Yugoslavia itself. As a result, the foreign workforce had become something unexpected and unwelcome, "a carrier of the idea of the sovereignty of the consumer into self-management society."[8]

All these factors worked together to encourage the shift of many Yugoslavs toward a consumerist orientation and to promote the development of a new sense of social belonging derived from participation in modern modes of consumption. They helped create a great reservoir of consumerist demand—the "genuine, avid hunger among all strata of the population" that Bogdan Denitch has described. But, as I have suggested throughout this book, the most important force for stimulating and channeling those desires was the country's own aggressive industry of commercial promotion. When we look for those elements that generated and defined the new New Class, the messages constantly communicated by the creators of Yugoslav advertising, and with them the implicit ideology of consumer sovereignty carried by those appeals, stand out as among the most significant.

Yugoslavia's economy never really became a market economy, but to a profound extent the country's business establishment did endorse and produce a market culture. Advertising set the tone, marketing provided the "science" and the ideology, and a new conception of retailing delivered it all to consumers as attractively and persuasively as possible. Through it all, it was the industry's cautious but unmistakably Western orientation toward commercial promotion that made Yugoslavia look and feel so different from every other socialist society and made life there so often reflect the classic capitalist manifestations of consumer culture.

Preference, Escape, Obsession, Distinction: "Social Differentiation" and the Products of Yugoslav Consumer Culture

With its lively, unmistakable crackle and hum, this spectacular cultural transformation was, as shown earlier, almost always described with a heavy

---

8. References are to Taboroši, *Odnosi potrošnje u socijalizmu*, 169–170. The author further argued that, while in Western Europe, the migrant workers constituted a specially targeted market segment and were, as a result, subjected to "the most aggressive form of advertising." Ibid.

dose of seemingly obligatory self-criticism. But, often enough, the *nostra culpas* betrayed some obvious satisfaction, too. Dušan Bilandžić's widely circulated history text on postwar Yugoslav society offers a fine example of how the country's new emphasis on buying and owning was offered up as both a self-management success story and at the same time a darker intimation of some basic failure to build socialism. "Toward the end of the 1960s," Bilandžić wrote, "the masses were caught up in a fever of consumption and money-making: in every part of the country, peasants and workers were building houses and buying durable consumer goods, while the richer people were getting vacation houses, ever more expensive cars, and so forth."[9] Along with the impressive increase in living standards, Yugoslav society in this view had also "gradually acquired all the principal characteristics of so-called consumer society."[10] In his typically measured style, Bilandžić acknowledged the ongoing polemic and even suggested its validity but did not himself engage in any open assault on consumerism. Yet even this account, which by the standards of "establishment" communist historiography is fairly balanced and moderate, was nevertheless shaped by the ideological imperatives of Yugoslav socialism. As a result, Bilandžić also read consumerism as, above all, part of a suspect process of social differentiation. "Is Yugoslav society," he asked, "increasingly being stratified into richer and poorer?"[11] His history, like the interpretations put forward by many of the outright critics of consumer culture, faulted the economic expansion of the 1960s and 1970s for reinforcing a dangerous tendency toward the creation of an unwelcome "middle class." (Party archival records show that Bilandžić had, as early as 1972, voiced to his colleagues in the highest circles of the League of Communists much the same concerns about a rising, potentially even dominant middle-class "that is taking over the management of the society.")[12] The perceived threat to the class goals of Yugoslav socialism was practically palpable:

> Because the Yugoslav economy toward the end of the 1960s was mainly transformed into a market economy system, the question thus arose: must this form of economy necessarily give rise to a new social class, one that in its fundamen-

---

9. Bilandžić, *Historija Socijalističke Federativne Republike Jugoslavije*, 394.

10. Ibid., 378. The author noted that the structure of the country's personal consumption had likewise "drawn ever nearer to the type associated with industrial consumer society." Expenditures for food had fallen from 53.9% of the total in 1952 to 39.5% in 1972, while outlays for furniture and equipment for the home had increased in the same twenty-year period from 4.8% to 10.2%, and the fraction spent on culture and recreation had risen from 0.7% to 3.8%. Energy consumption had increased astronomically, from 17.3 kWH to 369.4 kWH per capita. Ibid.

11. Ibid., 400.

12. Bilandžić, excerpts from presentation quoted in Centar za društvena istraživanja Predsedništva SKJ, Izvodi iz studija i diskusije, Naučni skup "Ocena sadašnjeg istorijskog trenutka Jugoslovenskog društva i analiza njegovih razvojnih mogućnosti" Bled 10-13.I.1972 [internal materials for use by the LCY Presidency], 21. Hrvatski Državni Arhiv, collection Centralni komitet, Savez komunista Hrvatske, HDA-1220-6209.

tal characteristics is distinguished from the working class by its place in the system of productive relations, by its status, and by its economic situation—and one that will turn into a "counter-class"?[13]

Here, as in the writings of many other contemporary observers, the analysis of consumer society was thus fused (and, I maintain, confused) with the ongoing battles against "enrichment," against private enterprise, and against the evil influence of "managers" and "technocrats," that is, those directors and other leaders of business enterprises and financial institutions who were seen as the core of a rising "middle class" and who now seemed to eclipse the old statist "bureaucrats" as the bogeys of self-management.

Yet for all the valuable insights it provides into the very real changes taking place across the country, the wide-ranging argument within Yugoslavia over the relationship between consumerism and social differentiation ultimately missed one critical and fundamental point. Driven as it was by the rhetorical imperatives of communism, with its antipathies to the bourgeoisie and its dedication to the struggle to create a classless society, the domestic critique of consumer society failed to fully appreciate the sweeping, inclusive quality of the Yugoslav version of consumer culture. The resistance was largely blind to its homogenizing and hence potentially *unifying* effects.

En colère about the *nouveaux riches* and ready to see a *petit bourgeois* in every *petite Peugeot*, the domestic critics missed some of the more subtle but just as important manifestations of their country's consumer culture. For the underlying vision of modernity, abundance, cosmopolitanism, and reward for hard work was present in all manner of lesser instances as well. In the workplace, the schools, the mass media, and elsewhere, public discourse constantly drove home the official message that Yugoslavs, through self-management, enjoyed a system uniquely attuned to the interests of workers and protective of their rights. Beginning in the 1960s, through the workings of consumer culture, that message was blended with the idea that none of this need come at the cost of progress and prosperity. Critically, this idea about the uninterrupted flow of progress could be communicated through acts as common and simple as flipping through the ads in a women's magazine, watching television commercials for snack foods, and perusing the well-stocked shelves of the local market. Often, when dealing with consumer culture, it's the little things that matter most.

As described earlier, the assault on consumerism in Yugoslavia focused, for the most part, on the largest, easiest targets: automobiles, weekend houses, high-fashion clothes, televisions, and other big-ticket items that, though now available to more than just a privileged few, still smacked of luxury

---

13. Bilandžić, *Historija Socijalističke Federativne Republike Jugoslavije*, 400; see, generally, 399–402.

and ill-gotten gain. Conflated with the domestic debates over corruption, technocracy, and unwarranted personal "enrichment," and grafted onto a dogged if mostly symbolic campaign against the country's tiny class of small-scale entrepreneurs, the controversy over consumerism missed a different and arguably much deeper transformation of Yugoslav society. Contrary to what much of the domestic criticism insisted, Yugoslavia's consumer culture was not driven exclusively or even predominantly by the major milestone acquisitions, that is, by rare and relatively expensive high-status purchases. The ideal that prevailed was instead one of abundance for the masses. As such, it was a much more ordinary occurrence—a daily thing, in fact—for ordinary Yugoslavs to reinforce their connection to consumer culture through equally ordinary shopping and spending.

Yugoslav consumerism surely was inspired by the grander aspirations and wealth of the West, but it was sustained by all sorts of much more minor consumer behaviors: shopping for cosmetics, buying a pair of stylish shoes, browsing through a rack of blouses in a gleaming, modern, self-service department store, or picking up cleansers and laundry powder in a supermarket styled along contemporary European lines. As inconsequential as they might seem at first glance, all these activities worked to connect Yugoslav citizens with an image of pleasurable, rewarding, convenient, and modern living.[14] Because they took place so frequently, their cumulative effects were likely equal to or even greater than those that came with milestone purchases. Although little acts like these did not communicate high status in the sense that so troubled those critics who decried the appearance of consumption-driven "snobbism," they did convey (and confer) status in a different, less obvious, and yet perhaps more important way: all the many minor, quotidian indulgences in consumer culture offered Yugoslavs a means of constant reassurance that they, too, were full participants in modern life. The most important manifestations of status associated with Yugoslav consumption were therefore not sneering or self-congratulatory displays of *superior* status directed at neighbors and coworkers; instead, they were hopeful assertions of a status *equal* to that enjoyed by citizen-consumers in the developed capitalist countries.

Most assuredly, a quest for "high status" was involved here, but it was high status of a very different sort from that which motivated most of the

---

14. See Jukka Gronow and Alan Warde, eds., *Ordinary Consumption* (London, 2001). On the possible cultural significance of everyday shopping, see Daniel Miller, *A Theory of Shopping* (Ithaca, 1998). Miller's insight that shopping is not necessarily an arena for materialism and hedonism but rather a means for practicing thrift may well be applicable to the Yugoslav case. In the popular press, for example, we see repeatedly how Yugoslav shoppers were strongly motivated by the idea of getting excellent value for their money; much of their cross-border shopping was predicated precisely on this idea. In the end, however, Miller's approach may not prove most useful for the purposes at hand here, as it tends to downplay the ways in which shopping functioned as a reward and an expression of status (even if the communication of status was often simply a reassuring message to oneself).

Marxist critiques of Yugoslavia's consumerist appetites. In this respect, the symbolic communication was primarily reflexive, a reassuring message to oneself rather than a bold declaration to others (though many Yugoslavs were well aware that the outside world was watching their success with keen interest).

In addition, a distinctly communitarian quality marked Yugoslavia's mass culture of consumerism. Certainly there were plenty of opportunities to use spending to create a sense of individual distinction, and yet a central idea communicated through the country's advertising and mass media was one of high *collective* status: as a people, the message went, "we" have succeeded. And, importantly, because of the system's pronounced emphasis on building and serving a unified Yugoslav market, "we" in such cases often signified the broadest possible community of *Yugoslav* citizens, undifferentiated along ethnic lines. In this respect, consumer culture became one of the relatively rare factors that worked to reinforce a pan-Yugoslav identity: though there were obviously clear differences in living standards from republic to republic, people in the country did not participate in the new consumerist abundance on the basis of their ethnicity. Rather, the consumerist ideal was a genuinely *Yugoslav* ideal, something that all the country's citizens were supposed to be able to share. It was, in other words, something that could work to lessen regional and "national" distinctions, something that, as a result, helped Yugoslavia survive and even thrive as a complex multiethnic federation.

Drawing attention to the smaller, more common incidents of everyday consumerism does not imply that the high-status items that drew most of the critics' ire and fire were of little importance. Quite to the contrary, the perceived need to make acquisitions of this sort clearly did exert a strong pull over many people. But as acknowledged by even a number of the critics themselves, Tito among them, such items had rapidly become fairly "ordinary" luxuries. They were increasingly available to all sorts of Yugoslav citizens, many of them quite unexceptional: yes, the suspect bureaucrats, technocrats, and white-collar types all found these consumer pleasures more easily within their grasp, but such things were also accessible, albeit with more of a struggle, to villagers living in some of the most undeveloped and remote parts of the country and to workers in the smaller cities and little towns all across the state where Yugoslav factories had been situated as a result of the government's policy of distributing industrial development beyond the historical, prewar manufacturing centers of the urban north and west.[15] As the domestic critique itself makes clear, Yugoslavia's consumer culture was remarkably expansive, intimately involving most of the

---

15. For a more detailed picture of both the impressive general level of consumption and the lingering differences attributable to socioeconomic and educational status, see, for example, Peter Klinar, "O življenskem stilu družbenih slojev na Slovenskem (II)," *Teorija in praksa* 16, no. 2

country's citizens. The wealthiest snobs may have received much of the attention, but people who were hardly "rich," even by a more inclusive, politicized definition of the term, were also participating avidly in the country's new consumerist spirit.

Moreover, for many, their hopes of having at least some scaled-down version of the markers of luxury and success were not, in fact, in vain. With patience, hard work (and extra work), and considerable sacrifice, they, too, had reasonable prospects of owning a car, a television, perhaps even a modest *vikendica*. We may well question, as did the adversaries of consumer society, whether the sacrifices were sensible. But the fact remains that many ordinary citizens did feel that they could share in the Yugoslav Dream, and their conclusions were largely justified, since the Yugoslav Dream had itself been scaled down, made more modest and reasonable, in order to ensure that it remained available and attractive to the masses. Yugoslav workers may have been laboring too hard in their quest to live the dream, but they were not laboring under an illusion: the vision of abundance sold by the country's advertisers and by the "economic propagandists" who promoted their wares was, when all is said and done, remarkable precisely for its accessibility.

One related aspect of consumer culture that went largely overlooked—probably because of its disturbing implications about the propriety of the prevailing system—was the way in which Yugoslav consumers could use their time spent shopping and buying as a means of sharing and joining in a broader, transnational culture of consumption, a lifestyle that was frequently understood not only to be modern but also either explicitly or implicitly Western (and often specifically Western European). In this, of course, they were prodded on by their country's marketing and advertising specialists, who were, as we have seen, thoroughly in the thrall of Western notions of what successful advertising should look like, how it worked, and what it was supposed to represent as part of a larger, marketing-inspired concept of "business." As open as Yugoslavia was to outside influences, Yugoslavs often did not feel that they were fully European. They were, in the minds of many at least, doubly severed from the main currents of life in Europe: first by a heritage of economic underdevelopment and "backwardness," and then again by a crimped, inefficient system that left the country unable to participate fully in the spectacular postwar affluence of Western Europe. It was sometimes uncertain exactly where Yugoslavia was: In the Balkans? In Eastern Europe? At the epicenter of the Non-Aligned World? But it was clear enough that "Europe" often still seemed to be somewhere else.

Consumer culture helped dissipate those feelings of alienation and cultural distance. When Yugoslavs snapped up jeans, maxi-skirts, "two-storey

(1979): 196–215; *Društveni slojevi i društvena svest: sociološko istraživanje interesa, stilova života, klasne svesti i vrednosno-ideoloških orijentacija društvenih slojeva* (Belgrade, 1977).

shoes," and all sorts of other fashions that radiated across the continent from Paris and Milan, when they purchased the very deodorants and lipsticks and skin creams that made people all over Europe feel more elegant, modern, and attractive, and when they saw in their own stores some of the same brands of soup and soap that they knew were on the shelves in Klagenfurt and Cologne, in Graz and Trieste, they were, in a subtle but important way, at one with a contemporary way of life that was grounded in consumption, cultivated by advertising, television, film, and the popular press, and, perhaps as never before, genuinely pan-European. A set of fine new furniture styled in Danish Modern would, quite obviously, have the desired effect of making a Yugoslav living room considerably more "modern" itself. Not so obviously, however, it could also render the room ever so slightly "Danish."

This last point bears further reflection: just as many democratic socialists in the West looked to Yugoslavia as a model, many Yugoslavs hoped just as sincerely that their version of socialism might over time evolve toward the more social-democratic Scandinavian paradigm. Consumer purchases that evoked the progressive, prosperous, and secure lifestyles of Scandinavia thus appear to have had a special cultural valence in Yugoslavia. This is, of course, simply a species of a more general phenomenon. When Yugoslavs bought perfumes with French-sounding names, Italian-style shoes, or American-label jeans, they were cloaking themselves just as certainly in French elegance, Italian flash, and the casual optimism of American youth. Of course, the fundamental premise of the Scandinavian design style was probably better matched than most to the economic realities that helped keep the Yugoslav Dream modest and measured: Danish Modern achieved its elegance through its simplicity. By adopting the style, Yugoslavs could purchase European modernity at a suitably low cost. (This thorough acquaintance with European styles, of course, was a two-edged sword: Yugoslavs also knew all too well what their system could not or would not deliver.)

Such considerations of "national" and "European" style evoke the insights of the classic essay on this subject by Roland Barthes, who argues that essential(ized) ideas of national identity or culture may be communicated succinctly through coded advertising images. Barthes builds his interpretation using the example of a pasta advertisement featuring visual and linguistic elements intended—he insists such representations are thoroughly *deliberate*—to connote "Italianicity" [*l'italianité*].[16] In terms of image and style, at least, Yugoslav commercial promotion did not often strive to summon up any distinctive "Yugoslavicity"—much less any narrower identity such as "Serbicity," "Croaticity," "Slovenicity," or the like. Rather, in the country's advertising messages, *jugoslovenstvo*, Yugoslav-ness, tended to be

---

16. Roland Barthes, "La rhétorique de l'image," *Communications* 4 (1964): 40–51.

shunted off to the sidelines in favor of an advanced, prosperous, modern European-ness. In many ads, either a cosmopolitan emphasis on European quality replaced any special Yugoslav identity of the goods, or the Yugoslav product was implicitly or explicitly equated with European standards and attributes.

It was not necessary that these "modern" and "European" experiences of shopping and buying be oriented toward real luxuries. Admittedly there had been some upward creep in tastes and expectations. *Svijet*'s review of newspaper headlines from the years of the Yugoslav boom noted, for example, that the automobile market had arrived at a new status quo as of 1966: "Yugoslavs are able to get a Fića after ten days, but they are increasingly oriented toward larger cars."[17] But the tokens of European citizenship that Yugoslavs sought and used most frequently were rather ordinary items, not BMWs and champagne and the other playthings of the wicked rich of the West.

Accordingly, in the "specific circumstances of Yugoslav self-management society" we encounter an interesting modification of the key process whereby the consumption practices of groups with lower social status come to mirror the habits and tastes of those placed more securely in the hierarchy. Thorstein Veblen, who produced one of the earliest and yet most durable critiques of consumerist behavior, called attention to the mechanisms through which, in a given society, upper-class, "highbrow" tastes become the model for others. "In modern civilized communities," Veblen observed, "the lines of demarcation between social classes have grown vague and transient, and wherever this happens the norm of reputability imposed by the upper class extends its coercive influence with but slight hindrance down through the social structure to the lowest strata." A certain trickle-down *avant la lettre* ensued: "The result is that the members of each stratum accept as their ideal of decency the scheme of life in vogue in the next higher stratum, and bend their energies to live up to that ideal."[18] The process Veblen identifies here was undoubtedly at work in Yugoslavia as well, at least on some levels. But, importantly, the fairly radical social leveling of the first postwar years had largely eliminated real wealth in the country. Yugoslav communism had, in this respect, succeeded: there was no longer any "upper" or "leisure" class in the traditional senses of those terms. In this case, however, it appeared that hierarchy, like nature, abhorred a vacuum, and thus almost immediately a reconstituted system of differentiation began to appear along the lines that Djilas identified. But in contrast to the Yugoslav past and the capitalist present, this new "upper" class was composed not of the rich but of those in power.[19]

---

17. Zlatar, "Vremeplov standarda," 5.
18. Veblen, *The Theory of the Leisure Class*, 84.
19. Consumerism and prosperity, however, worked as a great leveling force in this respect. As Yugoslav-American journalist Duško Doder noted in his assessment of Yugoslav society

With time, of course, some few Yugoslavs did manage to find ways to become genuinely rich, whether through private enterprise, celebrity, crafty speculation in real estate, or corruption, which of all the options was probably the most mundane path to wealth. Still, truly rich Yugoslavs were rarities, and, importantly, they were not necessarily deemed suitable for emulation, at least not in the official scheme of values. So, like its socialist cohorts, Yugoslav society remained noteworthy for the extent to which it lacked any substantial élite whose position was based on great wealth. Accordingly, in the absence of any firmly rooted, respectable "upper class," what Veblen called the "scheme of life in vogue in the next higher stratum" had to be, to a great extent, communicated to Yugoslavs from abroad.

The processes of intra-societal stratification, distinction, and top-down vertical modeling that analysts such as Veblen, Bourdieu, and others have identified were attenuated in Yugoslavia, clearing the way instead for comparatively greater *horizontal* modeling and the more generalized operation of a mass domestic "demonstration effect." By now a classic element of consumption studies, the phenomenon of demonstration effects is mainly the legacy of James Duesenberry, who argued that rising levels of consumption spark even greater increases in spending: as more people encounter more expensive, higher-quality goods more often, the social pressure to adjust consumption practices in order to buy those higher-quality goods is increased. As a result, even when incomes do not grow, consumption itself may rise, at the expense of savings and investment.[20]

This observation is painfully applicable to the state of affairs in Yugoslavia. The communist egalitarianism that was imposed at home among Yugoslav citizens may well have had the curious consequence of intensifying a *transnational* demonstration effect. Something like this seems to have been at work in Yugoslav consumption, pushing up both absolute levels of consumption and the relative quality of the goods consumed (and, fatefully, slighting investment in the future productive capacity of the economy).[21] Yugoslav critics of consumerism did not ignore the importance of foreign tastes, of course. But in this respect as well, the Marxist tendency to focus on social differentiation and to identify the styles and values of consumer

---

in the late 1970s, "the introduction of the consumer society...has succeeded remarkably in one thing and that has been *to eliminate or at least obscure economic and social differences between the elite and the great majority of the Yugoslav population.* The New Class, as Milovan Djilas described the ruling elite in his book of the same name, is still highly visible in Soviet bloc countries, with special stores, government limousines, villas and other privileges. Yet, except for a small circle around Tito—and there are fewer than five hundred persons who actually run the country—the system of economic privileges has largely disappeared in Yugoslavia." Doder, *The Yugoslavs,* 59–60 (emphasis added).

20. On the "demonstration effect" generally, see James S. Duesenberry, *Income, Saving and the Theory of Consumer Behavior* (Cambridge, Mass., 1949).

21. Regarding the "international demonstration effect," see Ragnar Nurkse, *Problems of Capital Formation in Underdeveloped Countries* (New York, 1966 [1953]).

culture with "the rich" obscures rather more than it illuminates. It was not the spending of the Yugoslav rich but the massive spending of ordinary Yugoslavs that drove the society's indebtedness.

One related point bears further consideration here. This is the idea that, as suggested by a number of the interpretations I have advanced just above, consumption practices in modern conditions may render group identities less distinct and hence may serve to *reduce* social differentiation. Although the processes found in the Yugoslav case do not, as we have seen, conform neatly to the intra-societal dynamics Veblen described, it nevertheless does appear that in Yugoslavia "the lines of demarcation between social classes" did, through the sharing of tastes and attitudes, become ever more "vague and transient," to use Veblen's terms. Because of the country's characteristic political and economic circumstances, consumer culture encouraged precisely this sort of blurring of social distinctions. To begin with, Yugoslavia's fundamental economic policy clearly discouraged social differentiation, especially at the top end of the scale. Admittedly, throughout the history of the federation, the relatively poor remained relatively common, and at the extremes, as in Slovenia and Kosovo, the pay differentials between workers could be substantial. But a significant number of the country's poorer residents found ways to improve their financial situations, enabling them to participate more fully in the prevailing culture of consumption. Moreover, incomes policies depressed salaries at the top end, with the result that it was almost impossible to become wealthy just by holding down a single job in the social sector of the economy. Aggressive taxation did much the same for those in the private sector. Coupled with these very real economic restraints were similarly powerful political pressures against social differentiation. As the concerted attack on "enrichment" during the early 1970s demonstrates, to appear conspicuously wealthy entailed some considerable risk. Yugoslavia's version of Marxist-Leninist governance was soft and tolerant, but it was definitely communist in its aspirations, and the goal of the classless society never disappeared from official public discourse. Both economic and political factors thus pushed consumption practices toward a very expansive middle. In such circumstances, it was just much harder for the wealthy to defend social distinction in the complex and innovative ways that, as Bourdieu demonstrated, have so often been available to the upper strata of capitalist societies.

Responding to these economic and political realities, the advertising and marketing specialists who helped sustain Yugoslavia's consumer culture also tended to cultivate a satisfying, unexceptionable middle ground. They appealed to tastes for genuine luxury only infrequently, while at the same time they used the alluring imagery of modern, respectable, cosmopolitan consumption to pull those with lower incomes toward the secure center, the happy medium. People did not have to be "rich" in order to buy—and buy into—the elements of the Yugoslav Dream. As we have seen, they could sometimes be so far from rich that they lacked even the electricity needed to power the modern appliances they insisted on buying. Advertising and marketing leaders did at times, as suggested earlier, speak and write about their work with an inattention to its subversive qualities that I can only interpret as either shrewdly duplicitous or astoundingly innocent (and this was not, it should be noted, a profession of naïfs). In such instances, industry activities had the clear potential to undermine socialism. However, when it came to the construction of a target audience, advertising and marketing specialists really were rather more faithful to the palatable, socialist-sounding line they espoused in their textbooks and journals and at industry conferences.

The creators of the country's advertising often said they were tailoring messages for "our Yugoslav man" [*naš čovek*], and on this particular count there was not much deception, either of themselves or of others. In practice, Yugoslav commercial promotion was actually much more noteworthy for its efforts to reach an expansive middle ground of potential consumers than for any attempt to slice the audience into desirable, wealthy "haves" and less favored, poorer "have-nots." Thus we find, for example, abundant advertisements for Zastavas and simple little Yugoslav-built Renaults but not much promotion of German luxury cars. The *ways* in which items were advertised increasingly inclined toward Western models, but *what* was advertised remained true to the modest, moderate Yugoslav Dream. Much of Yugoslav advertising was, as industry specialists themselves sometimes suggested, designed to make almost everyone feel securely average and, furthermore, to make the Yugoslav average seem respectable enough—and "average" enough—to satisfy both the egalitarian, anti-bourgeois ideology of the party and the standards of prosperity and modernity projected by the internationalized culture of the developed capitalist world.

In this way, the New Class of Yugoslav consumers ended up occupying a safe, respectable middle ground, even though it could not, as critics suggested, be equated with any "middle class." As a consequence of all these pressures toward the center, Yugoslav consumer culture did not promote social differentiation through consumption nearly as much, or nearly as openly, as did Western practice, which embraced the notion of precise market segmentation and sought to exploit it for commercial advantage, tailoring advertisements and marketing campaigns to target audiences identified with all the scientific precision the discipline could muster. Yet there do appear to be some instructive parallels in Western experience, despite the presence of more extreme examples of wealth and poverty in capitalist settings. The creation of a *cultural* "middle class" defined largely via consumption has been seen most conspicuously in the United States, where even persons earning many times the median income, members of a group that by any rational objective standards can only be defined as an economic élite, live in the unshakeable conviction that they are still middle-class (and where, conversely, workers earning much less than the average cling to the salvific notion that they, too, are part of the Great American Middle).

What Made It Special Made It Dangerous: The Contradictions of Consumerism and the End of the Yugoslav Dream

Since the Cold War era, analysts of Eastern Europe and the Soviet Union have frequently cited dysfunctional consumption policy among the chief causes of the failure of socialism. Almost always the connection has been taken for granted and noted in passing, as if the workings of consumption were self-evident and required no deeper exploration. Recently, however, a few scholars have sought a more complex understanding of the relationship between the material and the political in those societies. Communist governance was meant, of course, to offer a liberating alternative to capitalist acquisitiveness, but the evidence that has accumulated thus far suggests that the socialist experiment in Europe did not do much to disrupt what may well be a more pervasive (and thus perhaps more troubling) modern tendency to find status, satisfaction, identity, and meaning through consumption.

Examining the GDR, for example, Jonathan Zatlin concludes that the Socialist Unity Party's unsatisfying attempt to manage the treacherous concept of consumer sovereignty "illustrates the failure of Marxism-Leninism to provide a politically stable solution to the problem of consumer desire."[22] In Zatlin's view, the East Germans' frustrating experience with consumer culture holds a much larger lesson about the fate of state socialism. "If the effectiveness of capitalism lies in its ability to manufacture desire and sell it as need, thereby deflecting much systemic criticism into the activity of consuming the objects of desire," he observes, "then the ineffectiveness of the planned economy lies in its understanding of desire in terms of need." The policies pursued by the East German Communists, Zatlin concludes, produced recurring shortages which in turn prompted "an inflation of desire" that the party simply could not accommodate. In the end, "it was the accrual of desire, symbolized by the long waits for scarce goods, which helped undermine the socialist value system financially as well as morally."[23] Other scholars of the East German case have also identified consumer policy and the disappointments of the consumer experience as central to the long-term failure of the communist enterprise there.[24] For the GDR, then, attitudes

---

22. Jonathan R. Zatlin, "The Vehicle of Desire: The Trabant, the Wartburg and the End of the GDR," *German History* 15, no. 3 (1997): 358–380, at 380.

23. Ibid.

24. See Merkel, *Utopie und Bedürfnis;* Merkel, "Consumer Culture in the GDR, or How the Struggle for Antimodernity Was Lost on the Battleground of Consumer Culture," in *Getting and Spending: European and American Consumer Societies in the Twentieth Century,* ed. Susan Strasser, Charles McGovern, and Matthias Judt (Cambridge, 1998), 281–299; Landsman, *Dictatorship and Demand;* Heldmann, "Negotiating Consumption in a Dictatorship: Consumer Politics in the GDR in the 1950s and 1960s," in *The Politics of Consumption: Material Culture and Citizenship in Europe and America,* ed. M. J. Daunton and Matthew Hilton (Oxford, 2001), 185–202; André Steiner, "Dissolution of the 'Dictatorship over Needs'? Consumer

toward and efforts to manage consumption have emerged as key determinants of the socialist predicament.

But consumer markets in East Germany, the best-studied case, were always more characterized by limits and shortages than by widespread satisfaction. In comparison with Yugoslavia, the consumer culture of the GDR seems anxious, cramped, and gray. There were real achievements, to be sure, and in a number of aspects living standards in the GDR actually outranked those of Yugoslavia, but the East German consumer experience did not match the exhilaration of Yugoslavia at its most prosperous, when critic after critic was fretting about a slide into consumer society, and ordinary Yugoslavs were, by all accounts, "grabbing, just grabbing."[25] In both countries, consumer dissatisfaction contributed mightily to the collapse of socialist authority, but there was an essential difference: in Yugoslavia, the "inflation of desire" came not from unending frustration and scarcity but instead from the *fulfillment* of desire—from the lived experience of abundance. If a failure of the consumption regime ultimately proved fatal to the fortunes of the East German Communists, then in Yugoslavia, where a grievous mismatch between heightened expectations and diminished realities compounded the structural difficulties of socialist economics, consumption was likely even more critical to the destiny of the party and the state.

What we encounter in Yugoslavia, then, is something like a boomerang effect. The Yugoslav system succeeded in creating the image, and often enough the reality, of a Good Life for Everyman (and Everywoman). That the consumerist New Class ended up situated comfortably "in the middle" long worked as a sort of social glue, creating a sense of unity and thereby increasing the stability of the system and the legitimacy of its leaders. Yugoslav abundance was understood to be "ours," something distinctively Yugoslav, and the system and its leaders collected the credit for that. Expanding material abundance became, in many ways, the life of the party.

But the New Class of ordinary consumers not only loved the Yugoslav Dream. It needed the dream as well. Needing it was, indeed, a primary reason for the existence of the new New Class as a collectively constituted (or if you will, collectively imagined) social group. The very process of sharing and fulfilling those wants and desires was what produced this broad new cultural constellation.

Here lay the danger, since such need could not sit well with economic decline. Yet by the time that decline came, the cultural patterns were long since well in place to keep the popular sense of need alive and vital. As we saw in

Behavior and Economic Reform in East Germany in the 1960s," in Strasser, McGovern, and Judt, *Getting and Spending*, 167–185.

25. A particularly vivid depiction of East German consumer culture is found in Annette Kaminsky, *Illustrierte Konsumgeschichte der DDR* (Erfurt, 1999; see also Kaminsky, *Wohlstand, Schönheit, Glück: kleine Konsumgeschichte der DDR* (Munich, 2001).

chapter 2, the country's market culture, fueled by the industry of commercial promotion, had become "a machine that would go of itself," and in the years of the downturn the machine ended up doing just that.

The effects were profound. On the level of the economic elites, market culture fostered values that could and did lead to a rejection of the socialist status quo. Increasingly members of the country's business community insisted on the priorities and mechanisms of the market. When the economic slide revealed just how much market medicine Yugoslav society would likely require and how resistant the communist authorities and even much of the public would be to swallowing it, the most passionate and most assertive of the market disciples lost not just their faith in the system but their patience with it as well. In this sense, a growing insistence on market values as the foundation of economic organization was, as Slovenia's marketing *macher* Jure Apih argued, an "idea that turned the state and its future upside down."[26]

It is one thing for the ideology of "business" to spread *among* business professionals. The problems that arise from such processes are undoubtedly important, but this sort of diffusion and culture creation is to be expected. It is another matter entirely for an ideology associated with and borne by business to take root in business circles and then spread to the wider society. The evidence suggests that is just what happened in socialist Yugoslavia, and this is why the focus on the key vectors of advertising, marketing, and retailing is so important. The realm of commercial promotion and sales is where business values met the values of ordinary consumers: the central nexus with everyday life. This is where not just the goods and services that businesses offered but "business" itself was bought and sold. Central to that ideological transfer was the idea that the purpose of commerce, and of economic life more generally, was to deliver on the desires of the ordinary shopper. The consumer, not planners or producers, was to be sovereign.

This is not to say that the members of the consumerist New Class came to demand that the system would always meet their wishes in full. Rather, the Yugoslav public was evidently content if, first, the modest and moderated desires of the large group "in the middle" were fulfilled, more or less, on an ongoing basis and, second, there were genuine prospects of improvement in the future. What was needed, in other words, was enough now, and more to come. If the system managed to deliver on that, Yugoslavs could overlook the occasional shortage as a minor annoyance, just as they could be at peace with having to do some shopping abroad. In fact, those cross-border excursions even took on a positive light as a shared, consummately Yugoslav experience, and the opportunity to take them was credited to the system, not debited against Yugoslav socialism, as could easily have been the case.

---

26. See Apih, *Oglašanja v A-duru,* 5–6.

Sifting through the rubble of the multiethnic federation, the Croatian essayist and cultural critic Slavenka Drakulić has identified Yugoslavia's consumerist orientation as one of the most distinctive forces in the country's history, and a surprisingly powerful force as well. In *The Balkan Express*, she reminds readers just how remarkable the Yugoslav version of the Good Life really was, and she points to some of its deeper meanings:

> People in the West always tend to forget one key thing about Yugoslavia, that we had something that made us different from the citizens of the Eastern bloc: we had a passport, the possibility to travel. And we had enough surplus money with no opportunity to invest in the economy (which was why everyone who could invested in building weekend houses in the mid-sixties) and no outlet but to exchange it on the black market for hard currency and then go shopping. Yes, shopping to the nearest cities in Austria and Italy. We bought everything— clothes, shoes, cosmetics, sweets, coffee, even fruit and toilet paper.... Millions and millions of people crossed the border every year just to savour the West and to buy something, perhaps as a mere gesture.[27]

The interpretation that Drakulić offers here calls attention, naturally enough, to the exceptional Yugoslav freedom to shop abroad, but as I have shown throughout this book, Yugoslavs also had built and enjoyed their own domestic version of the land of plenty. In tandem, these complementary worlds of shopping and spending worked to keep Yugoslavs, for the most part, satisfied with their country and even with those who ran it.

The juxtaposition of post-communist chaos and violence with the comfort and consumerist complacency that pervaded the country's culture not so long before is one of the most notable features of Yugoslav history and, as such, one of the key themes in Drakulić's analysis of what went right and what went wrong. She writes, for example, of the difficulty of making sense of the hatred to her daughter, a girl who had been raised in the sweetest hours of the Yugoslav Dream, in a life of new cars and television, of foreign travel and a weekend house, of Levi's, Nike, and Benetton.[28] And she tells poignantly of a Zagreb populated by Coke-drinking boys in Diesel sweatshirts and Levi's who now face the prospect of dying in a conflict they can hardly understand. The young people called on to fight the wars, born in the early 1970s, seemed especially ill-prepared for such hardships. This was a generation, as Drakulić observes, "reared on Humana instant milk formula and Fructal baby food," with "disposable nappies and baby clothes boutiques, collapsible baby carriages from Germany and dummies [that is, pacifiers] from Italy. Later came battery-operated cars—that was a generation

---

27. Slavenka Drakulić, *The Balkan Express: Fragments from the Other Side of War* (New York, 1994), 135–136.
28. Ibid., 131–132.

that already had too many toys—and colour TV, pinball machines, video games, walkmans, Jeans, Sneakers, Rock concerts, Madonna, MTV."[29] The inescapable point here is that whether they got it at home or abroad, Yugoslavs were, often enough, able to buy what they wanted.

In turn, that ability to participate in a vigorous, satisfying routine of buying and selling made a real difference in Yugoslav society and in Yugoslav history—but not without a price. Consumerism, according to Drakulić, worked as a kind of palliative, as compensation for the lack of genuine popular participation in the guidance of the country's affairs. Yugoslav citizens had, in this view, "a kind of contract with the regime: we realize you are here forever, we don't like you at all but we'll compromise if you let us be, if you don't press too hard."[30] In this analysis, however, the soothing effects came at a terrible cost: the sometimes heavy hand of the Yugoslav Communists was indeed cushioned by access to material comforts at home and abroad, but as a consequence of that softer style, consumerism and the pursuit of living well became the order of the day and distracted Yugoslavs from the more serious and urgently needed work of creating a healthy political culture that could sustain a democratic society in a reformed state. Thus, echoing the Praxists, Drakulić suggests that Yugoslavs failed to develop the sort of activist political culture rooted in genuinely democratic and liberal values that would have been necessary to avert the nationalist wars that followed the demise of communism.

Like so much else about Yugoslav society, the Good Life of the 1960s and 1970s has been eclipsed by the desperation and death of more recent times. The connections between the culture of abundance and the disintegration that followed it may, however, be stronger than is immediately apparent. As it happened, the great problem that consumerism caused for the Yugoslav government was not that rising living standards would create a widespread demand for real political democratization, as some believed, but rather that the great increases in prosperity simply could not be sustained and were, in fact, forfeited in the 1980s. The apparent success of government policy in the 1950s, 1960s, and most of the 1970s built up huge popular expectations that the good times would continue and that the future would, in fact, be even brighter.[31] From the beginning, much of the Yugoslav Dream was

---

29. Ibid., 91.
30. Ibid., 135–136.
31. Mihailo Marković, for example, argued that Yugoslav economic conditions had created, in effect, a constant upward push for more and higher-quality consumption. Developing his argument in the late 1960s and early 1970s, he was willing to acknowledge at least some positive aspects of consumerism: "Given the constantly rising income (it is now $650 per capita, and some Yugoslavs are confident that by 1985, it will reach $2000), the impossibility of investing money and becoming a capitalist, and a constant sharp inflationary tendency, a Yugoslav is naturally oriented toward immediate consumption. Having overcome material misery he has become rather selective: he travels a lot and has an opportunity to see and buy foreign products, both abroad and at home. Consequently, he exerts constant pressure on the Yugoslav economy

wrapped up in the idea of progress, and without the real prospect of further progress it was bound to falter. Given the structural inefficiencies and inflexibility of the Yugoslav economy, and given the further fact that a good part of the country's abundance had been purchased on credit, the orientation toward consumer satisfaction ultimately set Yugoslavia on a course for disaster. It is important to remember that the "borrowing binge" John Lampe has described was undertaken partly to finance a sustained consumerist *spending* binge.

As long as Yugoslavs could tell themselves that more or less everyone had more or less enough, it did not make a critical difference that some actually had more, or that those who did have more might have been even better off if they were not, as they saw it, subsidizing the less productive. But once this basic sufficiency was gone, the resentments over inequalities and injustices could and did come boiling out, exacerbating regional and ethnic divisions that may have had little to do with economic issues in the first place. One of the most important ways of creating a Yugoslav "us" and making Yugoslavia "ours" disappeared.

It thus becomes apparent that although consumerism long served as a stabilizing force in Yugoslav society, keeping ordinary Yugoslavs happy and enhancing the popular acceptance of the regime, it ultimately played a significant role in causing the collapse of the system. This view is supported, for example, in the analysis of the Yugoslav breakup offered by Svetozar Stojanović. Although with time he modified considerably the anti-market sentiments of his Praxist days, Stojanović nevertheless continued to see the consumerism that characterized Yugoslav life from the 1960s on as a tremendous drag on the country's capacities and the spirit of its people. Analyzing the ruin of Yugoslav communism and the disintegration of the federation, Stojanović has suggested that the embrace of consumerism was "one of the props of the regime," an important element of a larger strategy of "statist paternalism" endemic to communist governance. As a result of this tactic of popular appeasement, the Yugoslav economy was pushed beyond its limits: "Huge consumerist appetites" were released, fed and whetted yet again by the too easy availability of foreign and domestic credit. The Titoist bargain, according to Stojanović, "corrupted the people," coaxing them to trade away any real power for relative prosperity and leading them into a reckless wastefulness that was "based in good part on the illusion that we had unlimited resources and supported by abundant financial remittances sent by Yugoslavs employed abroad."[32]

---

to modernize and to introduce novelties." Marković, *From Affluence to Praxis*, 104. The writer noted, however, that in most respects Yugoslav consumerism was "deplorable." Ibid.

32. Stojanović, *The Fall of Yugoslavia*, 66; on the evolution of the writer's views toward the market, see ibid., 315. Stojanović's Praxist colleague Rudi Supek likewise interpreted the government's support of consumerist habits as a substantial drain on the economy, alleging that the habitual negative trade balances were due in large part to the importation of unnecessary

Such a view, in my judgment, overstates the extent to which consumerism was deliberately encouraged by the government in order to keep the Yugoslav population contented and manageable. As explained earlier, the New Class of Yugoslav consumers was also, in many important ways, created at lower levels of the social hierarchy, through innumerable interactions between enterprises, ordinary consumers, and the creators of advertising. The idea that the government knowingly and instrumentally engineered a consumerist orientation is, in the end, based more on suspicion and frustration than fact. Yet Stojanović is correct in one important sense: when it comes to consumption, Yugoslavia does appear to have been a victim of its own apparent successes. The prosperous times of the 1960s and much of the 1970s nurtured a set of consumerist attitudes and behaviors that simply could not be sustained once the country's economy ran out of steam beginning in the late 1970s. Rapidly expanding consumption unleashed expectations that could not be satisfied indefinitely.

What the critics called "consumer society" never disappeared in socialist Yugoslavia, but ordinary Yugoslavs' happiness about their ability to consume did vanish to a large extent. That sense of satisfaction had provided one of the strongest supports for the Yugoslav system, predicated as it was on Communist Party leadership, socialist economic policy, and a multinational federation. Without such support, each of those fundamental elements of the Yugoslav system proved vulnerable. For years, the Yugoslav Dream had been so appealing and so satisfying because it seemed so reassuringly close to reality: if the Good Life was not available to everyone right away, then at least the future—the near future—held great promise. In the eyes of many citizens, at least, the reversal of fortunes that came in the country's last years proved fatal. Once prosperity became only a fondly remembered thing of the past, the consumerist dream no longer seemed to have any real chance of coming true, and support for the system began to slip away.

---

consumer goods that benefited only a small fraction of the population. Supek, "Some Contradictions and Insufficiencies of Yugoslav Self-Managing Socialism," in Marković and Petrović, *Praxis: Yugoslav Essays*, 249–271, at 258.

Epilogue

Missing It: Yugo-Nostalgia and the Good Life Lost

Now I don't want to get into statistics, but I am old enough to remember
the time of abundance in the 1970s and the time of the crisis after Tito's
death when we had to wait for coffee, sugar, and oil, when we drove only
on odd or even days of the month (because there was no gasoline), and
things like that.... It's true, there was corruption during Tito's time, but
it's also true that even the little guy could live normally—he had a secure
job and could plan some sort of future for his family.
         —Arhandjeo, pseudonymous Fun Zone Web forum contributor, 2006

When Milovan Djilas first conceptualized the workings of his
"new class" of privileged political and administrative functionaries in the
mid-1950s, the subtle connections between political life and mass culture
in Eastern Europe seemed, to most observers, a minor concern at best.
Anchored as they were to the paradigm of the recalcitrant, principled, and
politically engaged dissident, the typical Western inquiries into "life under
socialism" throughout the Cold War era were suffused with a concern for
the towering issues of freedom and political leadership. This has long been
true of Yugoslavia as well, where the standard narratives of high politics
are, for the most part, well known.

Yet Yugoslavia continues to mystify. Much of the cultural history of the
country—like the culture of socialist Eastern Europe more generally—still
manages to elude us, even though what is at issue is a history usually not
more than fifty years distant, and one within the recollection of many still
living. Now, with the memories of the Cold War beginning to recede, we
might do well to set aside, temporarily at least, the long dominant fascination with high-level decision making if we hope to delve more deeply into
what happened "on the ground" in communist Europe and, in so doing, better understand its culture—and its politics, too. What mattered more consistently in the day-to-day lives of most ordinary Yugoslavs was not the drama
of high politics per se but instead the concrete opportunities that the unusual

---

Source for the epigraph: http://www.fun-zone.org/forum/lofiversion/index.php/t3825.html,
forum topic "Drug Tito i SFRJ," 24 November 2006 (last accessed 14 February 2008).

economic and cultural liberality of the country's curious, hybridized system afforded them.

The pains and joys of the socialist era are indeed fading in the popular mind, and communism has, for many, lost its sting and its ability to inspire. This ongoing process of distancing compounds the difficulties posed by the scarcity of contemporaneous evidence of the nature of everyday socialism, making it now even more difficult to understand a way of life that has largely been left behind. But not all is lost. If we pay careful attention to the question of what gets remembered even to this day, we stand to learn a great deal more about the ways in which socialism was experienced by the ordinary people who lived through it.

The Legend Lives: Remembering What's Left of the Yugoslav Dream

Since the late 1990s travelers visiting the Museum of Contemporary History in Ljubljana, the capital of a newly independent Slovenia, have been offered a surprising lesson along precisely these lines. In most respects, the museum is nothing out of the ordinary. It is a sight familiar to those who have spent any time wandering through the smaller museums of the main cities of former Yugoslavia—a grand enough old building, tucked away unobtrusively in a quiet park, with modest exhibitions that are carefully and professionally presented notwithstanding the lack of resources available to museum staff in wealthier countries. Much of what the curators have chosen to put on display is, it bears noting, really quite conventional and unsurprising: traditional, if engaging, exhibitions of image and text that focus on questions of political and military history, the time-honored subjects of war and diplomacy and nationalism—all more or less standard fare for museumgoers across Europe. In the rooms leading up to the interpretation of Yugoslavia under socialism, for example, patrons will find displays dedicated to the movement for the political unification of the South Slavs, to Slovenia's problematic experience in the troubled interwar Yugoslav state, and to the historiography of the Partisan resistance to German and Italian occupation, lately a delicate matter in the wake of the collapse of socialism and Slovenia's secession in 1991.

Leaving these spaces behind, visitors finally arrive at the exhibition on Tito's Yugoslavia. Should guests by this point be expecting more of the same, that is, a standard historical interpretation grounded upon the main themes and events of élite politics and international relations, they have quite a surprise coming.

Stepping into the hall, visitors are bombarded by images and things indelibly linked in the minds of ordinary consumers with the Yugoslav socialists' vision of the Good Life. Alongside a dizzying collection of commonplace material objects, there are advertisements, placards, signs, and store displays trumpeting all sorts of Slovenian brands and products, most instantly recognizable to anyone who lived and worked and shopped in the unusual Yugoslav blend of socialism and market experimentation. All over the walls in this room, jamming the display cases, and even suspended from the ceiling is the stuff of daily life in what used to be Yugoslavia: clothing, furniture, televisions, radios, vinyl LPs and the hi-fi sets to play them, an electric blender, clocks, lamps, skis, pots, pans, even a modern kitchen stove and other household appliances. A supermarket cart filled with food and grocery items sits in front of a poster advertising the much loved orange soda Jupi and shelves displaying a range of products that evoke the growing abundance of the time. High politics is nowhere; consumerism is everywhere. The message is clear, if unspoken: for the people of this, the first breakaway republic, *this* was Yugoslav socialism.

That Slovenia's many contributions to the exploding consumer culture of the old federation would be chosen to best convey to visitors the experience of Yugoslav socialism and the nature of life in that not-so-distant past is extraordinarily telling. For perhaps more than anything else, it was the ability to participate in at least some of the pleasures and follies of "modern" consumption that set Yugoslav citizens apart from their fellows in other European socialist states. To be sure, compared to the lands of the real Soviet bloc, Yugoslavia did offer considerably more freedom of expression, a looser press regime, and greater latitude for unorthodox political opinions. But these were often of immediate importance only for those individuals who sought to participate directly in the country's political life; in Yugoslavia, as elsewhere in both the East and West, such people were fairly rare. For this unusual form of state socialism that developed in this most unusual of socialist states, what counted more was the system's ability to deliver a version—and beyond that, as I hope I have managed to show throughout this book, a *vision*—of consumption-driven wealth and well-being to its citizens.

It may be, then, that more than the novel theory of worker self-management, more than the profitable posture of nonalignment in international affairs, more than the principle of interethnic brotherhood and unity, more than perhaps even the commanding presence of Tito himself, it was the promise of a distinctive home-grown variety of the Good Life—what I have described as the Yugoslav Dream—that made the country, for its citizens, something uniquely theirs, something perhaps worth preserving.

That the curators of a museum in post-secession Slovenia would select, as the dominant theme of their display on the socialist era, Yugoslavia's consumer culture during "the time of abundance" is revealing in still another critical respect. It illustrates the way that, in the new political communities that have succeeded the Yugoslav federation, the novel consumer culture of the predecessor state has emerged as one of the few permissible subjects of *positive* official or quasi-official remembrance. The lingering authoritarianism of Titoism, the repression of real or imagined political opposition, the unresolved disputes between the country's ethno-national communities—all these find (quite naturally) a strongly negative portrayal in the political culture and the public-history presentations of much of post-socialist Yugoslavia. Yet it seems easy enough to find a warm memory, a bit of what now is often called Yugo-Nostalgia, for the old freedom to shop.

Yugo-Nostalgia is not some simple and straightforward thing, nor is the remembrance of socialist Yugoslavia always charitable, by any means.[1] And even when the retrospection of the past two decades has been more favorably disposed to the Yugoslav project, some aspects have focused on other memorable features of the shared experience—for example, the compelling figure of Tito himself,[2] the often masterful all-Yugoslav sports teams, and especially the powerhouses in soccer and basketball,[3] and, perhaps surprisingly, the inter-regional mixing and young male camaraderie of compulsory military service.

Socialism came with its share of burdens, of course, but even hardships, if communal, can be the basis for nostalgia of this sort, as we see, for example, in Rajko Grlić's film *Karaula* [Border Post], a popular dark-comedy parable of indulgence gone wrong that ends in a fratricidal shootout when the enlisted men of a conspicuously multiethnic unit of the Yugoslav National Army, falsely warned of a coming attack from Albania by an officer seeking to cover up his own sexual indiscretions, turn their fire on their fellow soldiers. Set in 1987 during the waning years of Yugoslavia's famed "brotherhood and unity," *Karaula* communicates with its allegory the message that Yugoslavs and their leaders came to tragedy by telling stories about threats that were not really there, and by believing stories that led them to see comrades as enemies. The film rose to prominence when it was released almost simultaneously across the old federation in 2006, with the much celebrated participation of actors—and characters—from each of the former Yugoslav

---

1. Key contributions to the study of Yugo-Nostalgia include Nicole Lindstrom, "Yugonostalgia: Restorative and Reflective Nostalgia in Former Yugoslavia" *East Central Europe/L'Europe du Centre Est/Eine wissenschaftliche Zeitschrift* 32, no. 1–2 (January 2006): 231–242; Mitja Velikonja, "'Red Shades': Nostalgia for Socialism as an Element of Cultural Pluralism in the Slovene Transition," *Slovene Studies* 30, no. 2 (2008): 171–184; Zala Volčič, "Yugo-Nostalgia: Cultural Memory and Media in the Former Yugoslavia," *Critical Studies in Media Communication* 24, no. 1 (March 2007): 21–38; Monika Palmberger, "Nostalgia Matters: Nostalgia for Yugoslavia as Potential Vision for a Better Future," *Sociologija* (Belgrade) 50, no. 4 (2008): 355–370. On the phenomenon of post-communist memory more generally, see, for example, Charity Scribner, *Requiem for Communism* (Cambridge, Mass., 2003); Maya Nadkarni and Olga Shevchenko, "The Politics of Nostalgia: A Case for Comparative Analysis of Post-Socialist Practices," *Ab Imperio* no. 2 (2004): 487–519.

2. See, for example, Mitja Velikonja, *Titostalgija: Študija nostalgije po Josipu Brozu* (Ljubljana, 2008).

3. See, for example, Vjekoslav Perica, "United They Stood, Divided They Fell: Nationalism and the Yugoslav School of Basketball, 1968–2000," *Nationalities Papers* 29, no. 2 (2001): 267–291; on soccer, see the documentary film *The Last Yugoslavian Football Team* [*Het laatste joegoslavische elftal*], director Vuk Janić, 2000.

republics, and production support from governments and cultural institutions in Croatia, Slovenia, Macedonia, Serbia, and Bosnia-Herzegovina—that is, from all the successor states at the time. Though the filmmakers have insisted that *Karaula* looks to the recent past "with no nostalgia and no hatred,"[4] it is hard not to see the story and the public reception of it as tinged with some affection and admiration for the old bonds and the old ways.

But while a few other subjects such as these can occasionally elicit a Yugo-friendly appraisal, these other themes are overwhelmed by continual upwellings of nostalgia for the shared abundance of the 1960s and 1970s. Above all else, it is a reference to the Good Life of the old days that keeps surfacing most prominently and most generously in the literature of *Jugonostalgija*. Even when what is recalled is the way in which the Yugoslav system sometimes could not manage to deliver, this, too, can form the foundation of happy memories. Here again, as with the remembrance of the mutual sacrifices and common annoyances of military service, we see how memory work may make a virtue out of shared communal hardship. In their joint endeavors to confront and overcome the occasional defect in the country's consumer offerings—the perceived weaknesses of domestic fashion, a shortage here and there, the need to use purchases made abroad to fill the luxury gap—Yugoslav shoppers showed themselves to be savvy, flexible, creative, and enterprising. They were then, and still remain, proud of that resourcefulness. Now, the commemoration of those efforts as "something we all did together, to make a go of it" may indeed function as powerfully as the celebration of what was plentiful, pleasurable, good, fun, and satisfying.[5]

These acts of remembrance offer, moreover, strong (if admittedly imperfect) evidence about the historical questions that form the foundation of the account I have presented here. Through this ongoing work of collective and individual memory, the potent consumer culture of socialist Yugoslavia, with all its pleasures and all its shortcomings, is once again revealed to be a vital element of the country's history.

The Good Life Lost surely has become the subject of nostalgia; that there is no denying. It is not, however, a mere museum piece, something to be visited on occasion, viewed at some safe distance as a curious thing of the past, and otherwise forgotten.

Instead, all across Yugoslavia, the years following the breakup have offered up example after example of how the consumption-driven Yugoslav Dream remains, to a surprising extent, alive: a vital and dynamic subject of popular historical memory. These retrievals and commemorations of the familiar old culture of the market, and of the experiences and pleasures it

---

4. See http://www.borderpostmovie.com/synopsis.php (last accessed 22 June 2009) (official website for the film *Border Post*, director Rajko Grlić).

5. Compare Paul Betts, "Twilight of the Idols: East German Memory and Material Culture," *Journal of Modern History* 72 (September 2000): 731–765.

promised, remind us once again just what it was about Yugoslav socialism that had the power to make ordinary Yugoslavs buy the visions that were so painstakingly sold to them, feel with their fellow citizens the solidarity of shared satisfaction and shared desire, and create a way of life that people around the country could experience then—and remember now—as "*naš*," "ours." These, then, are memories that matter.

Proof of that comes, in abundance, from ex-Yugoslavs themselves. Some of the richest and most compelling evidence of the tight link between the consumerism of the past and the wistfulness of the present is found in the fascinating online collection of contributions to a *Lexicon of Yugoslav Mythology* compiled by Dubravka Ugrešić, Dejan Kršić, and Ivan Molek, a frank and unapologetic Yugo-nostalgic project launched in the first decade after the demise of the federation, and one that has more recently come to life in a new way through a successful and well-received print version.[6] The online version of the *Leksikon* is crammed with references to the fondly remembered consumption practices of the past, submitted by a wide variety of ordinary ex-Yugoslavs from across ex-Yugoslavia. Such reminiscences also fairly spill from the pages of the later book version of the project, which was released, not coincidentally, by publishers in both Zagreb and Belgrade, and which sets forth its entries as contributed in the various dialects of Serbo-Croatian as well as Slovenian and Macedonian—reproducing them without translation, with the obvious implication that there would be no need, given a remembered history that remains "*naš*." Obviously this work presumes a past that was commonly experienced, and, as a result, one that may now be commonly retrieved, commonly held, commonly understood, and commonly enjoyed.

In this project, as indeed in so many other popular manifestations of Yugo-Nostalgia, we find in abundance the stuff that dreams were made of. There are, to be sure, quite a number of images of a rather more global notion of the Affluent Society, seen here as they came to Yugoslavia through such channels as the importation of Western brands and broadcasts of the American serial *Dynasty*, a veritable iconostasis of 1980s-era images of luxury, wealth, and status. But these glimpses of the capitalist world are counterbalanced, if not outweighed entirely, by the profusion of Yugoslavia's own distinctive versions of the many-splendored things that made the Good Life.

The *Leksikon*'s list is a long one, cataloguing (in addition to plenty of content from the worlds of politics, public life, and the arts) feature after feature of the consumer landscape: must-have rock albums and favorite movies, the well-loved evocations of the Good Life of the 1960s in the hit

---

6. Dubravka Ugrešić, Dejan Kršić, and Ivan Molek, eds., "Leksikon YU-mitologije," http://www.geocities.com/ yu_leksikon/home.html (last accessed 24 June 2009); Iris Adrić, Vladimir Arsenijević, and Djordje Matić, eds., *Leksikon YU mitologije*, 2nd ed. (Belgrade, 2005). See also http://www.leksikon-yu-mitologije.net/index.php (last accessed 24 June 2009).

TV series *Grlom u jagode*, Iskra electronic appliances, the short and stylish *šimike* and *Dikanke* boots of the 1970s, getaways taken on the national airline JAT, Zagreb's first Konzum/Unikonzum self-service grocery stores, Univerzalke athletic shoes, cigarettes with famous marks such as Opatija, Filter 57, and Filter 160, the supposedly indispensable Valera hair gel of the 1980s (remembered also for its notable TV ads with the exclamation "Va-va-va-lera!!"), Ledo and Pekabela ice cream treats, Majburger hamburgers and the Hambi fast-food restaurants, Perion detergent, Cedevita and Fla-Vor-Aid drink mixes, Obod refrigerators ("one of the all-Yugoslav symbols of household-appliance technology, and one still to be found even today in many homes"), Jugoplastika rubber sandals for jaunts to the seaside, Cockta soft drinks, Elan skis, Minas coffee, Euroblok chocolate snacks and Eurokrem chocolate spread (the Yugoslav answer to Nutella), the stone-washed jeans of the 1980s, candies marketed under the Fru-Fru, Kraš 505, and Kiki labels, Plazma cookies, the ubiquitous Vegeta seasoning mix, Kalodont and Vademecum toothpastes, and Argo packaged soups ("mandatory supplies for all trips and excursions").[7] *Šoping*—the colloquial word for "shopping," and an activity that one Macedonian contributor called "recreation for the working class"—gets no fewer than four separate entries.[8]

Some of the purchases recalled in the print and online versions of the *Lexicon of Yugoslav Mythology* were, naturally enough, big-ticket items. The Zastava 1300 and 101 automobiles and their little brother the beloved Fića take a prominent place, as do the ill-fated Yugo and the more respected Citroen 2CV (affectionately called the *spaček* or "freak" because of its odd looks), along with *vikendica* vacation homes and the inescapable furniture trend of the *kombinovana soba* (literally, "combination room"—a complete living-room set with a sofa, loveseat, armchair, coffee table, and étagère), a style that anyone who had spent much time in living rooms around the country would recognize as immensely popular, and one that led the lexicographers of the Yugoslav Dream to observe tartly that "after the *kombinovana soba* appeared on the market, all Yugoslav homes looked the same."[9]

But, notably, many if not most of the consumer goods and experiences evoked in the *Leksikon* are, quite to the contrary, simple everyday indulgences—examples, in other words, of the very sort of "ordinary luxuries" that allowed Yugoslavs to feel that they, too, had managed to grab a bit of the Good Life for themselves. Yes, many Yugoslavs may have contented themselves with soup mix from a packet when they were away on their camping

---

7. See, in particular, Dragan Jovanović, entry for "Argo juha/supa," in Adrić, Arsenijević, and Matić, *Leksikon YU mitologije*, 40; Anonymous, entry for "Frižider Obodin Cetinje," 140.

8. See Branko Rosić, Ira Payer, Iris Adrić, and Igor Toševski, entries for "Šoping," in Adrić, Arsenijević, and Matić, *Leksikon YU mitologije*, 382–383.

9. See Zorana Gajić, entry for "Kombinovana soba," in Adrić, Arsenijević, and Matić, *Leksikon YU mitologije*, 195.

adventures or spending weekends at the *vikendica,* but the bigger point is that they were, in fact, taking those trips, and enjoying themselves quite a bit along the way.

To be sure, there are regional variations in the kindly backward gaze of Yugo-Nostalgia, with the tendency most resilient among Serbs, Macedonians, and Slovenes, and, by contrast, weakest among Croats, where the term often functions pejoratively, sometimes as nothing less than an indictment for perceived disloyalty. As Maja Mikula has observed, many of the dominant registers of post-Yugoslav political culture, especially in the secessionist polities, have treated expressions of fond appreciation for the common past as the mark of a disreputable, retrograde politics. In these circles Yugo-Nostalgia was, she concludes, "a synonym for domestic treason and nemesis of patriotism."[10]

Yet the Yugo-Nostalgia of consumer abundance has proved remarkable for its tenacity, its variety, and, yes, its ubiquity. It shows no signs of abating any time soon, and it has not yet been squelched by the most insistent nationalist antipathy. Even in Croatia, where the phenomenon is most suspect, hostility toward Yugo-Nostalgia has not been enough, as Ines Prica concludes, to quell a sense of longing for the comparative personal economic security and reduced social differentiation of the past, and, stemming from this, the continued expression of "a feeling that 'things, nevertheless, used to be better then.'"[11]

In these displays of nostalgia for the commonly shared consumer opportunities of the past, we see repeatedly a sense of melancholy desire for the time when, as expressed by the Web forum contributor quoted in the epigraph to this closing section, "even the little guy could live normally," with employment security, sunny expectations for the future, and—not least of all—the lived experience of abundance in the present as well. Much the same sense is echoed in the sentiments of Srđan Karanović, director and cowriter of the popular 1970s television show *Grlom u jagode.* The series is, it should be remembered, at once a nostalgic enterprise in its own right, with its reflections on the early heyday of the Yugoslav Dream, and now a prime subject of post-socialist Yugo-Nostalgia.[12] "From today's perspective," Karanović

---

10. Maja Mikula, "Virtual Landscapes of Memory," *Information, Communication & Society* 6, no. 2 (2003): 169–186, at 172. Catherine Baker notes how such charges were used in post-independence Croatia in an effort to blunt the appeal of Serbian singer Đorđe Balašević, a fixture of the Yugoslav music scene since the 1970s: "The major accusation against both Balašević and his fans was of 'Yugo-nostalgia': in Croatian political life, this concept had served as a catch-all insult for any individual or idea which failed to correspond to Tudjmanist ideology and which was therefore assumed self-evidently to prefer the inimical previous regime." Catherine Baker, "The Politics of Performance: Transnationalism and Its Limits in Former Yugoslav Popular Music, 1999–2004," *Ethnopolitics* 5, no. 3 (2006): 275–293, citing Dubravka Ugrešić, *The Culture of Lies: Anti-Political Essays* (London, 1998), 231.

11. Ines Prica, "In Search of Post-Socialist Subject," *Narodna umjetnost: hrvatski časopis za etnologiju i folkloristiku* 44, no. 1 (2007): 163–186, at 167 n. 7.

12. On the abiding popularity of *Grlom u jagode* with television audiences in the former Yugoslavia, see, for example, Sonja Ćirić, "TV reprize—'Grlom u jagode': Odrastanje Baneta

reflects, "I can say that I am very happy that I grew up in those years of the '60's. I don't remember from that time any sort of political pressure either on my parents, on me, or on my friends. We lived very modestly, but we had the feeling that things were getting better both around us and with us, and that is a fantastic feeling."[13]

Yugoslavia's culture of consumption, abundance, and satisfaction was indeed, in a number of ways, "fantastic," and yet at the same time it was agreeably, reassuringly *real*. For the best part of three decades, most Yugoslavs could be justified in feeling that "things were getting better both around us and with us." If the vibrant consumer experience of the one-time socialist federation has become one of those rare things that can now be remembered fondly, as an element of the prior system unthreatening to the new, capitalist, post-Yugoslav political and cultural order of the successor states, that is because this distinctive feature of the old Yugoslavia played such a critical part in forming the broader popular culture of the separate societies that are now taking shape on its ruins. When the ordinary citizens of those successor states look for a happy memory of their former country, it is, with remarkable frequency, to the life of market-centered abundance—so important to the life and death of Yugoslavia—that they turn.

Remembered in this way, Yugoslavia *was* its consumer culture. This was what made the Yugoslavs Yugoslavs, what made the Yugoslavs dream, and what made the Yugoslav Dream.

Bumbara," *Vreme* no. 656 (31 July 2003), http://www.vreme.com/cms/view.php?id=347018 (last accessed 8 December 2010).

13. Srđan Karanović, quoted in Goran Tarlać, entry for "Grlom u jagode," in Adrić, Arsenijević, and Matić, *Leksikon YU mitologije*, 151.

Selected Bibliography

Archival Materials

Arhiv Jugoslavije, Belgrade
Hrvatski Državni Arhiv, Zagreb

Video Materials

Grlom u jagode (television series). DVD. Directed by Srđan Karanović. Belgrade TV2, 1976. Belgrade: PGP/RTS (Radio-Televizija Srbije), Zlatne Serije series, item number DV-1130204, 2004.

Vruć vetar (television series). DVD. Directed by Aleksandar Đorđević. Televizija Beograd, 1980. Belgrade: PGP/RTS (Radio-Televizija Srbije), Zlatne Serije series, item number 1140204, 2005.

Journals, Magazines, and Newspapers

Ambalaža
Beogradska nedelja
Bilten: glasilo Društva ekonomskih propgandistov Slovenije
Delo
Ideja: časopis za pitanja ekonomske propagande
Interpublic: list za pitanje ekonomske propagande, industrijske estetike i psihologije rada
Itd: ilustrirani tednik Dela
Jana
JFTK novosti: novine jugoslovenskog festivala tržišnih komunikacija
Kreativne komunikacije
Marketing: časopis Jugoslavenskog udruženja za marketing—JUMA
MEDIJ: glasilo Društva ekonomskih propagandistov Slovenije
MM: marketing magazin

Naš dom
Naš publicitet
NIN: Nedeljne informativne novine
Oslobođenje
Politika
Pregled Medjunarodnih sajmova
Privredna propaganda: jugoslovenski časopis za privrednu propagandu i publicitet
Propaganda: časopis za ekonomsku propagandu i publicitet
Savremena privredna propaganda: list za ekonomsku propagandu
Savremeno pakovanje
Standard: časopis za unapredjenje privredne propagande
Start
Supermarket: časopis za praksu suvremene trgovine
Svijet
Teleks
Tovariš
UEPS (newsletter of the Udruženje ekonomskih propagandista SR Srbije)
Večernje novosti
Vjesnik

Published Statistical Sources

Jugoslavija 1945–1985: Statistički prikaz. Belgrade: Savezni zavod za statistiku, 1986.
Jugoslavija, 1918–1988: Statistički godišnjak. Belgrade: Savezni zavod za statistiku, 1989.

Books, Articles, and Manuscripts

Adrić, Iris, Vladimir Arsenijević, and Djordje Matić, eds. *Leksikon YU mitologije,* 2d ed. Belgrade: Rende/Zagreb: Postscriptum, 2005.
Apih, Jure. *Oglašanja v A-duru.* Ljubljana: Slon, 1996.
Baćević, Ljiljana, Firdus Džinić, Gordana Kaćanski, Milan Matić, and Sergije Pegan. *Jugoslovensko javno mnenje o aktuelnim političkim i društvenim pitanjima.* Vol. 3, 1964. Jugoslovensko javno mnenje, Series A: Izveštaji o rezultatima anketnih istraživanja. Belgrade: Institut društvenih nauka, Centar za Istraživanje Javnog Mnenja, 1964.
Baćević, Ljiljana, Toma Djordjević, Firdus Džinić, Gordana Kaćanski, Zoran Pandurović, and Bratislav Valčić. *Jugoslovensko javno mnenje o aktuelnim političkim i društvenim pitanjima 1965.* Vol. 6, 1965. Jugoslovensko javno mnenje, Series A: Izveštaji o rezultatima anketnih istraživanja. Belgrade: Institut društvenih nauka, Centar za Istraživanje Javnog Mnenja, 1965.
Bajt, Aleksander. *Alternativna ekonomska politika.* Zagreb: Globus, 1986.
———. *Osnovi ekonomske politike i analize.* Zagreb: Informator, 1979.
Baker, Catherine. "The Politics of Performance: Transnationalism and Its Limits in Former Yugoslav Popular Music, 1999–2004." *Ethnopolitics* 5, no. 3 (2006): 275–293.

Barker, Adele Marie, ed. *Consuming Russia: Popular Culture, Sex, and Society since Gorbachev.* Durham, N.C.: Duke University Press, 1999.

Barthes, Roland. "La rhétorique de l'image." *Communications* 4 (1964): 40–51.

Baskin, Mark Allan. "Political Innovation and Policy Implementation in Yugoslavia: The Case of Worker Migration Abroad." Ph.D. diss., University of Michigan, 1986.

Bećković, Matija. "O Jugoslovenima." In Bećković, *Dr Janez Paćuka o meduvremenu,* 81–84. Novi Sad: Matica srpska, 1969.

Betts, Paul. "Twilight of the Idols: East German Memory and Material Culture." *Journal of Modern History* 72 (September 2000): 731–765.

Bilandžić, Dušan. *Historija Socijalističke Federativne Republike Jugoslavije: glavni procesi,* 2d ed. Zagreb: Školska knjiga, 1979.

Bird, William J., Jr. *"Better Living": Advertising, Media, and the New Vocabulary of Business Leadership, 1935–1955.* Evanston, Ill.: Northwestern University Press, 1999.

Bourdieu, Pierre. *Distinction: A Social Critique of the Judgment of Taste.* Cambridge, Mass.: Harvard University Press, 1984.

Božović, Ratko R. *Suočavanja.* Nikšić: Univerzitetska riječ, 1988.

Bracewell, Wendy. "Adventures in the Marketplace: Yugoslav Travel Writing and Tourism in the 1950s–1960s." In *Turizm: The Russian and East European Tourist under Capitalism and Socialism,* edited by Anne E. Gorsuch and Diane P. Koenker, 248–265. Ithaca: Cornell University Press, 2006.

Brkljač, Branimir. *Efekti ekonomsko-propagandnog programa koji se emituje na radiju i televiziji.* Novi Sad: Radio-Televizija Novi Sad, 1990.

Brubaker, Rogers. *Ethnicity Without Groups.* Cambridge, Mass.: Harvard University Press, 2004.

Bryson, Philip J. *The Consumer under Socialist Planning: The East German Case.* New York: Praeger, 1984.

Campbell, Colin. "Consumption: The New Wave of Research in the Humanities and Social Sciences." In *To Have Possessions: A Handbook on Ownership and Property.* Special issue. *Journal of Social Behavior and Personality* 6, no. 6 (1991): 57–74.

Castillo, Greg. *Cold War on the Home Front: The Soft Power of Midcentury Design.* Minneapolis: University of Minnesota Press, 2010.

Chandler, Alfred D., Jr. *The Visible Hand: The Managerial Revolution in American Business.* Cambridge, Mass.: Belknap Press of Harvard University Press, 1977.

Chelcea, Liviu. "The *Culture* of Shortage during State Socialism: Consumption Practices in a Romanian Village in the 1980s." *Cultural Studies* 16, no. 1 (2002): 16–43.

Cigoj, Stojan. *Varstvo potrošnikov in naloge javne uprave,* 1. zvezek. Ljubljana: Inštitut za javno upravo pri Pravni fakulteti, 1982.

Ćirić, Darko, et al. *Beograd šezdesetih godina XX veka.* Belgrade: Muzej grada Beograda, 2003.

Ćirić, Sonja. "TV reprize—'Grlom u jagode': Odrastanje Baneta Bumbara." *Vreme* no. 656, 31 July 2003.

Čobeljić, Dušan. *Problemi planiranja lične potrošnje.* Belgrade: Nolit, 1958.

Cohen, Lenard J. *Broken Bonds: The Disintegration of Yugoslavia.* Boulder: Westview, 1993.

Cohen, Lizabeth. *A Consumers' Republic: The Politics of Mass Consumption in Postwar America*. New York: Vintage Books, 2003.

Condee, Nancy, and Vladimir Padunov. "The ABC of Russian Consumer Culture: Readings, Ratings, and Real Estate." In *Soviet Hieroglyphics: Visual Culture in Late Twentieth-Century Russia*, edited by Nancy Condee, 130–172. Bloomington: Indiana University Press, 1995.

Cox, Randi. "All This Can Be Yours! Soviet Commercial Advertising and the Social Construction of Space, 1928–1956." In *The Landscape of Stalinism: The Art and Ideology of Soviet Space*, edited by Evgeny Dobrenko and Eric Naiman, 125–162. Seattle: University of Washington Press, 2003.

Crew, David F., ed. *Consuming Germany in the Cold War*. Oxford: Berg, 2003.

Crocker, David A. *Praxis and Democratic Socialism: The Critical Social Theory of Marković and Stojanović*. Atlantic Highlands, N.J.: Humanities, 1983.

Crowley, David. "Warsaw's Shops, Stalinism, and the Thaw." In *Style and Socialism: Modernity and Material Culture in Post-War Eastern Europe*, edited by Susan E. Reid and David Crowley, 25–47. Oxford: Berg, 2000.

Crowley, David, and Susan E. Reid, eds. *Socialist Spaces: Sites of Everyday Life in the Eastern Bloc*. Oxford: Berg, 2002.

Ćulibrk, Svetozar. *Želje i strahovanja naroda Jugoslavije*. Belgrade: Institut društvenih nauka, 1965. (Published in one volume with Zlata Grebo's *Želje i strahovanja jugoslovenske žene*.)

Damjanović, Mijat, Toma Đoršević, Firdus Džinić, Petar Gledić, Gordana Kaćanski, Milan Matić, Zoran Pandurović, Sergije Pegan, and Bratislav Valčić. *Jugoslovensko javno mnenje o privrednoj reformi 1965*. Vol. 7. Jugoslovensko javno mnenje, Series A: Izveštaji o rezultatima anketnih istraživanja. Belgrade: Institut društvenih nauka, Centar za Istraživanje Javnog Mnenja, 1965.

Davis, Deborah S., ed. *The Consumer Revolution in Urban China*. Berkeley: University of California Press, 2000.

de Grazia, Victoria. *Irresistible Empire: America's Advance through 20th-Century Europe*. Cambridge, Mass.: Belknap Press of Harvard University Press, 2005.

Denitch, Bogdan Denis. *The Legitimation of a Revolution: The Yugoslav Case*. New Haven, Conn.: Yale University Press, 1976.

———. *Limits and Possibilities: The Crisis of Yugoslav Socialism and State Socialist Systems*. Minneapolis: University of Minnesota Press, 1990.

Deželak, Bogomir. *Ekonomska propaganda*. Maribor: Visoka ekonomsko komercialna šola, 1973 [1966].

———. *Marketing*. Maribor: Založba Obzorja, 1971.

———. *Politika in organiziranje marketinga*. Maribor: Založba Obzorja, 1984.

Dimitrijević, Radmilo, ed. *Ekonomska propaganda i privredna reforma u SFRJ*. Belgrade: Jugoslovenska izložba ekonomske propagande i publiciteta, 1968.

Dinter, Čedo. *Ekonomsko-propagandna služba u poduzeću*. Zagreb: Savezni centar za obrazovanje rukovodnih kadrova u privredi, 1961.

Djilas, Aleksa. *The Contested Country: Yugoslav Unity and Communist Revolution, 1919–1953*. Cambridge, Mass.: Harvard University Press, 1991.

Djilas, Milovan. *The New Class: An Analysis of the Communist System*. New York: Praeger, 1957.

Doder, Dusko. *The Yugoslavs.* New York: Random House, 1978.

Donia, Robert J., and John V. A. Fine, Jr. *Bosnia and Hercegovina: A Tradition Betrayed.* New York: Columbia University Press, 1994.

Drakulić, Slavenka. *The Balkan Express: Fragments from the Other Side of War.* New York: Harper Perennial, 1994.

Drasinover, Julije. "Juridical and Institutional Marketing Framework." In *Marketing East/West: A Comparative View: Report on the Work of the ESOMAR East/West Marketing Group,* European Society for Opinion and Marketing Research/World Association for Public Opinion Research, 1–6. Amsterdam: ESOMAR, n.d. (ca. 1973).

Drugo jugoslavensko savjetovanje propagandista. Proceedings of the Second Yugoslav Conference of Advertising Specialists, Zagreb, 22–23 February 1963. Zagreb: Udruženje ekonomskih propagandista Hrvatske, 1963.

Društveni slojevi i društvena svest: sociološko istraživanje interesa, stilova života, klasne svesti i vrednosno-ideoloških orientacija društvenih slojeva. Belgrade: Centar za sociološka istraživanja Instituta društvenih nauka, 1977.

Dubey, Vinod. *Yugoslavia: Development with Decentralization.* Baltimore: Johns Hopkins University Press, 1975.

Duda, Igor. *Pronađeno blagostanje: svakodnevni život i potrošačka kultura u Hrvatskoj 1970-ih i 1980-ih.* Zagreb: Srednja Europa, 2010.

———. *U potrazi za odmorom i blagostanjem: o povijesti dokolice i potrošačkog društva u Hrvatskoj 1950-ih i 1960-ih.* Zagreb: Srednja Europa, 2005.

———. "Tehnika narodu! Trajna dobra, potrošnja i slobodno vrijeme u socijalističkoj Hrvatskoj." *Časopis za suvremenu povijest* 37, no. 2 (2005): 371–392.

Duesenberry, James S. *Income, Saving and the Theory of Consumer Behavior.* Cambridge, Mass.: Harvard University Press, 1949.

Easterlin, Richard. "Does Economic Growth Improve the Human Lot?" In *Nations and Households in Economic Growth: Essays in Honor of Moses Abramovitz,* edited by Paul David and Melvin Reder. 89–125. New York: Academic Press, 1974.

———. "Will Raising the Incomes of All Increase the Happiness of All?" *Journal of Economic Behavior and Organization* 27 (1995): 35–48.

Ewen, Stuart. *Captains of Consciousness: Advertising and the Social Roots of Consumer Culture.* 25th anniversary edition. New York: Basic Books, 2001.

Fehérváry, Krisztina. "In Search of the Normal: Material Culture and Middle-Class Fashioning in a Hungarian Steel Town, 1950–1997." Ph.D. diss., University of Chicago, 2005.

———. "American Kitchens, Luxury Bathrooms, and the Search for a 'Normal' Life in Postsocialist Hungary." *Ethnos* 67, no. 3 (November 2002): 369–400.

Fine, Ben, and Ellen Leopold. *The World of Consumption.* London: Routledge, 1993.

Fitzpatrick, Sheila. *Everyday Stalinism: Ordinary Life in Extraordinary Times: Soviet Russia in the 1930s.* New York: Oxford University Press, 1999.

Fox, Stephen. *The Mirror Makers: A History of American Advertising and Its Creators.* Urbana: University of Illinois Press, 1997.

Francetić, Marija. "Semiologija reklame?" *Sol* 1 (1986): 83–90.

Fruht, Miroslav. *Kreacija privredne propagande.* Belgrade: Savremena administracija, 1975.

Galbraith, John Kenneth. *The Affluent Society.* New York: New American Library, 1958.

Gams, Ivan. "Skozi Srednjo Evropo v Evropo?" *Nova revija* 9, nos. 101–102 (September–October 1990): 1338–1340.

Gécser, Ottó, and Dávid Kitzinger. "Fairy Sales: The Budapest International Fairs as Virtual Shopping Tours." *Cultural Studies* 16, no. 1 (2002): 145–164.

Goldman, Robert. *Reading Ads Socially.* London: Routledge, 1992.

Grebo, Zlata. *Želje i strahovanja jugoslovenske žene.* Belgrade: Institut društvenih nauka, 1965. (Published in one volume with Svetozar Ćulibrk's *Želje i strahovanja naroda Jugoslavije.*)

Gronow, Jukka, and Alan Warde, eds. *Ordinary Consumption.* London: Routledge, 2001.

Gronow, Jukka. *Caviar with Champagne: Common Luxury and the Ideals of the Good Life in Stalin's Russia.* Oxford: Berg, 2003.

——. "Caviar with Champagne: Good Life and Common Luxury in Stalin's Soviet Union." *Suomen Antropologi/Finnish Journal of Anthropology* 23, no. 4 (1998): 29–40.

Guevara, Ernesto "Che." "Man and Socialism." In *The Cuba Reader: History, Culture, Politics,* edited by Aviva Chomsky, Barry Carr, and Pamela Maria Smorkaloff, 370–374. Durham, N.C.: Duke University Press, 2003.

Hamilton, Shane. "Supermarket USA Confronts State Socialism: Airlifting the Technopolitics of Industrial Food Distribution into Cold War Yugoslavia." In *Cold War Kitchen: Americanization, Technology, and European Users,* edited by Ruth Oldenziel and Karin Zachmann, 137–159. Cambridge, Mass.: MIT Press, 2009.

Hankiss, Elémer. *The Toothpaste of Immortality: Self-Construction in the Consumer Age.* Washington, D.C.: Woodrow Wilson Center Press, 2006.

Hanson, Philip. *Advertising and Socialism.* White Plains, N.Y.: International Arts and Sciences Press, 1974.

Heldmann, Philipp. *Herrschaft, Wirtschaft, Anoraks: Konsumpolitik in der DDR der Sechzigerjahre.* Gottingen: Vandenhoeck & Ruprecht, 2004.

——. "Negotiating Consumption in a Dictatorship: Consumer Politics in the GDR in the 1950s and 1960s." In *The Politics of Consumption: Material Culture and Citizenship in Europe and America,* edited by M. J. Daunton and Matthew Hilton, 185–202. Oxford: Berg, 2001.

——. "Konsumpolitik in der DDR: Jugendmode in den sechziger Jahren." In *Konsumpolitik: Die Regulierung Des Privaten Verbrauchs Im 20. Jahrhundert,* edited by Hartmut Berghoff, 135–158. Göttingen: Vandenhoeck & Ruprecht, 1999.

Hessler, Julie. *A Social History of Soviet Trade: Trade Policy, Retail Practices, and Consumption, 1917–1953.* Princeton, N.J.: Princeton University Press, 2004.

——. "A Postwar Perestroika? Toward a History of Private Enterprise in the USSR." *Slavic Review* 57, no. 3 (fall 1998): 516–542.

Hilton, Marjorie L. "Retailing the Revolution: The State Department Store (GUM) and Soviet Society in the 1920s." *Journal of Social History* 37, no. 4 (summer 2004): 939–964.

Hilton, Matthew. "The Legacy of Luxury: Moralities of Consumption since the 18th Century." *Journal of Consumer Culture* 4, no. 1 (2004): 101–123.

Hladnik, Mario, ed. *Mediji komuniciranja s tržištem danas i sutra: referati s međunarodnog simpozija ekonomske propagande '75*. Papers presented at the International Advertising Conference, Cavtat, 11–14 March 1975. Zagreb: Društvo ekonomskih propagandista SR Hrvatske, 1975.

——. *Zbornik predavanja sa seminara vizuelnog komunikacije*. Papers presented at the seminar "Visual Communication and Advertising," Zagreb, 1975. Zagreb: Društvo ekonomskih propagandista Hrvatske, 1976.

Horkheimer, Max, and Theodor W. Adorno. "The Culture Industry: Enlightenment as Mass Deception." In Adorno and Horkheimer, *Dialectic of Enlightenment: Philosophical Fragments*, edited by Gunzelin Schmid Noerr, translated by Edmund Jephcott, 94–136. Stanford: Stanford University Press, 2002.

Horvat, Branko. *Jugoslavenska privreda, 1965–1983*. Ljubljana: Cankarjeva Založba, 1984.

——. *ABC jugoslavenskog socijalizma*. Zagreb: Globus, 1989.

——. *An Essay on Yugoslav Society*. White Plains, N.Y.: International Arts and Sciences Press, 1969 [1967].

——. *The Yugoslav Economic System*. Armonk, N.Y.: M. E. Sharpe, 1976.

Humphery, Kim. *Shelf Life: Supermarkets and the Changing Cultures of Consumption*. Cambridge: Cambridge University Press, 1998.

Humphrey, Caroline. *The Unmaking of Soviet Life: Everyday Economies after Socialism*. Ithaca: Cornell University Press, 2002.

——. "Creating a Culture of Disillusionment: Consumption in Moscow, a Chronicle of Changing Times." In *Worlds Apart: Modernity through the Prism of the Local*, edited by Daniel Miller, 43–68. London: Routledge, 1995.

Ikels, Charlotte. *The Return of the God of Wealth: The Transition to a Market Economy in Urban China*. Stanford: Stanford University Press, 1996.

Ilić, Stanko. *Put u humano društvo: od socijalizma ka komunizmu*. Belgrade: Ekonomika, n.d. (ca. 1984).

Janeković, Dara. Interview with Josip Broz Tito. *Vjesnik*, 8 October 1972, 1–4.

Jelenić, Čedomir. *Ekonomska propaganda u trgovinskom preduzeću*. Belgrade: Naša reč, n.d.

Jogan, Maca. "Potrošniška usmerjenost in vprašanje emancipacije." *Teorija in praksa* 18, no. 10 (1981): 1218–1223.

Johnson, A. Ross Johnson. *The Transformation of Communist Ideology: The Yugoslav Case, 1945–1953*. Cambridge, Mass.: MIT Press, 1972.

Jugoslovensko javno mnenje 1966. Vol. 8, 1966. Jugoslovensko javno mnenje, Series A: Izveštaji o rezultatima anketnih istraživanja. Belgrade: Institut društvenih nauka, Centar za Istraživanje Javnog Mnenja, 1967.

Kaminsky, Annette. *Wohlstand, Schönheit, Glück: kleine Konsumgeschichte der DDR*. Munich: Beck, 2001.

——. *Illustrierte Konsumgeschichte der DDR*. Erfurt: Landeszentrale für politische Bildung Thüringen, 1999.

Kaplan, Robert D. *Balkan Ghosts: A Journey Through History*. New York: St. Martin's, 1993.

Kapor, Momo. "Reklamokracija." *MM: Media Marketing*, no. 12 (April 1982): 6.

Keat, Russell, Nigel Whitely, and Nicholas Abercrombie, eds. *The Authority of the Consumer*. London: Routledge, 1994.

Kelly, Catriona. "Ordinary Life in Extraordinary Times: Chronicles of the Quotidian in Russia and the Soviet Union." *Kritika: Explorations in Russian and Eurasian History* 3, no. 4 (fall 2002): 631–651.

Kersnik, Aleš. *Struktura potrošnje narodnega dohodka in njen vpliv na razvoj našega gospodarstva.* Ljubljana: RSS, 1958.

Klinar, Peter. "O življenskem stilu družbenih slojev na Slovenskem (II)." *Teorija in praksa* 16, no. 2 (1979): 196–215.

Kornai, János. *The Socialist System: The Political Economy of Communism.* Princeton, N.J.: Princeton University Press, 1992.

Kotler, Philip. *Marketing Management: Analysis, Planning, and Control.* Englewood Cliffs, N.J.: Prentice Hall, 1967.

Kozak, Primož. *Peter Klepec v Ameriki.* Maribor: Založba Obzorja, 1971.

Kuvačić, Ivan. "Middle Class Ideology." In *Praxis: Yugoslav Essays in the Philosophy and Methodology of the Social Sciences,* edited by Mihailo Marković and Gajo Petrović, translated by Joan Coddington et al., 333–356. Dordrecht: D. Reidel, 1979.

——. "Potrošačko društvo." In Ivan Kuvačić, *Znanost i društvo,* 167–173. Zagreb: Naprijed, 1977.

Lampe, John R. *Yugoslavia as History: Twice There Was a Country,* 2d ed. Cambridge: Cambridge University Press, 2000.

Lampe, John R., and Marvin R. Jackson. *Balkan Economic History, 1550–1950: From Imperial Borderlands to Developing Nations.* Bloomington: Indiana University Press, 1982.

Landsman, Mark. *Dictatorship and Demand: The Politics of Consumerism in East Germany.* Cambridge, Mass.: Harvard University Press, 2005.

Leach, William. *Land of Desire: Merchants, Power, and the Rise of a New American Culture.* New York: Pantheon, 1993.

——. "Transformations in a Culture of Consumption: Women and Department Stores, 1890–1925." *Journal of American History* 71 (September 1984): 319–342.

Lears, T. J. Jackson. *Fables of Abundance: A Cultural History of Advertising in America.* New York: Basic Books, 1994.

Lebergott, Stanley. *Pursuing Happiness: American Consumers in the Twentieth Century.* Princeton, N.J.: Princeton University Press, 1993.

Leiss, William. *The Limits of Satisfaction: An Essay on the Problem of Needs and Commodities.* Toronto: University of Toronto Press, 1976.

Leiss, William, Stephen Kline, and Sut Jhally. *Social Communication in Advertising: Persons, Products, and Images of Well-Being.* New York: Methuen, 1986.

Letić, Franjo. *Društveni život vanjskih migranata.* Zagreb: Radničke novine, 1989.

Lilly, Carol S. *Power and Persuasion: Ideology and Rhetoric in Communist Yugoslavia, 1944–1953.* Boulder: Westview, 2001.

Lindstrom, Nicole. "Yugonostalgia: Restorative and Reflective Nostalgia in Former Yugoslavia." *East Central Europe/L'Europe du Centre Est/Eine wissenschaftliche Zeitschrift* 32: 1–2 (January 2006): 231–242.

Lorbek, Franc. *Osnove komuniciranja v marketingu.* Ljubljana: Delo/Gospodarski vestnik, 1979.

Lüdtke, Alf. "Introduction: What Is the History of Everyday Life and Who Are Its Practitioners?" In *The History of Everyday Life: Reconstructing Historical Experiences and Ways of Life,* edited by Alf Lüdtke, 3–40. Translated by William Templer. Princeton, N.J.: Princeton University Press, 1995.

Luthar, Breda. "Remembering Socialism: On Desire, Consumption and Surveillance." *Journal of Consumer Culture* 6, no. 2 (2006): 229–259.

Lydall, Harold. *Yugoslavia in Crisis.* Oxford: Clarendon, 1989.

Magaš, Branka. *The Destruction of Yugoslavia: Tracking the Break-up 1980–92.* London: Verso, 1993.

Mandel, Ruth, and Caroline Humphrey, eds. *Markets and Moralities: Ethnographies of Postsocialism.* Oxford: Berg, 2002.

Marchand, Roland. *Advertising the American Dream: Making Way for Modernity, 1920–1940.* Berkeley: University of California Press, 1985.

Marković, Mihailo. "Self-governing Political System and De-alienation in Yugoslavia (1950–1965)." *Praxis International* 6, no. 2 (July 1986): 159–174.

———. *Democratic Socialism: Theory and Practice.* New York: St. Martin's, 1982.

———. *From Affluence to Praxis: Philosophy and Social Criticism.* Ann Arbor: University of Michigan Press, 1974.

———. *The Contemporary Marx: Essays on Humanist Communism.* Nottingham: Spokesman Books, 1974.

Marković, Mihailo, and Gajo Petrović, eds. *Praxis: Yugoslav Essays in the Philosophy and Methodology of the Social Sciences.* Translated by Joan Coddington et al. Dordrecht: D. Reidel, 1979.

Marković, Predrag J. *Beograd između Istoka i Zapada, 1941–1965.* Belgrade: Službeni list SRJ, 1996.

———. "Ideologija standarda Jugoslovenskog režima 1948–1965." *Tokovi istorije: Časopis Instituta za noviju istoriju Srbije,* nos. 1/2 (1996): 7–20.

———. *Trajnost i promena: društvena istorija socijalističke i postsocijalističke svakodnevice u Jugoslaviji i Srbiji.* Belgrade: Javno preduzeće "Službeni Glasnik," 2007.

Martinić, Tena. "Potrošačka kultura." *Kultura: časopis za teoriju i sociologiju kulture i kulturnu politiku,* no.27 (1974): 8–24.

Mattelart, Armand. *Advertising International: The Privatisation of Public Space.* London: Routledge, 1991.

Mazurek, Malgorzata, and Matthew Hilton. "Consumerism, Solidarity and Communism: Consumer Protection and the Consumer Movement in Poland." *Journal of Contemporary History* 42, no. 2 (2007): 315–343.

Medvedev, Katalin. "Ripping Up the Uniform Approach: Hungarian Women Piece Together a New Communist Fashion." In *Producing Fashion: Commerce, Culture, and Consumers,* edited by Regina Lee Blaszczyk, 250–272. Philadelphia: University of Pennsylvania Press, 2008.

Merkel, Ina. *Utopie und Bedürfnis: die Geschichte der Konsumkultur in der DDR.* Cologne: Böhlau, 1999.

———. "Alternative Realities, Strange Dreams, Absurd Utopias: On Socialist Advertising and Market Research." In *Socialist Modern: East German Everyday Culture and Politics,* edited by Katherine Pence and Paul Betts, 323–344. Ann Arbor: University of Michigan Press, 2008.

——. "Consumer Culture in the GDR, or How the Struggle for Antimodernity Was Lost on the Battleground of Consumer Culture." In *Getting and Spending: European and American Consumer Societies in the Twentieth Century,* edited by Susan Strasser, Charles McGovern, and Matthias Judt, 281–299. Cambridge: Cambridge University Press, 1998.

Mikula, Maja. "Virtual Landscapes of Memory." *Information, Communication & Society* 6, no. 2 (2003): 169–186.

Milenkovitch, Deborah Duff. *Plan and Market in Yugoslav Economic Thought.* New Haven, Conn.: Yale University Press, 1971.

Miller, Daniel. *A Theory of Shopping.* Ithaca: Cornell University Press, 1998.

——. *Material Culture and Mass Consumption.* Oxford: Blackwell, 1987.

——. "Introduction: Anthropology, Modernity, and Consumption." In *Worlds Apart: Modernity through the Prism of the Local,* edited by Daniel Miller, 1–22. London: Routledge, 1995.

Miller, Michael B. *The Bon Marché: Bourgeois Culture and the Department Store, 1869–1920.* Princeton, N.J.: Princeton University Press, 1981.

Mills, C. Wright. *White Collar: The American Middle Classes.* New York: Oxford University Press, 1956 [1951].

Mitrović, Borislav B. *O+P+P=: priručnik za upravljanje propagandom.* Belgrade: Korisne knjige, 1989.

"Moments and Movements in the Study of Consumer Culture: A Discussion between Daniel Miller and Don Slater." *Journal of Consumer Culture* 7, no. 1 (2007): 5–23.

Možina, Stane. "Vloga potrošniških svetov." *Delo,* 12 January 1974, 19

——. "Zaščita potrošnikov in proizvajalcev." *Delo,* 9 March 1974, 16.

Mrvoš, Dušan P. *Propaganda reklama publicitet: teorija i praksa.* Belgrade: OZEHA Zavod za ekonomsku propagandu i publicitet, 1959.

Nadkarni, Maya, and Olga Shevchenko. "The Politics of Nostalgia: A Case for Comparative Analysis of Post-Socialist Practices." *Ab Imperio* no. 2 (2004): 487–519.

Nava, Mica, et al., eds. *Buy This Book: Studies in Advertising and Consumption.* London: Routledge, 1997.

Neuburger, Mary. "Veils, *Shalvari,* and Matters of Dress: Unravelling the Fabric of Women's Lives in Communist Bulgaria." In *Style and Socialism: Modernity and Material Culture in Post-War Eastern Europe,* edited by Susan E. Reid and David Crowley, 169–187. Oxford: Berg, 2000.

Niketić, Radoslav R. *Privredno planiranje: osnovi planiranja privredne propagande.* Belgrade: Viša ekonomska škola, 1972.

Norris, James D. *Advertising and the Transformation of American Society, 1865–1920.* New York: Greenwood, 1990.

Novak, Jana. "Razvoj slovenskega televizijskega oglaševanja v obdobju 1960–1980." *Diploma* thesis, University of Ljubljana, Faculty of Economics, 1997.

Novković, Bogdan. *Tehnika privredne propagande.* Belgrade: Savremena administracija, 1973.

Nurkse, Ragnar. *Problems of Capital Formation in Underdeveloped Countries.* New York: Oxford University Press, 1966 [1953].

Odnos sredstava informisanja prema potrošačkom društvu. Belgrade: Jugoslovenski institut za novinarstvo, 1981.

Packard, Vance. *The Hidden Persuaders.* New York: McKay, 1957.

Paić, Ivo. "Reklamno nebo i njegova svjetovna osnova. *Komunist,* 22 February 1976.

Palmberger, Monika. "Nostalgia Matters: Nostalgia for Yugoslavia as Potential Vision for a Better Future." *Sociologija* (Belgrade) 50, no. 4 (2008): 355–370.

Patten, Simon N. *The Consumption of Wealth.* Philadelphia: T. & J. W. Johnson, 1899.

Pavlić, Zrinka. *Svijet i praktična žena.* Zagreb: Jesenski i Turk, 2006.

Pence, Katherine Helena. "From Rations to Fashions: The Gendered Politics of East and West German Consumption, 1945–1961." Ph.D. diss., University of Michigan, 1999.

Perica, Vjekoslav. "United They Stood, Divided They Fell: Nationalism and the Yugoslav School of Basketball, 1968–2000." *Nationalities Papers* 29, no. 2 (2001): 267–291.

Pernek, Franc. *Potrošnik in njegovo varstvo: marketinški, pravni, in organizacijski vidik.* Maribor: Založba Obzorja, 1986.

Petz, Boris. *Psihologija u ekonomskoj propagandi.* 3d ed. Zagreb: Društvo Ekonomskih Propagandista SR Hrvatske, 1980.

Pirjevec, Jože. *Jugoslavija 1918–1992: nastanek, razvoj ter razpad Karadjordjevićeve in Titove Jugoslavije.* Koper: Lipa, 1995.

Potrošnja: zasebne prakse, javni užitki. Special issue. *Časopis za kritiko znanosti* 26, no. 189 (1998).

Prica, Ines. "In Search of Post-Socialist Subject." *Narodna umjetnost: hrvatski časopis za etnologiju i folkloristiku* 44, no. 1 (2007): 163–186.

Puhar, Alenka. "Krivda in nekrivda potrošništva." *Delo,* 14 April 1979, 21.

Ramet, Sabrina P. *The Three Yugoslavias: State-Building and Legitimation, 1918–2005.* Washington, D.C.: Woodrow Wilson Center Press, 2006.

Randall, Amy E. *The Soviet Dream World of Retail Trade and Consumption in the 1930s.* Basingstoke, England: Palgrave Macmillan, 2008.

——. "Legitimizing Soviet Trade: Gender and the Feminization of the Retail Workforce in the Soviet 1930s." *Journal of Social History* 37, no. 4 (summer 2004): 965–990.

Reid, Susan E. "Cold War in the Kitchen: Gender and the De-Stalinization of Consumer Taste in the Soviet Union under Khrushchev." *Slavic Review* 61, no. 2 (2002): 211–252.

——. "The Khrushchev Kitchen: Domesticating the Scientific-Technological Revolution." *Journal of Contemporary History* 40, no. 2 (2005): 289–316.

Richards, Thomas. *The Commodity Culture of Victorian England: Advertising and Spectacle, 1851–1914.* Stanford: Stanford University Press, 1990.

Ristović, Milan. "Pogled kroz ogledalo: reklama i istorija." *New Moment,* no. 6 (1996): 102–110.

Sagrak, Mirko. *Ekonomska propaganda: programi.* Zagreb: Radničko sveučilište "Moša Pijade," 1958.

Savez komunista Jugoslavije. *Nova inicijativa u SKJ (Pismo predsednika SKJ i Izvršnog biroa Predsedništva SKJ; Intervju Predsednika SKJ Josipa Broza Tita Vjesniku.* Belgrade: Izdavački centar Komunist, 1972.

Schudson, Michael. *Advertising, the Uneasy Persuasion: Its Dubious Impact on American Society.* New York: Basic Books, 1984.

Scribner, Charity. *Requiem for Communism*. Cambridge, Mass.: MIT Press, 2003.

Sedej, Ivan. "Kupite si zadovoljstvo in srečo." *Delo*, 2 February 1974, 20.

Šetinc, Franc. *Jesmo li potrošačko društvo*. Belgrade: Politika, 1979.

——. *Smo potrošniška družba*. Ljubljana: Zveza delavskih univerz Slovenije/ Dopisna delavska univerza Univerzum, 1980.

Sfiligoj, Nada. "Trg in tržno komuniciranje v našem gospodarstvu." *Bančni vestnik* 35, no. 12 (December 1986): 367–372.

Singleton, Fred. *A Short History of the Yugoslav Peoples*. Cambridge: Cambridge University Press, 1985.

——. *Twentieth Century Yugoslavia*. New York: Columbia University Press, 1976.

Skobe, Mihovil. *Organizacija privredne propagande*. Belgrade: Viša ekonomska škola, 1973.

Snoj, Jože. "Tisoč let samote." *Nova revija* 9, no. 95 (March 1990): 250–259.

Spahić, Besim. *Aspekti reklame u jugoslovenskom društvu*. Sarajevo: Oslobođenje, 1983.

——. *Strategija savremene propagande: prilog demitologizaciji savremene građanske reklame*. Sarajevo: Oslobođenje, 1985.

Splichal, Slavko, and France Vreg. *Množično komuniciranje in razvoj demokracije*. Ljubljana: Komunist, 1986.

Sproule, J. Michael. "Authorship and Origins of the Seven Propaganda Devices: A Research Note." *Rhetoric & Public Affairs* 4, no. 1 (spring 2001): 135–143.

Sredl, Katherine. "Consumption and Class during and after State Socialism." In *Research in Consumer Behavior*. Vol. 11, *Consumer Culture Theory*, edited by Russell Belk and John Sherry, 187–205. Oxford: Elsevier, 2007.

Štahan, Josip. *Životni standard i osobna potrošnja u Jugoslaviji*. Zagreb: Ekonomski institut Zagreb, 1973.

——. *Strukturne promjene i razvojne tendencije osobne potrošnje u Jugoslaviji u razdoblju od 1953. do 1967. godine*. Zagreb: Ekonomski institut, 1970.

Stanković, Slobodan. "Campaign Against Belgrade and Zagreb Professors." RAD Background Report/6 (Yugoslavia), Radio Free Europe Research series, 17 January 1975, 3.

Steiner, André. "Dissolution of the 'Dictatorship over Needs'? Consumer Behavior and Economic Reform in East Germany in the 1960s." In *Getting and Spending: European and American Consumer Societies in the Twentieth Century*, edited by Susan Strasser, Charles McGovern, and Matthias Judt, 167–185. Cambridge: Cambridge University Press, 1998.

Stitziel, Judd. *Fashioning Socialism: Clothing, Politics and Consumer Culture in East Germany*. Oxford: Berg, 2005.

Stojanović, Biljana. "Exchange Rate Regimes of the Dinar 1945–1990: An Assessment of Appropriateness and Efficiency." In *Workshops—The Proceedings of OeNB Workshops*, The Experience of Exchange Rate Regimes in Southeastern Europe. *Proceedings of the Second Conference of the South-Eastern European Monetary History Network, 13 April 2007*, no. 13 (2008): 198–243.

Stojanović, Svetozar. *Between Ideals and Reality: A Critique of Socialism and Its Future*. Translated by Gerson S. Sher. New York: Oxford University Press, 1973.

——. *The Fall of Yugoslavia: Why Communism Failed*. Amherst, N.Y.: Prometheus Books, 1997.

Stoković, Živorad K. *Štampa naroda i narodnosti u SFRJ 1945–1973: građa za istoriju štampe*. Belgrade: Jugoslovenski institut za novinarstvo, 1975.

Strasser, Susan. *Satisfaction Guaranteed: The Making of the American Mass Market*. New York: Pantheon Books, 1989.

Sudar, Josip. *Promotivne udruženog rada na tržištu*. Zagreb: Informator, 1984 [1979].

———. *Ekonomska propaganda: predavanja na postdiplomskom studiju Ekonomskog fakulteta u Zagrebu*. Zagreb: n.p., 1975.

———. *Ekonomska propaganda*, 3d ed. Zagreb: Informator, 1971.

———. *Ekonomska propaganda u teoriji i praksi*. Zagreb: Informator, 1958.

Supek, Rudi. "Some Contradictions and Insufficiencies of Yugoslav Self-Managing Socialism." In *Praxis: Yugoslav Essays in the Philosophy and Methodology of the Social Sciences*, edited by Mihailo Marković and Gajo Petrović, translated by Joan Coddington et al., 249–271. Dordrecht: D. Reidel, 1979.

———. "Stabilno društvo kao revolucionarna suprotnost potrošačkom društvu." In Rudi Supek, *Ova jedina zemlja: idemo li u katastrofu ili u treću revoluciju?*, 219–229. Zagreb: Naprijed, 1973.

Susman, Warren I. *Culture as History: The Transformation of American Society in the Twentieth Century*. New York: Pantheon Books, 1984.

Šuvar, Stipe. "Elementi potrošačkog društva i potrošačkog mentaliteta" (1976). In Stipe Šuvar, *Samoupravljanje i alternative*, 163–183. Zagreb: Centar za kulturnu djelatnost, 1980.

Švab, Alenka. "Consuming Western Image of Well-Being—Shopping Tourism in Socialist Slovenia." *Cultural Studies* 16, no. 1 (2002): 63–79.

Taboroši, Svetislav. *Odnosi potrošnje u socijalizmu: potrošač u sistemu udruženog rada*. Belgrade: NIO Poslovna Politika, 1986.

Tepavac, Mirko. "Tito: 1945–1980." In *Burn This House: The Making and Unmaking of Yugoslavia*, edited by Jasmina Udovički and James Ridgeway, 64–79. Durham, N.C.: Duke University Press, 1997.

Tippach-Schneider, Simone. *Messemännchen und Minol-Pirol: Werbung in der DDR*. Berlin: Schwarzkopf & Schwarzkopf, 1999.

Todorović, Živojin. "Izložba najmodernih dostignuća ali i najostalijih navika." *Politika*, 31 October 1960, 5.

Topham, S.W. *Advertising and Socialist Self-Management in Yugoslavia*. Bradford, UK: Postgraduate School of Yugoslav Studies, University of Bradford, 1984.

Toš, Niko, P. [Peter] Klinar, B. [Boštjan] Markič, Z. [Zdravko] Mlinar, Z. [Zdenko] Roter, and C. [Cveto] Trampuž. *Slovenski utrip: rezultati raziskav javnega mnenja, 1988–1989*. Ljubljana: Fakulteta za sociologijo, politične vede in novinarstvo, n.d. (ca. 1989).

Trentmann, Frank. "Knowing Consumers—Histories, Identities, Practices: An Introduction." In *The Making of the Consumer: Knowledge, Power and Identity in the Modern World*, edited by Frank Trentmann, 1–27. Oxford: Berg, 2006.

Tyson, Laura D'Andrea. *The Yugoslav Economic System and Its Performance in the 1970s*. Berkeley: Institute of International Studies/University of California, 1980.

Udovički, Jasmina, and James Ridgeway, eds. *Burn This House: The Making and Unmaking of Yugoslavia*. Durham, N.C.: Duke University Press, 1997.

Veblen, Thorstein. *The Theory of the Leisure Class.* Boston: Houghton Mifflin, 1973 [1899].

Velikonja, Mitja. *Titostalgija: Študija nostalgije po Josipu Brozu.* Ljubljana: Mirovni inštitut, 2008.

———. "'Red Shades': Nostalgia for Socialism as an Element of Cultural Pluralism in the Slovene Transition." *Slovene Studies* 30, no. 2 (2008): 171–184.

Volčič, Zala. "Yugo-Nostalgia: Cultural Memory and Media in the Former Yugoslavia." *Critical Studies in Media Communication* 24, no. 1 (March 2007): 21–38.

Vračar, Dragutin S. *Uloga privredne propagande u politici prodaje jugoslovenskih preduzeća.* Ph.D. diss., University of Belgrade, 1972.

———. *Privredna propaganda.* Skopje: Ekonomski fakultet Univerziteta Kiril i Metodij Skopje, 1974.

Vrčon, Branko, ed. *Reklama v gospodarski propagandi.* Ljubljana: Delo, 1967.

West, Richard. *Tito and the Rise and Fall of Yugoslavia.* New York: Carroll & Graf, 1994.

Williams, Rosalind H. *Dream Worlds: Mass Consumption in Late Nineteenth-Century France.* Berkeley: University of California Press, 1982.

Woodward, Susan L. *Balkan Tragedy: Chaos and Dissolution after the Cold War.* Washington, D.C.: Brookings Institution, 1995.

———. *Socialist Unemployment: The Political Economy of Yugoslavia, 1945–1990.* Princeton, N.J.: Princeton University Press, 1995.

Zatlin, Jonathan R. *The Currency of Socialism: Money and Political Culture in East Germany.* New York: German Historical Institute, 2007.

———. "Consuming Ideology: Socialist Consumerism and the Intershops, 1970–1989." In *Arbeiter in der SBZ-DDR,* edited by Peter Hübner and Klaus Tenfelde, 555–572. Essen: Klartext-Verlag, 1999.

———. "The Vehicle of Desire: The Trabant, the Wartburg and the End of the GDR." *German History* 15, no. 3 (1997): 358–380.

Zapiski s posvetovanja ekonomskih propagandistov Slovenije, od 20. do 22. marca 1964. Ljubljana: Društvo ekonomskih propagandistov Slovenije, 1964.

Zbornik referata sa II međunarodnog simpozijuma privrednih propaganda. Belgrade: Privredna propaganda, n.d.

Zekić, Slobodanka. "Ne emotivno o interesima." *Komunist,* 19 January 1979, 9.

Zimmerman, William. *Open Borders, Nonalignment, and the Political Evolution of Yugoslavia.* Princeton, N.J.: Princeton University Press, 1987.

Životić, Miladin. "Between Two Types of Modern Culture." In *Praxis: Yugoslav Essays in the Philosophy and Methodology of the Social Sciences,* edited by Mihailo Marković and Gajo Petrović, translated by Joan Coddington et al., 187–197. Dordrecht: D. Reidel, 1979.

Zukin, Sharon. *Point of Purchase: How Shopping Changed American Culture.* New York: Routledge, 2005.

Index